TEACHER PREP

MERRILL PRENTICE HALL

Teacher Preparation Classroom

See a demo at
www.prenhall.com/teacherprep/demo

Your Class. Their Careers. Our Future. Will your students be prepared?

We invite you to explore our new, innovative and engaging website and all that it has to offer you, your course, and tomorrow's educators! Preview this site today at www.prenhall.com/teacherprep/demo. Just click on "go" on the login page to begin your exploration.

Organized around the major courses preservice teachers take, the Teacher Preparation site provides media, student/teacher artifacts, strategies, research articles, and other resources to equip your students with the quality tools needed to excel in their courses and prepare them for their first classroom.

This ultimate online education resource will provide you and your students access to:

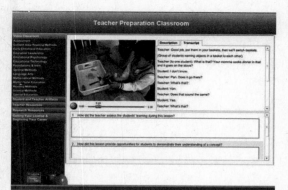

Online Video Library. More than 250 video clips—each tied to a course topic and framed by learning goals and Praxis-type questions—capture real teachers and students working in real classrooms

Student and Teacher Artifacts. More than 200 student and teacher classroom artifacts—each tied to a course topic and framed by learning goals and application questions—provide a wealth of materials and experiences to help your students observe children's developmental learning.

Lesson Plan Builder. Step-by-Step guidelines and lesson plan examples support students as they learn to build high-quality lesson plans.

Articles and Readings. Over 500 articles from ASCD's renowned journal *Educational Leadership* are available. The site also includes Research Navigator, a searchable database of additional educational journals.

Strategies and Lessons. Over 500 research-supported instructional strategies appropriate for a wide range of grade levels and content areas.

Licensure and Career Tools. Resources devoted to helping your students pass their licensure exam; learn standards, law, and public policies; plan a teaching portfolio; and succeed in their first year of teaching.

How to ORDER *Teacher Prep* for you and your students:

For students to receive a *Teacher Prep* Access Code with this text, instructors must provide a special value pack ISBN number on their textbook order form. To receive this special ISBN, please e-mail Merrill.marketing@pearsoned.com and provide the following information:
- Name and Affiliation
- Author/Title/Edition of Merrill text

Upon ordering *Teacher Prep* for their students, instructors will be given a lifetime *Teacher Prep* Access Code.

Assistive Technology in the Classroom

ENHANCING THE SCHOOL EXPERIENCES OF STUDENTS WITH DISABILITIES

Amy G. Dell
The College of New Jersey

Deborah A. Newton
Southern Connecticut State University

Jerry G. Petroff
The College of New Jersey

PEARSON

Merrill
Prentice Hall

Upper Saddle River, New Jersey
Columbus, Ohio

Library of Congress Cataloging-in-Publication Data

Dell, Amy G.
  Assistive technology in the classroom : enhancing the school experiences of students
with disabilities / Amy G. Dell, Deborah A. Newton, Jerry G. Petroff.
    p. cm.
  Includes bibliographical references and index.
  ISBN-13: 978-0-13-119164-8
  ISBN-10: 0-13-119164-0
1. Educational technology—United States.   2. Students with disabilities—United States.
I. Newton, Deborah A.   II. Petroff, Jerry G.   III. Title.
  LB1028.3.D43 2007
  371.33—dc22   2007024218

Vice President and Executive Publisher: Jeffery W. Johnston
Executive Editor: Ann Castel Davis
Editorial Assistant: Penny Burleson
Senior Production Editor: Sheryl Glicker Langner
Production Coordination: Rebecca K. Giusti, GGS Book Services
Design Coordinator: Diane C. Lorenzo
Cover Designer: Kristina Holmes
Cover Image: Kevin Cohen
Production Manager: Laura Messerly
Director of Marketing: David Gesell
Marketing Manager: Autumn Purdy
Marketing Coordinator: Brian Mounts

This book was set in Sabon by GGS Book Services.

Pearson Prentice Hall™ is a trademark of Pearson Education, Inc.
Pearson® is a registered trademark of Pearson plc.
Pearson Hall® is a registered trademark of Pearson Education, Inc.
Merrill® is a registered trademark of Pearson Education, Inc.

Pearson Education Ltd.   Pearson Education Australia Pty. Limited
Pearson Education Singapore Pte. Ltd.   Pearson Education North Asia Ltd.
Pearson Education Canada, Ltd.   Pearson Educación de Mexico, S.A. de C.V.
Pearson Education—Japan   Pearson Education Malaysia Pte. Ltd.

PEARSON
Merrill
Prentice Hall

10 9 8
ISBN-13: 978-0-13-119164-8
ISBN-10:   0-13-119164-0

DEDICATION

In memory of my husband, James E. Dell,
a master problem solver, who taught me "there's a right tool for every job."
Amy G. Dell

To my son, Sean, who taught me how to use a computer so many years ago, and
to my husband, John, for encouraging and supporting the pursuit of all my dreams.
Deborah A. Newton

To my partner, David, and our sons Parker and Borey,
for their unconditional love and support.
Jerry G. Petroff

About the Authors

Amy G. Dell is chairperson of the Department of Special Education, Language and Literacy at The College of New Jersey. She has been involved in assistive technology training for over 20 years, developing and teaching a master's-level course in assistive technology, leading initiatives to infuse assistive technology into undergraduate and graduate coursework, and establishing an Alliance for Technology Access (ATA) center in northern New Jersey. She serves as director of the Adaptive Technology Center for New Jersey Colleges, which is funded by the New Jersey Commission on Higher Education, and directs the Center for Assistive Technology and Inclusive Education Studies (CATIES) at The College of New Jersey.

Deborah A. Newton is currently an associate professor in the Department of Special Education and Reading at Southern Connecticut State University in New Haven, Connecticut, where she teaches graduate courses in adaptive technology. She taught for many years at the elementary level, then served as assistive technology specialist at the Center for Enabling Technology in Whippany, New Jersey. She holds a doctorate in curriculum and instruction from the University of Cincinnati, a master's degree from The College of New Jersey, and a bachelor's degree from the State University of New York at New Paltz. Dr. Newton regularly presents at assistive technology conferences and remains active as an assistive technology consultant.

Jerry G. Petroff is an assistant professor in the Department of Special Education, Language and Literacy at The College of New Jersey. He is project director of the New Jersey Deafblind Project and director of outreach and research for the Center for Assistive Technology and Inclusive Education Studies (CATIES). Dr. Petroff has over 30 years of experience working on behalf of students, youth, and adults with disabilities. Holding a doctorate in psychological studies in special education and a master's degree in speech pathology and audiology, he teaches courses and consults with local school districts on inclusive education, assistive technology for students with severe disabilities, and the transition of students with disabilities from school to adult life.

Preface

Assistive Technology in the Classroom emphasizes the *integration of assistive technology into the curriculum*—how assistive technology can be used in schools to enhance the teaching and learning of students with disabilities. It specifically addresses how *teachers* can use assistive technology in all kinds of classrooms to teach new skills to students with all kinds of disabilities and to provide students with access to the general education curriculum. The context for our discussions of technology use is always the classroom, the school, and other environments in which students learn. This approach reflects the philosophy of the leading professional organization in educational technology, the International Society for Technology in Education (ISTE), which articulates that "learning with technology should not be about the technology itself but about the learning that can be facilitated though it."[1]

This focus on teachers and their role in assistive technology implementation stems from our recognition that one of the major problems contributing to the gap between the *possibilities* of assistive technology and the successful implementation of it in our schools is that teachers lack the necessary knowledge and skills. Even in school districts in which assistive technology teams conduct assistive technology evaluations on student with disabilities and make recommendations for appropriate technology tools, many students do not benefit from the recommendations because the professionals with whom they interact on a daily basis—that is, their teachers—are not aware of what assistive technology can do, do not know how to use it within the context of their classrooms, and do not know how to support their students' use of it.

By maintaining a focus on what *teachers* need to know about assistive technology, this text is not a survey of the entire field of assistive technology. Discussions of assistive technology for positioning and mobility, sports and recreation, architecture, and transportation are not included. Although these are important applications of assistive technology, they typically fall within the domain of rehabilitation professionals such as physical therapists and do not rely on the involvement of classroom teachers for their successful implementation.

The technology solutions included in this text are appropriate for students with a wide range of disabilities. Technology tools that benefit students with low-incidence disabilities such as autism and multiple disabilities are presented, as well as technology solutions for students with high-incidence disabilities such as learning disabilities and attention deficit disorders. Although some states have teacher certification requirements that are categorical in nature, other states have generic special education education certifications, and as such, teacher candidates need to be prepared to implement assistive technology with *all* students.

We assume (based on our experience in higher education) that today's undergraduate and graduate students bring a basic familiarity with using computers to an assistive technology course. Most know, at a minimum, how to use e-mail, word processing software, and an Internet browser. Therefore, the book does not include

---

[1]From "Identifying Key Research Issues," by G. Knezek, R. Christensen, L. Bell, and G. Bull, 2006. *Learning and Leading with Technology, 33*(8), pp. 18–20.

introductory chapters on parts of a computer, what the Internet is, different storage devices, or similar background material.

ORGANIZATION OF THE BOOK

The link between technology and teaching and learning drives this text's organization as well as its content. Part I is organized by *school-related tasks* that students must perform on a daily basis to be successful—writing, reading, practicing academic skills, demonstrating what they have learned, communicating with teachers and peers, and understanding what their teachers and peers express. Each chapter in Part I begins with a description of the problems students with disabilities face with the specific school-related task, and then goes on to describe how assistive technology can help overcome the problems related to this activity. Some recommended solutions are found in easily obtained commercial products that have been universally designed, whereas other solutions involve more specialized products that are produced by assistive technology manufacturers. This structure helps teacher candidates understand how assistive technology fits into their classrooms and curricula. It shifts the focus from training on specific *devices* and the latest gizmos to training on how to use the technology *to learn*.

After Part I has established the benefits of assistive technology for students with disabilities, Part II addresses the question: How can we make computers and the Internet *accessible* to students who cannot type on a keyboard, use a mouse, hear an alert sound, or see a monitor? Chapters in this part discuss ways to adjust operating systems and conventional software programs to provide access; specialized access solutions for students with low-incidence disabilities; and the decision-making process for determining the most effective access method for a student.

Part III focuses on augmentative communication—the use of computer technology to provide a voice for students who cannot speak. The first two chapters provide essential background information on augmentative communication so that the third chapter can highlight the *teacher's role* in integrating augmentative communication in the classroom. The background information in Chapters 9 and 10 is provided because most teachers and teacher candidates have had little, if any, previous training in augmentative communication. Chapter 11 presents strategies for teachers to use in their classrooms to encourage students to develop and refine their augmentative communication skills. This chapter describes how to integrate communication objectives into classroom activities and daily routines and how to provide multiple opportunities for students to use their augmentative communication systems during the school day.

Part IV is titled "Making It Happen." The first three parts of the text established the value of assistive technology and presented a variety of assistive technology solutions. In this last part the book moves from possibilities to the nitty-gritty: How do we make these exciting possibilities happen for students with disabilities? What do we need to know, and what do we need to *do* to actually get assistive technology to the students who stand to benefit from it? The answers to these questions are complex and involve a wide range of issues, including the laws related to assistive technology, the integration of assistive technology into IEPs, the "digital divide," the knowledge and skills of professionals who work with students with disabilities, administrative issues, and funding sources. Chapter 12 summarizes the typical barriers to assistive technology implementation and presents recommendations for getting around these barriers. Chapter 13 addresses implementation issues specifically related to transitioning from high school.

Although disability categories are mentioned within the context of technology-based solutions, this text in *not* organized around disability categories. There is a common misconception in special education that Disability X = Technology Tool Y, but this is overly simplistic and misguided. There are multiple factors involved in selecting appropriate technology tools for students with disabilities, and it is a mistake to base selection decisions simply on a child's diagnosis. Therefore, this text discusses disability categories within the context of school-related tasks and technology-based solutions.

PEDAGOGICAL ELEMENTS

The book was designed following the principles of "considerate text:" Each chapter begins with a set of focus questions, is divided into sections that are labeled with headings, and concludes with a summary of key points. Sidebars highlight specialized information. An important pedagogical element is that the technology presented is continually *linked to real people* though the use of *user profiles*, which are concise summaries of how assistive technology tools have transformed students' school experiences. We recommend that as you proceed through the text, you consciously try to make connections between the information presented and the students whom you teach. Applying the lessons of the text to students with disabilities whom you know will help you understand the subtleties of the assistive technology decision-making process.

Because of the ever-changing nature of technology, the text purposefully presents only a brief sampling of assistive technology hardware, software, and related websites. A deliberate effort was made to minimize the use of specific product names, and they have been used only for purposes of illustration. For additional information on specific products, and to see photographs of them, go to the websites that are listed in the section called Web Resources at the end of each chapter. This section contains the URLs of manufacturers and publishers of hardware, software, and assistive devices, as well as links to informative resources. Every effort has been made to provide accurate URLs for all Web sites. However, if you are unable to access the site, we recommend that you go to the site's home page and try to navigate to the specific page using the links included on the home page.

A list of suggested activities is included at the end of each chapter. These are in-class or out-of-class activities that involve students more deeply in the chapter's subject matter. All of the suggested activities have proven successful over the past 12 years in assistive technology courses with students who are studying to be special education teachers or technology coordinators. Instructors are encouraged to assign one or more of these for each chapter, or to assign similar activities of their own design. Many of the activities are hands-on and require a computer and specific software to complete. Others involve interviews of people in the field. All of the activities are designed to engage students in active exploration of assistive technology tools or environments in which assistive technology is or could be used to help students make the connection between assistive technology and the learning process.

ACKNOWLEDGMENTS

We would like to express our sincere gratitude and deep appreciation to the many people who generously contributed their expertise to the writing of this text. Our colleagues at The College of New Jersey, Helene Anthony, Jean Slobodzian, and Shrivdevi Rao, provided essential information on reading and writing, deafness, and transition from school to community life, respectively. Christina Schindler researched the complicated topic of making websites accessible to people with disabilities. Kevin Cohen helped us refine our ideas on two key topics—universal design and augmentative communication—and assisted us in taking photographs. Pat Beaber, of TCNJ's Roscoe West Library, provided critical library support. Dianne Gibson and Mary Ann Peterson, office staff of the Department of Special Education, Language and Literacy, and Andrew Brunetto of Information Technology, rescued us numerous times. Anne Disdier, Tammy Cordwell, and Michelle Ragunan good-naturedly assisted with myriad screenshots, photographs, and permissions. Ellen Farr took on the onerous tasks of formatting the entire manuscript and organizing all the photos; without her superb organization skills and unflappable nature, this book would not exist.

We would also like to thank current and former students at The College of New Jersey for their contributions. Lisa Pacifico's research on math websites found its way into Chapter 5, and Lorrie Jo Dirienzo's research on blogs in education was incorporated into Chapter 2. Sara Best, Jennifer DiPersio, Torie Foma, Bryana Fogarty, Jenna Gnade, and Brenda Mason wrote the sample social story that appears in Chapter 13. Many of the user profiles that appear in the text were adapted from articles that were originally written for our newsletter *TECH-NJ* by TCNJ graduate students Patricia Mervine, Danielle Niemann, Meenakshi Pasupathy, Gerald Quinn, Wolf Shipon, Tina Spadafora, and Kavita Taneja. We would also like to acknowledge the many students in our courses over the years who provided us with valuable feedback on our teaching and assignments that influenced our planning and organizing of this text.

We are indebted to many people outside our college campuses, as well. Vicki Spence and students of the John C. Leach School in New Castle, Delaware, provided us with wonderful photographs of assistive technology in action. Vincent Varrassi of Fairleigh Dickenson University coined the phrase, "There are no IEPs in college," and cheerfully gave it to us to use in Chapter 13. Bill Ziegler of the Bucks County, Pennsylvania, Intermediate Unit was Amy Dell's first assistive technology teacher. (He taught us how to make switches to use with the Adaptive Firmware Card on Apple IIe computers.) His beliefs in the incredible possibilities of assistive technology permeate this text. His colleague, Patricia Mervine, a one-time student of Amy Dell, has moved to the other side of the desk to become her teacher of assistive technology for students with severe disabilities.

Over the years we have been inspired by many students with disabilities, their parents, and adults who have disabilities, and by their efforts to get assistive technology to work for them. Thank you to Anthony Arnold, Michael Williams, and Serena Cucco, for showing the world what is possible. Thank you to the Alliance for Technology Access for working to make assistive technology accessible to *all* people with disabilities. And thank you to Barbara Shiller at Southern Connecticut State

University, and parents Jeanne D'Aries, Fran Scuilli, Jeanne Earle, Jesse Bayer, Dan Daly, and Cathy Tamburello for working so hard to make assistive technology a reality in Connecticut and New Jersey.

We would also like to thank the following individuals for reviewing this edition: Lynne S. Arnault, Mississippi State University; Tamarah Ashton, California State University, Northridge; Emily C. Bouck, Purdue University; Kristy K. Ehlers, Oklahoma State University; Richard Evans, University of Texas of the Permian Basin; Kathleen Gruenhagen, North Georgia College and State University; Beth Hair, Greensboro College; Thomas S. Higbee, Utah State University; Daniel Kelly, State University of New York, Geneseo; Linda Mechling, University of North Carolina, Wilmington; Barbara B. Natalle, St. Norbert Collage; Thomas J. Simmons, University of Louisville; and Martha A. York, Pittsburg State University.

Discover the Merrill Resources for Special Education Website

Technology is a constantly growing and changing aspect of our field that is creating a need for new content and resources. To address this emerging need, Merrill Education has developed an online learning environment for students, teachers, and professors alike to complement our products—the *Merrill Resources for Special Education* Website. This content-rich website provides additional resources specific to this book's topic and will help you—professors, classroom teachers, and students— augment your teaching, learning, and professional development.

Our goal is to build on and enhance what our products already offer. For this reason, the content for our user-friendly website is organized by topic and provides teachers, professors, and students with a variety of meaningful resources all in one location. With this website, we bring together the best of what Merrill has to offer: text resources, video clips, web links, tutorials, and a wide variety of information on topics of interest to general and special educators alike. Rich content, applications, and competencies further enchance the learning process.

The *Merrill Resources for Special Education* Website includes:

- Video clips specific to each topic, with questions to help you evaluate the content and make crucial theory-to-practice connections.
- Thought-provoking critical analysis questions that students can answer and turn in for evaluation or that can serve as basis for class discussions and lectures.
- Access to a wide variety of resources related to classroom strategies and methods, including lesson planning and classroom management.
- Information on all the most current relevant topics related to special and general education, including CEC and Praxis™ standards, IEPs, portfolios, and professional development.
- Extensive web resources and overviews on each topic addressed on the website.
- A search feature to help access specific information quickly.

To take advantage of these and other resources, please visit the *Merrill Resources for Special Education* Website at

http://www.prenhall.com/dell

Brief Contents

Contents

PART IV   MAKING IT HAPPEN   281

CHAPTER 12   Implementation of Assistive Technology in Schools   283

CHAPTER 13   Implementation of Assistive Technology in Transition Planning   305

Note: Every effort has been made to provide accurate and current Internet information in this book. However, the Internet and information posted on it are constantly changing, so it is inevitable that some of the Internet addresses listed in this textbook will change.

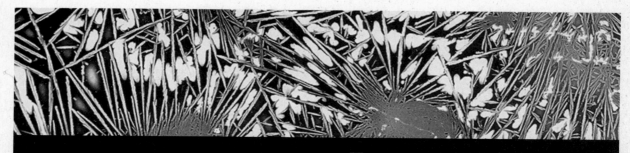

PART **I**

Benefits of Computer Use in Special Education

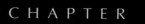

Introduction to Assistive Technology

FOCUS QUESTIONS
1. How is assistive technology defined in IDEA 2004?
2. What is the assistive technology continuum?
3. What laws mandate the provision of assistive technology to students with disabilities?
4. What is the promise of assistive technology?
5. What principles underlie the philosophy of this text?
6. What are universal design and universal design for learning?

INTRODUCTION

In 1972, when I was a sophomore in college, I met an unusual middle-aged man who made a deep impression on me. Bernie had severe cerebral palsy, a neuromuscular condition that significantly affected his movement and posture. He could not walk and had no control over his arms or hands; in fact, he had one of his arms tied across his chest to prevent it from jerking involuntarily and hitting someone. His head control was poor. Most people looking at him sitting in his wheelchair with his head hanging down assumed he could do nothing; they assumed he was as cognitively disabled as he was physically disabled, and they made no attempt to discover the person inside.

Bernie, however, did not accept other people's low expectations of him. He was determined to find a way around his physical limitations so he could be an active participant in the world around him. Bernie knew that he had a little control over one of his legs, and he wondered if he might be able to do something with that little voluntary movement. A handy friend attached a metal dowel to the bottom of one of his shoes and placed a rubber tip on the end. With this simple contraption, Bernie was able to type on a typewriter. The only assistance he needed was someone to put the shoe with the dowel on his foot and place the typewriter on the floor next to his foot. His typing speed was slow, but he was now able to write letters to his friends (this was before e-mail), type letters to legislators, and write articles expressing his points of view. Although the term did not exist at this time, this kind of creative problem solving is an early example of assistive technology.

I never forgot Bernie. Today, 35 years later, I still remember what I learned from him: (1) Regardless of how disabled a person may appear, inside is a person who wants to be part of life. (2) Taking a problem-solving attitude, instead of a too-bad-there's-nothing-that-can-be-done attitude, can lead to creative solutions that eliminate or bypass obstacles such as physical disabilities. (3) Simple technology can change a person's life. These lessons are what led me to personal computers when they became available many years later. I had seen with my own eyes that "having a disability no longer has to mean that things cannot be done; it means that we can find new ways to get them done" (Alliance for Technology Access [ATA], 2004, p. 3). And I wanted to be one of those problem solvers—"people who ask not *whether* something can be done, but rather *how* it can be accomplished" (ATA, 2004, p. 3, italics added). Marc Gold, an early leader in the field of severe disabilities, expressed this philosophy succinctly: (1980) "Try another way."

WHAT IS ASSISTIVE TECHNOLOGY?

The term *assistive technology* is defined in the federal law that provides the foundation for all special education services—the Individuals with Disabilities Education Improvement Act (IDEA 2004). This law's definition of assistive technology consists of two parts: assistive technology *devices* and assistive technology *services*. Both are important and will be discussed in this section.

IDEA 2004 defines an assistive technology *device* as "any item, piece of equipment, or product system, whether acquired commercially off the shelf, modified, or customized, that is used to increase, maintain, or improve functional capabilities of a child with a disability" (IDEA 2004, Sec. 1401(1)(A)). (See Figure 1.1 for the complete definition.) Let's examine this definition in reverse. An assistive technology device must have an impact on the *functioning* of a child with a disability. For example, a portable magnifier enables a child who has a visual impairment to read a worksheet, thereby improving his or her ability to complete schoolwork. A motorized wheelchair increases the ability of a child who has a physical disability to move around the classroom to participate in activities. A talking augmentative communication system that enables a child who has autism to express preferences increases the child's ability to communicate. These three examples show how an assistive technology device can "increase, maintain, or improve functional capabilities of a child with a disability."

If we look at the first part of the definition—an assistive technology device can be bought in a store ("acquired commercially off the shelf"), it can be a purchased item that has been modified, or it can be something that has been customized for an individual's particular needs. A large computer monitor is an example of an assistive technology device that can be bought in a store (for students with visual impairments who need to enlarge the visual display). Another example of off-the-shelf assistive technology is a talking calculator, which provides auditory feedback to a student with learning disabilities who has a problem typing numerals correctly.

Examples of modifications to off-the-shelf products include adding wooden blocks to the pedals of a tricycle so a child who has short legs can reach the pedals; building up the handle of a pencil or eating utensil with foam so a child with poor motor skills can grip and manipulate it better; and adding special software to a standard computer so a child with autism can learn new academic skills.

FIGURE 1–1   IDEA 2004 definition of assistive technology

Individuals with Disabilities Education Act (IDEA) of 2004, 20 U.S.C. § 1401

1) ASSISTIVE TECHNOLOGY DEVICE—
   (A) IN GENERAL—The term 'assistive technology device' means any item, piece of equipment, or product system, whether acquired commercially off the shelf, modified, or customized, that is used to increase, maintain, or improve functional capabilities of a child with a disability
   (B) EXCEPTION—The term does not include a medical device that is surgically implanted, or the replacement of such device.

2) ASSISTIVE TECHNOLOGY SERVICE—
The term 'assistive technology service' means any service that directly assists a child with a disability in the selection, acquisition, or use of an assistive technology device. Such term includes—
   (A) the evaluation of the needs of such child, including a functional evaluation of the child in the child's customary environment;
   (B) purchasing, leasing, or otherwise providing for the acquisition of assistive technology devices by such child;
   (C) selecting, designing, fitting, customizing, adapting, applying, maintaining, repairing, or replacing assistive technology devices;
   (D) coordinating and using other therapies, interventions, or services with assistive technology devices, such as those associated with existing education and rehabilitation plans and programs;
   (E) training or technical assistance for such child, or, where appropriate, the family of such child; and
   (F) training or technical assistance for professionals (including individuals providing education and rehabilitation services), employers, or other individuals who provide services to, employ, or are otherwise substantially involved in the major life functions of such child.

Source: http://www.law.cornell.edu/UScode/20/USC_Sec_20_0000/40/----000-.html.

Customized assistive technology devices include a wide variety of items. Communication boards created with pictures and talking computerized devices that serve as augmentative communication systems are usually customized for each individual student. Teacher-made computer-based activities to teach specific skills are another example of customized assistive technology devices.

As you can see from these examples, the definition of assistive technology devices is quite broad. A helpful way of organizing all of these possibilities is to place them on an assistive technology continuum—that is, a continuum from low tech to high tech. Low-tech devices use no electronic components and are relatively inexpensive. They are what are often called "gadgets," "gizmos," "doodads," or "thingamajigs," that is, "simple tools that make life's daily activities easier or even possible" (Collins, n.d.). The kitchen is a good place to find examples of low-tech devices. Can openers and jar openers with thick handles make opening cans and jars easier for people with limited strength. Color-coded measuring spoons with big numbers help people with low vision. Cookbook holders hold open the pages of a cookbook to the correct recipe so the cook can refer to it easily. In the classroom, typical low-tech devices include pencil grips (see Figure 1.2) for writing (building up the shaft of a pencil to improve a student's control), clipboards for holding papers steady, masking

FIGURE 1–2
A pencil grip is an example of a low-tech writing tool

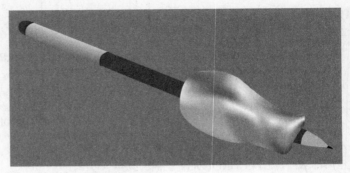

Onion Mountain Technology

cards to help struggling readers keep their eyes on the correct line of text, and simple communication boards made out of pictures.

High-tech devices are items that often are based on computer technology. In general, high-tech devices are more complicated to operate and require more training than low-tech devices, and are considerably more expensive. However, high-tech devices offer unique benefits that often make their expense and training demands worthwhile. They are powerful and flexible devices, and can be used for many different tasks. For example, desktop computers and laptop computers connected to the Internet and equipped with specialized software can be used for writing, reading, information gathering, corresponding via e-mail, and learning new skills. Sophisticated augmentative communication systems can be used for these same tasks, with the important addition of providing a voice for students who cannot speak.

In between sophisticated high-tech and nonelectronic low-tech devices are items classified as mid-tech devices. Mid-tech devices are electronic in nature but are much less expensive and require less training than high-tech devices. Tape recorders and digital recorders for recording teachers' lectures and handheld electronic dictionaries and spell-checkers are examples of mid-tech devices. Oversized calculators and calculators that talk are other examples. As you will see in Chapter 8, decisions about selecting appropriate assistive technology for students should always consider the low-tech to high-tech continuum.

Before leaving our discussion of IDEA's definition of assistive technology devices, it is important to note that the law includes an exception: "The term [assistive technology device] does not include a medical device that is surgically implanted, or the replacement of such device" (IDEA 2004, Sec. 1401(1)(B)). Implanted devices include feeding tubes for students who cannot eat and cochlear implants for students who are deaf (see Chapter 4).

The second part of IDEA's definition of assistive technology discusses assistive technology *services*. *Assistive technology service* refers to "any service that directly assists a child with a disability in the selection, acquisition, or use of an assistive technology device" (IDEA 2004, Sec. 1401(2)). Assistive technology services include evaluating a child for assistive technology, purchasing or leasing an assistive technology device for a child, customizing a device to meet a child's specific needs, repairing or replacing a broken device, teaching the child to use the device, providing training for professionals who work with the child and/or for family members and are "substantially involved in the major life functions" of the child (IDEA 2004, Sec. 1401(2)(F); see Figure 1.1). The inclusion of assistive technology services in the law is extremely important as it recognizes that simply *providing* a device is not enough. Making a device available without providing essential supports does not lead to successful implementation of assistive technology. This concept will be discussed in detail in Chapter 12.

Related Terms

Other terms are sometimes used to refer to technology that helps students with disabilities. *Rehabilitation technology, special education technology, educational technology, instructional technology,* and *information technology* often overlap and may mean different things to different people (Golden, 1998). Golden points out that this "definitional ambiguity has fostered an atmosphere of confusion in the development and implementation of assistive technology policies in many settings, especially education" (p. 6). This text uses *assistive technology* to refer to any kind of technology (low-tech to high-tech) that helps students with disabilities succeed in school. The following section explains the focus and limitations of this use of the term.

Assistive technology is also used in rehabilitation fields such as physical therapy, occupational therapy, speech-language therapy, adapted recreation, and adaptive driving to refer to a wide range of technology applications (Church and Glennen, 1992).

> Assistive technologies include mechanical, electronic, and microprocessor-based equipment, non-mechanical and non-electronic aids, specialized instructional materials, services, and strategies that people with disabilities can use either to (a) assist them in learning, (b) make the environment more accessible, (c) enable them to compete in the workplace, (d) enhance their independence, or (e) otherwise improve their quality of life. (Blackhurst & Lahm, 2000, p. 7)

This broad definition encompasses devices such as wheelchair-accessible elevators and lifts, sit-skis, cars and vans with adapted steering mechanisms, environmental controls, and power wheelchairs and motorized scooters. Although these devices are important to quality-of-life issues, they do not directly relate to the instructional process and students' success in schools and therefore are not covered in this text. Furthermore, selection of and training to use these devices usually fall under the domain of professionals other than teachers. For example, when a student needs a power wheelchair, it is primarily the physical therapist, not the teacher, who conducts an evaluation to determine the best fit. Teachers are not involved in selecting wheelchair-accessible vans for families or in making homes more physically accessible.

What teachers *do* become involved in is teaching and learning: teaching reading and writing, listening and speaking, math, science, and social studies. Because this book's focus is on teaching and learning in the classroom, our use of *assistive technology* refers primarily to technology that meets the *learning and communication needs* of children and youth with disabilities in school.

Educational and Instructional Technology

Educational technology and *instructional technology* have come to be used interchangeably, but as Roblyer (2003) points out, "no single acceptable definition of these terms dominates the field" (p. 5). To ease this confusion, Roblyer has developed the following definitions:

> Educational technology is a combination of the processes and tools involved in addressing educational needs and problems, with an emphasis on applying the most current tools: computers and their related technologies. (p. 6)
>
>   "Integrating educational technology" refers to the process of determining which *electronic tools* and which methods for implementing them are appropriate for given classroom situations and problems. (p. 8)

A close reading of these definitions reveals that *assistive technology* could be considered a subset of Roblyer's definition of *educational technology*. Insert the phrase "students with disabilities" and this becomes a good working definition of assistive technology:

> [Assistive] technology is a combination of the processes and tools involved in addressing educational needs and problems [of students with disabilities], with an emphasis on applying the most current tools: computers and their related technologies. (p. 6)

Insert the phrase "integrating assistive technology" into the second definition and it accurately describes that process as well:

> "Integrating [assistive] technology" refers to the process of determining which *electronic tools* and which methods for implementing them are appropriate for given classroom situations and problems. (p. 8)

Although some writers have used *special education technology* to refer to these processes (e.g., Edyburn, 2003), we have chosen to use the more neutral *assistive technology* because it does not imply that the technology is limited to students who are educated in special education settings.

THE LEGAL BASIS FOR ASSISTIVE TECHNOLOGY

As noted in the previous section, the definition of *assistive technology* is specified in federal special education law. IDEA 2004 includes this definition because the law mandates that assistive technology devices and services be provided to students with disabilities if the technology is essential for accessing education and education-related resources.

Individuals with Disabilities Education Act

Although IDEA 2004 is the most recent reauthorization of the federal law that governs the education of students with disabilities in P–12 settings, it was the 1997 reauthorization that changed the role of assistive technology. Reauthorizations of IDEA prior to 1997 mentioned assistive technology only in provisions related to supplementary aids

FIGURE 1–3   Brief timeline of assistive technology laws

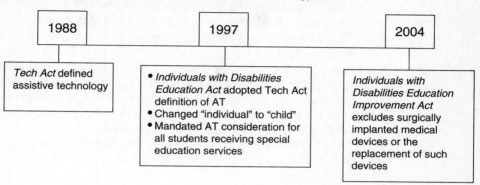

and services. As a result, consideration of assistive technology was typically limited to students with severe disabilities. The reauthorization of IDEA in 1997 dramatically changed this situation by clearly defining assistive technology and requiring consideration of the assistive technology needs of *every* student receiving special education services. IDEA 1997 adopted the definition of assistive technology established by the Technology-Related Assistance for Individuals with Disabilities Act of 1988 (Tech Act). (See Figure 1.3 for a brief timeline.) By inserting assistive technology consideration into every individualized education program (IEP) development process, IDEA 1997 significantly increased the number of students, as well as the range of disabilities, for which assistive technology solutions are now considered.

IDEA 2004 alters only slightly the 1997 definition of assistive technology by specifically excluding surgically implanted medical devices or replacement of such devices. Assistive technology consideration remains as one of the "special factors" that must be considered during the development of the IEP. IDEA 2004 reiterates its importance in the education of students with disabilities by giving priority status to funding "projects that promote the development and use of technologies with universal design, assistive technology devices, and assistive technology services to maximize children with disabilities' access to and participation in the general education curriculum" (Sec. 1481(d)(4)(6)).

In addition to IDEA 2004, two other federal laws have had an impact on the provision of assistive technology to students with disabilities. Section 504 of the Rehabilitation Act of 1973 (and subsequent reauthorizations) and the Americans with Disabilities Act (ADA) of 1990 ensure that students with disabilities have equal access to education and that they are protected from discrimination based on having a disability. Each of these laws has relevance to our discussion of assistive technology.

Section 504 of the Rehabilitation Act of 1973

Section 504, which has been reauthorized several times since its original passage, states:

> No otherwise qualified individual with a disability in the United States . . . shall, solely by reason of her or his handicap, be excluded from participation in, be denied the benefits of, or be subjected to discrimination under any program or activity receiving Federal financial assistance. (Sec. 794(a))

As recipients of federal funds, school districts must comply with Section 504. Because it is a civil rights provision, Section 504 applies to a broader range of students than those who fall within 1 of the 13 categories of disabilities specified by IDEA 2004. Section 504 applies to *all* students with disabilities, even those who are not eligible for special education. Students with medical conditions such as heart malfunctions, blood disorders, chronic fatigue syndrome, respiratory conditions, epilepsy, and cancer would be considered to have a disability and are entitled to accommodations under Section 504 if the condition impacts their education (Copenhaver, 2005). They are entitled to educational accommodations, so they will not be denied an education equal to that provided for their typical peers. Therefore, students who are considered to have a disability under Section 504 may be entitled to assistive technology to avail themselves of educational opportunities.

Americans with Disabilities Act

The Americans with Disabilities Act (ADA) is civil rights legislation aimed at preventing discrimination against individuals that is based on disability. The ADA extends civil rights protection to public places, including educational institutions, places of employment, transportation, and communication services whether or not the institution or business receives federal funds. With respect to education, the ADA is especially important for students pursuing postsecondary education because these students are no longer covered by IDEA. Assistive technology is not specifically mentioned in the ADA, but it is generally considered to fit under the phrase "auxiliary aids and services" that must be provided to make programs accessible. Many colleges and universities provide assistive technology as a reasonable accommodation to make their programs accessible to students with disabilities. Chapter 13 provides more detailed information on college students' rights under the ADA. Figure 1.4 shows a visual representation of the relationship between IDEA, Section 504, special education, general education, and the ADA.

BRIEF HISTORY OF ASSISTIVE TECHNOLOGY

Before the passage of the laws discussed previously, there were no legal mandates to provide assistive technology to students with disabilities. However, a few people recognized the value of what we now call low-tech devices. The manual typewriter was one of the first pieces of technology adopted by people who could not write due to a disability. The first typewriter was developed in 1808 by a man named Pellegrino Turri who built it for his friend Countess Carolina Fantoni da Fivizzono, who was blind, to help her write legibly (Jacobs, 1999). In more recent times, Bob Williams, a commissioner in the U.S. Department of Health and Human Services during the Clinton administration, who has physical disabilities and cannot speak, identifies

FIGURE 1–4 Laws affecting assistive technology

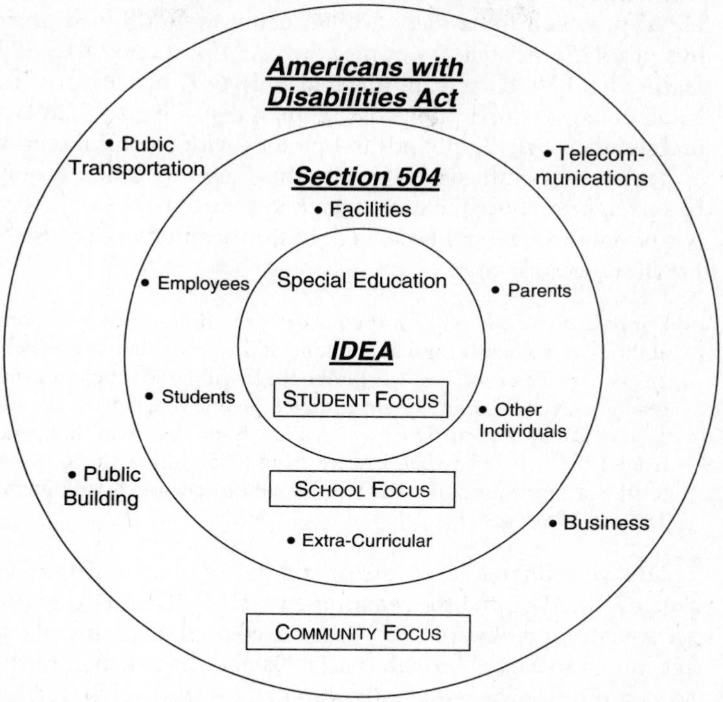

Americans with Disabilities Act
- Pubic Transportation
- Telecommunications
- Employees
- Students
- Public Building

Section 504
- Facilities
- Parents
- Other Individuals
- Business
- Extra-Curricular

Special Education

IDEA
STUDENT FOCUS

SCHOOL FOCUS

COMMUNITY FOCUS

Source: Reprinted with permission from *A Parent and Educator Guide to Section 504: Another Service Option for Children with Disabilities,* by J. Copenhaver, 2005. Retrieved from the Mountain Plains Regional Resource Center website: http://www.rrfcnetwork.org/images/stories/MPRRC/Products/Generic/Section 504/504parentguide.pdf

a typewriter as his first piece of technology. He was 7 years old when his parents provided with him an IBM electric typewriter. He learned years later that his teacher had not believed he would ever learn to read. His reflection on this first piece of technology provides important insights:

I am convinced that had I not had the typewriter, my teacher's perception would have likely become very much of a self-fulfilling prophecy. I would have become, like an estimated 50% of my contemporaries with cerebral palsy who, despite their typical intelligence, now face significant difficulties with reading, writing, and comprehending much of the printed word. (Williams, 2000, p. 247)

Fast-forward to the early 1980s when the first affordable personal computers became available. The ability to delete and insert text without having to retype entire pages was quickly recognized as a powerful feature by problem solvers like Bernie (from the chapter introduction) and Bob Williams. Peripherals that turned PCs into talking machines for people who could not speak quickly followed. The first book on this topic, *Personal Computers and the Disabled*, was published in 1984 (McWilliams) with illustrations of the latest computers such as Hewlett-Packard's HP-150, which for a mere $3,995 came with a 9-inch green screen and 256K of memory (256 *kilo*bytes, not megabytes). The Radio Shack TRS-80 was $1,999 and featured a 12-inch screen, but had only 64K of memory. Texas Instruments marketed one of the first "portable" computers"—it cost $2,695, had 128K of memory, and weighed *only* 37 pounds (44 pounds with a color monitor)!

Technology enthusiasts thought they saw the future: If only the technology could be faster, have more memory, weigh less, and cost less, the problems facing students with disabilities would be solved. In the introduction to his 1984 book, McWilliams predicted exactly that:

> I hope that people will soon consider providing a personal computer for certain disabilities as automatic and as fundamental as providing a wheelchair or a leader [guide] dog or a pair of crutches. . . . I hope there will be so much information on and action in getting personal computers to disabled people that this book will be but a minor footnote in a major campaign. . . . Let's just hope that what happened to word processing from 1982 to 1984 [when it went from being unknown to being a ubiquitous writing tool] is a forerunner of what will happen to personal computers for the disabled from 1984 to 1986. (p. 16)

Did McWilliams say 1986? It still has not happened in 2007. Even with the passage of the ADA and the reauthorizations of IDEA that require the consideration of assistive technology for every student who receives special education services, it still has not happened. Through the 1990s and the first half of the next decade the technology did improve—steadily, rapidly, impressively—yet McWilliams's prediction has not come to pass. The problems of getting technology to students with disabilities and getting the technology used effectively have not been solved. At the time of this writing, numerous assistive technology products are available, many easy to use and at affordable prices, but problems with identifying appropriate tools and implementing plans in schools remain major obstacles that keep students with disabilities from benefiting from assistive technology.

Bob Williams (2000), the disability advocate, identifies additional barriers to assistive technology implementation—society's negative stereotypes and low expectations of people with disabilities:

> Why are so many people consigned to lead lives of needless dependence and silence? Not because we lack the funds or because we lack the federal policy mandates needed to gain access to those funds. Rather, many people lead lives of silence because many others still find it difficult to believe that people with speech disabilities like my own have anything to say or contributions to make. (p. 250)

Assistive technology has the potential to empower people with disabilities with the ability to participate in their communities and achieve more than ever before (ATA, 2004). Technology has been called "the great equalizer" for people with disabilities because it offers "better opportunities to communicate, learn, participate, and achieve greater overall levels of independence. Perhaps most importantly, new technologies enable people with disabilities to perform competitively in the workplace" (National Organization on Disability, 2006).

Also called "electronic curb cuts," computers provide access to activities and opportunities that people without disabilities take for granted. In education they can provide access to the general education curriculum and key educational experiences such as typical reading, writing, and assessment activities that take place daily in every classroom. Providing access to the curriculum is an essential component of the successful inclusion of students with disabilities in their neighborhood schools (Nolet & McLaughlin, 2000; Salend, 2004; Villa & Thousand, 2000). Computers can enable students with disabilities to demonstrate their understanding of academic subjects even if they cannot write legibly or speak intelligibly (Male, 2003). They can make textbooks understandable to students who are poor readers (Meyer & Rose, 1998). They can decrease students' reliance on teachers and other adults by increasing students' independence in completing academic tasks (Bryant, Bryant & Rieth, 2002). Computer technology can provide a voice for students who cannot speak (Williams, 2006). The list of benefits goes on.

However, after 20 years of exploring new assistive technology products and teaching teachers, parents, and students how to use them, we have reached one very clear conclusion: Technology alone is not enough. Assistive technology is exciting and fun, no question about it, but a computer alone will not increase a student's success in school. A school's simply purchasing an expensive site license for a software program will not lead to student gains. Providing students who have disabilities with the latest, most dazzling devices in the world will not make a difference in their lives—unless the initiative integrates the technology into the curriculum and addresses the details of implementation.

Therefore, this text's emphasis is on the *integration of assistive technology into the curriculum*; how assistive technology can be used in all kinds of classrooms to enhance the teaching and learning of students with a wide range of disabilities. It is easy to be seduced by the razzle-dazzle of the latest electronic gimmick, but we have tried to resist that temptation and instead have focused on the *link* between technology and the teaching–learning process. The context for our discussions of technology use is always the classroom, the school, and other environments in which students learn. This approach reflects the philosophy of the leading professional organization in educational technology, the International Society for Technology in Education (ISTE), which articulates that "learning with technology should not be about the technology itself but about the learning that can be facilitated through it" (Knezek, Christensen, Bell, & Bull, 2006, p. 19).

In addition to this curriculum integration philosophy, we share the core principles of the Alliance for Technology Access (ATA), a national network of technology resource centers, organizations, and businesses who seek to connect people with disabilities to technology that will empower them to participate fully in their communities (ATA, 2004).

These principles explain how technology relates to people with disabilities obtaining their basic rights:

- People with disabilities have the right to maximum independence and participation in all environments, without barriers.
- Technology can be harnessed to diminish or eliminate environmental barriers for people with disabilities.

- People with disabilities have the right to control and direct their own choices, and the right to access the information they need in order to make informed decisions according to their goals and interests.
- People with disabilities have the right to employ assistive technologies, strategies for implementation, and necessary training support to maximize their independence and productivity. (ATA, n.d.)

Independence, self-sufficiency, personal choice, participation, inclusion, dignity—these principles are a direct outgrowth of the disability rights movement. In the late 1960s, motivated and educated by the protest strategies and successful outcomes of the civil rights movement, a handful of college students with disabilities began their own self-determination movement in Berkeley, California (Shapiro, 1993). Calling themselves the Rolling Quads and led by Ed Roberts, a young man with severe physical disabilities as a result of polio, these students rebelled against the patronizing, controlling, and limiting bureaucracy, and set out to break down "the common barriers they faced—from classrooms they could not get into to their lack of transportation around town" (p. 48). Their goals expanded to "total self-sufficiency," and eventually they founded the first independent living center in the country. The Rolling Quads wanted to be their own case managers, "so they would never again have to kowtow to a bureaucrat who controlled their funding" (p. 48), and they decided that they needed to change the way they thought of themselves—no longer would they be clients of the state; from now on they were "consumers of state services."

With this dramatic change in attitude, the traditional medical model of diagnosis and treatment prescribed by professionals was called into question. Shapiro (1993) explains this change:

> The medical model of disability measured independence by how far one could walk after an illness or how far one could bend his legs after an accident. But [Ed] Roberts redefined independence as the control a disabled person has over his life. Independence was measured not by the tasks one could perform without assistance but by the quality of one's life with help. . . . Disabled people themselves, the newly christened "independent living movement" assumed, knew better than doctors and professionals what they needed for daily living. And what disabled people wanted most of all was to be fully integrated in their communities, from school to work. (p. 51)

The continuing efforts of these and other disability activists eventually led to the passage in 1990 of the ADA. This civil rights law for people with disabilities provides the legal basis for the inclusion of people with disabilities in all walks of life, from the workplace to public places like educational institutions. Assistive technology is a means to these ends. Therefore, we believe that students with disabilities must be provided with access to the assistive technology tools that will increase their independence and participation in school. We also believe that teachers and other school personnel have a responsibility to help students with disabilities find and learn how to use these tools.

In keeping with the philosophy of the disability rights movement, this text does not advocate the medical model of diagnosis and treatment that is accepted practice in rehabilitation fields. Instead the text advocates a decision-making process that places the student at the center (ATA, 2000).

This consumer-directed approach is in direct opposition to the traditional medical model and its reliance on "experts" who prescribe solutions for the "patient." Instead, we believe that the individual with a disability, their family members, or their authorized representatives are in charge of the decisions about their own lives. They set their own goals and direct the process of finding technology that meets their needs.

How does this consumer-directed approach fit in an educational setting? We believe that students and their parents need to be active participants in the decision-making process; that is, in figuring out which technology tools they are comfortable with and which technology tools will best help them with their schoolwork. The selection of these technology tools ties in to the goals and dreams students (and their parents) have. Teachers and assistive technology specialists need to ask students for their input and honor their preferences during the assistive technology selection process (Grady, Kovach, Lange, & Shannon, 1993; Moore, Duff, & Keefe, 2006). This process is discussed in detail in Chapter 8.

UNIVERSAL DESIGN

Another concept that is woven throughout this book is *universal design*, which supports increased independence, participation, and inclusion of individuals with disabilities in all aspects of life and at the same time maintains the dignity of the individual. Universal design is defined as "the design of products and environments to be usable by all people, to the greatest extent possible, without the need for adaptation or specialized design" (Center for Universal Design, 1997, para. 3). Before a product or environment is developed and marketed, universal design recommends considering "the needs of the greatest number of possible users, [thereby] eliminating the need for costly, inconvenient, and unattractive adaptations later on" (Center on Applied Special Technology, 2006). This concept began in the field of architecture, then broadened to the fields of hardware and software development, and is now a key principle in instructional design.

Three popular conveniences today clearly illustrate the concept of universal design: automatic doors, curb cuts, and captioning of television programs. Automatic doors make stores, airports, and other public spaces accessible to individuals with disabilities, but they also make those places accessible to a broader range of people: shoppers pushing shopping carts, travelers wheeling suitcases, parents pushing children in strollers, elderly people, and others who lack the strength to open heavy doors. In sum, automatic doors benefit a wide range of people and all of them, including individuals with disabilities, can access the facilities in a dignified manner—independently, through the same entrance.

Curb cuts are another good example of universal design. Originally designed to make navigating city streets more accessible to wheelchair users, curb cuts turned out to benefit many more people than just wheelchair users (Jacobs, 1999). Curb cuts are now used by workers making deliveries with hand trucks, elderly people using walkers, roller bladers and skateboarders, as well as people pulling city shopping baskets and pushing baby strollers.

A curb cut benefits many people, not only those who use wheelchairs.

Moving from the field of architecture to the field of media, our third example of universal design is the captioning of television programs. Closed captioning was originally developed to enable people who are deaf to access and enjoy television shows. When its use was limited to the deaf, the technology was expensive and cumbersome to find. Today, however, captioning is built into television production because it benefits many people. As Jacobs (1999) explains:

> Television (TV) manufacturers in the U.S. will tell you that their caption decoders for the deaf wound up benefiting tens-of-millions more consumers than originally intended. As the electronic curb cut effect has shown in the past, televisions with decoders are simply better than those without. For example, captioning can enable TV viewers to: . . . listen to programs in silence while someone is sleeping; and listen to programs in noisy environments like sports bars.

Captioning for television and film has also become a widely used instructional tool for people who are learning English as a second language (National Council on Disability, 2005).

In the field of computer technology, a good example of a design feature that is convenient for all but a necessity for some is placing the power switch on the keyboard, rather than in the back of a computer (ATA, 2004). This design change enables independent computer access to people with physical disabilities who cannot reach a rear-mounted switch, while providing a welcome convenience to every computer user.

SIDEBAR

Other Examples of Technology Innovations Benefiting Large Numbers of People

The list of technology innovations that were originally developed to meet the needs of people with disabilities but ended up benefiting everyone is long (Jacobs, 1999). It includes:

- Alexander Graham Bell's invention of the telephone, which he developed while trying to help his deaf students
- Bell Labs' scientists' invention of the transistor, which they developed while trying to develop more reliable, powerful, smaller, and cheaper hearing aids (Jacobs, 1999)
- Ray Kurzweil and his team's invention of the flat-bed scanner, which was an unexpected result of their work on a "reading machine" for the blind.

Seven principles comprise the concept of universal design. They are as follows:

1. equitable use
2. flexibility in use
3. simple and intuitive use
4. perceptible information
5. tolerance for errors
6. low physical effort
7. size and space for approach and use (Center for Universal Design, 1997)

All seven principles are applied, to some degree, in computer design. However, it is principle 2, flexibility in use, that is most relevant to this text because of its direct impact on students with disabilities.

Flexibility in use encourages designers to make products that offer choices in methods of use. Current computer operating systems, for example, follow this guideline by presenting users with the choice of using either the mouse or the keyboard to control the computer. Both Macintosh and Windows operating systems offer keyboard shortcuts that provide access to all operating systems functions directly from the keyboard. For example, in Windows XP an item can be permanently deleted by pressing Shift + Delete, rather than by using the mouse to drag the item to the Recycle Bin. Having the option to use the keyboard instead of the mouse provides computer access for users who find it difficult or impossible to control a mouse. This includes students with fine motor control difficulties, limited range of motion, or visual impairments that interfere with seeing or tracking the mouse pointer on the computer screen.

FIGURE 1–5
Selecting larger
icons using
Windows
Accessibility
Wizard

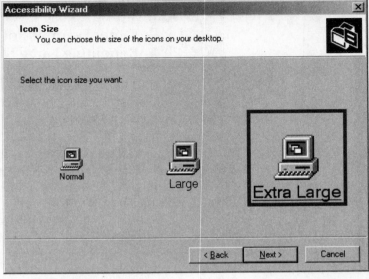

Source: Microsoft Product. Screen shot reprinted with permission from
Microsoft Corporation.

The principle of flexibility in use also encourages designers to take into account variations among the precision and accuracy of computer users, and variations in users' speeds. Both the Macintosh and Windows operating systems provide the means to enlarge the size of icons on the monitor (Figure 1.5). Larger icons provide a larger target area to accommodate some students' lack of precision and accuracy in directing the mouse pointer. The larger icons may promote successful computer use for students with cognitive deficits, hand-eye coordination problems, visual perceptual issues, low vision, hand tremors, or poor fine motor control. Both operating systems also provide the means to speed up or slow down the speed of double-clicking a mouse or tracking the mouse pointer across the screen. The benefits to these and other features are discussed in more detail in Chapter 6.

UNIVERSAL DESIGN FOR LEARNING

Universal design for learning (UDL) draws on the concept of universal design in architecture and products, and combines it with current brain research about how students learn, resulting in an approach that increases flexibility in teaching and decreases the barriers that prevent students from accessing materials and classroom activities (Rose & Meyer, 2002). Just as the original concept of universal design intended to make structures and products usable by the broadest range of individuals, UDL seeks to make curricular content available to the broadest range of students. For example, software programs that provide spoken directions with a simple click of the mouse enable students who cannot read, students who forget directions, and students with attention problems to complete activities without teacher intervention. Digital media, especially electronic text, offer many opportunities to engage students in learning and to enable them to demonstrate what they have learned even if they struggle with traditional reading and writing tasks. Upcoming chapters, Chapter 5 in particular, provide additional information about UDL. Readers should note that UDL makes the curriculum accessible to a broad range of students, including general education students who are auditory learners, visual learners, or difficult to engage or motivate, as well as students with disabilities. When the principles of UDL are applied in classrooms, the need for additional assistive technology solutions for individual students may be reduced or eliminated.

Even in classrooms where UDL is practiced, however, some students will continue to need specialized technology solutions. For example, because the number of students who are blind is comparatively low, the potential market for Braille keyboards is small. As a result, Braille keyboards are not likely to become a standard option on conventional computers. Similarly, the number of students who cannot speak and who benefit from augmentative communication systems is relatively low. Technology-based augmentative communication systems are not likely to be integrated into off-the-shelf computers. Therefore, whereas universal design is an outstanding development for people with disabilities and it remains an essential part of the assistive technology decision-making process, it does not completely eliminate the need for specialized products. Throughout the text, we will provide information on both universally designed features and specialized technology devices, with the emphasis always placed on identifying the appropriate match between students' needs and possible technology solutions.

CONCLUSION

Do you remember Bernie, the person profiled at the beginning of this chapter who typed on a typewriter with his foot? The dowel that was bolted to the bottom of his shoe was a good example of a low-tech device, and it served him well. However, think of how much more Bernie could have written, how much more he could have interacted with the world, had he lived today and could use his low-tech dowel to access a high-tech computer with a high-speed Internet connection. As you read the following chapters, think of what Bernie could have accomplished with the technology tools that are highlighted. Think of other people you know who have difficulties writing or reading or learning or communicating. Try to make connections between their particular needs and the opportunities offered by assistive technology. You will find powerful solutions to the problems they face, and we hope you will be as excited as we are by the promise of assistive technology.

SUMMARY

- Lessons from people with disabilities: (1) Regardless of how disabled a person may appear, inside is a person who wants to be part of life. (2) Taking a problem-solving attitude can lead to creative solutions that eliminate obstacles caused by disabilities. (3) Simple technology can change a person's life.

- Assistive technology is defined in the Individuals with Disabilities Education Improvement Act of 2004 (IDEA 2004). The definition consists of two parts: assistive technology devices and assistive technology services.

- The assistive technology continuum spans low-tech to high-tech devices. Low-tech devices, such as pencil grips and clipboards, use no electronic components and are relatively inexpensive. High-tech devices, such as laptop computers and augmentative communication devices, are usually based on computer technology, require training to use, and are expensive. However, their power and flexibility usually make the expense and training worthwhile.

- The term *assistive technology* is related to several other terms—*rehabilitation technology, special education technology, educational technology, instructional technology,* and *information technology.* However, this text uses it to refer primarily to technology that meets the learning and communication needs of students with disabilities.

- The 1997 reauthorization of IDEA was the first law to require that assistive technology be considered for every student receiving special education services.

- Two other two federal laws have had an impact on the provision of assistive technology to students with disabilities: Section 504 of the Rehabilitation Act and the Americans with Disabilities Act (ADA).

- Despite these laws, serious problems remain in getting appropriate assistive technology to students with disabilities who stand to benefit from it.

- This text's philosophy: People with disabilities have the right to independence, self-sufficiency, personal choice, participation, inclusion, and dignity, and technology can be harnessed to achieve these goals.

- The text's emphasis is on the integration of assistive technology into the curriculum—the link between assistive technology and the teaching and learning of students with disabilities.

- Universal design is defined as "the design of products and environments to be usable by all people, to the greatest extent possible, without the need for adaptation or specialized design" (Center for Universal Design, 1997, para. 3).

- Universal design principle 2, flexibility in use, is the principle that is most relevant to this text because of its direct impact on students with disabilities.

WEB RESOURCES

For additional information on the topics listed, go to the following websites:

Low-Tech Tools

Arizona Technology Access Program
http://www.nau.edu/ihd/aztap/geriatric/article.shtml
Onion Mountain Technology, Inc.
http://www.onionmountaintech.com

Michigan's Assistive Technology Resource: *Now You See It . . . Now You Don't! Three dozen cheap tricks*. Download PDF from
http://www.cenmi.org → Handouts/Training Materials

Other Kinds of Assistive Technology

Family Center on Technology & Disability
http://www.fctd.info/resources/search.php

Laws Governing Assistive Technology

Wrightslaw
http://www.wrightslaw.com

Benefits of Assistive Technology in the Workplace

National Organization on Disability
http://www.nod.org → Technology

Philosophy of This Text

International Society for Technology in Education (ISTE)
http://www.iste.org
Alliance for Technology Access (ATA)
http://www.ataccess.org
Norman Kunc
http://www.normemma.com → Schools

Disability Rights Movement

Smithsonian's Disability Rights Movement Virtual Museum
http://www.americanhistory.si.edu/disabilityrights/welcome.html

Universal Design

Center for Universal Design at North Carolina State University
http://www.design.ncsu.edu/cud/about_ud/udprinciples.htm
Center on Applied Special Technology (CAST)
http://www.cast.org/research/udl/ index.html

Universal Design in Computer Operating Systems

Keyboard shortcuts in Windows Vista
http://www.microsoft.com/enable/training/windowsvista/accesskeys.aspx

SUGGESTED ACTIVITIES

1. *Recognize the power of assistive technology.* Observe or interview a person with a disability who uses assistive technology in daily life. The technology could be a computer, an augmentative communication system, or any low-tech or mid-tech device.
   a. *Introduce the user:* Write a paragraph introducing the person. Make him or her come alive as an individual first and foremost. Mention school or work and the person's interests. Then include some information about his or her disability.
   b. *Discuss the benefits and purpose of assistive technology use:* What does assistive technology enable this person to do? Discuss specific activities.

2. *Demonstrate low-tech assistive technology.* Visit a dollar store and find an item that could be used as low-tech assistive technology. Bring the item to class to share your idea and demonstrate its use (for example, a clipboard to hold papers securely, or rubberized shelf liner to keep books from slipping).

3. *Research universal design.* Visit the website of the Center for Applied Special Technology (CAST) at http://www.cast.org. Read up on the latest research and developments in universal design for learning. Write a summary of one of them and post it to your class' discussion board.

4. *Start an assistive technology portfolio.* Begin gathering resources on assistive technology. The portfolio can be compiled and presented electronically using PowerPoint or a website, or it can be compiled in hard copy, using a binder or accordion file. The key is to organize the materials and clearly label them. The following categories are suggested: product flyers and catalog excerpts; standards or guidelines from your professional organization regarding assistive technology skills; informative websites or print materials that would be useful resources for colleagues and parents. Add relevant materials to the portfolio after reading each subsequent chapter in the text.

REFERENCES

Alliance for Technology Access. (n.d.). *Principles*. Retrieved June 2, 2006, from http://www.ataccess.org/about/principles.html

Alliance for Technology Access. (2000). *1999–2000 Impact Report*. Retrieved June 2, 2006, from http://www.ataccess.org/about/impact2000/default.html

Alliance for Technology Access. (2004). *Computer resources for people with disabilities* (4th ed.). Alameda, CA: Hunter House.

Blackhurst, A. E., & Lahm, E. A. (2000). Foundations of technology and exceptionality. In J. Lindsey (Ed.), *Technology and exceptional individuals* (3rd ed., pp. 3–45). Austin, TX: Pro-Ed.

Bryant, B. R., Bryant, D. P., & Rieth, H. J. (2002). The use of assistive technology in postsecondary education. In L. Brinckerhoff, J. McGuire, & S. Shaw (Eds.), *Postsecondary education and transition for students with learning disabilities* (pp. 389–429). Austin, TX: Pro-Ed.

Center for Universal Design. (1997). *About universal design*. Retrieved June 20, 2006, from http://www.design.ncsu.edu/cud/about_ud/about_ud.htm

Center on Applied Special Technology. (2006). *Research and development in universal design for learning*. Retrieved June 20, 2006, from http://www.cast.org/research/index.html

Church, G., & Glennen, S. (1992). *The handbook of assistive technology.* San Diego, CA: Singular.

Collins, R. (n.d.). *Independence can be cheap and easy with low tech assistive technology.* Retrieved August 24, 2006, from the Arizona Technology Access Program (AzTAP) website: http://www.nau.edu/ihd/aztap/aztap

Copenhaver, J. (2005). *A parent and educator guide to Section 504: Another service option for children with disabilities.* Logan, Utah: Mountain Plains Regional Resource Center website: http://www.rrfenetwork.org/images/stories/MPRRC/Products/General/Section504/504parentguide.pdf

Edyburn, D. L. (2003). Technology in special education. In M. D. Roblyer (Ed.), *Integrating educational technology into teaching* (3rd ed., pp. 315–333). Upper Saddle River, NJ: Merrill/Prentice Hall.

Gold, M. (1980). *Try another way: Training manual.* Austin, Texas: Marc Gold & Associates. ERIC# ED172507

Golden, D. (1998). *Assistive technology in special education: Policy and practice.* Reston, VA: Council for Exceptional Children's Council of Administrators in Special Education and Technology and Media Division.

Grady, A. P., Kovach, T., Lange, M., & Shannon, L. (1993, February). "Consumer knows best": Promoting choice in assistive technology. *PT: Magazine of Physical Therapy, 1*(2), 50–56.

Individuals with Disabilities Education Act of 2004, 20 U.S.C. §§ 1401, 1481.

Jacobs, S. I. (1999). Section 255 of the Telecommunications Act of 1996: Fueling the creation of new electronic curbcuts. Retrieved June 20, 2006, from the Center for an Accessible Society website: http://www.accessiblesociety.org/topics/technology/theelectriccurbcut

Knezek, G., Christensen, R., Bell, L., & Bull, G. (2006). Identifying key research issues. *Learning and Leading with Technology, 33*(8), 18–20.

Male, M. (2003). *Technology for inclusion: Meeting the needs of all students.* Boston: Allyn & Bacon.

McWilliams, P. A. (1984). *Personal computers and the disabled.* Garden City, NY: Quantum Press/Doubleday.

Meyer, A., & Rose, D. H. (1998). *Learning to read in the computer age.* Newton, MA: Brookline Books.

Moore, V. M., Duff, F. R., & Keefe, E. B. (2006, October/November). The importance of student preferences, human rights, and dignity. *Closing the Gap, 25*(4), 1, 12.

National Council on Disability. (2005). *Information technology and Americans with disabilities: An overview of innovation, laws, progress and challenges.* Retrieved June 20, 2006, from http://www.ncd.gov/newsroom/publications/2005/innovation.htm

National Organization on Disability. (2006). *Economic participation: Technology.* Retrieved June 20, 2006, from http://www.nod.org/index.cfm?fuseaction=Page.viewPage&pageId=16

Nolet, V., & McLaughlin, M. J. (2000). *Accessing the general curriculum: Including students with disabilities in standards-based reform.* Thousand Oaks, CA: Corwin Press.

Rehabilitation Act of 1973, Section 504, Pub. L. No. 93–112, 29 U.S.C. § 794 (1977).

Roblyer, M. D. (2003). *Integrating educational technology into teaching* (3rd ed.) Upper Saddle River, NJ: Merrill/Prentice Hall.

Rose, D., & Meyer, A. (2002). *Teaching every student in the digital age: Universal design for learning.* Alexandria, VA: Association for Supervision and Curriculum Development.

Salend, S. J. (2004). *Creating inclusive classrooms: Effective and reflective practices* (5th ed.). Upper Saddle River, NJ: Merrill/Prentice Hall.

Shapiro, J. P. (1993). *No pity: People with disabilities forging a new civil rights movement.* New York: Times Books.

Villa, R. A., & Thousand, J. S. (Eds). (2000). *Restructuring for caring and effective education: Piecing the puzzle together* (2nd ed.). Baltimore: Brookes.

Williams, B. (2000). More than an exception to the rule. In M. Fried-Oken & H. Bersani (Eds.), *Speaking up and spelling it out* (pp. 245–254). Baltimore: Brookes.

Williams, M. B. (2006). *How far we've come, how far we've got to go: Tales from the trenches* [DVD]. Monterey, CA: Augmentative Communication, Inc.

CHAPTER 2

Assistive Technology to Support Writing

FOCUS QUESTIONS

1. What are the major components of the writing process?
2. What kinds of problems do students with disabilities have with writing?
3. Which technology tools can address these problems, and how?
4. What else, in addition to appropriate technology selection, is essential to improve the writing of students with disabilities?

THE CONTEXT—PROCESS WRITING

Before we can discuss how assistive technology can support writing, we need to define the term *writing*. What *is* writing? Is it simply holding a pen and moving your hand from left to right to leave meaningful marks on a page? Of course it is more than that. What *else* is involved in the process of getting your thoughts down on paper?

There is a huge body of literature that addresses these questions, including the specification of content standards for language arts developed by the National Council of Teachers of English and the International Reading Association (1996). Although it is beyond the scope of this text to present this literature in detail, a brief summary of it will provide a helpful context to our discussion.

Writing is a complex problem-solving activity that involves thinking, planning, and decision making as well as the mechanics of transcription. Flower and Hayes (1981) present a cognitive process model in which emphasis is placed on the underlying *thinking skills* involved in writing. They characterize the act of writing as consisting of three major elements: the task environment, the writer's long-term memory, and the writing process itself:

> The task environment includes all of those things outside the writer's skin, starting with the rhetorical problem or assignment. . . . The second element is the writer's long-term memory in which the writer has stored knowledge, not only of the topic, but of the audience and of various writing plans. The third element . . . contains writing processes themselves, specifically the basic processes of Planning, Translating, and Reviewing (p. 369)

The process Flower and Hayes (1981) call "planning" has come to be known as **prewriting**. This process takes place before any sentence is put on paper. Prewriting involves planning for writing; generating ideas, which may include brainstorming activities and/or collecting relevant information; organizing the ideas into some kind of meaningful structure and sequence that may take the form of a concept map or outline; and setting goals for the composing activity. Tomkins (2000) suggests that 70% of writing time should be spent on these prewriting activities.

The second process, translating, is usually referred to **drafting**. In this process students develop their ideas and thoughts into meaningful words, sentences, and paragraphs (Scott & Vitale, 2003). Drafting requires both thinking and mechanical processes such as handwriting or keyboarding.

In the third process, **reviewing**, students *reread* and *evaluate* what they have written. In the fourth process, **editing**, they *edit* and *revise* their drafts. These self-evaluations, edits, and revisions focus on all aspects of writing—spelling, grammar, organizational structure, word choice, and content.

Although these concepts at first glance may look like an ordered sequence, it is important to emphasize that in good writing these processes do not proceed in a linear fashion. Good writers continually generate new ideas, reorganize their thoughts, and set new goals as they compose, edit, and revise (Flower & Hayes, 1981). The writing process, then, is more like a series of interconnected loops than a straight line. This recursive nature of the writing process has important implications for the teaching of writing (Lipson, Mosenthal, Daniels, & Woodside-Jiron, 2000) and for the use of technology to enhance writing.

Once the writing process is completely finished (usually after multiple drafts and revisions), a fifth and culminating activity is **sharing** the final product with others, or **publishing** it. Publishing can be done in a variety of ways, such as through bulletin board displays, class books or newsletters, school newspapers, or postings on class websites or discussion boards. The purpose of publishing is to provide a specific audience for the writing and "to instill pride of authorship" in student writers (Scott & Vitale, 2003).

PROBLEMS THAT STUDENTS WITH DISABILITIES HAVE WITH WRITING

Students with disabilities often have difficulty with all of the processes previously described, and it is not uncommon for them to try to avoid any kind of writing assignment. " 'I don't like to write. It's hard and it hurts my brain to think so hard,'" wrote a student in a journal that was part of a research study on struggling writers (Tompkins, 2002, p. 179). Another student in Tompkins's study said, "'When I have to write, I'm thinking about being done because I really don't like to write'" (p. 179). Students with learning disabilities and attention deficits, in particular, find the writing process overwhelming. In their research on the perceptions of students with language and learning disabilities (LLD) about instruction in the writing process, McAlister, Nelson, and Bahr (1999) found that "students with LLD may not plan because they do not know how to plan" (p. 170). The students in their study could not articulate what it means to plan or why they should plan. One interviewee said, "'I just do [planning] in my head, and sometimes I just type words out, and it becomes a story.'" These researchers summarize writing samples of students with LLD as being "shorter, less coherent, and less refined" than those of normally achieving students (p. 160). Other experts have characterized their writing as "lifeless" (Baker, Gersten, & Scanlon, 2002).

Spelling is particularly troublesome for students with learning disabilities. Their writing is often filled with misspelled words that are not corrected because students with learning disabilities have difficulty detecting the spelling errors in their writings (Darch, Kim, Johnson, & James, 2000; Jones, 2001). MacArthur, Ferretti, Okolo, and Cavalier (2001) summarize the writing problems displayed by students with learning disabilities:

> Their revisions are limited primarily to correction of mechanical errors. . . . They experience difficulties with transcription processes, both spelling and handwriting, and these struggles affect the overall quality of their writing because cognitive resources devoted to transcription are not available for higher-order processes. . . . Students with writing difficulties are also less knowledgeable about criteria for good writing and about writing strategies. . . . Their written products, in comparison to those of their normally developing peers, are typically shorter; contain more errors in spelling, punctuation, and capitalization; lack organization; are less cohesive; omit important genre components; and are lower in overall quality. (p. 288)

Students with other kinds of disabilities may also face obstacles when writing. Students who are deaf and communicate primarily through sign language have literacy levels well below grade level. Students with cerebral palsy, muscular dystrophy, and other physical disabilities struggle with the mechanics of writing. They cannot hold a pencil or do not have the fine motor skills needed to manipulate a pencil. Others may be minimally able to hold a writing implement but their movements are so slow and tedious that they are unable to work at a comfortable rate. These students may have lots of ideas and may be strong editors, but they cannot get their thoughts on paper. Some students with autism, Down syndrome, or visual-motor learning disabilities may have poor fine motor coordination that results in dysgraphia, which, in the context of writing, means their handwriting is illegible. Not only are they unable to share their final products with others, but their handwriting is illegible to themselves as well, making the rereading and revising process impossible.

One final problem related to writing faced by many students with disabilities is notetaking. Taking notes, which is an essential activity in many educational situations, is a specialized form of writing. Although it does not require prewriting and revising per se, it requires the ability to listen and write at the same time, the ability to organize the ideas that are presented, and the ability to distinguish what is important from what is not, all carried out simultaneously and speedily. This is a serious obstacle to learning for all students with disabilities.

TECHNOLOGY TOOLS THAT SUPPORT THE WRITING PROCESS

SIDEBAR

Low-Tech Adaptations for Writing

For students who have poor fine motor control, there are several low-tech items that can improve their ability to manipulate a pencil and write legibly. For example, building up the shaft of a pencil with modeling clay, foam, or a commercially available pencil grip can help a student control the pencil better (Georgia Assistive Technology Project Tools for Life, n.d.). Sometimes placing the paper on a board that is slanted (at a 15- to 30- degree angle) provides better control. Students who have use of only one hand can sometimes benefit from anchoring the paper on a clipboard. Paper that has raised lines or bold lines helps students stay on the lines when writing. This can help students with learning disabilities, as well as students with visual impairments. Students who are blind need to be taught to use signature guides, which are small plastic cards that have a cutout the size of a typical signature. A sighted person places the signature guide on the appropriate spot on the paper, and person with vision loss signs his or her name in the cutout space.

Other low-tech solutions are available for students who cannot manipulate a pen or pencil at all. Some students who have a whole-hand grasp can use rubber stamps for certain writing activities. For example, number and operation sign stamps are available and can be used for simple arithmetic worksheets. Having a stamp made with a student's name can enable a student with physical disabilities to sign his or her name. Rubber stamps with a wide variety of pictures are available in craft stores and could be used to answer questions on worksheets or quizzes. These are all examples of easy-to-use, inexpensive items that can support the activity of writing.

Prewriting: Graphic Organizers

Most writers, both professional and amateur, are apprehensive when faced with a blank piece of paper or a blank computer screen (optimistically called a "new document"). How can students get past this hurdle?

Remember that the writing process does not begin with drafting. It begins with prewriting activities such as brainstorming and getting organized. Even before computers, teachers discovered that using diagrams called graphic organizers could help students in the planning process. Sometimes called "think sheets" (Englert, Raphael, Anderson, Anthony, & Stevens, 1991), these prewriting activities encouraged students to think about what they wanted to write and helped them organize their ideas into a logical order. Now with computers, graphic organizer software programs offer students a seamless connection between a concept map and a text outline. Students no longer have to copy their ideas from the concept map to their paper or word processing document. They can spend their time thinking about their ideas and manipulating their graphical representation on a computer screen, and then—with one click of the mouse—they can turn their concept map into a text outline.

Graphic organizer software is particularly well suited for brainstorming activities. Inspiration software (by Inspiration Software, Inc.) has a feature called "rapid fire" that enables users to record ideas quickly; then the ideas can be manipulated on the screen until they are arranged into a meaningful structure and sequence, and the connections and subconnections among them are clearly represented (see Figure 2.1). This kind of activity can help students organize information and their ideas for a writing assignment.

Many students with learning disabilities or attention deficits do not yet have the skills needed to turn a brainstorming activity into an organized concept map. For these students, teachers have found that **templates** are a helpful scaffolding technique.

FIGURE 2–1   Sample graphic organizer: Concept map and related text outline

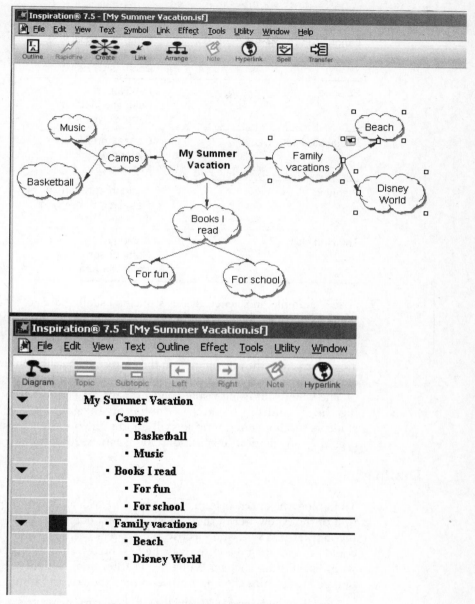

Source: Diagrams created in Inspiration® by Inspiration Software, Inc.

Templates provide a predesigned format that matches the specific organizing task. The student's responsibility is simplified to filling in the content only. With the organization being provided by the template, the student is free to concentrate on the subject matter. Table 2.1 lists various templates provided in Inspiration 7.5.

TABLE 2–1   Sample templates provided in Inspiration®

Subject Matter	Template Title
Language arts	Literary Web Literary Analysis Persuasive Essay
Science	Lab Report Scientific Method Simple Cycles
Social studies	Cause and Effect Historical Period Pro and Con
Planning	Assignment Plan Research Strategy Goal Setting
Thinking skills	Analogy Comparison Venn Diagram

For example, in science classes students usually have to write science lab reports. Students with learning disabilities or attention deficits often fail to demonstrate their understanding of the lab because their lab reports are disorganized and poorly written. With the science lab template that is provided in Inspiration 7.5, these students are able to enter the information in the correct place, click on the Outline button, and create an organized text outline from which they can finish the lab (see Figure 2.2).

The benefits of using visual concept maps are supported by both cognitive learning theory and the research. Graphic organizers have been shown to improve students' outlining and writing skills, and to help students with learning disabilities organize information (Inspiration, 2003; James, Abbott & Greenwood, 2001).

Drafting

Technology has been helping people get their ideas down on paper since the invention of the typewriter in the 1800s. (The first commercial typewriter was placed on the market in 1874, and electric typewriters became available in the 1950s.) You could say that the typewriter was the first high-tech writing tool used by individuals with disabilities. Michael Williams, a writer and disability advocate who has cerebral palsy, explains the importance of the typewriter to him:

> I was born in the late 1930s and these technologies [computers and augmentative communication devices] weren't even dreamt of then. My first piece of assistive technology was my grandfather's standard manual typewriter. I used typewriters to communicate all through grade school, high school, and during my undergraduate years in college. (Microsoft Corporation, 1999)

Bob Williams (no relation to Michael Williams), who held administrative positions in the U.S. Department of Health and Human Services during the Clinton

FIGURE 2–2
Inspiration's
science lab template
and outline

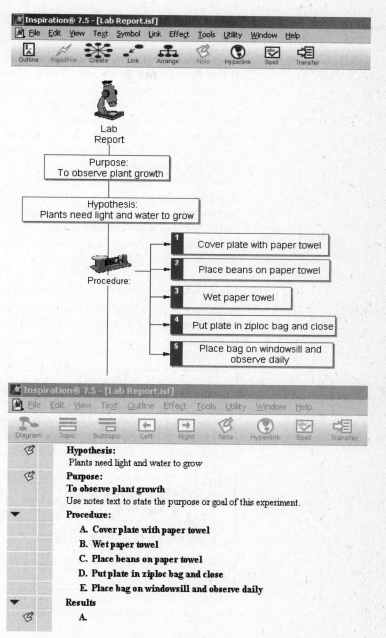

Source: Diagrams created in Inspiration® by Inspiration Software, Inc.

administration, also identifies the typewriter as his first piece of writing technology (Williams, 2000), as mentioned in Chapter 1. Unable to control his fingers due to cerebral palsy, he typed by grasping a small dowel in his fist. And Dick Boydell, an Englishman with cerebral palsy who could not use his hands at all, taught himself to type on a typewriter using his big toe. (See Chapter 7 for discussion of alternative access methods for students who cannot use a standard keyboard.)

Word Processing Software. These three individuals illustrate the first solution offered by technology: the ability to create clear, legible text by students who do not have the motor skills to grasp a pencil or the fine motor coordination to master the mechanics of penmanship. This, of course, is accomplished through the use of **word processing software** such as Microsoft Word. Even the simplest document created in Word is neat in appearance and legible. There are no smudges or tears in the paper where the writer had tried to erase a phrase. There are no messy cross-outs or arrows going in every direction to indicate changes in the order of sentences or paragraphs (see Figure 2.3). Richard Wanderman (2000), a leading educational technology consultant who has learning disabilities himself, explains why he embraces word processing for composing: "Being able to make perfectly formed letters by hitting a key is a lot easier than struggling to write by hand."

FIGURE 2–3 Word processing software allows students to write clear, legible text

A portion of a handwritten draft prepared by a fourth grader who has learning disabilities for the writing assignment "Should Peanuts Be Banned in School?"

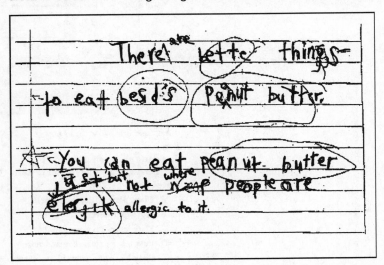

Here is a final draft prepared by the same student using word processing.

3/11/99

Should Peanuts Be Banned?

I am [author deletion] and I think peanuts should be banned from schools. I see more lives have been lost because, when people that even touch it, they can die. That's how bad peanut butter is. There are better things to eat besides peanut butter. You can eat peanut butter but not where people are allergic to it.

Source: From "AlphaSmart a Success in Inclusive Classroom," by K. Taneja, 2000, *TECH-NJ, 11*(1), p. 4.

When viewed in the context of the writing process, you can see that word processing programs support the generative nature of writing. The tasks of inserting new text, deleting unwanted text, and replacing text through cut-and-paste commands become effortless, allowing writers to change their minds about sentence constructions and idea development without penalty. There is no drudgery involved in recopying. Quoting Richard Wanderman (2000) again:

> Just being able to change things without a rewrite frees us from worry about making mistakes. With the ability to change things comes:
> - no emphasis on spelling during composition
> - less emphasis on getting the ideas in the right order the first time
> - more emphasis on content. . . .
>
> Being able to concentrate on what you are trying to say rather than struggling to get the spelling right, or worse, choosing only words you know how to spell, is . . . what electronic editing allows.

Word Prediction Software. The drafting (composing) process can also be supported through the judicious use of **word prediction software**. Word prediction programs, such as Word Q (Quillsoft) make an educated guess about the next word a student wants to type and presents a list of choices (see Figure 2.4).

FIGURE 2–4 WordQ word prediction software used in conjunction with Microsoft Word

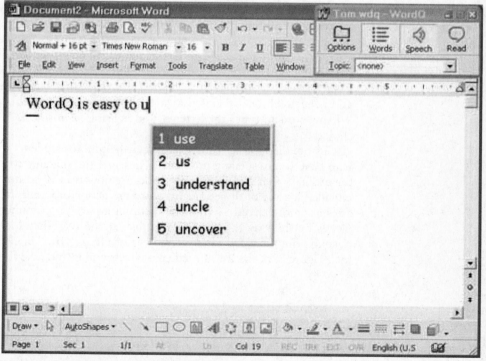

Source: Reprinted with permission of Quillsoft.

The student glances over the list of choices and, if his or her word appears in the list, selects it simply by clicking on it or typing the corresponding number. The word then appears in the sentence followed by an appropriate space. Most word prediction software must be used in conjunction with a second software program, such as a word processing or e-mail program. In this way, word prediction can support users in all writing environments.

The use of word prediction technology can reduce the number of keystrokes needed to express a thought and therefore has been widely used by individuals with physical disabilities. It is especially helpful for students who type with a single finger (or dowel like Bob Williams) or those who use an alternate access method (see Chapter 7) and whose typing speed is extremely slow. It has also become a helpful writing tool for students with learning disabilities who have severe spelling problems. This use is discussed in more detail in the following text.

Word prediction programs usually predict based on the initial letter that is typed by the user. Sophisticated programs can also predict based on the rules of grammar. For example, if a student types "Yesterday we . . ." a grammatically sensitive word prediction program will guess that the next word is going to be a verb and will present mostly verbs in its initial list of guesses. These programs can also be set to "favor" previously used words: The program "remembers" the words a user typed earlier and presents these words first in the lists of guesses. For example, if the user's name is Jujuan, anytime he types a Shift-J and the program infers a noun may be needed, "Jujuan" will appear as one of the choices in the list.

One of the most powerful features of word prediction programs is the ability to set up **custom dictionaries**. Custom dictionaries include vocabulary that is specific to a particular writing activity or subject. Often they include technical terms that are not included in a program's standard dictionary. For example, if a student is writing a paper on dinosaurs, a custom dictionary can be set up that includes words such as *Triassac, Jurassic, Early Cretaceous, Late Cretaceous, Allosaurus, Plateosaurus, Coelophysis, Erythrosuchus, Scutellosaurus, Heterodontosaurus, Megalosaurus,* and other technical terms that are not found in a typical spell-check dictionary. When a student types the letter *A*, for example, *Allosaurus* is likely to be one of the choices.

Custom dictionaries can be extremely helpful for students with learning disabilities who have severe spelling problems. These are the students whose spelling is so out of the ordinary that standard spell-checks are not effective because they cannot guess the intended word. For these students word prediction programs that use **phonetic dictionaries** are more effective. Phonetic dictionaries are programmed to identify misspelled words by the way they sound, not just by the way they look. So if a student tries to sound out the word *physical* and begins typing "fzic" in Co:Writer (Don Johnston, Inc.; Figure 2.5), the list of predicted words will include the following:

1. physics
2. physical
3. fickle
4. FICA
5. fiction

FIGURE 2–5   Co:Writer word list with custom dictionary

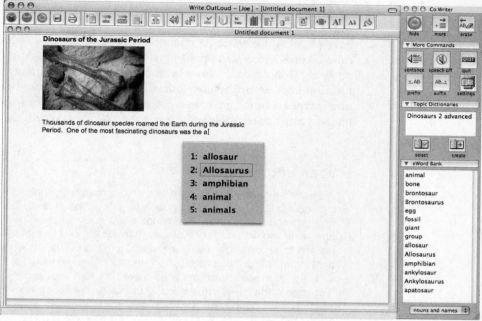

Source: Don Johnston, Inc.

Or if a student tries to sound out the word *photosynthesis* by typing "fotosi," the program will provide the following choices:

1. fantasy
2. photosensitive
3. photostatic
4. photostatting
5. photosynthesis

An additional feature that helps poor spellers is that when the mouse is moved over a choice in the predicted words list, the program speaks aloud the word. Students who cannot visually recognize the correct spelling of a word can often make their selection based on the way the word sounds.

Research on the use of word prediction by students with learning disabilities provides helpful direction regarding its use. The size of the vocabulary available in the dictionary or custom dictionary, as well as the content, must be tailored to the specific writing task (MacArthur et al., 2001). Early writers perform better when the dictionary selected is a small one and includes a focused set of words. Students writing a research paper on a particular topic will perform better if a larger dictionary is selected and relevant proper names and technical vocabulary are added to the dictionary. When the match between a writing task and predicted words is a good one, students can easily find the words they are attempting to spell. Conversely, if the match is a poor one, students can quickly become overwhelmed by lists of irrelevant choices and will not find word prediction to be a helpful tool.

AutoCorrect and AutoText.   For students who enter text very slowly because they have physical disabilities, a common feature of standard word processing programs called AutoCorrect can speed up the drafting process. AutoCorrect, usually found under the Tools menu, allows users to create typing shortcuts. Using abbreviations or function keys set by the user, AutoCorrect enters an entire phrase after the abbreviation is typed. For example, in typing this chapter we recorded a macro ("AT") for the phrase "assistive technology." Every time "AT" was typed, the entire phrase "assistive

USER PROFILE: Josh

Josh is an eighth-grade student who enjoys many of the pastimes that other 14-year-olds do. He listens to music and talks to girls on the phone. He likes to play baseball, soccer, and roller hockey and attends sleep-away camp in the summer. At a young age, Josh was found to have severe learning disabilities that resulted in significant academic deficits, specifically in written language. Josh's learning disabilities are evident in any subject that requires organization, handwriting, spelling, or composition.

In the short amount of time that I spent with Josh and his parents, I was able to catch a glimpse of the intense frustrations that they have all experienced due to these deficits. Josh's parents handed me a stack of letters that Josh had written the previous summer from sleep-away camp. I glanced through the crumpled pages trying to make out a word here or there. In most of the letters, I was able to decipher only the date, the greeting "Mom & Dad," and the closing "Love, Josh." The illegible words were not even written on any lines. They zigzagged up and down the page, looking as if they were not organized in any logical fashion. His parents described to me how they would sit together and try to read the letters. Usually, they could not decipher more than a sentence or two. They explained the frustration of not knowing what their son was trying to tell them.

Josh's parents pointed out that even if you can get used to his handwriting, the next obstacles are spelling and composition. Josh has difficulty understanding the connection between sounds and letters. This, in turn, creates big problems with spelling. His phonemic unawareness was evident as I tried to read through the camp letters.

When Josh was in seventh grade, his parents were referred to an Alliance for Technology Access (ATA) center in their state. The assistive technology specialist at the center tried several different software programs to help him with his writing. When she introduced him to word prediction, Josh typed a complete sentence, then turned to his mother and asked, "Can I write some more?" Josh's mother was overcome—this was the first time she had ever seen her son show any competence or interest in writing.

Josh uses word prediction to complete his writing assignments in school and homework assignments. For example, he now does his weekly vocabulary assignments on the computer. For these assignments, he has to write original sentences using his vocabulary words. In the past, Josh would either write out the sentences, which usually meant that they were illegible, or he would dictate the sentences to his mother and she would type them on a word processor. Now, Josh is able to do these types of assignments on his own. This is important progress for an adolescent in middle school. His parents are very pleased with the way his writing has progressed.

Source: From "Word Prediction Makes the Differences: Learning Disabilities in Middle School," by D. Niemann, 1996, *TECH-NJ, 8*(1), p. 4.

technology" was automatically entered. This feature is especially useful for students' names and specialized vocabulary words that are needed for a writing assignment.

Microsoft Word also offers a feature called AutoText. AutoText is similar to word prediction in that when the user starts to type a word or phrase that it recognizes, it presents an option to enter the entire word or phrase. A pop-up box appears with the complete word or phrase and the instructions "press ENTER to insert." Users can add new phrases to the AutoText submenu for additional shortcuts. The major difference between AutoText and AutoCorrect is that AutoCorrect allows the user to specify abbreviations or other shortcuts for frequently used words and phrases, reducing keystrokes significantly. However, it requires memorization of the shortcuts. Students with certain disabilities may prefer one of these methods over the other, depending on their strengths.

Speech Recognition Software. One final technology tool that must be mentioned in a discussion of drafting or composing is **speech recognition software**. Speech recognition software such as Dragon NaturallySpeaking (Nuance) or SpeakQ (Quillsoft) enables a user to dictate his or her words into a computer that is equipped with a microphone (see Figure 2.6). This technology bypasses the keyboard completely and holds promise

FIGURE 2–6   Dragon NaturallySpeaking dictation box as it appears in Microsoft Word

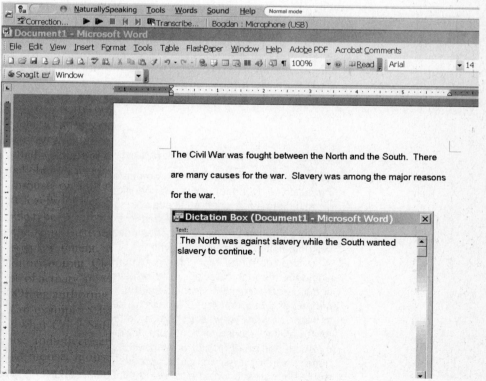

Source: Nuance.

for people who struggle with handwriting and keyboards. However, at the time of this writing speech recognition continues to have a number of limitations that make it a useful writing tool for only a small number of students with disabilities.

Although the accuracy rates of programs such as Dragon NaturallySpeaking are said to be 95% when used by trained users, the accuracy rate is likely to be lower for children with disabilities (MacArthur, 1999a), and any percentage of inaccuracies poses problems for the writing process for students with disabilities. Consider that speech recognition requires students to do the following tasks, sometimes simultaneously:

- Think about what they are going to say
- Speak the thought aloud
- Speak any punctuation and capitalization
- Read on the monitor what the program understood them to say
- Decide if that was actually what was said (recognize mistakes)
- Correct the program if it misunderstood
- Go back to picking up the train of thought

Therefore, instead of making writing easier, speech recognition adds a substantial burden to the writing process. It is not likely to help the composition process for students who are weak in reading or have difficulty multitasking.

However, for a small number of older students with disabilities who meet the following criteria, speech recognition has been shown to be an effective writing tool: (1) the students are computer savvy and enjoy solving technical problems, rather than getting discouraged by them; (2) they have strong oral language skills and understand the differences between spoken and written language; (3) they and their teachers and parents receive extensive training on how to use speech recognition; and (4) they are highly motivated to make it work and are willing to persevere (Speaking to Write, 1999).

USER PROFILE: Megan M. (adapted from Schindler, 2005)

Megan M., a 23 year-old college graduate, uses *Dragon NaturallySpeaking Professional* (Nuance), a voice recognition program, to write on her computer. By dictating into a microphone, she is able to control both the mouse and the keyboard solely with her voice. Megan needed to explore different access methods because she has very limited use of her arms due to a form of muscular dystrophy called Werdnig-Hoffmann's Disease Type II.

Before Learning *Dragon*, Megan's computer access was very limited and she was dependent on other people to write for her. Typing "just became too troublesome and time-consuming, so I would end up dictating in the end. Dictation was my method of 'typing' for years." Megan typically relied on "my student aides or brother or sister, or whoever was around, to do the physical typing while I dictated. It was extremely time-consuming, not only for me, but for the people helping me as well."

At the age of 18 Megan worked with an assistive technology specialist to find a better solution for her computer access. "The technician evaluating me thought I would be a great candidate for using *Dragon* because I had fine speech and the cognitive ability to handle the training." Megan began using the program at college where she received technical support from the director of the disability support office. She started with a tutorial, but it was through use over time, and much trial-and-error, that Megan fully grasped the program's capabilities.

"As time went on and I began mastering *Dragon*, I began doing my own work completely independently. I started out with small papers and assignments, then I started surfing the internet for research and whatnot, and before I knew it, I was doing a 22-page senior seminar paper, research and all."

Megan emphasizes that this efficiency did not occur overnight. It took her 3 to 5 months to feel comfortable with the program, and it was not until a year of use that she felt she had truly mastered the software. "Learning this program is very much like learning another language. At first I was very slow, saying only short sentences and making sure the process was actually working. It's a very strange feeling talking to a computer and seeing visual results in front of you immediately. As time went on and I had a better understanding of how the program worked and how I could work with the program, my speed and accuracy became faster and greater. The language of *Dragon* has become second nature to me. Now I can talk for sentences without worrying about how the program is responding. If a problem arises, I know I can fix it."

Reviewing

The reviewing part of the writing process, which is so difficult for students who have poor reading skills, is made easier by the use of **talking word processing** programs or a feature in some software called **text-to-speech.** Text-to-speech reads aloud whatever a student writes. It can read aloud word by word, sentence by sentence, or entire paragraphs or documents. The "reading chunk" feature is easily set by the user from a menu or submenu. The speed of the reading and the quality of the voice are also easily adjustable. "Just being able to hear your writing read aloud is enough . . . to allow some writers to hear problems in their syntax or even spelling where they might not be able to see them" (Wanderman, 2000). Figure 2.7 shows the menu toolbar for IntelliTalk (IntelliTools). Note the four "read aloud" icons on the second row. A study of college students with learning disabilities using text-to-speech supports the idea that the feature can help students find errors in their writing on their own (Raskind & Higgins, 1995).

The more sophisticated text-to-speech programs also offer a **highlighting** feature that helps students read and evaluate what they have written. Users can choose to have their writing highlighted word by word, phrase by phrase, sentence by sentence,

FIGURE 2–7   Screenshot of IntelliTalk 3 toolbar

Source: Imagery provided courtesy of Intellitools®, Inc.

FIGURE 2–8
Write:OutLoud
highlighting

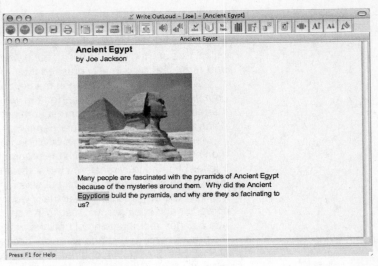

Source: Don Johnston, Inc.

or paragraph by paragraph. A common choice is to have the chunk of text being read aloud (such as a sentence) highlighted in one color, while having a second color highlight what is being spoken word by word. This arrangement supports students with reading difficulties by helping keep their eyes on the chunk of text they are trying to evaluate and revise. Figure 2.8 shows an example of highlighting using Write:OutLoud (Don Johnston, Inc.).

Editing

We have already mentioned that the ability to manipulate text afforded by word processing software "makes revision possible without tedious recopying" (MacArthur et al. 2001). In addition to this editing power of word processing, the revising process can be significantly enhanced through the use of several other technology tools, some that we have already described. In the following text we will discuss spell-checks, thesauruses, grammar checkers, homonym finders, and Track Changes and Insert Comments features.

Spell-Checks. Built in to all word processing programs and many Internet browsers, spell-checks quickly find words that have been misspelled. If the writer chooses, spell-checks also guess which word the writer intended by presenting a list of possibilities and will spell each guess correctly. This is an extremely helpful tool for skilled readers and writers because it picks up typographical errors as well as true spelling errors, and these users can quickly correct their mistakes by choosing the right word from the word list. However, for many students with learning disabilities, standard spell-checks present a new set of problems: (1) For students who are poor readers, the list of suggested words can add to the confusion. For example, a student who types "redy" for "ready" is presented with the following choices:

reedy

red

rely

redeem

ready

redo

reds

redeye

Many of the words look similar and the poor reader or speller cannot distinguish the correct word from the list of choices. (2) For students who have severe spelling problems, conventional spell-checks often do not guess correctly, and as a result, the list of choices presented does not include the student's intended word. For example, if a writer spells the word *reference* as "refrins," the spell-check in Microsoft Word presents the following choices:

refrains

refries

refines

This list of choices will not help the writer who needed to spell *reference*.

Spell-checks that use phonetic dictionaries are a better choice for poor spellers. As mentioned, phonetic dictionaries are programmed to identify misspelled words by the way they sound, not just by the way they look (see the earlier example). Spell-checks based on phonetic dictionaries are available in Franklin's handheld dictionaries and in most text-to-speech and word prediction software designed for people with learning disabilities.

Poor spellers are also helped by spell-checks that talk. **Talking spell-checks** (also called **talking dictionaries**) read aloud the misspelled word and every suggestion in the list of correctly spelled words. Students who are poor readers can listen to the words and choose the correct word based on how it sounds. If the student is still uncertain of the correct word, talking dictionaries read aloud the words' definitions, and the student can make a choice based on the correct definition. (See Figure 2.9.)

Thesauruses. Many skilled writers use a **thesaurus** to help them with their word choices. This is another electronic tool that can help improve the writing of students with learning disabilities. Sometimes called a "synonym finder," these tools present a list of words with similar meanings to the selected word. If users find the choices in Microsoft Word's thesaurus too limiting, there are several websites that offer more comprehensive lists of choices. (See Sidebar.)

Using a talking dictionary is one way to deal with the problem of homonyms. Homonyms are words that sound the same but have different meanings (e.g., *there* and *their*; *to*, *two*, and *too*). A conventional spell-check presents homonyms as choices in its word lists, but this does not help the writer who does not know which spelling goes with which meaning. The Franklin handheld dictionaries include a "confusable checker," and some word processing programs include a feature called **homonym**

FIGURE 2–9
Spell-check in
IntelliTalk 3

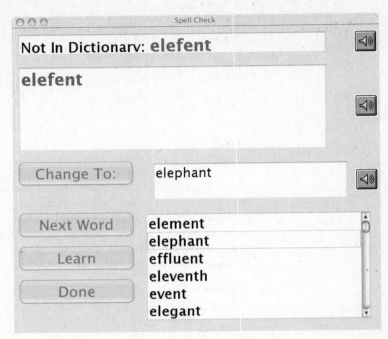

Source: Imagery provided courtesy of Intellitools®, Inc.

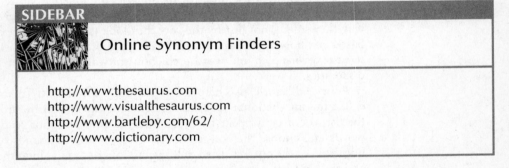

SIDEBAR

Online Synonym Finders

http://www.thesaurus.com
http://www.visualthesaurus.com
http://www.bartleby.com/62/
http://www.dictionary.com

finder which identifies words that are homonyms and presents definitions of them to assist the writer in selecting the correct word. A website launched in 2004 called Confusing Words offers an extensive inventory of homonyms and helpful definitions, taking into account regional differences in pronunciation (Wanderman, Wanderman, Clark, & Koethnig, 2004; see Figure 2.10).

Grammar Checkers. Professional writers and teachers are divided on the value of grammar checkers. Grammar checkers are tools that are available within word processing programs such as Microsoft Word. When activated, they underline grammatical errors such as incomplete sentences, capitalization errors, punctuation errors, subject–verb disagreement, and a whole host of other errors in syntax.

The problem is Word's grammar checker also looks for and underlines phrases and sentences that do not match its particular writing style. Unless you specifically tell

FIGURE 2–10 Confusing Words website

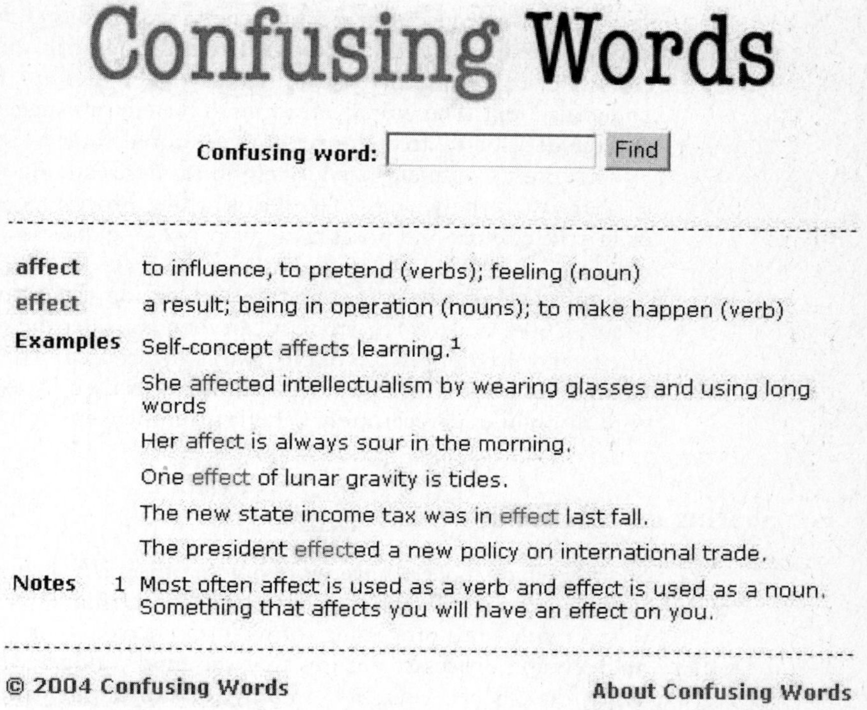

Confusing Words

Confusing word: [   ] [Find]

----

affect	to influence, to pretend (verbs); feeling (noun)
effect	a result; being in operation (nouns); to make happen (verb)
Examples	Self-concept affects learning.[1]
	She affected intellectualism by wearing glasses and using long words
	Her affect is always sour in the morning.
	One effect of lunar gravity is tides.
	The new state income tax was in effect last fall.
	The president effected a new policy on international trade.
Notes	1 Most often affect is used as a verb and effect is used as a noun. Something that affects you will have an effect on you.

© 2004 Confusing Words   **About Confusing Words**

Source: Reprinted with permission of R. Wanderman.

it not to, it will underline passive sentences, sentences that are longer than 60 words, clichés and colloquialisms, successive nouns (more than three), first-person uses, gender-specific words, and "wordiness." Professional writers strongly object to what they consider Word's "dubious advice on grammar" and Microsoft's attempt to "reengineer the language" (Teresi, 2000). To check the accuracy of Word's grammar checker, Teresi ran the Preamble to the Constitution through it and was told, "Consider revising. Very long sentences can be difficult to understand." The Gettysburg Address was also criticized. When Word's grammar checker encountered the phrase "dedicated to the proposition that all men are created equal," it said, "men is a gender-specific expression. Consider replacing with person, human being or individual" (Teresi, 2000)

The most recent versions of Word do allow users (including teachers) to specify which aspects of the grammar checker they want activated. This is easily done through Word's Preferences menu (click on Spelling and Grammar, then Settings). It is possible, therefore, to turn off any stylistic evaluations and limit the grammar checker to identifying only a few selected grammatical errors. A creative teacher could integrate this focused use of the grammar checker into students' writing assignments.

Track Changes and Insert Comments Features. Technology also offers a convenient way for teachers to communicate with students about the editing process. An important component of writing instruction is that student writers receive feedback on their drafts—from either their teacher or peer editors—in a timely manner (Zeitz, 2003). Using two tools in Microsoft Word, Track Changes and Insert Comments, and the speed and convenience of e-mail, teachers or peer editors can provide feedback quickly without erasing the student's original writing. When Track Changes is activated, an editor's deletions are marked in ~~strikethrough~~ font and insertions are indicated by underlined text. The writer can see both the editor's suggestions and the original text, and the decision to accept or reject the editorial changes is left to the writer.

The Insert Comments tool is helpful for notes and questions that the editor wants to share with the writer. "The real learning process occurs when the reviewer discusses the content and poses thought-provoking questions about how the material is presented. . . . [Track Changes] allows the reviewer to make annotations in a separate window on the screen without changing the actual text of the document" (Zeitz, 2003, p. 16). The student can then consider the editor's questions and comments and decide how he or she wants to proceed. The Track Changes and Insert Comments features are powerful editing tools used by experienced writers; students with disabilities can certainly benefit from their use in writing instruction.

Sharing or Publishing

Sharing what students have written with others is the culminating experience of most writing activities. Technology has much to contribute to this stage. Simply using computers (with word processing software) connected to printers for the drafting, editing, and revising processes ensures that the final product will be legible and attractive. When the teacher assembles a library of stories published by his or her students, or posts students' writings on the bulletin board, students with disabilities—even those with illegible handwriting and poor spelling—can be proud of their printed stories.

Sharing what students have written can also be accomplished through the creation of class (or school) newsletters and newspapers. This is easily done using advanced features of word processing programs such as formatting a document in columns, changing text direction, inserting graphics and digital photos, and automatically wrapping text around pictures. Publishing newsletters that can be distributed around the school or community often motivates students who have come to dread any writing assignment. It gives them a clear purpose and a real audience for their writing—not just the teacher, but their families and peers as well.

Combining graphics, video, and sound with text can be an enjoyable method of getting students interested in writing. Story-writing programs combine features of word processing programs with features of graphics programs and seamlessly integrate the two. Just as in the primary grades students may be asked to draw a picture in preparation for a writing assignment, story-writing programs allow students to begin their writing activity by creating elaborate images on the computer. Not only is the final printed product enhanced by the creative illustrations, but anecdotal evidence suggests that the added dimension of images enhances the prewriting process, motivates students to write, and leads to more intricate writing (Daiute, 1992). One concern expressed by researchers is that students may become distracted by the bells and whistles of graphics, video, and sound, and will end up paying less, not more, attention to the writing of text (MacArthur et al., 2001).

SIDEBAR

Students Sharing Writing on the Internet

A good example of using the Internet to share students' writings is described by Strassman and D'Amore (2002). Seeking to provide opportunities for her high school students, who are deaf and hard of hearing, to think and write about controversial issues, the teacher arranged online synchronous chats (a technical term for a form of "instant messaging") and Electronic Read Arounds. Students were asked to discuss their opinions about school uniforms on an online chat, which served as a prewriting activity. A printout of the completed dialogue was given to students to help them organize their thoughts. From there students expanded their ideas and edited them into a document.

The Electric Read Arounds combined the sharing process with the editing process. Students' written drafts were shared with other students who added questions and comments about the effectiveness of the writing. This helped the writer see the strengths of his or her writing and the sections that were unclear; getting feedback from fellow students, rather than just the teacher, provided students "practice in real-world styles of writing while simultaneously helping them to improve the process by which they write" (Strassman & D'Amore, 2002, p. 31).

Multimedia presentation software such as PowerPoint offers another method for publication that combines graphics, video, and sound. The strength of a PowerPoint presentation is that it neatly presents a summary of complicated information or a longer document through the skillful use of bulleted phrases. As such, creating a PowerPoint presentation does not lend itself to improving students' composing skills. What it can do is (1) provide an engaging environment for prewriting—in particular, for determining an appropriate organization for a writing assignment; and (2) offer an alternative to writing a paper in a content area for students who have weak writing skills but need to demonstrate knowledge of a topic.

Digital storytelling is another option for motivating students to write and for sharing their writing with a wider audience. It has been described as "a new twist on the ancient art of the oral narrative" (Salpeter, 2005, p. 18). Students are encouraged to tell their own personal story through a process sometimes called "PowerPoint on steroids." The process begins with the writing of a story or script. After editing and rewriting the story, students add photographs, other images, sound, and/or video to further personalize the story. Students' emotional attachment to the people or events in the story is considered a key to the success of this use of technology.

The Internet offers additional avenues for publication. Discussion boards are useful for sharing short pieces of writing. Teachers can begin a discussion thread by posting questions or topics on a class discussion board. These questions or topics establish a clear purpose for this writing activity. Students can be required to post replies to each thread and to read what their peers have written. On class discussion boards the audience for students' writing is clear, and knowing that their peers, not just their teacher, will be reading their words often motivates students to put forth an effort.

Blogs are the latest online method for sharing students' writing. The origin of the word *blog*—a blending of *web* and *log*—explains its basic characteristic: it is an online journal. But for educators, the characteristic that makes it a valuable writing tool is that it is interactive: Students can easily respond to the writer with their own comments (Britt, 2006). Teachers can set up a blog on a particular unit of study, assign students to research different topics and post their writeups on the blog, and require students to provide feedback to their fellow students. This can be used to teach editing and revising skills, as well as to encourage ongoing written dialogues about the topic of study.

TECHNOLOGY TOOLS THAT SUPPORT NOTETAKING

As mentioned at the beginning of this chapter, taking notes during lectures is a specialized form of writing. It requires students to listen and write at the same time, and it must be done quickly. Students need to be able to see the instructor and the blackboard or whiteboard. In most middle schools, high schools, and colleges, methods of notetaking must also be portable because students typically attend classes in different rooms. These requirements preclude the use of desktop computers for most

Students using a Neo by AlphaSmart.
Printed with permission of AlphaSmart, Inc. A Renaissance Learning Brand.

notetaking. Laptops are one alternative but present another set of shortcomings: (1) Battery life on laptop computers is limited, meaning students either need to sit near a power source (not always possible in typical classrooms), or they need to carry an extra battery with them and remember to change it before the laptop loses its charge. (2) Laptops take a few minutes to boot up. While they are starting up, students may miss the first part of lectures. (3) Laptops are vulnerable to damage. They will not withstand being thrown on the ground in their users' backpacks or being accidentally knocked off a desk. (4) Laptops are expensive.

For students who can take their own notes by typing on a keyboard there are portable devices available that meet the following criteria: (1) They have a longer battery life than a laptop; (2) they have a simple on/off switch and require no time to start; (3) they are durable and are less likely to break than a laptop; and (4) they are relatively inexpensive. These devices are called portable word processors or portable notetakers. The Neo (AlphaSmart, Inc.) is an example of this kind of technology tool. It has a full-sized keyboard and is lightweight, plus it connects easily to a printer for printing or to a computer for downloading files for later editing (wireless versions are available). Its visual display is relatively small, so it is not appropriate for in-depth editing, but for notetaking, the Neo is ideal.

The Dana, also by AlphaSmart, is a portable notetaker with an additional function—it is also a personal digital assistant (PDA). The Dana functions like a Palm Pilot attached to a full-sized keyboard; in fact, the Dana runs on the Palm Operating System. This means that any software that runs on a Palm PDA will run on the *Dana*, including AlphaWord (AlphaSmart, Inc.) Inspiration, ThoughtManager (Hands High Software) TextPlus (a word prediction program by SmartCell Technology), and 4.0Student (a student-focused personal organizer by Handmark).

In the business world, many people have started to use their PDAs as notetakers by attaching foldable keyboards to them. This is another option for students, but it must be remembered that PDAs are somewhat fragile and will not withstand being thrown on the floor or accidentally being stepped on.

For students who are blind, a line of portable notetakers, such as the Braille Note by HumanWare, is available that provides a choice of adaptive inputs and outputs.

Dana portable notetaker and personal digital assistant
Printed with permission of AlphaSmart, Inc. A Renaissance Learning Brand.

Some students prefer a portable notetaker that has a standard Braille keyboard while other prefer a regular QWERTY keyboard (see the User Profile of Serena in Chapter 13). Both kinds of devices can be connected to a computer, a printer, or a Braille printer for downloading of files and printing. The use of Braille as a computer access method will be discussed in more detail in Chapter 7.

Some students with disabilities are not able to take their own notes in class. In the past they have had to rely on photocopies of notes taken by fellow students, or they were provided with a personal notetaker who may or may not have been familiar with the subject matter. This was particularly problematic for students in math and science classes. Today technology tools called capturing devices offer notetaking alternatives.

By attaching a portable captioning device to any whiteboard, notes can be digitally recorded in real time and color format. These notes can then be disseminated through print, e-mail, a class website, or any other type of electronic media. One such capturing device, the mimio (Virtual Ink), can be attached directly to any whiteboard, and notes can be displayed in real time on a student's computer, or they can be stored in the device for upload later. (See Figure 2.11.)

Another type of captioning device, the SMART Board (SMART Technologies Inc.), functions as an interactive whiteboard. Using SMART Board software, all notes written on the device can be digitally recorded in real time so students can rewind and fast-forward to specific sections of lectures for review. Additionally, the SMART Recorder feature of the software allows audio to be added to notes for an extra level of support.

For students who are deaf or hard of hearing, two methods of notetaking have been developed that rely on professional notetakers. Communication Access

SMART Board
Copyright 2001–2006 SMART Technologies Inc. All rights reserved.

Realtime Translation, or CART, is a system that is used in the courts because it results in a verbatim record of proceedings. CART captionists are specially trained to transcribe every word that is spoken, much like a court stenographer. The verbatim transcription is displayed on a large light-emitting diode (LED) display or a laptop computer so that individuals with hearing loss can read it. This kind of verbatim record is required in legal proceedings. Some colleges provide CART for students who are deaf as a complete record of class meetings. For students who need only lecture notes, however, CART is usually considered excessive.

For these students a more affordable accommodation is C-Print. C-Print was designed by the National Technical Institute for the Deaf specifically as a notetaking system. Using a special software program and trained captionists, C-Print produces paraphrased records of class lectures. For students who want to see the notes as the instructor lectures, the captionist's laptop can be connected to a student's laptop for simultaneous display or to a projected display. Some students prefer that the captionist e-mail them the notes after they have been edited.

Table 2.2 summarizes technology tools that can enhance the writing process.

TABLE 2–2 Linking technology tools to the writing process

Writing Process	Technology Tool	Sample Products
Prewriting	Graphic organizer Outlining software	Inspiration DraftBuilder
Drafting	Word processing software Word prediction software Macros Speech recognition software	Microsoft Word WordQ Co:Writer Microsoft Word Dragon Naturally- Speaking SpeakQ
Evaluating what was written	Talking word processing (text-to-speech)	WordQ Write: OutLoud Read & Write
Editing and revising	Talking word processing with talking spell-checks (text-to-speech) Homonym finder Word prediction Grammar checker	WordQ Write:OutLoud Read & Write Confusingwords.com WordQ Co:Writer Microsoft Word
Sharing and publishing	Track Changes and Insert Comment features Multimedia software (combining text with graphics, sound, and video)	Microsoft Word PowerPoint

(*continued*)

TABLE 2–2   (continued)

Writing Process	Technology Tool	Sample Products
Notetaking	Portable notetakers PDAs with keyboards	Neo Dana Palm
	Braille notetakers	Braille Lite M40 BrailleNote
	Software with captionist and second display Capturing devices	C-Print CART mimio SMART Board

TECHNOLOGY ALONE WILL NOT IMPROVE STUDENTS' WRITING

Although technology offers powerful tools that can improve the writing of students with disabilities, the research on computers and writing conveys a consistent message: Assistive technology will succeed in helping students improve their writing skills *only if* it is paired with good teaching strategies. Simply providing graphic organizers, word processing software, word prediction software, speech recognition software, text-to-speech, talking spell-checks, homonym finders, or portable notetaking devices will not lead to improvements in the writing skills of students with disabilities (MacArthur, 1996, 2000). Students need to receive three-pronged training: (1) instruction on the *writing* process, (2) training on specific *technology tools*, and (3) training on how to use these technology tools to enhance the writing process.

Instruction on the Writing Process

The literature on how to teach the writing process is extensive. Tompkins (2002) recommends instructional scaffolding such as having the teacher model the writing process—that is, directly demonstrate in a step-by-step fashion how to plan, create a draft, evaluate what was written, and then revise and edit. She also recommends teaching mini-lessons on specific writing-related skills, collaborative writing assignments, and guided writing assignments, in addition to independent writing activities. Baker et al. (2002, p. 70) suggest that teachers model the "inner dialogue expert writers engage in during the writing process." James and colleagues (2001) describe a model for teaching writing to students with learning disabilities that combines process writing with an assessment process for monitoring student progress. They recommend providing explicit instruction on the skills that are included in their Six-Trait Writing Assessment Rubric such as organization, voice, word choice, and writing conventions (e.g., punctuation and grammar).

Scott and Vitale (2003) developed a scaffolding technique called the Writing Wheel that serves as a visual guide to the writing process for students who need help focusing and sequencing (see Figure 2.11). The Writing Wheel is divided into five

FIGURE 2–11 The Writing Wheel

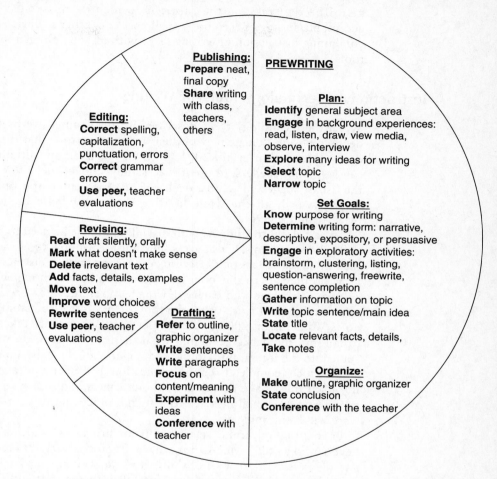

Source: From "Teaching the Writing Process to Students with LD," by B. J. Scott and M. Vitale, 2003, *Intervention in School and Clinic, 38*(4), p. 222. Reprinted with permission.

unequal sections, each devoted to a major subprocess of the writing process and each containing a list of the activities students need to do. By allocating half of the circle to prewriting, the Writing Wheel conveys at a glance the relative amount of time students should spend on each stage. An overlay with a cutout can be placed on the wheel to help students focus on one task at a time. The Writing Wheel can help students with learning disabilities be more aware of the processes involved in writing, provide monitoring information for teachers and students, and help students focus on the individual components of the writing process.

Loeffler (2005) provides a helpful strategy to teach students with learning disabilities how to monitor their misspelling of words. She points out that traditional spelling tests have a narrow focus on memorization and do not teach students spelling strategies. As an alternative, she recommends modeling a "spelling self-check routine" and using a spelling rubric that teaches students a variety of strategies. The first task on the rubric is to identify misspelled words. One of the acceptable strategies is to use a spell-check. Loeffler's rubric is a good example of combining instruction in writing tasks with instruction on appropriate technology tools.

Instruction on Technology Tools for Writing

When the technology tools described in this chapter are first introduced to students, the tools "create new burdens at the same time that they remove other burdens" (MacArthur et al., 2001, p. 298). For example, although word prediction can help poor spellers, to use it successfully students need to continually read over the list of suggested words, decide if one of them is appropriate, and select the desired word, all the while holding their intended sentence in their memory (MacArthur, 1999b).

To be helpful to students with disabilities, students need to be *comfortable* using the technology tools. This means they must learn how to use them *skillfully* so that their minds can focus on the writing process and not be distracted by the technology. How do they get to this point? They need to be taught explicitly how to use each software program and each relevant feature, and they need plenty of time and opportunity to *practice* using the tool. "Do a lot of something and it gets easier," notes Wanderman (2003), adding "Once enough practice takes place the tool starts to fall into the background and what the user wants to do with the tool starts to come into the foreground. In the end, the tool ought to be almost taken for granted and the focus completely on the application." Wanderman reminds us that the practice itself must have meaning. Without a meaningful task to accomplish, such as composing an e-mail message to a friend, practicing using a piece of writing software will be meaningless.

In addition to learning specific software programs, students need to acquire basic keyboarding skills (MacArthur, 1996). Typing is very different from handwriting and requires a different set of skills. Students who are not familiar with the conventional keyboard will be forced to spend their time and attention "hunting and pecking" for keys instead of focusing on the content of their writing. It is not necessary for students to become skilled touch-typists, but they need to reach a level of proficiency at keyboarding. Several good software programs exist that teach keyboarding in an entertaining way. (See Web Resources.)

Putting It All Together

Just as teachers need to model the writing process, they need to model the use of technology to support writing. They need to teach skills like using a graphic organizer to brainstorm and/or organize a writing assignment, using a talking spell-check to find the correct spelling of a word for students who are extremely poor spellers, or using the Confusing Words website (http://www.confusingwords.com) to identify and correct homonym errors. Word prediction requires that students learn how to scan a list of choices, decide if the word they want appears on the list, and hit another key if the desired word does not appear. These steps must be taught to students in the context of writing and spelling strategies (MacArthur et al., 2001). In fact, all of the technology tools described in this chapter need to be demonstrated, taught, and practiced within the context of writing activities if students with disabilities are to benefit from their use.

SUMMARY

- Writing is a complex problem-solving activity that involves thinking, planning, and decision making, as well as the mechanics of transcription.
- Writing is an iterative process that can be broken into various steps: prewriting, drafting, reviewing, editing, and sharing or publishing. Students with disabilities often have difficulty with all of the processes involved in writing, so it is not uncommon for them to try to avoid writing assignments.
- There are a variety of helpful writing tools available to assist individuals with disabilities in each part of the writing process:
  - *Prewriting:* graphic organizers (e.g., Inspiration)
  - *Drafting:* word processing, including macros, word prediction software, speech recognition software
  - *Reviewing:* talking word processing, text-to-speech
  - *Editing:* talking word processing, text-to-speech, phonetic spell-checks, talking dictionaries, thesaurus
  - *Sharing or publishing:* word processing software, multimedia presentation software
- Assistive technology will succeed in helping students improve their writing skills only if it is paired with good teaching strategies.
- Students need to receive three-pronged training: (1) instruction on the writing process, (2) training on specific technology tools, and (3) training on how to use these technology tools to enhance the writing process.

WEB RESOURCES

For additional information on the topics listed, go to the following websites:

Writing Process

ReadWriteThink, Project of International Reading Association, National Council of Teachers of English & the Verizon Foundation
http://www.readwritethink.org

Graphic Organizers

Inspiration Software, Inc.
http://www.inspiration.com/resources/index.cfm

Word Processing for Drafting

LD Resources
http://www.ldresources.org/?p=171

Word Prediction

Co:Writer
http://www.donjohnston.com/products/cowriter/index.html

WordQ
http://www.wordq.com
Read & Write www.texthelp.com → Education

Using Autocorrect and Autotext

Michigan's Assistive Technology Resource *Using MS Word Tools to Differentiate for Diverse Learners*, Download PDF from
http://www.cenmi.org/MATR/uploaded/2006/MAR/7292572923_DiffMSW.pdf

Speech Recognition

Dragon Naturally Speaking
http://www.nuance.com/naturallyspeaking/home/

SpeakQ
http://www.wordq.com

iListen
http://www.macspeech.com

IBM ViaVoice
http://www.306.ibm.com/software/voice/viavoice

Text-To-Speech

ReadPlease
http://www.readplease.com

TextAloud
http://www.nextup.com

WordQ
http://www.wordq.com

Read & Write
http://www.texthelp.com → Education

IntelliTalk
http://www.intellitools.com

Phonetic Dictionary

Write:OutLoud
http://www.donjohnston.com/products/write_outloud/index.html
Insert comments feature in Microsoft Word
Microsoft Education
http://www.microsoft.com/education/atschool.mspx

Digital Storytelling

Center for Digital Storytelling
http://www.storycenter.org/index1.html
Adobe Digital Kids Club
http://www.adobe.com/education/digkids/
Educational Uses of Digital Storytelling
http://www.coe.uh.edu/digital-storytelling

Blogs in Education

Free site designed by a teacher
http://www.classchatter.com

Portable Notetakers

AlphaSmart, Neo & Dana
http://www.alphasmart.com/
Videos on the Alphasmart site
http://www.alphasmart.com/k12/solutions/index.html
BrailleNote
http://www.humanware.com/Products/Notetakers/BrailleNoteQT.asp

Capturing Devices

mimio
http://www.mimio.com
SmartBoard
http://www.smarttech.com
Teacher resources
http://www.education.smarttech.com/ste/en-US/Ed+Resource/

Captioning for People Who are Deaf/Hard of Hearing

CART
http://www.rit.edu/~itvcaps/basics.htm

C-print
http://www.ntid.rit.edu/cprint/

Keyboarding

Type to Learn free demo
http://store.sunburst.com/trials.aspx
Mavis Beacon Teaches Typing® Deluxe 16
http://www.riverdeep.com
SpeedSkin
http://www.speedskin.com
Talking Typer (for blind users)
http://www.aph.org/tech/tt_info.htm

Low-Tech Tools for Writing

Georgia Assistive Technology Project Tools for life
http://www.gatfl.org/ldguide/write.htm
Onion Mountain Technology
http://onionmountaintech.com

SUGGESTED ACTIVITIES

1. *Explore word prediction.* Type a short paragraph (3–4 sentences) and count the total number of keystrokes you needed to make (every letter, number, punctuation mark, space, and Shift key hit). Now type that same paragraph using a word prediction program that is set to "remember recent words." Keep track of the number of keystrokes you use. What is the difference in the number of keystrokes between the two times you typed the paragraph? Now type the paragraph a third time. Again, keep track of the number of keystrokes you use. What is the difference in the number of keystrokes between the first time you typed the paragraph (without word prediction) and the third time, when the word prediction program had had a chance to learn your vocabulary? What are the implications of this finding for students with disabilities?

2. *Make the writing components of a unit accessible to students with disabilities.*
   a. Select a unit of study for a grade level. It can be a unit you that you currently teach, have taught in the past, would like to teach in the future, or one that you have been asked to support by another teacher. Or you can select lesson plans from a website such as www.teachnology.com.
   b. Identify the writing components in the unit (e.g., completing worksheets, taking a quiz, writing a story, writing a letter). Then explain how you would make the writing components accessible to a student who has learning disabilities and a student who has physical disabilities. Be specific. Make sure your recommended solution or solutions match the task and the students' needs.

3. *Create topic dictionaries in word prediction.* Using vocabulary from your unit, create a topic dictionary in Co:Writer or another word prediction program. Include at least 10 words in it. Type a writing sample using the topic dictionary, and take a screenshot of the topic dictionary in use. Print the screenshot. Then write a brief narrative explaining the formatting options you would select to meet your student's needs (e.g., number of choices, flexible spelling, background color).

4. *Find low-tech solutions for writing.* Put together a kit of simple low-tech writing aids. Go to a local crafts store and an office supply store and gather items such as clipboards, pencil grips, appropriate rubber stamps, items that can be used as a slant board, pens and markers with wide diameters, different kinds of paper, and so on. Organize them in a plastic bin.

REFERENCES

Baker, S., Gersten, R., & Scanlon, D. (2002). Procedural facilitators and cognitive strategies: Tools for unraveling the mysteries of comprehension and the writing process and for providing meaningful access to the general curriculum. *Learning Disabilities Research & Practice, 17*(1), 65–77.

Britt, J. (2006). Go blogging with social studies field trips. *Learning and Leading with Technology, 33*(6), 29.

Daiute, C. (1992). Multimedia composing: Extending the resources of kindergarten to writers across the grades. *Language Arts, 69,* 250–260.

Darch, C., Kim, S., Johnson, S., & James, H. (2000). The strategic spelling skills of students with learning disabilities: The results of two studies [Electronic version]. *Journal of Instructional Psychology, 27*(1), 15–27.

Englert, C. S., Raphael, T. E., Anderson, L. M., Anthony, H. M., & Stevens, D. D. (1991). Making writing strategies and self-talk visible: Cognitive strategy instruction in regular and special education classrooms. *American Educational Research Journal, 28,* 337–372.

Flower, L., & Hayes, J. R. (1981). A cognitive process theory of writing. *College Composition and Communication, 32*(4), 365–387.

Georgia Assistive Technology Project Tools for Life. (n.d.). *Learning disabilities and assistive technologies: Reading.* Retrieved June 29, 2006, from http://www.gatfl.org/ldguide/read.htm

Inspiration Software®, Inc. & Institute for the Advancement of Research in Education (IARE) at AEL. (July 2003). Graphic organizers: A review of scientifically based research. Retrieved April 2, 2007, from http://www.inspiration.com/vlearning/research/index.cfm

James, L. A., Abbott, M., & Greenwood, C. R. (2001). How Adam became a writer: Winning writing strategies for low-achieving students. *Teaching Exceptional Children, 33*(3), 30–37.

Jones, C. J. (2001). Teacher-friendly curriculum-based assessment in spelling. *Teaching Exceptional Children, 34*(2), 32–38.

Lipson, M. Y., Mosenthal, J., Daniels, P., & Woodside-Jiron, H. (2000). Process writing in the classrooms of eleven fifth-grade teachers with different orientations to teaching and learning. *The Elementary School Journal, 101*(2), 209–231.

Loeffler, K. A. (2005). No more Friday spelling tests? An alternative spelling assessment for students with learning disabilities. *Teaching Exceptional Children, 37*(4), 24–27.

MacArthur, C. A. (1996). Using technology to enhance the writing processes of students with learning disabilities. *Journal of Learning Disabilities, 29*(4).

MacArthur, C. A. (1999a). Overcoming barriers to writing: Computer support for basic writing skills. *Reading & Writing Quarterly, 15,* 169–192.

MacArthur, C. A. (1999b). Word prediction for students with severe spelling problems. *Learning Disabilities Quarterly, 22*(3), 158–172.

MacArthur, C. A. (2000). New tools for writing: Assistive technology for students with writing difficulties. *Topics in Language Disorders, 20*(4), 85–100.

MacArthur, C. A., Ferretti, R. P., Okolo, C. M., & Cavalier, A. R. (2001). Technology applications for students with literacy problems: A critical review. *The Elementary School Journal, 101*(3), 273–301.

McAlister, K. M., Nelson, N. W., & Bahr, C. M. (1999). Perceptions of students with language and learning disabilities about writing process instruction. *Learning Disabilities Research & Practice, 14*(3), 159–172.

Microsoft Corporation. (1999). *Enable, people with disabilities and computers* [Video]. Retrieved transcript of script from http://depts.washington.edu/enables/vdescription/vd_mw_multimodalities.htm

National Council of Teachers of English and the International Reading Association. (1996). *Standards for the English language arts.* Urbana, IL: Authors.

Niemann, D. (1996). Word prediction makes the difference: Learning disabilities in middle school. *TECH-NJ, 8*(1), 4, 8. Retrieved from http://www.tcnj.edu~technj/fall96/writeaway.html

NOVA. (1982). *Finding a voice* [Video]. (Originally broadcast on PBS February 7, 1982.)

Raskind, M. H., & Higgins, E. (1995). Effects of speech synthesis on the proofreading efficiency of postsecondary students with learning disabilities. *Learning Disability Quarterly, 18,* 141–158.

Salpeter, J. (2005). *Telling tales with technology.* Retrieved from the Tech Learning website: http://www.techlearning.com/showArticle.Php?articleID=60300276

Schindler, C. (2005). Voice. Recognition provides Independence for Ramapo College Student. *TECH-NJ,* Vol. 16, No. 1, Retrieved April 2, 2007: http://www.tcnj.edu/~technj/2005/ramapo.htm

Scott, B. J., & Vitale, M. R. (2003). Teaching the writing process to students with LD. *Intervention in School and Clinic, 38*(4), 220–224.

Speaking to Write. (1999). *Spotlight on speech recognition.* Retrieved from http://www.edc.org/spk2wrt/

Strassman, B. K., & D'Amore, M. (2002). The write technology. *Teaching Exceptional Children, 34*(6), 28–31.

Taneja, K. (2000). AlphaSmart a success in inclusive classroom. *TECH-NJ, 11*(1), 4.

Teresi, D. (2000). Call me Fishmeal. *Forbes, 166*(13), 39.

Tompkins, G. E. (2000). *Teaching writing: Balancing process and product* (3rd ed.). Upper Saddle River, NJ: Merrill/Prentice Hall.

Tompkins, G. E. (2002). Struggling readers are struggling writers, too. *Reading & Writing Quarterly, 18,* 175–193.

Wanderman, R. (2000). *How computers change the writing process for people with learning disabilities* (First Person feature). Retrieved July 7, 2004, from the LD OnLine website: http://www.ldonline.org

Wanderman, R. (2003). *Tools and dyslexia: Issues and ideas* (LD Resources). Retrieved July 7, 2004, from the LD Resources website: http://www.ldresources.org/?p=17/

Wanderman, R., Wanderman, A., Clark, D., & Koethnig, M. (2004). *Confusing words.* Retrieved from the Confusing Words website: http://www.confusingwords.com

Williams, B. (2000). More than an exception to the rule. In M. Fried-Oken & H. Bersani (Eds.), *Speaking up and spelling it out* (pp. 245–254). Baltimore: Brookes.

Zeitz, L. E. (2003). Electronic editing. *Learning & Leading with Technology, 30*(7), 14–17, 27.

CHAPTER **3**

Assistive Technology to Support Reading

FOCUS QUESTIONS

1. What is the difference between learning to read and reading to learn?

2. What are the five areas of reading instruction that were identified by the National Reading Panel as being essential for children to learn to read?

3. How can computers be used as a reading remediation tool (to teach reading skills)?

4. How can computers be used as a reading compensation tool (to help students compensate for their reading difficulties)?

5. What does the research say about the impact of scan/read programs on students with learning disabilities?

INTRODUCTION

Reading is both a subject area that students must master *and* a means by which students learn other subject areas. In the early grades (K–3) the primary focus of schools is on reading *instruction*, on children "learning to read," whereas it is said that in Grades 4 and up, the focus shifts to children "reading to learn." Computer technology has a powerful role to play in both learning to read and reading to learn.

This chapter is divided into four parts. The first part provides a *context* for using computer technology as a tool to teach reading. It presents what we know about teaching children to read (evidence-based strategies). The second part summarizes the typical reading problems faced by children who have trouble reading. Children with reading difficulties are given many labels: struggling readers, learning disabled, dyslexic, print disabled. The strategies discussed in this chapter apply to all of these children, regardless of their label. In the third part of this chapter the focus shifts to how computer technology can be used to teach children to read (i.e., as an instructional tool). The fourth part addresses how computer technology can help older students whose reading remains inadequate even after intensive instruction (i.e., how computer technology can be used as a compensatory tool to provide access to grade-level texts).

WHAT WE KNOW ABOUT TEACHING CHILDREN TO READ: EVIDENCED-BASED STRATEGIES

In 2000 the National Reading Panel (NRP), a group that had been convened at the request of the U.S. Congress, published a seminal report titled *Teaching Children to Read*. The report reviewed the published research on reading, pinpointed the types of skills children need to learn to become independent readers, and summarized the evidence relating to how those skills are best taught to beginning readers (NRP, 2000). The panel recommended specific instructional approaches and strategies ("evidence-based practices") that its members believed "hold substantial promise for application in the classroom at this time." These findings and recommendations have had far-reaching effects on reading instruction in the early 21st century, and therefore are summarized in the next section.

Findings of the NRP: Topic Areas

To become proficient readers, children need to be taught skills in five topic areas. These areas are described in the following sections and listed in Table 3.1.

Phonemic Awareness. Phonemes are the smallest units of sound in the spoken language, and *phonemic awareness* refers to the ability to "focus on and manipulate phonemes in spoken words" (NRP Subgroup on Alphabetics, 2000, p. 3). The term relates to children's understanding of the *sounds* of their language. English, for example, consists of 41 different phonemes. The word *book*, for example, consists of three sounds or phonemes /b/, /u/, and /k/. Explicitly teaching children to recognize and manipulate phonemes is the first recommendation of the NRP's report.

Phonics. Phonics instruction teaches the correspondence between sounds and letters. "The primary focus of phonics instruction is to help beginning readers understand how letters are linked to sounds (phonemes) to form letter-sound correspondences and spelling patterns and to help them learn how to apply this knowledge in their reading" (NRP, 2000, p. 3). The NRP's report found that "systematic phonics instruction produces significant benefits for students in kindergarten through 6th grade and for children having difficulty learning to read" (p. 4). Instruction in phonics also "improved the ability of good readers to spell" (p. 4). The NRP concluded

TABLE 3–1 Topic areas identified by the National Reading Panel

Phonemic awareness: Understanding the *sounds* of a language
Phonics: Recognizing the correspondence between sounds and letters
Fluency: Reading orally with speed, accuracy, and proper expression
Comprehension: Understanding the meaning of the text
Vocabulary: Understanding the meaning of words both orally and in print

that "explicit, systematic phonics instruction is a valuable and essential part of a successful classroom reading program" (p. 5).

Fluency. "Fluent readers are able to read orally with speed, accuracy, and proper expression" (NRP, 2000, p. 6). Fluency is necessary for reading comprehension; disfluent readers have difficulty gaining meaning from what they read. One major approach to teaching fluency is guided oral reading. The NRP report found that "guided oral reading procedures that included guidance from teachers, peers, or parents had a significant and positive impact on word recognition, fluency, and comprehension" (p. 7).

Comprehension. Reading comprehension is defined as "intentional thinking during which meaning is constructed through interactions between text and reader" (Harris & Hodges, 1995). Reading comprehension is enhanced when students "actively relate the ideas represented in print to their own knowledge and experiences and construct mental representations in memory" (NRP, 2000, p. 10). This is usually accomplished through the use of various cognitive strategies such as making predictions, questioning, summarizing, clarifying, visualizing using graphic organizers, and self-monitoring (Rose & Dalton, 2002). Palincsar and Klenk (1991) point out that children learn to use these strategies when their teachers explicitly model them. For example, a good reading teacher will pause while reading aloud and say, "I'm predicting that he is going to get in trouble." Or the teacher might say, "I don't know what this word means so I'm going to try to figure it out by reading the rest of the sentence."

Vocabulary. The larger the child's vocabulary—both oral and print vocabulary—the easier it is to understand text. A child with a weak vocabulary will have difficulty comprehending what he or she is trying to read. The findings of the NRP show that direct and indirect instruction in vocabulary leads to improvements in reading comprehension. The report recommends both repetition and multiple exposures to vocabulary as approaches to teaching vocabulary.

READING PROBLEMS IN STUDENTS WITH DISABILITIES

Which of the five topic areas discussed present problems for children with disabilities? You probably know children who have difficulties in *all* of the areas. Some reading experts today believe that decoding or "phonological processing is the core deficit in dyslexia" (Ross-Kidder, 2004). For these children explicit instruction on phonemic awareness and phonics is critical to improving their reading skills. Reading programs such as the Wilson Reading Program (www.wilsonlanguage.com) and Orton-Gillingham (www.orton-gillingham.com) stress these phonological skills. Other reading experts emphasize the need for children with reading disabilities to be taught specific reading comprehension strategies *and* how to use these strategies. For example, struggling readers need to be taught to monitor their comprehension *and* to take some kind of productive action when they do not understand what they are reading (Lipson & Wixson, 1997).

One group of students who often have problems with reading comprehension are those who have attention disorders (Schulte, Conners, & Osborne, 1999). These students have difficulty focusing on the text; they may "lose their place, have trouble keeping what they read in short-term memory, and have to read the same paragraph repeatedly to get any meaning out of it. As a result, reading becomes mentally fatiguing" (Robin, 1998). For students with these kinds of reading problems, access to content is severely diminished. This results in problems with *learning* because their weak comprehension skills interfere with their ability to read to learn (National Center to Improve the Tools of Educators [NCITE], 1996). Many students with learning disabilities "find that books and other texts that constitute the general curriculum function as *barriers* rather than gateways to learning. Decoding difficulties block students from access to important content, and comprehension problems block students from responding to and learning from text in meaningful ways" (Rose & Dalton, 2002, p. 9, italics added).

HOW TECHNOLOGY CAN ADDRESS THESE PROBLEMS

Learning to Read: The Computer as a Remediation Tool

The computer can be a powerful teaching tool. Its ability to present systematic, repetitive, and individualized instruction makes it particularly well suited for providing students who have disabilities with the practice they need to master specific skills (Wehmeyer, Smith, Palmer, & Davies, 2004). In this section we examine how computers can be used specifically to teach the five skill areas identified in the NRP's report.

Phonemic Awareness and Phonics. Well-designed educational software is particularly good at teaching phonemic awareness and sound–letter correspondence. This is due to the computer's ability to present both visual displays (color and animation) and sounds to highlight patterns and to engage students. Whereas the workbooks and worksheets typically used in elementary school classrooms can represent sound only with letters, computers can speak phonemes orally and can provide practice with the actual sounds that students need to learn (Meyer & Rose, 1998). Both the short /a/ sound in *apple* and the long /a/ sound in *gate*, for example, can be presented and practiced when the computer says the actual sounds aloud.

There is an abundance of software programs on the market that claim to teach phonological processes. The key is to select programs that (a) are designed around the principles of good reading instruction, and (b) meet the criteria for effective instructional software (Meyer & Rose, 1998) (see Chapter 5). Good reading software does the following:

- It highlights patterns among sounds, letters, and letter–sound correspondence.
- It provides multiple opportunities for meaningful practice.
- It engages students through interactive activities and interesting displays (colors, animation, sounds) that motivate students to practice and learn.
- It allows for customization for individual differences. (Meyer & Rose, 2000)

One special application of computers for teaching phonological processes to students with learning disabilities involves slowing down, exaggerating, and altering sounds to make sound patterns easier to recognize. Intensive interventions using software or Internet-based programs such as Fast ForWord (Scientific Learning Corp.) or Earobics (Cognitive Concepts Inc.) are designed "to train the brain to speed its auditory information processing. . . . As the child becomes more proficient at recognizing the sounds, the Fast ForWord Language program adjusts to the child's improving level of competence by continually shortening the duration of the sound, requiring the brain to process at faster rates of speech" (Ross-Kidder, 2004). This specialized intervention seems to be most effective with children whose reading difficulties are due to problems in phonological processing. The developers of Fast ForWord have published several studies whose results show "significant improvements in reading and oral language skills on a number of assessments" in children with dyslexia who used the program for 8 weeks (Temple et al., 2003). These kinds of results are achieved only when students follow a rigorous schedule of completing the Fast ForWord activities for at least an hour each day for a minimum of 8 weeks.

Reading Comprehension. One of the most exciting changes in reading software in recent years has been the shift from primarily "drill and practice" formats to the more constructivist approach of computer-supported strategy instruction (Rose & Dalton, 2002). The ability of the computer to manipulate text, read text aloud, provide a range of supports, and maintain records of performance is now being put to use in programs that model and explicitly teach strategies for reading comprehension. Thinking Reader (Tom Snyder Productions) is a good example of a software series that teaches comprehension strategies to struggling readers (see Figure 3.1).

Thinking Reader presents the unabridged text of high-quality middle school–level literature on a computer so that students can (1) listen to the story being read, (2) read along with a visual display that has been adjusted to meet their individual preferences, (3) observe on-screen characters model reading comprehension strategies, (4) quickly access definitions of unfamiliar vocabulary, and (5) practice using the reading comprehension strategies. The books in the series include *The Giver* (Lois Lowry), *Tuck Everlasting* (Natalie Babbitt), *Roll of Thunder, Hear My Cry* (Mildred Taylor), and *Bud, Not Buddy* (Christopher Paul Curtis). Because the story can be read aloud by the computer, students who are poor decoders (i.e., those who have not mastered phonemic awareness and phonics) can still enjoy the books and can still work on improving their comprehension by learning the reading comprehension strategies. The seven strategies that are embedded in the program are summarizing, questioning, clarifying, predicting, visualizing, feeling, and reflecting (Tom Snyder Productions, 2004; see Table 3.2). Students are reminded of the strategies at appropriate times while they are reading and listening to the text via an elaborate system of prompts, hints, models, and feedback (see Figures 3.2 and 3.3). For teachers the series includes an extensive system for gathering assessment data on every student and for providing feedback to each student.

The Internet also offers several subscription services that are designed to improve the higher level reading skills of fluency, comprehension, and vocabulary. KidBiz3000 and TeenBiz3000 (Achieve3000) are good examples. Every day, KidBiz3000 sends grade 2 to 5 students a news-based reading assignment that is customized for their

FIGURE 3–1   Text of a Thinking Reader book

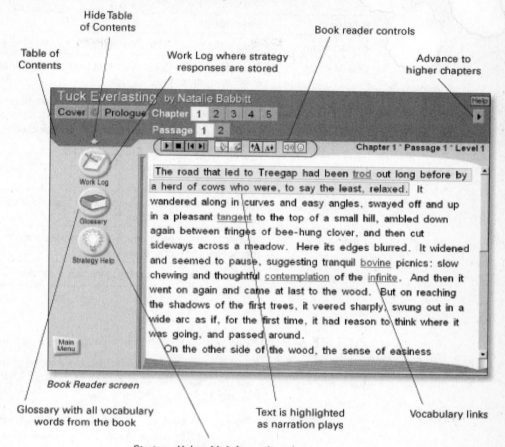

Source: Reprinted with permission from Tom Snyder Productions.

reading level. TeenBiz3000 focuses on grades 6–12. The reading passage could be about national or world events, science, technology, trends, or sports. All children read about the same topic and complete a set of related writing activities, but the levels of the passages differ depending on how the students performed on a reading pretest. A customized dictionary and reference materials are also provided. So although each student works at his or her own level, all students read about the same topics and can participate in class discussions (Achieve3000, n.d.).

Interesting Reading Materials on the Internet.   In addition to the strategies and technology tools already discussed, children who struggle with reading can benefit from careful selection of their reading material. Meyer and Rose (1998) point out that "engagement is essential to successful reading" (p. 56), and that "deep engagement . . . depends on *interesting material*. . . . For individuals with skill deficits,

TABLE 3–2 Seven reading comprehension strategies taught in Thinking Reader

Strategy	Description
Summarizing	Students are asked to summarize what they have read.
Questioning	Students pose a question about book content that is important to know and remember.
Clarifying	Students have the opportunity to ask about something they do not understand in the text. Their question may be about a word or phrase, historic/background information, or anything else requiring additional explanation.
Predicting	Students use what they know to make a prediction about what will happen next.
Visualizing	Students visualize the setting or an important event. They can either record or write their visualization.
Feeling	Students are asked to make a personal connection to the text or to put themselves in a character's place.
Reflecting	Students reflect on their progress as a reader.

FIGURE 3–2 Thinking Reader hint for the strategy of feeling

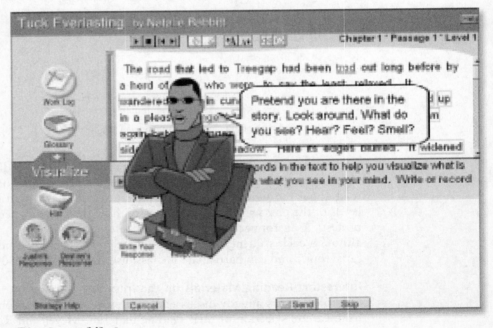

Strategy Hint

Source: Reprinted with permission from Tom Snyder Productions.

FIGURE 3–3
Thinking Reader
Strategy Help
screen

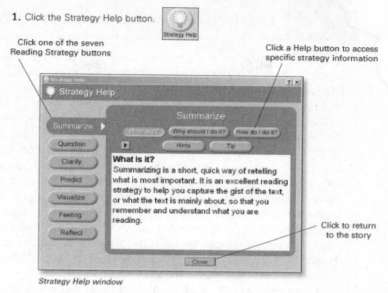

Strategy Help window

Source: Reprinted with permission from Tom Snyder Productions.

interest can lead to remarkable engagement and success. It can motivate them to make extraordinary efforts to overcome difficulties that would stop them cold if they did not care so much about the subject" (p. 61, italics added). Letting students *choose* their own reading material is one way to enhance their engagement with the text (Rothman, 2004).

How is this related to computer technology? Today finding reading material that matches students' interests is as simple as a few mouse clicks. Teachers can find all kinds of reading material on the Internet—books, articles, and newspaper stories, as well as websites, discussion boards, and blogs. Teachers (or students) can download these materials, save them as text documents in a word processing program, manipulate the text for a comfortable visual display (e.g., increase the font size, double-space the text, increase the margins so the line of text is shorter), and then print them for reading or save them to be read aloud by a computer using software that we discuss in the next section (Meyer & Rose, 1998).

Reading to Learn: The Computer as a Compensation Tool

In the upper elementary grades, just as direct reading instruction begins to taper off, the nature of the material students must read begins to change. Whereas in K–3 children read mostly narrative fiction and nonfiction stories, in fourth grade they begin to read textbooks in the content areas, called expository texts (Rothman, 2004). Being able to read and understand these textbooks is critical for academic success, especially as the student moves on to middle school, high school, and college.

Low-Tech Adaptations That Support Reading

Special education teachers and reading specialists use a range of strategies to improve the literacy of students with reading problems. Students are taught to use highlighter pens and sticky notes, for example, to call attention to certain text passages or pages, especially when reading long selections. Highlighting makes important information stand out and helps students locate important information (Assistive Technology Training Online Training Project [ATTO], 2005). This is especially helpful for students who cannot skim text when studying. Using different-colored highlighters for different types of information can help cue students to where in the passage they can find the information they need (Georgia Assistive Technology Project Tools for Life, n.d.). For example, students can be taught to use a yellow highlighter for topic sentences, a blue highlighter for unfamiliar vocabulary, and a green highlighter for important names. Sticky notes can be used to jot down reminders and questions about the reading passage. For library books or other books that cannot be marked, removable highlighter tape is a good alternative.

For students who have physical disabilities, book holders can be an essential low-tech device. A good one holds a book of nearly any size at a comfortable reading angle, and provides adjustable pegs that prevent pages from flipping inadvertently (ATTO, 2005). Some students can use a pencil eraser or rubber-tipped head stick or chin stick to turn pages when the book is positioned in a book holder. To make it easier for students to read worksheets and other single sheets of paper, teachers can place them in an inexpensive holder called a Page Up (MTM Corp). These simple adaptations enable many students who have physical disabilities to read independently, freeing them from the need to ask another person to hold the paper or turn the page for them.

Middle, high school and college students are required to complete extensive amounts of reading on a daily basis—textbooks, works of literature, journal articles, reference materials—most of which have readability levels well beyond the skills of most students with disabilities (Boyle et al., 2002). Slow readers and students with reading comprehension problems struggle to complete their reading assignments and fall behind in their work because they cannot keep up with all the reading. This is not only frustrating and stressful, but it also interferes with their learning of the subject matter.

Some students get through high school by having their parents or instructional aides read their textbooks to them. (Some simply do not complete the reading and get by through paying attention to class lectures.) These may be short-term solutions, but in the end they are a disservice to students; when teenagers attempt to attend college or hold a job they find they are unable to complete their reading assignments on their own. Therefore, students with reading difficulties stand to benefit significantly from computer technology that can increase their independence in reading. One such application is called *scan/read systems*.

USER PROFILE: Anthony M.

Meet Anthony M.: A graduate of a well-known college in the northeast, he now works in his field of choice—business. His elementary school teachers would be very surprised to hear this. In the primary grades Anthony could not read. Although his parents thought he was reading along with them, he was actually listening to them read and then reciting the books from memory. "Functionally I did not know how to read until the fourth grade, and even then it was at a first-grade level. One school district attempted to classify me as mentally retarded." Eventually he was diagnosed with a perceptual impairment, poor fine motor skills, low mathematical reasoning, and poor spelling ability, and in the third grade, he entered a self-contained special education class. "You could tell that the teacher did not have high expectations for any of us," Anthony recalls.

How did he get from being a nonreader to graduating from college? Anthony credits his strong motivation, hard work, and his discovery of scan/read systems. He found using the Kurzweil 3000 helped him immensely with his 12-credit course load. "It was beyond my expectations," he said.

If I were to read a book like *Marketing Principles* [without scan/read], if I were to persevere through all the reading, it would probably take me 2.5 hours to read one chapter. By the time I finished reading the last page of the chapter I would have forgotten the first part of the chapter and remembered maybe 40 percent of the rest. When using the Kurzweil 3000, it took me half the time to read the chapter, and I'd remember 75 to 80 percent.

I literally had 700 pages of retail management, 980 pages of market research, 650 pages of consumer behavior, and 2,000 pages of econ/stats to read. Reading with the Kurzweil 3000 made it easier for me to digest the information. If I had been trying to read all that without the help of the Kurzweil, I would know just a whole bunch of pieces and it would be difficult. It made a real difference in my comprehension. (Shipon, 2002)

Scan/Read Systems. Scan/read systems combine the use of a computer, a scanner, optical character recognition software, and speech output to read aloud any printed text while providing a visually enhanced display on a computer monitor. Users of scan/read systems place the pages to be read on a flatbed scanner and click the Scan button. (Using a document scanner instead of a flatbed scanner is a faster alternative.) The print is then converted into an electronic file, similar to a word processing file. Scan/read programs then speak the words on the screen while highlighting the corresponding text. This provides a "synchronized auditory and visual presentation of the text" (Hecker, Burns, Katz, Elkind, & Elkind, 2002). Optional highlighting in color helps readers keep their eyes on a line of text, while the speech output provides ongoing auditory feedback.

Two of the most popular, full-featured scan/read systems, Kurzweil 3000 (Kurzweil Educational Systems) and WYNN (Freedom Scientific), offer features that are designed to meet the needs of people who struggle with reading comprehension (see Figures 3.4 and 3.5). Both programs offer options to change the appearance of the visual display and to set the reading speed to match the user's preference. They also offer what Anderson-Inman and Horney (1997) call "embedding tools"—a talking dictionary and thesaurus; electronic highlighters to assist students in taking notes and preparing study guides; voice notes; and yellow "sticky notes" for inserting hidden prompts and reminders.

The talking dictionary is a good example of how embedding tools can help students who have reading comprehension problems. When a student with reading problems encounters an unfamiliar word, the suggestion to "look it up in the dictionary" is not terribly helpful. Dictionaries, even electronic dictionaries, tend to cram a lot of text onto a single page; the font is quite small and spacing is tight. The student with reading problems often cannot find the word in the dictionary to begin with, and if he or she manages to locate it, reading the small print and understanding it present additional difficulties. Contrast that with the talking dictionaries that are embedded in scan/read systems. The student simply clicks on the unfamiliar word, then clicks on the dictionary icon, and the program immediately displays the dictionary entry for that word and will read it aloud when the student clicks the Read button. In addition, another simple click of the mouse will copy the definition to the computer clipboard so the student can create a customized vocabulary list that can be studied later.

The impact of scan/read software on the reading performance of postsecondary students with attention disorders was demonstrated in a research study by Hecker and Colleagues (2002). Twenty students were trained to use the Kurzweil 3000 and over

FIGURE 3–4
WYNN text highlighting

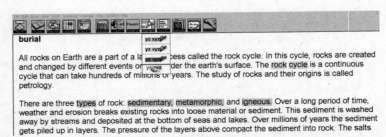

Source: Used with permission from Freedom Scientific.

FIGURE 3–5
Kurzweil 3000
dictionary

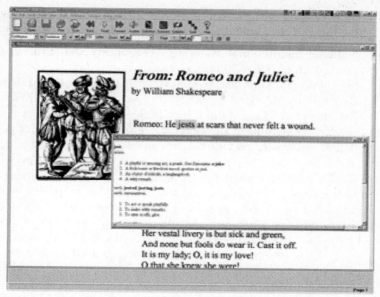

Source: Used with permission from Kurzweil Educational Systems.

the course of a semester used it to read assignments in English class and take tests. The results revealed that scan/read software "allowed the students to attend better to their reading, to reduce their distractibility, to read with less stress and fatigue, and to read for longer periods of time. It helped them to read faster and thereby to complete reading assignments in less time" (p. 243).

Scan/read programs are powerful tools that can help students with learning disabilities compensate for their reading and study skills problems. However, Anderson-Inman and Horney (1997) emphasize that students need to be *taught* how to use the features in these programs. Their study found, for example, that embedding tools can improve student achievement only if struggling readers are taught to use them properly. Simply providing students with software is not enough. This and other implementation issues are discussed in more detail in Chapter 12.

Alternative to Scanning Text: e-Text. One of the obstacles standing in the way of widescale implementation of scan/read technology is that scanning documents takes quite a bit of time. Unless a school has access to a high-speed scanner and it is acceptable to tear the bindings off books, scanning requires a person to stand at a flatbed scanner and scan one page at a time. This is easily done for a few pages of reading material, but when it comes to entire books, it can take hours. Therefore, it is important for teachers to become knowledgeable about Internet sites that provide files of text that are already in electronic format. Called e-text, these are files of books or other printed material that someone else has already converted into a computer file. Most literature that is in the public domain, such as all of Shakespeare's plays, are available for free download from Internet sites such as Project Gutenberg (http://www.gutenberg.net). Instead of scanning in *Hamlet* for a high school student, for example, the file can be downloaded from the Internet and read aloud using a scan/read system such as WYNN or Kurzweil 3000. The student benefits from all of the features and embedding tools in the software, but the need for time-consuming scanning is eliminated.

National Instructional Materials Accessibility Standard. In the most recent reauthorization of IDEA 2004, a provision was added to ease the problem of procuring textbooks in alternate formats. Called the National Instructional Materials Accessibility Standard (NIMAS), this provision was clarified in 2006 when the U.S. Department of Education, Office of Special Education Programs (OSEP) published specific regulations in the *Federal Register*. NIMAS guides publishers in producing digital versions of textbooks that can be easily converted to accessible formats such as Braille, audio, e-text, and large print (Center for Applied Special Technology [CAST], 2006). Publishers are now required to use this standard when preparing source files for textbooks and need to provide these files when requested by state and local education agencies. The regulations also reaffirm the responsibilities of state and local education agencies to provide students who have print disabilities with alternate-format versions of textbooks in a timely manner (CAST, 2006).

K–12 textbook publishers are now required to prepare NIMAS file sets for deposit in a national repository of digital materials (CAST, 2006). Known as the National Instructional Materials Access Center (NIMAC), the repository is hosted by the American Printing House for the Blind. NIMAC provides states and local education agencies with textbook files that follow NIMAS and therefore should be easily converted to alternate formats.

SIDEBAR

What Is Electronic Text?

Electronic Text or e-Text is text that has been saved in a form that can be opened on any computer: no formatting, no html markup. A Microsoft Word document or an AppleWorks document is not an e-text document unless it is saved as plain text. You may know the acronym ASCII (American Standard Code for Information Interchange); any text file that is saved as plain text usually conforms to this standard.

Why collect it? Plain text versions of writing that is out of copyright is usually compact enough (*Alice in Wonderland* is about 140K) that it can easily be shared on disks or downloaded from the Web. Once you have an electronic version of a book or other text, you can have your computer read it aloud, change its font and the size of the type, use color to highlight key words, and manipulate the text in ways that you just can't do with a printed book.

What about copyright? At this point . . . copyrights in the United States on books and other material last for 70 years. After 70 years, unless the copyright is reapplied for, the printed material moves into the public domain.

From *What Is Electronic Text?* by Richard Wanderman, n.d. Retrieved from the LD Resources website: http://www.LDResources.org

Internet Sites Offering e-Text

Bookshare.org

http://www.bookshare.org

Bookshare.org is an online community that enables people with visual and other print disabilities to legally share scanned books. Bookshare.org takes advantage of a special exemption in the U.S. copyright law that permits the reproduction of publications into specialized formats for individuals with disabilities.

Electronic Text Center at the University of Virginia

http://etext.lib.virginia.edu

The Electronic Text Center's holdings include approximately 70,000 humanities texts in 12 languages. They include classic British and American fiction, major authors, children's literature, American history, Shakespeare, African American documents, and the Bible.

EServer

http://eserver.org

The EServer, formerly at Carnegie Mellon and the University of Washington, is now based at Iowa State University. It contains over 32,419 works in 45 collections on such diverse topics as contemporary art, race, Internet studies, sexuality, drama, design, gender studies, accessible publishing, and current political and social issues.

Google Book Search

http://Books.Google.com

This repository differs from the previous ones in that it contains copyrighted books as well as books in the public domain. Books that are protected by copyright may show up in a search but the full content of the book may not be available for download. This is a growing area of the Internet and the publishing field and we are likely to see changes in the near future.

Internet Public Library

http://www.ipl.org

The IPL Online Texts Collection housed at Drexel University contains over 19,000 titles including various online books, stories, essays, poems, articles, dramas, letters, and speeches. They can be browsed by author, title, or Dewey Decimal classification.

Louis Database

http://www.aph.org/louis.htm

This free database includes 200,000 titles in accessible formats including Braille, large print, sound recording, and electronic files from over 180 agencies throughout the United States.

Project Gutenberg

http://www.Gutenberg.net

At the time of this writing there are 17,000 books in the Project Gutenberg Online Book Catalog. Two million e-books are downloaded each month.

Scan/Read for Students Who Are Blind or Visually Impaired. Students who are blind or visually impaired also benefit from scan/read technology. Their needs are different from students with learning disabilities. They do not have reading comprehension problems—in fact, many are fluent Braille readers—but they face significant barriers in gaining access to printed materials in a timely manner. They often use scan/read systems when they need quick access to print, for example, the morning newspaper, their mail, professional reports, and legal documents. The Kurzweil 1000 (Kurzweil Educational Systems) and OpenBook (Freedom Scientific) are two popular scan/read systems designed to meet the needs of people who cannot see printed text. These systems offer many of the same features as WYNN and Kurzweil 3000, but their interface is easier to use for people who cannot see the screen. Tasks that users with learning disabilities do with a mouse, such as navigating through documents, managing documents, or selecting a tool, can be accomplished through the use of "hot keys" and function keys. Although these commands require some memorization, they are far more efficient than using the mouse for users who are blind.

Other Compensatory Reading Tools: Recorded Books. In addition to scan/read programs, there are other forms of technology that can help older students who struggle with reading comprehension. Books-on-tape is a service that has been available for many years. The books were read aloud by readers and recorded on four-track tapes that had to be played back on special four-track tape recorders.

K-NFB Reader:
The Kurzweil-National Federation of the Blind Reader is the first handheld scan/read device. The user holds the Reader's build-in digital camera over any kind of point—a worksheet, a journal article, or a restaurant menu—and snaps a picture. In seconds the device speaks the contents of the printed document in clear synthetic speech.

Photo courtesy of Kurzweil Educational Systems, Inc.

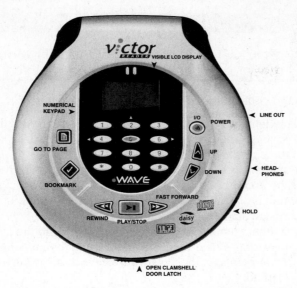

The Victor Reader Wave is a lightweight portable playback device for digital books. It can be used with headphones or speakers. Its numeric keypad makes it easy for students to navigate by page, chapter or section.
Photo courtesy of Humanware.

Today organizations like Recording for the Blind and Dyslexic (RFB&D) have moved from four-track tapes to digital books on CD, a format they call AudioPlus. The advantage to digital recordings is that, unlike tapes, they do not have to be navigated in order from beginning to end. Users can start the book at any place, can insert bookmarks at any point, and can easily navigate from one page or chapter to another, or from one bookmark or heading to the next. This ease of navigation affords students the opportunity to use prereading strategies that can increase their comprehension and learning. One such strategy is SLiCK, short for Set up, Look ahead, Comprehend, Keep it together (Boyle et al., 2002). This strategy is described in the sidebar.

Another advantage digital books have over analog recordings is that digitally recorded books can be stored on CDs, which have a much greater storage capacity than cassettes. A book recorded on 10 RFB&D cassettes will now fit onto a single CD, so a student listening to five textbooks may have to carry only five CDs rather than 50 cassettes. To listen to RFB&D's digital books, students need either a special portable CD player or a standard computer equipped with specialized software. It is important to note that for copyright reasons, organizations like RFB&D require their members to provide documented evidence of a print disability before they can borrow digital books.

Other sources of recorded books are commercial bookstores and Web-based businesses that are targeted at the general public. With the popularity of portable CD players, car audio systems, and MP3 players such as the iPod, listening to recorded books has become a popular activity in our society. People listen to books as they commute, work out in gyms, jog, or just walk around. They borrow recorded books from public libraries, buy them in bookstores, and download them

SLiCK Strategy for Use with Audio Books

Boyle and colleagues (2002) explain the SLiCK strategy:

1. The student gets all materials set up: He or she opens the textbook to the correct page, places a SLiCK worksheet on the desk, and loads the CD into the playback device.
2. The student looks ahead through the chapter (both the printed textbook and the audio book), noting the headings, subheadings, keywords, and vocabulary, in order to think about what is coming up and access prior knowledge about the subject.
3. The student comprehends the text by listening to the audio book and following along in the text. This step includes pausing the CD to write important points on the SLiCK worksheet and writing a summary of what was learned.
4. The student now must keep it together—must combine the summaries to comprehend the entire reading "to get the bigger picture" (Boyle et al., 2002, p. 54).

Based on "Reading's SLiCK with New Audio Texts and strategies," by E. A. Boyle, S. G. Washburn, M. S. Rosenberg, V. J. Connelly, L. C. Brinckerhoff, and M. Banerjee, 2002, *Teaching Exceptional children, 35*(2), 50–55.

from Web-based services such as Audible.com or iTunes. At the time of this writing, commercially available recorded books typically focus on bestsellers and popular fiction and nonfiction titles, not on textbooks. However, anecdotal evidence suggests that if given a choice, teenagers would prefer to listen to a recorded book on an iPod, rather than a "special" device. For students who do not need to see modified or enhanced text on a computer monitor, it is likely that in the next few years schools will see the format of compensatory reading tools shift from special playback devices to MP3 players and other popular electronics.

Other Compensatory Reading Tools: Adapted Books. The compensatory tools previously presented are particularly well suited for students who understand material at their grade level when they hear it, even though they struggle with decoding and comprehending written text. There are other students, however, who have not yet mastered the skills needed to understand grade-level material. These students need additional reading supports and can benefit from another kind of assistive technology.

It has been estimated that 90% of students with multiple disabilities never learn to read above the second-grade level (Koppenhaver & Yoder, 1992). Many students with cognitive disabilities get "stuck" at the emergent literacy level (Erickson, Musselwhite, Ziolkowski, n.d.). They may listen to stories for enjoyment and participate in reading activities, but they do not progress to being able to read new text independently. Part of the problem has been a lack of appropriate materials, that is, of reading material

SIDEBAR

DAISY Format

Digital Accessible Information System (DAISY) is an international consortium of libraries and organizations for people with print disabilities. Its mission is to ensure that all people have access to published material through the development of an international standard and implementation strategies for the production, exchange, and use of digital talking books. This international standard features an accessible, feature-rich, easily navigable format. RFB&D's AudioPlus recordings use the DAISY format.

that is age appropriate, engaging, and written at a level the students can understand (Erickson et al., n.d.). Without such materials, reading development is hampered further because the students do not have many opportunities to read successfully. To break this cycle, these students need reading materials that match their reading abilities and interests, and they need multiple opportunities to read (Erickson et al., n.d.).

Computer technology has proven to be an excellent medium for addressing this problem. A series called Start-to-Finish Books (Don Johnston, Inc.) provides a

Student reading a book using an iPod for auditory support.
Photo by Anne M. Disdier

FIGURE 3–6
Start-To-Finish
book

Source: Image provided courtesy of Don Johnston, Inc.

library of abridged books that are written at lower grade levels but designed for the interests and curricula of higher grade levels (Figure 3.6). Each book is packaged in three formats: a paperback book to read, an audio book to listen to, and a computer book that provides visual and auditory supports. To help with fluency, the computer book highlights the text as it reads it aloud. The narration is digitized speech, not synthesized, so different characters speak differently and the reading sounds more like a dramatization than typical computerized voices. This captivates students and involves them in the story. Students can click on unfamiliar words to hear them spoken aloud.

The Start-to-Finish books enable students who are reading on a second- or third-grade level to read a version of *Treasure Island, Huck Finn,* or *Romeo and Juliet.* So if their middle school or high school English class is reading one of these classics, a student whose reading is far below grade level can still enjoy the story and participate in class activities. There are also titles available about sports figures such as Jackie Robinson and Muhammad Ali, and historical figures such as Sacagawea and Rosa Parks. As students' reading skills improve, the series offers another set of titles at the fourth- to fifth-grade reading level.

In 2005 the Start-to-Finish series expanded to include supplements to textbooks called Core Content. These nonfiction packages provide access to topics covered in middle school and high school curricula such as evolution (*Adaptation and Change on the Galapagos Islands*) and history (*Fighting Back Against Hitler: Heroes of the Holocaust*). In addition to offering electronic supports, these books have been designed to provide considerate text. Considerate text is written at an appropriate level, is organized in a meaningful way, and provides helpful headings and questions to the reader (Armbruster & Anderson, 1988). It limits the amount of new vocabulary and carefully introduces new words. In the Start-to-Finish Core Content series, for example, all new subject-specific terms are printed in boldface and defined in the glossary. Students can read the book on the computer, following along as the text is

USER PROFILE: Carol

Carol is a middle school student who has been receiving special education services since second grade. She is a star soccer player and attends a public school in her hometown. She has been described as having learning disabilities, a central auditory processing disorder, and/or attention deficits. Whatever label you use, the fact remains that she has a very difficult time gaining meaning from text, and as a result, is reluctant to do any reading. In typical teenage fashion, Carol also does not want to "look different," to draw attention to her learning difficulties, so her mother has tried a variety of technology tools to help her succeed in reading.

In the summer before sixth grade Carol was finally able to enjoy a book when she read *Anne of Green Gables* from the Start-to-Finish series. It was shorter than the original and it was read aloud by the computer, but for the first time Carol understood what she was reading. The following summer her mother downloaded and reformatted *The Hobbitt* from Bookshare.org, and Carol read it using the scan/read program WYNN. Being tied to a computer was inconvenient, so the following summer (between seventh and eighth grade), Carol chose to listen to the latest Harry Potter book on a portable CD player, following along in the book. During eighth grade, for "personal choice book" assignments she read the Thinking Reader version of *Esperanza Rising*. Then she discovered that she could purchase books from iTunes and downloaded *Heartbeat* (by Sharon Creech) onto her iPod. Now she can listen to age-appropriate books on her iPod, not be tied to a computer, and not look different from the other middle schoolers.

highlighted and spoken aloud; they can listen to the audio book; or they can read the paperback book independently. Curriculum content that was previously inaccessible to students who were poor readers is now accessible through this use of technology.

Listening to books on MP3 players such as an iPod is becoming a popular compensatory reading strategy. Many programs, including the latest versions of Kurzweil 3000 and WYNN, offer the ability to convert electronic files to MP3 format for this exact purpose.

DECISION MAKING: INSTRUCTIONAL TOOL OR COMPENSATORY TOOL?

Earlier in this chapter we explained how computer technology can be used to help students *learn to read*. In the last section we discussed that computers can also be used as a compensatory strategy for students who need to *read to learn* but whose reading skills are inadequate. This section addresses the following questions: How does a teacher *decide* which application of technology to use? *When* does a teacher switch the emphasis from learning to read to using computer technology to help a student read to learn? Edyburn (2003) asks, "How do we decide if the best course of action is remediation (i.e., additional instructional time, different instructional approaches) versus compensation (i.e., recognizing that remediation has failed and that compensatory approaches are needed to produce the desired level of performance)? . . . When should students be provided with compensatory technologies when they can't read?" (p. 18).

In answering this question Edyburn (2003) finds guidance in the field of occupational therapy. If a student has cerebral palsy and cannot use an arm, a therapist teaches the student alterative ways of completing tasks that require the use of two arms. Compensatory approaches are often used in occupational therapy because with physical disabilities "there are [often] no other ways to complete the task" (p. 19). He parallels this to education: Technology should be considered as a compensatory tool when a student routinely fails "to attain appropriate levels of academic performance" (p. 19). If these students are provided with appropriate compensatory tools, they will "experience success and achieve the functional outcome expected in their academic classes" (p. 20).

A helpful framework for this decision-making process is provided by Dyck and Pemberton (2002). Although their article focuses on text adaptations and is not specific to assistive technology, the issues they raise are very relevant to our discussion. They recommend asking the question, "Can this student read and understand this text with sufficient speed and accuracy? . . . If the answer is 'No, the student is struggling with the printed word,' text adaptation should be considered" (p. 29). They provide a decision tree to help teachers select one of six adaptations. We focus on the first four options in the following text and summarize them in Figure 3.7.

The first option to consider for the student who cannot comprehend a text is the substitution of an **alternative text,** "one the student can read and understand but that contains the same content material" (p. 29). Dyck and Pemberton (2002) recommend locating substitute books that use "considerate text." Which technology application was presented in this chapter that uses considerate text? The Start-to-Finish Core Content series uses considerate text. These packages provide access to core curriculum content to poor readers; they are intentionally designed as substitutions to conventional textbooks.

Next, Dyck and Pemberton (2002) suggest asking the question, "Can this student achieve the lesson goal or objective if the **text is read to** the student?" **(p. 30, bold face added).** They call this "bypass reading," and mention books-on-tape or books-on-CD as examples. The Thinking Reader series discussed in this chapter and scan/read programs like WYNN and Kurzweil 3000 are also examples of this option; the student experiences the same text as the other students but benefit from being able to *listen* to the text.

The third option Dyck and Pemberton (2002) discuss is **decreasing the amount** of reading a student is required to complete. This can be done simply by reducing the student's assignment, but other options include using the AutoSummarize feature in Microsoft Word, using abridged versions of books-on-tape or books-on-CD, or using the abridged Start-to-Finish Books. The Web-based program KidBiz3000, which was described earlier in this chapter, also reduces the amount of reading for struggling readers.

The fourth option for adapting text recommended by Dyck and Pemberton (2002) is to **support reading**. "Supported reading means placing aids right in the text to make it more interesting and understandable" (p. 32). This is easily done in scan/read programs like WYNN and Kurzweil 3000. Talking dictionaries and thesauruses are available at the click of a mouse. Teachers can embed text notes and voice notes in the text that, for example, remind students to look up a word in the

FIGURE 3–7 Using technology to adapt text for students who struggle with reading comprehension

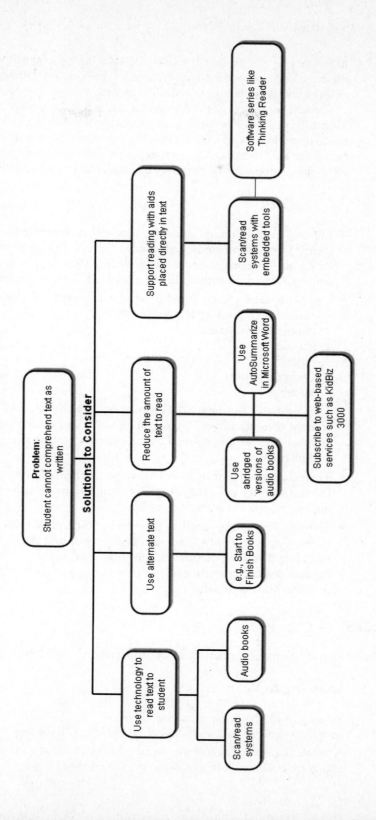

dictionary or signify that the next sentence is important or prompt students to use their reading comprehension strategies. The Thinking Reader series regularly provides prompts for comprehension strategies.

Clearly, regardless of the type of support needed, assistive technology offers multiple means to scaffold reading success. Assistive technology tools can meet the reading needs of students who have disabilities, whether they require remediation or compensation for skill deficits. Appropriate applications of assistive technology can support all of the components of effective reading instruction as identified by the NRP.

SUMMARY

- Reading instruction in Grades K–3 focuses on learning to read; that is, learning to identify letters and sounds, decode words, and glean meaning from printed text. By Grade 4, students are reading to learn. They are relying on printed text to gain contextual understanding. Instruction focuses on improving comprehension.

- The National Reading Panel identified five areas of reading instruction that are essential for children to learn to read:
  1. Phonemic awareness
  2. Phonics
  3. Fluency
  4. Comprehension
  5. Vocabulary

- The computer can be used as a reading remediation tool by increasing access to content through improving decoding skills and teaching phonological processes. It improves learning to read by providing systematic, repetitive, and individualized instruction.

- There has been a shift in software program design from drill and practice to focusing on strengthening overall reading comprehension strategies using interesting and popular reading materials.

- Scan/read programs, such as Kurzweil 3000 and WYNN, offer a variety of tools to increase a student's reading independence and overcome reading difficulties, including a talking dictionary and thesaurus, electronic highlighters for notetaking and preparing study guides, voice notes, and sticky notes for inserting hidden prompts and reminders.

WEB RESOURCES

For additional information on the topics listed, go to the following websites:

Learning to Read

Finding of the National Reading Panel
http://www.nichd.nih.gov/publications/nrp/smallbook.cfm
Schwab Learning: Learning to Read—Research Informs Us
http://www.schwablearning.org/articles.aspx?r=22

International Reading Association
http://www.ira.org

Reading Problems in Students with Learning Disabilities

Georgia Assistive Technology Project
http://www.gatfl.org/ldguide/read.htm

Phonemic Awareness Instruction

Wilson Reading Program
http://www.wilsonlanguage.com
Orton-Gillingham approach
http://www.orton-gillingham.com
Free demos of phonics software
http://www.riverdeep.com → Products → Reading or Educator Tools →
Free Demos & Trials

Intensive Training in Phonological Processes

Fast Forward
http://www.scilearn.com/
Earobics
http://www.earobics.com

Thinking Reader Software Series

www.tomsnyder.com → Reading → Thinking Reader → User Resources

Assistive Technology Tools for Reading

Schwab Learning
http://www.schwablearning.org/ariticles.aspx?r=1071&f=tech&x=9&y=3

Scan/Read Software

Kurzweil 1000 and 3000
http://www.kurzweiledu.com
WYNN
http://www.freedomscientific.com/LSG/products/index.asp

Text Readers

ReadPlease
http://readplease.com

gh Player
http://www.ghbraille.com/ghplayer.html

Additional Internet Sites for e-Text

TECH-NJ 2007
http://tcnj.edu/ntechnj/2007/etext.htm

National Instructional Materials Accessibility Standards

NIMAS updates
http://nimas.cast.org

National Instructional Materials Accessibility Center

Frequently Asked Questions
http://nimac.us/faq.html

Audio Books

Recording for the Blind and Dyslexic
http://www.rfbd.org
Storyline Online
http://www.storylineonline.net
Commercial audio books
http://www.audible.com

Adapted Books

Start-to-Finish books
http://www.donjohnston.com/products/start to finish/library/index.html
News-2-You: Subscription service to online news stories written at beginning
literacy levels.
http://www.news-2-you.com/about.aspx

Low-Tech Tools for Reading

Assistive Technology Training Online Project
http://atto.buffalo.edu/registered/ATBasics/populations/Lowtech/reading.php

SUGGESTED ACTIVITIES

1. *Try out software or Internet-based activities that teach reading skills.* Choose one
   of the titles in the Thinking Reader series (Scholastic) or a software program or
   Internet-based activity that teaches specific reading skills (for example, Riverdeep's

Destination Reading or Scholastic's WiggleWorks). Explore the program thoroughly. Deliberately make wrong answers to see how the program responds and find out what kind of teacher options are available. Does the program teach the reading skills it claims to teach? How would you use this program in your classroom?

2. *Locate and use e-text.* You are an in-class support teacher in a high school English class. The class will be reading Shakespeare's *Romeo and Juliet*. Some of your students read on a fourth-grade level and will not be able to keep up with the reading assignments. Your school has scan/read programs available. Go online and locate e-text versions of the play. Download three different versions, check them for accuracy and style, then choose one to import into SOLO (Don Johnston, Inc.), Kurzweil 3000, or WYNN.

3. *Convert e-text to MP3 format.* Go to http://www.nextup.com and listen to the variety of voices available. Download a trial version of the software program TextAloud (NextUp.com). Use it to listen to a Web page or a Word document. Then convert the file to MP3 format and listen to it again on an MP3 player. Write a narrative commenting on the ease or difficulty of the technical aspects of the task and the implications of this technology for students with disabilities.

4. *Make the reading components of a unit accessible to students with disabilities.*
   a. Select a unit of study for a grade level. It can be a unit you that you currently teach, have taught in the past, would like to teach in the future, or one that you have been asked to support by another teacher. Or you can select lesson plans from a website, such as www.teachnology.com.
   b. Identify the **reading components** in the unit (e.g., reading questions on worksheets or quizzes, reading a story, reading nonfiction for preparing a report). Then explain how you would make the reading components accessible to a student who has learning disabilities and a student who has physical disabilities. Be specific. Make sure your recommended solution or solutions match the task and the students' needs. Use a chart like the one below to organize and present your information. It will help show the relationship between the specific reading activity and the specific technology solution.

Reading Activity	Adaptations for Student with Learning Disabilities			Adaptations for Student with Physical Disabilities		
	Type of Technology	Product Name & Publisher	Rationale	Type of Technology	Product Name & Publisher	Rationale

5. *Find low-tech solutions for reading.* Add low-tech reading aids to the low-tech writing kit you began in Chapter 2. Go to a local craft store and an office supply store and gather items such as highlighters, highlighter tape, different-sized sticky notes, a page up paper holder, a cookbook holder, and other items that could be used to support reading.

REFERENCES

Achieve3000. (n.d.). *KidBiz3000.* Retrieved April 11, 2007, from http://www.achieve3000 .com/article/a3k/?c=7

Anderson-Inman, L., & Horney, M. (1997). Electronic books for secondary students. *Journal of Adolescent and Adult Literacy, 40*(6), 486–491.

Armbruster, B. B., & Anderson, T. H. (1988). On selecting "considerate" content area textbooks. *Remedial and Special Education, 9*(1), 47–52.

Assistive Technology Training Online Training Project. (2005). *Low-tech tools: Reading aids.* Retrieved September 7, 2006, from http://atto.buffalo.edu/registered/ATBasics/Populations/ LowTech/reading.php.

Boyle, E. A., Washburn, S. G., Rosenberg, M. S., Connelly, V. J., Brinckerhoff, L. C., & Banerjee, M. (2002). Reading's SLiCK with new audio texts and strategies. *Teaching Exceptional Children, 35*(2), 50–55.

Center for Applied, Special Technology (2006). What is the National Instructional Materials Accessibility Standard (NIMAS)? Retrieved April 6, 2007 from http://nimas.cast.org/ about/nimas/index.html

Dyck, N.,& Pemberton, J. B. (2002). A model for making decisions about text adaptations. *Intervention in School and Clinic, 38*(1), 28–35.

Edyburn, D. L. (2003, March/April). Learning from text. *Special Education Technology Practice*, pp. 16–27.

Erickson, K., Musselwhite, C. R., & Ziolkowski, R. (n.d.). *The beginning literacy framework.* Volo, IL: Don Johnston, Inc.

Georgia Assistive Technology Project Tools for Life. (n.d.). Learning disabilities and assistive technologies: Reading. Retrieved June 29, 2006, from http://gatfl.org/ldguide/read.htm

Harris, T. L., & Hodges, R. E. (1995). *The literacy dictionary: The vocabulary of reading and writing.* Newark, DE: International Reading Association.

Hecker, L., Burns, L., Katz, L., Elkind, J., & Elkind, K. (2002). Benefits of assistive reading software for students with attention disorders. *Annals of Dyslexia, 52*, 243–272.

Koppenhaver, D., & Yoder, D. (1992). Literacy learning of children with severe speech and physical impairments in school settings. *Seminars in Speech and Language, 13*(2), 143–153.

Lipson, M. Y., & Wixson, K. K. (1997). *Assessment and instruction of reading and writing disability: An interactive approach* (2nd ed.). New York: Longman.

Meyer, A., & Rose, D. H. (1998). *Learning to read in the computer age.* Newton, MA: Brookline Books.

National Center to Improve the Tools of Educators. (1996). *Learning to read/reading to learn campaign.* Retrieved February 14, 2006, from http://idea.uoregon.edu/~ncite/programs/read.html

National Reading Panel. (2000). Findings and determinations of the National Reading Panel by topic areas. In *Report of the National Reading Panel: Teaching children to read.* Retrieved

January 21, 2006, from the National Institute of Child Health & Human Development website: http://www.nichd.nih.gov/publications/nrp/smallbook.cfm

National Reading Panel Subgroup on Alphabetics. (2000). Alphabetics: Part 1, Phonemic awareness instruction. In *Report of the National Reading Panel: Teaching children to read.* Retrieved January 21, 2006, from the National Institute of Child Health & Human Development website: http://nichd.nih.gov/publications/nrp/findings.cfm

Palincsar, A. S., & Klenk, L. J. (1991). Dialogues promoting reading comprehension. In B. Means, C. Chelemr, & M. S. Knapp (Eds.), *Teaching advanced skills to at-risk students: Views from research and practice* (pp. 112–130). San Francisco: Jossey-Bass.

Robin, A. (1998). *ADHD in adolescents: Diagnosis and treatment.* New York: Guilford Press.

Rose, D., & Dalton, B. (2002). Using technology to individualize reading instruction. In C. C. Block, L. B. Gambrell, & M. Pressley (Eds.), *Improving comprehension instruction: Rethinking research, theory, and classroom practice* (pp. 257–274). San Francisco: Jossey-Bass. Retrieved January 21, 2006, from http://udl.cast.org/udl/UsingTechnologytoIndividualizeReadingInstruction3096.cfm

Ross-Kidder, K. (2004). "Reading disability" or "learning disability": The debate, models of dyslexia, and a review of research-validated reading programs. Retrieved January 21, 2006 from the LD OnLine website: http://www.ldonline.org/ld_indepth/reading/reading_approaches.html

Rothman, R. (2004). Adolescent literacy: Are we overlooking the struggling teenage reader? *Harvard Education Letter, 20*(1), 1–3.

Schulte, A., Conners, C., & Osborne, S. (1999). Linkages between attention deficit disorders and reading disability. In D. D. Duane (Ed.), *Reading and attention disorders* (pp. 161–184). Baltimore: York Press.

Shipon, W. (2002). College student combines motivation and technology to succeed. *TECH-NJ, 13*(1). Retrieved January 15, 2006, from http://www.tcnj.edu/~technj/2002/anthony.htm

Temple, E., Deutsch, G. K., Poldrack, R. A., Miller, S. L., Tallal, P., Merzenich, M. M., et al. (2003). Neural deficits in children with dyslexia ameliorated by behavioral remediation: Evidence from functional MRI. *Proceedings of the National Academy of Sciences, 100*(5), 2860–2865.

Tom Snyder Productions. (2004). *Thinking Reader teacher's guide.* Watertown, MA: Author.

Wehmeyer, M., Smith, S., Palmer, S., & Davies, D. (2004). Technology use by students with intellectual disabilities: An overview. *Journal of Special Education Technology, 19*(4), 7–21.

CHAPTER 4

Assistive Technology to Enhance Communication

FOCUS QUESTIONS

1. What kinds of obstacles do students who cannot speak face in school?
2. What is augmentative communication, and why is it important?
3. What kinds of obstacles do students who are hard of hearing face in a typical classroom?
4. What is hearing assistive technology and how can it help students who are hard of hearing?
5. Why is Internet technology considered "an instrument of liberation" (Kisor, 1990) by people who are deaf or hard of hearing?

INTRODUCTION

Being able to communicate your thoughts, feelings, and ideas is absolutely critical to being successful in school and the workplace. Being able to understand other people's communication attempts is equally essential. For people who cannot speak or hear speech, technology offers an exciting range of solutions. In this chapter we discuss assistive technology tools that can enhance communication between students with disabilities and their teachers and peers. We introduce the area of assistive technology called augmentative communication, which helps students who cannot speak, and we summarize hearing assistive technology tools that support students who cannot hear.

THE IMPORTANCE OF COMMUNICATION—PART 1

Have you ever had laryngitis or another illness that took away your ability to speak? Or have you ever been in a foreign country in which nobody understood your speech? If so, you will have had some experience with the frustration and powerlessness of being voiceless. Bob Williams (2000), a disability advocate who cannot speak due to cerebral palsy, expresses it this way: "The silence of speechlessness is never golden. We all need to communicate and connect with each other. . . . It is a basic human need, a basic human right" (p. 248). This intense hunger to communicate is strikingly conveyed by Ruth Sienkiewicz-Mercer, a woman with quadriplegia cerebral palsy. Although Ruth cannot walk, feed, or dress herself, these limitations do not compare with her inability to speak: "Without a doubt, my inability to speak has been the single most devastating aspect of my handicap. If I were granted one wish and one wish only, I would not hesitate for an instant to request that I be able to talk, if only for one day, or even one hour" (Sienkiewicz-Mercer & Kaplan, 1996, p. 12).

Problems Students with Physical Disabilities or Autism Have with Communication

Many students who have physical disabilities like cerebral palsy cannot speak. They do not have the oral motor control necessary to articulate words and sentences. One estimate is that 41% of the school-aged population with cerebral palsy have some speech problems, with 22% being reported to have no understandable speech (Blackstone, 1993). Dysarthria is the technical term for speech disorders that are due to the inability of the oral motor muscles to move to their proper positions because of neuromotor control issues (Stuart, 2002). Dysarthria has been reported in 88% of children with athetoid cerebral palsy, and in 52% of those with spastic cerebral palsy (Blackstone, 1993). Although speech therapy can help some children with mild dysarthria develop some functional speech, many will never develop intelligible speech.

Another group of students who cannot speak have neurological disabilities like autism. Communication problems are one of the defining characteristics of individuals with autism (Wing, 1996). Although they do not have physical disabilities and some may be able to recite television commercials or sing songs by rote, many students with autism have dyspraxia, which is an interruption in the ability to program the position of the speech musculature (Stuart, 2002). They do not have the motor planning skills necessary to express themselves meaningfully.

Problems Resulting from Communication Problems

How can students actively participate in class activities if they cannot speak? How can they demonstrate knowledge and understanding if they do not speak? How can they make choices, express their opinions, reveal their interests if they cannot speak? How can they socialize and develop friendships if they cannot speak? Bob Williams (2000), an augmentative communication user himself, highlights the serious problems of not being able to speak:

If I could not express myself clearly and accurately [with my augmentative communication device], I could not tell my physician and others how I feel or describe the health problems I may be having. Similarly, I could not let others know what I know or what I am capable of learning. Nor could I go to work or vote. (p. 250)

Unfortunately, many people in our society—including education professionals—tend to equate an inability to speak with an inability to think (Williams, 2000). They often hold very low expectations for children who cannot speak, and as a result, do not offer challenging educational opportunities. Williams expresses it best:

Why are so many people consigned to lead lives of needless dependence and silence? Not because we lack the funds, nor because we lack federal policy mandates needed to gain access to those funds. Rather, many people lead lives of silence because many others still find it difficult to believe that people with speech disabilities like my own have anything to say or contributions to make. (p. 250)

The inability to communicate often leads to intolerable frustrations that, in many students with autism or severe cognitive disabilities, lead to temper tantrums, screaming, biting, hitting, and self-abusive behaviors (Carr et al., 1994; Durand, 1993). This connection between communication frustrations and challenging behaviors has received increasing attention in the last 20 years. A major component of current educational programs for students with autism involves strategies for teaching functional communication skills as alternatives to challenging behavior (Koegel, Koegel, & Dunlap, 1996). Because many students with autism have dyspraxia, functional communication for them often involves augmentative communication systems.

ASSISTIVE TECHNOLOGY THAT PROVIDES A VOICE

Having the power to speak one's heart and mind changes the disability equation dramatically. (Bob Williams, 2000, p. 249)

One of the most powerful applications of computer technology has been the development and ongoing refinement of devices that can speak. The technical term for this technology is alternative and augmentative communication, which is shortened for convenience to augmentative communication. Simply put, augmentative communication is "about helping individuals who cannot speak to interact with others" (Beukelman & Mirenda, 2000, p. 13). Augmentative communication systems serve as an alternative to speech for people who cannot talk. The word *augmentative* is emphasized because we all—whether we can or cannot speak—also use other, nonverbal means to communicate with others. For example, we all use facial expressions, gestures, and body language when we communicate. Augmentative communication systems are designed to "augment" whatever existing communication a person has. Blackstone (1993), a leading researcher, summarizes the benefits of augmentative communication: "For a person with a severe motor impairment

SIDEBAR

Rick Creech

Rick Creech, who has cerebral palsy, offers a simple way for students to get a hint of what it feels like to be unable to speak:

> Go to a party and don't talk. Play mute. Use your hands if you wish but don't use paper and pencil. . . . Here is what you will find: people talking; talking behind, beside, around, over, under, through, and even for you. But never with you. You are ignored until finally you feel like a piece of furniture. (Musselwhite & St. Louis, 1988)

who does not speak, communication . . . is the key that unlocks the door, . . . letting the individual *Out* and the rest of the world *In*. It is language that truly connects one human to the other" (p. 4).

Augmentative communication systems can be *unaided* or *aided*. Unaided systems use only a person's body for communication. Sign language is a good example of an unaided system. A person does not need to carry anything with him or her; the communication system (sign language) is always available in every environment. In contrast, aided systems involve the use of an external piece of equipment to convey a message. An alphabet board is an aided communication method. So are assistive technology–based systems. An inconvenience of aided systems is that they must be transported by the user, and they may present problems in inclement weather. However, unlike sign language, aided systems have the advantage of being easily understood by most listeners (Stuart, 2002).

USER PROFILE: Anthony Arnold

My name is Anthony Arnold, and I'm from North Dakota. I was born on May 22, 1977. Right before birth, I had a lack of oxygen in my brain, which is needed for normal development. Due to this, I have cerebral palsy, which affects my whole physical body and my speech abilities. I now use a power chair and an augmentative communication device to gain independence.

Before my first communication board, I pointed at sales fliers and objects in my house to communicate with my family. I know sometimes my parents got frustrated by my pointing and their having to guess, but I feel it also offered them some encouragement. It helped them realize that I did know something.

Early Communication Boards
From this discovery, my parents went to a rehab clinic to meet with my team and suggested developing a communication board that could be easily understood by anyone. It took my parents some time to sell my therapists on this idea. During this time I also began to attend to preschool, which helped create some interaction between other children and me. This built more interest in communication board use and led to more communication boards with more symbols.

By the time I reached elementary school I had a communication board with almost 100 symbols on it. I knew more parts of speech than most five-year-olds. I was easily making 10 or more word sentences. This usually frustrated people trying to follow my hand movements (it wasn't easy to read as fast as I was building a sentence). From watching my progress with communication boards and realizing that there was no more physical room to put 200 words on a board, my parents and therapists started researching other methods. At that time, the Prentke Romich Company was just introducing the *Touch Talker*. Here was a portable device with a computer-generated voice, one of the first available in 1984. It was a wonderful and dependable device, so we decided to rent one for a trial period and eventually bought it.

Independence Through Technology
When I first received my *Touch Talker*, I remember that was the happiest day of my childhood. I finally had a way of communicating without having somebody always

(continued)

there reading my board. During this time I was seen by two speech-language pathologists who were truly dedicated to working with my parents and teachers to build my vocabulary and my interest level for using the device.

I would say that during my early teenage years was when I began to realize how much my *Touch Talker* (and then my *Liberator*) helped me gain independence. I wanted to help others receive what I had already received thanks to many people, including my parents. So I made a career goal of working for the Prentke Romich Company (PRC) or another place where I could use my knowledge and experiences to help.

The Dream Job

I began working for PRC as an Ambassador, traveling to conferences to display the powers of the *Liberator* (the successor to my *Touch Talker*). I still do that today. After seeing the success of the Ambassador program, PRC developed the Remote Troubleshooter Program for the Technical Service Department. I answer technical service calls about PRC's augmentative communication devices at night and on weekends when the company is closed. I feel we have had great success with this program. I have been doing it for five years now, and I love it . . . .

The commissioned painting of the progression of Anthony's communication boards

Photo by Anthony Arnold.

I recently commissioned a painting of all of my communication boards. . . .
Excerpts from my speech follow:

One of the things I most like about this painting is that it shows that communication
development doesn't just happen over night, which is a common misconception.
I received my first communication board with six pictures on it at the age of two. Now
I'm 27, using the most advanced communication device we have available today
(*Pathfinder*), and within these years, I have used a number of different communication
boards and augmentative communication devices.

From "Augcom User Helps Others as a Troubleshooter for Prentke Romich Company,"
by A. Arnold, 2003, *TECH-NJ, 14*(1), p. 14.

SIDEBAR

Listservs for Augmentative Communication Users

Anthony highly recommends joining a listserv to learn more about augmentative communication and to exchange ideas with augmentative communicators, family members, college students, and professionals. SpeakShare
(www.speakshare.com), is sponsored by the Prentke Romich Company. The
ACOLUG listserv (Augmentative Communication OnLine Users Group) is
hosted by Temple University's Institute on Disabilities (http://listserv
.temple.edu/archives/ACOLUG.html). Anthony also hosts hosts two listservs
on his website: the AAC-List (http://www.aac-list.net) and AAC-Pals (http://
www.aac-list.net/aacpals.html). AAC-Pals is geared toward augmentative communicators who are 7-12 years old.

The profile written by Anthony Arnold, an augmentative communication user,
introduces many of the basic principles of augmentative communication. Augmentative
communication devices can range from low tech to high tech. Anthony's first communication board, when he was a toddler, was simply a few pictures mounted on a piece
of wood (low tech). He pointed to what he wanted, and an adult who was present
would "read" his request. This low-tech board was expanded to over 100 picture symbols that were arranged categorically on a laminated, fold-out display. Today he uses a
high-tech device called a Pathfinder (Prentke Romich), which offers unlimited vocabulary, a high-quality computer-generated voice, strategies for increasing his speed of
communication (called "rate enhancement"), and access to the Internet.

Augmentative communication techniques existed before computer technology
was widely available (for example, Anthony's early picture board), but computer
technology has led to an explosion of options, features, and communication power.
Software programs like Boardmaker (Mayer-Johnson) have greatly simplified the
process of creating picture boards for teachers, parents, and speech therapists. When

The tango! augmentative communication device includes phrase banks, word banks, a built-in camera, photo albums, and voice morphing. It is designed to support social interactions and conversations in daily life.
Courtesy of Blink-Twice, Inc.

selecting a system, augmentative communication users can choose to use a picture-based system, text-based system, or a combination of the two. They can choose a male or female voice, an adult's voice, or a child's voice. Even inexpensive devices (less than $100) can now speak aloud with a good-quality voice. Speech output on a device enables an augmentative communication user to gain attention (for example, "Mrs. T, I need help!") and to communicate more elaborate messages more quickly. For his job as an augmentative communication troubleshooter, Anthony stores pre-programmed answers and instructions on his Pathfinder and accesses them when he is talking to a customer by simply pressing a few keys.

Which augmentative communication system is the best? No single augmentative communication device is appropriate for all students. Students have different needs and strengths that change over time (Beukelman & Mirenda, 2000). The augmentative

---

SIDEBAR

Gus Estrella

Gus Estrella (2000), a graduate of the University of Arizona who has cerebral palsy, describes one way his computerized augmentative communication system enhanced his life:

> When I finally had a more powerful VOCA [voice output communication appliance] . . . I started to have real conversations with people whom I had always wanted to talk. . . . My father was one person that I had always wanted to have a conversation with, but there was always a barrier. Finally that barrier was broken! Now we were able to carry on a real conversation without needing someone to translate my grunts into real words! We were able to talk about women. . . . Plus we were able to talk about all the beers we had the night before at the football game, without my mother knowing what we really did. Now we could have our little secrets that would drive my mother nuts! (p. 37)

FIGURE 4–1 Communication board for a music class made with BoardMaker.

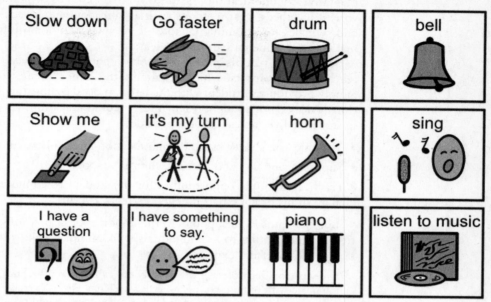

Source: The Picture Communication Symbols ©1981–2006 by Mayer-Johnson LLC.
All Rights Reserved–Worldwide. Used with permission.

communication system chosen for a student must match that particular student's abilities, communication needs, motor skills, and personal preferences. For example, a child who walks and runs needs an augmentative communication system that will not break easily. This was not a concern for Anthony, who uses a wheelchair for mobility; his first high-tech augmentative communication device was heavy and fragile, but it was mounted securely to his wheelchair tray. A young child or a child with developmental disabilities who cannot read or spell needs an augmentative communication system that uses picture symbols and not words. Anthony is a high school graduate with solid reading skills; although he uses a picture symbol system because it is fast, he needs a spell mode option when he wants to communicate something that is not represented by his picture symbols, or when he is programming his device.

The decision-making process in selecting and setting up an augmentative communication system for a student is complex. It must, at a minimum, involve a speech-language therapist, the student, the parents, and the classroom teacher. Usually a physical or occupational therapist is part of the team to help with issues related to motor skills. Many factors must be considered, including the communication demands of the student's various environments, the student's language development, the student's motor abilities, and the student's personal preferences. One study of augmentative communication evaluations reported that in a pool of 64 individuals with cerebral palsy, a total of 17 different types of augmentative communication devices were recommended (LaFontaine & DeRuyter, 1987). These included low-tech picture boards and word boards, and 13 different types of electronic devices.

Half of the individuals in this study were able to use a finger to access their augmentative communication system; those who could not point with a finger used a variety of other access methods such as chin pointers, joysticks, optical indicators, and switches for scanning. Chapter 9 provides additional information on decision making for augmentative communication.

Several times in his profile Anthony mentions his speech-language therapists, teachers, and parents, which highlights the importance of training and support. Simply providing a student with the latest, most dazzling augmentative communication devices is not enough. Augmentative communication will not make a difference in students' lives unless schools provide:

- **Training:** on strategies for communication and on how to use the specific device
- **Support:** ongoing and timely technical support
- **Practice:** multiple opportunities for the student to communicate with the device in all of his or her environments (Estrella, 2000)

Bob Williams (2002) points to the importance of providing access to augmentative communication to *all* individuals who cannot speak, calling for a transformation of attitudes and expectations:

> Every person, regardless of the severity of his/her disabilities, has the right . . . to communicate with others, express everyday preferences and exercise at least some control over his or her daily life. Each individual, therefore, should be given the chance, training, technology, respect and encouragement to do so. (2002, p. 2)

Specific strategies for classroom teachers to provide this kind of support are the focus of Chapter 11.

SIDEBAR

TASH Resolution on the Right to Communicate

The right to communicate is both a basic human right and the means by which all other rights are realized. All people communicate. In the name of fully realizing the guarantee of individual rights, we must ensure:

- that all people have a means of communication which allows their fullest participation in the wider world;
- that people can communicate using their chosen method; and
- that their communication is heeded by others.

Where people lack an adequate communication system, they deserve to have others try with them to discover and secure an appropriate system. No person should have this right denied because they have been diagnosed as having a particular disability. Access to effective means of communication is a free speech issue.

Originally adopted November 1992; revised December 2000.

From "TASH Resolution on the Right to Communicate," by TASH, 2002, *TASH Connections, 25*(5).

THE IMPORTANCE OF COMMUNICATION—PART 2

Computer technology "meant the beginning of the end of my isolation—isolation from other people" writes Hank Kisor, a Chicago journalist who is deaf (1990, p. 152). Kisor continues, "The microchip is probably the greatest aid to communication the twentieth century has . . . provided" (p. 225). E-mail, real-time chats, and instant messaging "enable me to 'talk'. . . with the hearing world at large. . . . To me they were truly an instrument of liberation" (p. 230).

The feeling of isolation Kisor refers to is common among people who are deaf or hard of hearing (Andrews, Leigh, & Weiner, 2004; Steinberg, 2000; Stinson & Foster, 2000). A student who cannot hear a teacher's question will not be able to answer the question or communicate his or her understanding of the subject matter. A student who cannot hear a fellow student's comment in class or at the lunch table will not be able to carry on a conversation or enjoy a social interaction. If your hearing has ever been diminished by an ear infection or a bad head cold, you may have some idea of the isolation caused by an inability to hear clearly.

Students Who Are Deaf or Hard of Hearing

Background Information. Before we discuss technology tools for students who are deaf or hard of hearing, it will be helpful to briefly define *deaf* and *hard of hearing*. Although they are similar, there are important differences between the terms, and these differences affect the usefulness of specific technology tools.

Students who are *deaf* have little or no functional hearing (DO-IT, 2004). They usually are not highly skilled or comfortable with speaking, and they communicate primarily through sign language. (American Sign Language [ASL] is one common form of sign language, but it is not the only form.) These students require a sign language interpreter to communicate with nonsigners and to participate in school activities.

Unlike students who are deaf, students who are *hard of hearing* do not typically use sign language. They usually can understand speech through a combination of personal hearing aids, which amplify sounds, and their skills in lip-reading. Students who are hard of hearing may have some speech impairments but they can usually speak well enough to be understood. In recent years increasing numbers of children who are hard of hearing have had cochlear implants surgically inserted in their inner ears (Northeast Technical Assistance Center [NETAC], 2000); with appropriate training, these implants are significantly increasing the hearing abilities of students who are hard of hearing.

Communication Problems in School. Students who are hard of hearing often have difficulty following lectures, particularly if the acoustics of the room are poor or if the teacher speaks quietly, quickly, or unclearly (DO-IT, 2004). Although their hearing aids may be adequate in one-on-one conversations, the poor acoustics of many classrooms (caused by cement floors and walls, noisy heating and cooling systems, and lack of soft materials to absorb sound) lessen the hearing aids' effectiveness for

SIDEBAR

Cochlear Implants

Cochlear implants are miniature electronic devices that are surgically implanted in the inner ear (the cochlea) to improve useful hearing. They are designed to bypass cochlear hair cells that do not work and to provide direct stimulation to the auditory nerve. Cochlear implant users will have, in addition to the miniature implant itself, a tiny microphone, a signal processor (older models are worn on a waistband; newer models use tiny behind-the-ear units), and a small signal coupler (transmitter and receiver). The microphone picks up sounds and sends them to the processor, which selects and codes the sounds. The coded sounds are then sent through the skin to a transmitting coil which converts them to electrical impulses, and the implanted electrode array stimulates the auditory nerve.

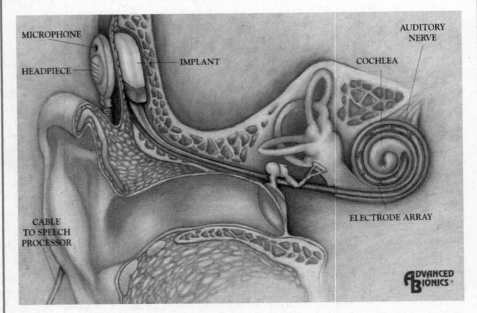

From *Serving Deaf Students Who Have Cochlear Implants* (NETAC Teacher Tipsheet Series), by Northeast Technical Assistance Center, 2000, Rochester, NY.

understanding lectures. "Whereas a young adult with normal hearing may experience a mild awareness of room reverberation and background noise, it may not significantly reduce the intelligibility of the spoken message for that student. For the person using a hearing aid, however, such conditions form an acoustic barrier to listening" (Warick, Clark, Dancer, & Sinclair, 1997).

SIDEBAR

Supporting Students Who Use Assistive Listening Devices: Guidelines for Teachers

1. Become knowledgeable about the assistive listening device. Request training from an audiologist and/or manufacturer of the system.
2. Discuss how the assistive listening device will be used with the student ahead of time.
3. Position the microphone carefully. It should not be near a noise source such as an overhead projector. It should be 3–5 inches from the teacher's mouth.
4. Consult with an audiologist about optimal positioning of the receiver or speakers.
5. Inform the entire class about how the assistive listening device will be used in classroom instruction. Remind students to speak one at a time. Be sure to repeat questions and comments from other students. When possible, pass the microphone/transmitter from student to student.
6. Try to face the student in case he or she relies on visual cues to aid understanding.
7. Use the assistive listening device for audiovisual presentations.
8. Perform a listening check with the equipment regularly. Establish and follow a regular maintenance routine and schedule.

From *The Role of Assistive Listening Devices in the Classroom* (NETAC Teacher Tipsheet Series), by Northeast Technical Assistence Center, 1998, Rochester, NY.

Exacerbating the problem of acoustics is the need for teachers to move around a classroom. If a teacher turns his or her back to the class—to write on the blackboard, for example—the student who is lip-reading can no longer hear the lecture. Similarly, if the teacher looks down while demonstrating a science lab activity, the student who reads lips cannot see the teacher's face. Class discussions and video presentations are two other classroom activities that present difficulties to students who are hard of hearing.

Outside the classroom, students who are deaf and hard of hearing also face obstacles in trying to communicate with their teachers and peers. Understanding speakers in face-to-face situations such as small-group discussions and social situations is hampered by the presence of background noise and several people talking at once. Communication over distances is problematic because they are usually not able to use standard telephones.

TECHNOLOGY TOOLS THAT ADDRESS COMMUNICATION PROBLEMS

Hearing assistive technology is a term for assistive technology that helps people who have hearing losses (Self Help for Hard of Hearing People [SHHH], 2004). It includes alerting devices that indicate the presence of sound in the environment, such as smoke detector indicators, shaking alarm clocks, and baby cry signalers. Hearing assistive technology also includes adaptations for telephones. Tables 4.1 and 4.2 provide examples of these kinds of assistive technology. This chapter, however, focuses on hearing assistive technology that can enhance students' communication in the classroom. (Specialized applications of technology that are used for note-taking for students who are deaf or hard of hearing are discussed in Chapter 2.)

TABLE 4–1 Alerting devices for people who are deaf or hard of hearing

Device	Function
Alarm clock with flasher or strobe light	A light or bright strobe flashes when the alarm clock goes off.
Shake Awake travel alarm clock	Placed under a pillow, this vibrates to wake up the user.
Alarm clock with flash and vibrator	Can use either the flashing light or vibrator or both simultaneously.
Door Beacon	When someone knocks at the door, the beacon flashes.
Wireless strobe door chime	The door chime sets off a strobe light.
Smoke detector with strobe light	A powerful strobe light flashes when the smoke detector is activated. Can also be connected to a bed vibrator.
Baby Cry Signaler	Emits a strobe light or vibrates a bed when a baby cries.
Blink Receiver	A strobe light flashes when hooked to a unit of your choice.
Super Phone Ringer	Rings the phone very loudly for people who are hard of hearing. Used in conjunction with amplified telephones.
Phone Flasher	A light flashes when the phone/TTY rings.
Silent Call wireless alerting system	An integrated system that can alert a person to the activation of any one of a number of common household devices. Can be connected to a strobe light, vibrator, or a regular household lamp, and can be used in various locations of a house. The advantage is that this system can indicate the presence of a sound at places *other* than where the sound occurred and it can be set to use different patterns to differentiate types of sounds.

From "Assistive Technology for People Who Are Deaf and Hard of Hearing," by J. Dodds, 2003, *TECH-NJ, 14*(1).

TABLE 4–2 Telecommunication devices for people who are deaf or hard of hearing

Device	Function
Amplified telephone	Allows the user to adjust the volume and control the tone, like boosting the treble or bass on a stereo.
Portable phone amplifier	This small gadget fits over a telephone handset. It can be taken and used anywhere.
TTY (also known as a TDD—Telecommunication Device for the Deaf)	Equipped with a keyboard and small visual display, this device enables users to type their messages and send them over telephone lines. Two deaf people using TTYs can communicate with each other directly.
Relay service	If the person on one end of a phone call uses a TTY and the person on the other end uses a regular (speaking) telephone, the services of a relay operator are needed. When the TTY user types, the relay operator speaks the message to the telephone user. When the telephone user speaks, the relay operator types the message to the TTY user. To comply with the Americans with Disabilities Act, all telephone companies now provide this service free of charge.
Pocket Speak-and-Read Portable VCO (Voice Carry Over)	For people who cannot hear on the phone but have use of their voice and prefer to use their voice (late-onset deafness, oral deafness), this device slides on the telephone handset and provides a screen readout like a TTY. The call must be placed through a relay service.

Hearing Lectures with Assistive Listening Devices

Called "binoculars for the ears" [SHHH], 2006), assistive listening devices (ALDs) help reduce the effect of an "acoustically unfriendly room" (Warick et al., 1997). They catch a desired sound (the teacher's voice, for example) as cleanly as possible, and amplify it for students who are hard of hearing. ALDs help these students by

- minimizing background noise such as chairs moving, fan motors whirring, and students talking;
- overcoming the weakening effect of sound traveling through air; and
- reducing the effect of poor room acoustics. (SHHH, 2006)

Providing a high-quality listening environment is known to have a major impact on the academic performance of students who are hard of hearing (NETAC, 1998).

ALDs do not replace hearing aids. Hearing aids are worn all day long and amplify all sounds in a student's environments. ALDs, on the other hand, are used when it is important to amplify a specific voice such as a teacher's. By placing a microphone close to the speaker's mouth, ALDs provide the most advantageous ratio between the intensity of speech and the level of background noise (NETAC, 1998). They also eliminate echoes. An ALD can be used along with hearing aids or as a stand-alone unit.

Types of Assistive Listening Devices

FM System. With a personal FM system, the teacher wears a wireless lavalier microphone clipped to his or her lapel or blouse and a small transmitter worn on a belt or waistband. The student wears a small receiver and some kind of coupling device—usually headphones, ear buds, or a direct connection to his or her hearing aid. Special cables are available to connect with the hearing aids of students who have cochlear implants. When the teacher speaks, an auditory signal is broadcast to the FM receiver worn by the student. The student hears the amplified teacher's voice either through headphones or directly through the hearing aid. The wireless unit is battery operated, portable, and unobtrusive.

Infrared System. Infrared ALDs have similar components to FM systems (microphone, transmitter, and receiver), but they use infrared light waves for transmission instead of FM radio waves. Infrared technology is used in everyday devices such as remote control units for televisions and garage door openers. The advantage to infrared systems is that there is minimal distortion and internal amplifier noise in its signal so the sound quality can be superior to FM systems. Infrared transmission is also private because, unlike the FM signal, light cannot travel through walls. This is why theaters and courtrooms prefer infrared ALDs over FM systems. Schools, however, tend to not use infrared ALDs because they require a direct line of sight between teacher and student, with no physical objects in between, and the teacher needs to limit his or her movement around the classroom.

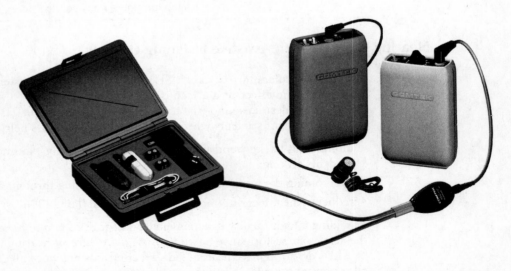

An FM system for a student who is hard of hearing: The teacher wears the lavalier microphone and transmitter, and the student wears the receiver and headphones (or a direct connection to a hearing aid—(not shown).
Courtesy of Comtek, Inc.

USER PROFILE: Nicole

The students in Mr. D.'s world history class are annoyed with his coteacher for not grading a project they did weeks ago. The class leader thinks of a way to show disapproval and comes to the front of the room to propose her plan to the rest of the students. After addressing the group, the leader turns to Nicole, who is sitting in the front row. She confirms that Nicole heard the idea and is in agreement. Nicole has a hearing impairment. Although this disability sometimes limits a student's participation in the classroom, Nicole is not excluded from the protest being planned, nor is she ever left out of classroom activities. Her inclusion is due, in part, to her classmates' awareness of her disability and her teachers' positive attitudes. Equally important, she stays involved with the help of an FM system. Because Nicole's classroom has two teachers, a DAISY chain system is set up with multiple transmitters. Mr. V. wears one transmitter while Mr. D. wears both a transmitter and receiver. Mr. V.'s voice is sent to Mr. D.'s receiver. In turn, his transmitter passes the sound along the chain to Nicole's receiver.

There are several advantages to this setup: (1) Although Nicole lip-reads, she misses a lot of information with lip-reading alone. (2) Lip-reading does not capture the inflection in a speaker's voice. (3) The coteachers are free to move around the classroom; with an FM system it is not necessary for them to face Nicole at all times or stand close by in order for her to hear them. (4) Nicole can hear the soundtrack on videos that are shown in class by simply having a teacher place the FM system microphone close to the monitor. (5) The FM system's ability to minimize background noise is especially helpful for Nicole because her school has an open layout, which tends to be very noisy.

Adapted from "FM System, C-Print Assist Hard-of-Hearing Student in High School," by T. Spadafora, 2003, *TECHNJ, 14*(1), p. 4.

Induction Loop System. Induction loop systems use electromagnetic waves for transmission and work directly with hearing aids. A wire is looped around the perimeter of a space such as a classroom or school auditorium. Sounds are picked up by the teacher's microphone, amplified, and sent through the loop, creating an invisible magnetic field. A telecoil (called a T-switch) in the student's hearing aid serves as a receiver and picks up the signal from the loop. The hearing aid then reconverts this signal into sound, amplifies it, and feeds it directly into the student's ear (NETAC, 1998).

Soundfield Amplification System. A soundfield amplification system broadcasts the teacher's voice through loudspeakers that are mounted on the walls or ceiling. A speaker can also be placed directly next to a student. Other components of the soundfield amplification system are a microphone and transmitter worn by the teacher. This kind of system has been successfully used with students who have attention deficit disorders and central auditory processing disorders. It helps them filter out distracting background noise and focus on the teacher's voice (Boswell, 2006).

Table 4.3 lists the advantages and disadvantages of the four systems. It is important to note that the effectiveness of all ALDs can be affected by a number of factors.

TABLE 4–3 Summary of assistive listening systems

Device	Advantages	Disadvantages
FM system	• Student can sit and face anywhere within the system's range. • System can be used inside or outside (not affected by light).	• Potential confidentiality issues: the sound broadcast may carry through walls. • Possible electrical interference.
Infrared system	• Privacy is protected because the broad cast signal is secure within the room. • Sound quality can be superior to FM systems.	• There must be a direct line of sight between teacher and student; they must face each other directly with no physical objects in between. • Teacher needs to limit movement around the classroom. • Not effective in direct sunlight.
Induction loop system	• Can be used by anyone with a hearing aid without requiring another piece of equipment for the listener. Users can simply switch their hearing aids to T-switch mode.	• Requires permanent installation. • Possible electromagnetic interference from nearby power transformers, heavy equipment, etc.
Soundfield amplification system	• Serves the entire classroom; all students benefit from the amplification.	• Helpful only for mild or moderate hearing losses.

The quality of the microphone used can improve or degrade the sound quality, as can the quality of the "coupling device"—headphones, T-switches, and cochlear implant patch cords (SHHH, 2006). Providing adequate training, of both the student and the teacher, is also a critical factor (NETAC, 1998). If a student indicates that an ALD is not working (or if a teacher suspects a problem), simple troubleshooting techniques should include checking for a dead battery or a break in the wiring, making sure the system has been turned on, checking for interference, and checking to see if the student's hearing aid's T-switch has been turned on (SHHH, 2004).

Interacting with Teachers and Peers Outside Class

An important part of learning often involves interacting with teachers and fellow students outside class. Before the advent of computer technology, students who were deaf or hard of hearing were at a significant disadvantage. Today common computer applications such as e-mail, instant messaging, chat rooms, and discussion boards present convenient alternatives for communicating with teachers and fellow students. They avoid the issue of hearing completely. As Kisor (1990) writes, "Computer chatting was a staggering revolution in communications. For the first time I could participate in group talks without worrying about whether people could understand my speech . . . and whether I could follow the bouncing ball of conversation among a large number of people" (p. 251).

Similarly the revolution in cell phone technology has freed people who are deaf and hard of hearing from the struggles of using the telephone. Text messaging, once an exotic add-on to cell phone plans but now a widely used feature, provides a mainstream alternative to specialized telecommunication devices for the deaf (TDDs, also know as TTYs). It offers a new independence for people who are deaf or hard of hearing because they can now carry a lightweight, easy-to-use cell phone with them anywhere and can communicate directly with anyone who also has text messaging activated on their cell phone (Schindler, 2003).

SUMMARY

- Students who lack the ability to speak are at a serious disadvantage in school: They are unable to express ideas and opinions, participate in class discussions, and engage in social situations.

- Augmentative communication is simply defined as a way to supplement an individual's method of communication to assist comprehension. It is, for some, essential in making themselves understood and for conveying clear messages to a variety of audiences.

- Augmentative communication increases an individual's independence and opens the door to numerous opportunities. See Table 4.4.

TABLE 4–4   Summary of technology tools that enhance communication

Communication Goal	Technology Tools	Sample Products	Who Benefits?
Participating in class activities, expressing yourself, making choices, interacting with others, demonstrating your knowledge	Augmentative communication systems	Pathfinder/Dynavox Springboard	Students who cannot speak (e.g., students with cerebral palsy or students with autism)
Hearing lectures and class discussions	Assistive listening devices	Phonak Personal FM System Phonic Ear Soundfield Amplication System	Students who are hard of hearing Students who have attention deficit disorder or central auditory processing disorder
Interacting with faculty and peers outside class	TTY/TDD	Ameriphone	Students who are deaf or hard of hearing
	Text messaging	Available in cell phone plans	
	E-mail	Any commercial e-mail program	
	Online discussion boards Instant messaging	Any online course system Instant Messenger	

- Students who are hard of hearing have difficulty following classroom instruction due to poor acoustics, classroom layout, and teacher style. They are also at a serious disadvantage during social interactions.

- Hearing assistive technology, a category of assistive technology that helps people who have hearing losses, can help students who are hard of hearing by amplifying specific sounds while minimizing background distractions. There are a variety of assistive listening devices available to meet specific needs.

- Common computer applications such as e-mail, instant messaging, chat rooms, and discussion boards have made the computer "an instrument of liberation" by people who are deaf or hard of hearing because they open avenues of communication that do not rely on hearing or speaking.

WEB RESOURCES

For additional information on the topics listed, go the following websites:

Autism and Communication

Communication Interventions for Children with Autism
http://www.autismnetwork.org/modules/comm/aac/index.html

Perspectives of Augmentative Communication Users

Anthony Arnold's Website
http://www.anthonyarnold.net
Gus Estella's Distinguished Lecture
http://www.aacinstitute.org/Resources/PrentkeLecture/1997/GusEstrella.html
Rick Creech's Distinguished Lecture
http://www.aacinstitute.org/Resources/PrentkeLecture/2004/RickCreech.html

Cochlear Implants

National Institute on Deafness and Other Communication Disorders
http://www.nidcd.nih.gov/health/hearing/coch.htm

Hearing Assistive Technology

Soundbytes
http://www.soundbytes.com/Visual_Alerting_Systems.html

Assistive Listening Devices

Comtek
http://www.comtek.com/assistive_Listening.html

Williams Sound
http://www.williamssound.com/home.aspx

Other resources from the American Speech, Language and Hearing Association
http://www.asha.org/public/outreach/hearingweb/ald_resources.htm

Sound-Field Systems Guide for Classrooms in Alberta
www.infratrans.gov.ab.ca/INFTRA_Content/docType486/Production/
soundfieldguide.pdf

Augmentative Communication

Vermont Communication Resource Guide
www.dad.state.vt.us/DSwebsite/docs/ds/CommunicationResourceGuideV4-Updated
Oct2006.pdf

SUGGESTED ACTIVITIES

1. *Research a personal perspective.* Read *I Raise My Eyes to Say Yes* by Sienkiewicz-Mercer and Kaplan (1996). Then write a short paper discussing the following: (a) How significant was Ruth's inability to speak? How did it affect her life? (b) How has Ruth's story affected your attitude, expectations, and/or teaching practices toward students who are nonspeaking?

2. *Investigate assistive devices for people who are deaf or hard of hearing.* Locate a demonstration center near you that provides assistive devices for people who are deaf or hard of hearing. These centers are often funded by state agencies or organizations focused on hearing impairments. If you cannot visit a center, explore websites such as Gallaudet University's LeClerc Center at http://clerccenter.gallaudet.edu/InfoToGo/418.html, DeafWeb Washington at http://www.deafweb.org/assist.htm, or *TECH-NJ* at http://www.tcnj.edu/~technj/2003/dodds.htm. What kinds of assistive devices are available that help people who are deaf or hard of hearing carry out daily living activities independently?

3. *Research cochlear implants.* Write a short research paper on cochlear implants. How long have they been available? Who is the latest group to receive them? How are children who have cochlear implants being educated? What is the controversy surrounding cochlear implants?

4. *Investigate the function of cell phones and personal digital assistants.* Conduct an interview with a person who is deaf or hard of hearing to find out what technology tools he or she uses: cell phone, personal digital assistant (PDA) such as a Palm Pilot or BlackBerry, instant messaging, and so on. What specific things is this technology enabling the person to do?

REFERENCES

Andrews, J. F., Leigh, I. W., & Weiner, M. T. (2004). *Deaf people: Evolving perspectives from psychology, education, and sociology.* Boston: Allyn & Bacon/Pearson Education.

Arnold, A. (2003). Augcomm user helps others as a troubleshooter for Prentke-Romich Company. *TECH-NJ, 14*(1). Retrieved April 2007 from www.tcnj.edu/~technj/2003/arnold.com

Beukelman, D. R., & Mirenda, P. (2000). *Augmentative and alternative communication: Management of severe communication disorders in children and adults* (2nd ed.). Baltimore: Brookes.

Blackstone, S. (1993, November). Clinical news: AAC for people with CP. *Augmentative Communication News, 6(5)*.

Boswell, S. (2006, May 23). Sound field systems on the rise in schools: Improved test scores cited as benefit. *The ASHA Leader, 11(7)*, 1, 32–33.

Carr, E. G., Levin, L., McConnachie, G., Carlson, J. I., Kemp, D. C., & Smith, C. E. (1994). *Communication-based intervention for problem behavior: A user's guide for producing positive change*. Baltimore: Brookes.

DO-IT. (2004). *Disabilities, opportunities, internetworking, and technology*. Retrieved June 2006, from the Faculty Room website: http://www.washington.edu/doit/Faculty/

Dodds, J. (2003). *Assistive technology for people who are deaf and hard of hearing. TECH-NJ, 14(1)*. Retrieved April 2006 from www.tcnj.edu/~technj/2003/dodds.htm

Durand, V. M. (1993). Functional communication training using assistive devices: Effects on challenging behavior. *Augmentative and Alternative Communication, 9*, 168–176.

Estrella, G. (2000). Confessions of a blabber finger. In M. Fried-Oken & H. Bersani (Eds.), *Speaking up and spelling it out* (pp. 31–45). Baltimore: Brookes.

Kisor, H. (1990). *What's that pig outdoors? A memoir of deafness*. New York: Penguin Books.

Koegel, L. K., Koegel, R. L., & Dunlap, G. (1996). *Positive behavioral support: Including people with difficult behavior in the community*. Baltimore: Brookes.

LaFontaine, L., & DeRuyter, F. (1987). The nonspeaking cerebral palsied: A clinical and demographic database report. *Augmentative and Alternative Communication, 3*, 153–162.

Musselwhite, C., & St. Louis, K. (1988). *Communication programming for persons with severe handicaps*. Austin, TX: Pro-Ed.

Northeast Technical Assistance Center. (1998). *The role of assistive listening devices in the classroom* (NETAC Teacher Tipsheet Series). Rochester, NY: Author.

Northeast Technical Assistance Center. (2000). *Serving deaf students who have cochlear implants* (NETAC Teacher Tipsheet Series). Rochester, NY: Author.

Schindler, C. (2003). Text messaging: More than just an add-on to cell phone plans. *TECH-NJ, 14(1)*.

Self Help for Hard of Hearing People. (2006). *Facts on hearing loss*. Retrieved April 11, 2007, from http://www.hearingloss.org/learn/factsheets.asp

Sienkiewicz-Mercer, R., & Kaplan, S. B. (1996). *I raise my eyes to say yes*. West Hartford, CT: Whole Health Books.

Spadafora, T. (2003). *FM system & C-Print™ assist hard-of-hearing student in high school. TECH-NJ, 14(1)*. Retrieved April 2006 from www.tcnj.edu/~technj/2003/cprint.htm

Steinberg, A. (2000). Autobiographical narrative on growing up deaf. In P. E. Spencer, C. J. Erting, & M. Marschark (Eds.), *Essays in honor of Kathryn P. Meadow-Orlans: The deaf child in the family and at school* (pp. 93–108). Mahwah, NJ: Erlbaum.

Stinson, M. S., & Foster, S. (2000). Socialization of deaf children and youths in school. In P. E. Spencer, C. J. Erting, & M. Marschark (Eds.), *Essays in honor of Kathryn P. Meadow-Orlans: The deaf child in the family and at school* (pp. 191–209). Mahwah, NJ: Erlbaum.

Stuart, S. (2002). Communication: Speech and language. In M. L. Batshaw (Ed.), *Children with disabilities*. (5th ed., pp. 229–241). Baltimore: Brookes.

Stuckless, R., Ashmore, D., Schroedel, J., & Simon, J. (1997). *A report of the National Task Force on Quality of Services in the Postsecondary Education of Deaf and Hard of Hearing Students*. Rochester, NY: Northeast Technical Assistance Center NETAC, Rochester Institute of Technology, National Technical Institute for the Deaf. Retrieved August, 2004, from the NETAC website: http://netac.rit.edu/publication/taskforce/device/device7.html

TASH (2002). TASH resolution on the right to communicate. *TASH Connections, 28*(5).

Warick, R., Clark, C., Dancer, J., & Sinclair, S. (1997). Assistive listening devices. In R. Stuckless, D. Ashmore, J. Schroedel, & J. Simon (Eds.) *A report of the National Task Force on Quality of Services in the Postsecondary Education of Deaf and Hard of Hearing Students*. Rochester, N.Y.: Northeast Technical Assistance Center (NETAC), Rochester Institute of Technology, National Technical Institute for the Deaf. Retrieved April, 2007 from the Northeast Regional Center website: http://netac.rit.edu/ publication/taskforce/ device/ device7.html

Williams, B. (2000). More than an exception to the rule. In M. Fried-Oken & H. Bersani (Eds.), *Speaking up and spelling it out* (pp. 245–254). Baltimore: Brookes.

Williams, B. (2002). Preface. *Vermont communication resource guide*. Retrieved January 2005 from the Division of Developmental Services website: http://depts.washington.edu/ augcomm/03_cimodel/commind1_intro.htm

Wing, L. (1996). *The autistic spectrum: A guide for parents and professionals*. London: Constable.

CHAPTER 5

Computers and the Internet for Teaching Content Areas

FOCUS QUESTIONS

1. How can technology support the learning of students with disabilities in the classroom?
2. How can products designed for the popular market address problems faced by students with disabilities?
3. What software programs have been specifically designed for students with disabilities and what are their features?
4. How can the Internet be used to enhance learning for students with disabilities?
5. How does computer use support universal design for learning?
6. How do authoring software programs make the general education curriculum accessible to students with disabilities?

INTRODUCTION

Computers have become as commonplace in the classroom as pencils and notebooks, and their presence has expanded the options available to teachers of students with disabilities. In Chapter 2 the computer was discussed as a tool for enhancing writing; Chapter 3 discussed the computer as a tool for reading; this chapter explores how teachers can enhance instruction of students with disabilities using computer technology. The term *instruction* refers to teaching—reinforcing or assessing students' abilities to understand concepts or demonstrate skills. The emphasis of this chapter is using the classroom computer as a tool to teach content to students who have disabilities. Many textbooks are devoted entirely to using instructional technology or educational technology in classrooms, and this chapter is not intended as a substitute. Rather, it explores specific technologies that can facilitate the learning process, increase participation, and build independence for students with disabilities. The computer is an extremely flexible tool that can enhance all students' learning. It can provide students at all levels with myriad meaningful learning experiences. The computer "can emulate a book, an audio CD player, a video game, a telephone, a VCR, a spreadsheet, a drafting table, a musical instrument, an editing studio, or even a battlefield. Computers can be customized. Adaptable to many tasks, they can also be adapted to many users" (Meyer & Rose, 1998, p. 61).

ADDRESSING THE NEEDS OF STUDENTS WITH DISABILITIES

Students with disabilities who need extended practice and repetition especially can benefit from using the computer. Computer-assisted instruction is particularly promising for helping these students master needed skills because it can be customized to meet individual needs, provide sufficient repetition, and systematically present materials (Wehmeyer, Smith, Palmer, & Davies, 2004). Well-constructed software ". . . allows teachers to provide students with repeated practice opportunities, an unlimited number and variety of examples, and focused individual feedback" (Ayres & Langone, 2005).

Students who have difficulty with memory, auditory processing, visual perception, language, internal motivation, or attention often find it challenging to attend to a task that is without stimulation (Carroll, 1993, as cited in Wehmeyer et al., 2004 and Hickson, Blackman, & Reis, 1995). It is, therefore, essential to engage such students in interesting and motivating ways. Computer use in the classroom can provide students with external motivation and keep them engaged (Brown, Miller, & Robinson, 2003). Software can present information in the ways in which students learn best, and teachers can select topical software that matches students' interests.

Although students with disabilities can benefit from computer use in the classroom, there are significant issues that need to be considered for successful implementation. The following section identifies specific features of software programs or interactive Web-based activities that promote learning in students with disabilities, criteria for selecting software or Web-based activities, and various technology tools that address the specific learning challenges of students with disabilities.

FEATURES OF INSTRUCTIONAL SOFTWARE AND WEB-BASED LEARNING ACTIVITIES

Although the needs of each student are unique to the individual, there are general characteristics of software that assist a broad spectrum of students. The work of Wehmeyer et al. (2004) identifies features of software programs that are likely to accommodate individual preferences as well as meet the needs of students with a wide variety of disabilities. The features that they mention with regard to software apply equally well to interactive Web-based activities. They recommend the following features:

- Simplified screens and instructions
- Consistent placement of menus and control features
- Graphics along with text to support nonreaders and early readers
- Audio feedback
- Accessibility by a variety of methods
- Ability to set pace and level of difficulty

- Appropriate and unambiguous feedback
- Easy error correction

Simplified screens and instructions are beneficial for a variety of reasons. When the visual presentation is clear and uncluttered students can easily discern the important elements and identify where they should devote their attention. Students are not distracted or confused by graphics and animations that are not integral to their learning. Simplified instructions allow students who struggle with receptive language, following multiple-step directions, or other learning issues to understand what needs to be done for successful interaction with the program.

Consistent placement of menus and control features makes it easier for students to know which menu to access or where to point and click to appropriately engage with software- or Web-based activities. This reduces the complexity of working with activities so students are able to devote their energy and concentration to the content of the program, increasing the potential for learning.

Graphics provided along with text enable nonreaders and early readers to engage successfully with computer-based learning activities. The picture cues can provide the scaffolding needed by struggling readers. The graphics give students an opportunity to access the content of the software despite difficulty reading directions or text-based navigation controls.

Audio output provided by software programs or Web-based learning activities allows students who are struggling or nonreaders as well as students who are strong auditory learners to access content and benefit from frequent, relevant feedback. Auditory output can be understood more easily because it bypasses reading weaknesses and addresses the students' strengths. Students can spend their energy and cognitive resources on learning concepts, adjusting their strategies, and incorporating feedback provided as they continue to interact with the activities.

When software- and Web-based learning activities are *accessible by a variety of methods* (i.e., by either the keyboard or the mouse or with alternate computer access methods [see Chapter 7]), it can be used effectively by a greater number of students. Those students who can easily use both a mouse and keyboard can access most software programs. However, when *only* the mouse or *only* the keyboard can be used, students with disabilities may find their access to programs restricted or precluded altogether.

Pace can be considered as the speed at which students are expected to respond to or initiate interaction. Students finding it difficult to execute a quick response benefit from adjustable response rates; their knowledge, rather than their speed of response, is the most important factor in determining success. Pace can also be considered as the speed of progression from one concept to another or from one level of difficulty to another. Students who need extended practice benefit from being able to control the speed at which the program advances. This enables them to develop, practice, and master the skills associated with one concept or at one difficulty level before moving on. Being able to set the level of difficulty allows students to enter programs at the most appropriate level and makes it usable by students at different levels. When computer-based learning activities allow the user to control both the pace and the level of difficulty, they are accessible to a more diverse range of students.

Unambiguous and appropriate feedback is an important feature of software programs and Web-based learning activities for all students, but especially for students with special needs. When feedback is provided to inform students whether an answer is right or wrong (e.g., drill and practice on math facts), it is imperative that the feedback be delivered clearly and in a manner that students will understand. For students who have reading difficulty or those who are nonreaders, auditory feedback or graphic feedback—provided separately or combined with print-based feedback—are good choices. For example, when a student enters the correct answer, appropriate feedback would be auditory feedback saying, "That's correct. You're on a roll," displaying a picture of "thumbs up," or doing either one while displaying the text "Correct. 3 + 4 = 7." When the feedback is meant to inform students that their answer is incorrect it is important that it be done clearly, but with kindness and sensitivity. Simply displaying or speaking the message "Wrong" delivers feedback that may be perceived as harsh. It may diminish students' interest and motivation over time. Such feedback is not as meaningful as it could be because it does not provide information that will help students be successful in the future. Another consideration for appropriate feedback is that the feedback for correct answers should always be more stimulating and rewarding than the feedback for incorrect answers. If not, it can lead to confusion and misunderstanding; students may not realize that an enhanced response is due to making an error. Additionally, they may intentionally enter wrong answers because it is more interesting and entertaining to do so.

Ease of error correction can be a decisive factor between success and failure. For myriad reasons students may wish to change their initial computer input, whether it be to a software program or a Web-based learning activity. If input is immediately accepted, students will not have an opportunity to change answers or correct mistakes. Additionally, if error correction is overly burdensome (e.g., time-consuming or confusing), students with disabilities may not be able to make changes efficiently or effectively.

SOFTWARE PROGRAM AND WEB-BASED ACTIVITY SELECTION

Having discussed the implications of various software features, the conundrum becomes selecting one that is best suited to your students' needs. Although there are many factors to consider when purchasing software, the primary considerations should be that the software naturally fits instructional goals or objectives and that it meets the interests of the students. Software should not be a forced fit; it is imperative to match the software to the student and not vice versa. Teachers should assume a user-centered approach when selecting software, matching it to the student's IEP goals to keep the student on target with the curriculum.

Key questions to consider when selecting software programs to help meet students' goals and objectives are:

- What is the intended outcome of software use? For example, is it meant to strengthen math skills in problem solving or is it meant to build speed and accuracy with basic math facts?
- Is the software likely to fulfill its stated purpose? Some software programs purport to build skills in phonetics, but they just present letter identification tasks.

- Can the software be used as an alternative to traditional classroom activities to enhance students' participation? For example, will students learn as effectively dissecting a frog using Digital Frog (http://www.digitalfrog.com) as they would using the traditional hands-on method?

Teachers should select software with a specific outcome in mind. Although many software programs offer support in several areas, some focus on a specific subject or only one aspect of a subject. The teacher must be able to justify the intended purpose for using the software prior to purchasing. This will increase the likelihood of purchasing programs that meet the needs of the students and decrease the chances that software programs are purchased simply because they are affordable or have an attractive visual display.

Furthermore, students' interests must be considered. If the program matches the students' interest, they will be more apt to dedicate their attention to the activities. When students find learning activities, including software-based activities, meaningful and interesting they spend more time on task and are more likely to meet learning objectives.

Given the previous discussion about how to select software and Internet-based activities and the numerous options available, it may seem like a daunting task to make an appropriate selection. However, it need not be so. Figure 5.1 offers an easy, user-friendly checklist for guiding software evaluation. It represents a synthesis of the previous discussion and emphasizes the match between students' individual needs and specific features of software programs. It can be used as a quick tool for evaluating the appropriateness of a given software program or Web-based activity.

FIGURE 5–1   Quick guide for software and Web-based learning activity selection

What is the goal or purpose of computer use?

❏ Providing an alternative means of completing schoolwork, participating in classroom activities, or demonstrating knowledge
❏ Teaching basic concepts and academic skills
❏ Providing practice with basic concepts or academic skills
❏ Using as a tool for writing (mechanics), prewriting, and composition
❏ Providing opportunities to think critically and solve problems
❏ Finding information on the Internet or other reference tools
❏ Using for play, leisure, or for exploring interests
❏ Self-expressing or making choices
❏ Practicing basic concepts (such as colors, shapes, and classification)
❏ Encouraging emergent literacy (developing language, developing an interest in written language, etc.)
❏ Other _____

Content of the software program

❏ Does it match the goal or purpose of computer use?
❏ Does it match the students' interests?

Matching student needs

❏ Young children and nonreaders or struggling readers benefit from speech output (spoken instructions).

❏ Children with attention difficulties need software whose feedback, reinforcement, and visual presentation are not distracting.

❏ Children with perceptual problems need uncluttered screens and clear, easily readable fonts.

❏ Children with visual impairments often need speech output.

❏ Children with physical and/or cognitive disabilities need programs in which speed of response or input is not essential.

Flexibility of software program or Web-based activity

❏ Can the visual display be customized for student's individual needs?

❏ Can sound or music be turned off?

❏ Can levels be selected or modified?

❏ Can specific content be selected?

❏ Can speed and reaction time be modified?

Ease of use: Should be both easy to use and simple to customize.

Source: Adapted from "Content Software Makes the Grade," by D. A. Newton, A. G. Dell, and A. M. Disdier, 1998, *Exceptional Parent, 20*(12). Adapted with permission.

We strongly recommend that teachers try software programs and Web-based learning activities before adopting them. Many software companies offer free 30-day trials. Many trial versions are fully functioning versions of the software but are time-limited—they cease to work after a certain period (e.g., 30 days or 30 hours of use). Other demo versions may lack some of the functions available in purchased versions. For example, users may not be able to save, print, or enable options such as record keeping. If demo versions are available, they can usually be obtained by contacting the software publisher or downloading it from the Internet; visit the software publishers' websites to check availability. Many Web-based learning activities are available for free; however, some websites require users to pay subscription fees. Often fee-based subscription sites offer free, time-limited access. Teachers should take advantage of demo versions, 30-day free trials, and free subscription offers because the best way to determine if software programs or Web-based learning activities are appropriate is to try them out firsthand.

SOFTWARE SELECTION: FOCUS ON MATH

Software That Teaches Math Skills

In choosing software to teach math skills to students with disabilities, teachers find that many general education math programs offer appropriate features. For example, the programs in Riverdeep's Mighty Math series are highly customizable and engaging. The programs in this series are designed to meet the needs of students at widely disparate levels, and offer many of the recommended features already described. Mighty Math Number Heroes, for example, provides activities for upper elementary (Grades 4–6) students focusing on fractions, multiplication, division, 2D geometry, and probability. Embedded in the program is a "grow slide" (see Figure 5.2) that automatically records students' progress and adjusts to guide learning at the appropriate level; as students master skills at easier levels they are presented with material at increasingly challenging levels. The grow slide may also be set manually so students can begin interacting with the program at the most appropriate level or return to previous levels to refresh their skills.

Many supports are built into the program to accommodate students' varying abilities. Students can operate the program in two modes: Question & Answer (Q&A) and Explore (see Figures 5.3 and 5.4). Students with stronger skills can choose to use the program in Q&A mode, which requires that they solve a specific problem. Students with emerging or developing skills can elect to use the program in Explore mode initially. In this mode students are able to engage with the math concepts in a risk-free environment—investigating and experimenting to develop their skills. Then, when they are ready they can switch to the Q&A mode. Additional supports include an on-screen calculator, freeing students to concentrate on math concepts rather than math facts; a fact book to clarify confusing terms and concepts; and speech output so all text can be read aloud and repeated as needed.

Many students with learning disabilities in math have difficulty remembering as many facts as their typical peers, fail to transfer the math facts to long-term memory, and have difficulty retrieving quickly those math facts that have been transferred (Geary, 1999). Students who fail to develop math fact fluency are at a disadvantage

FIGURE 5–2
Mighty Math
Carnival
Countdown grow
slides

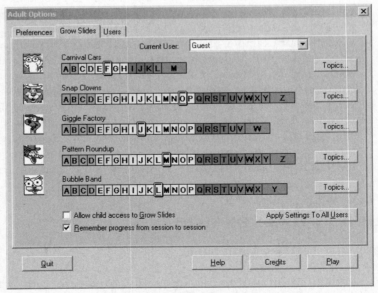

FIGURE 5–3
Mighty Math
Carnival
Countdown!
Annie's Pattern
Block in Question &
Answer mode

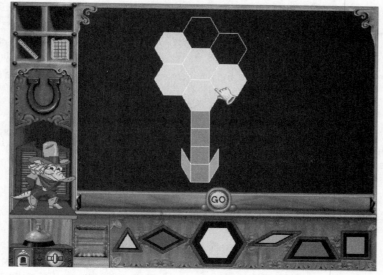

Source: Image used with permission. © 2007 Riverdeep Interactive Learning Limited. All rights reserved.

when it comes to developing computational fluency and understanding higher order mathematics concepts (Hasselbring, Lott, & Zydney, n.d.).

Figure 5.5 illustrates what is meant by math fact fluency and computational fluency.

By the end of sixth grade students should have developed computational fluency with whole numbers in all of the basic operations—addition, subtraction, multiplication, and division (National Council of Teachers of Mathematics, 2004). However,

FIGURE 5–4
Mighty Math
Carnival
Countdown Snap
Clowns Explore
mode

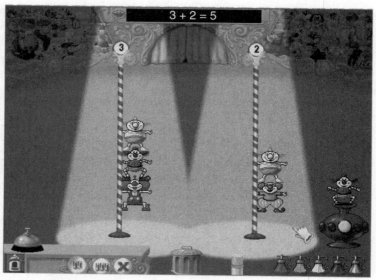

Source: Image used with permission. © 2007 Riverdeep Interactive Learning Limited. All rights reserved.

FIGURE 5–5   Math fact fluency and computational fluency

The National Council of Teachers of Mathematics (NCTM) Principle and Standards of School Mathematics (2000) indicate that students should develop both math fact fluency and computational fluency.

Math fact fluency means being able to quickly and accurately recall the answers to problems such as the following:

$$3 + 4 = \qquad 12 - 3 = \qquad 4 \times 5 = \qquad 12 \div 4 =$$

Computational fluency refers to having efficient and accurate methods for computing that are based on well-understood properties and number relationships. This means a student is able to quickly and correctly solve problems such as the following. Math fact fluency supports computational fluency.

$$\begin{array}{cccc} 45 & 71{,}623 & 908 & 68\overline{)5372} \\ +\,27 & -\,46{,}795 & \times\,320 & \end{array}$$

students who have not developed math fact fluency never achieve computation fluency. Throughout their math courses they may have to devote so much of their cognitive resources on the basic math facts that they fail to grasp the higher order concepts being presented or they understand the concept but cannot arrive at the correct answer. Based on an understanding of the importance of math fact fluency, Tom Snyder Productions published FASTT Math (Fluency and Automaticity through Systematic Teaching with Technology), a math intervention program that helps students acquire math fact fluency (Figure 5.6). The program assesses students' command of basic facts by measuring response time and then generates customized activities based on the results. Students progress through the customized series of

FIGURE 5–6
FASTT Math

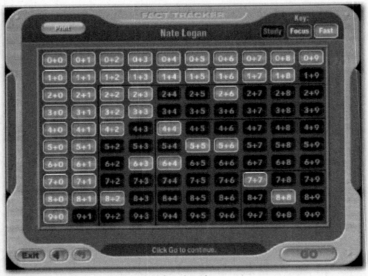

Fact Grid screen for a typical math-delayed student

Source: Reprinted with permission from Tom Snyder Productions.

activities to strengthen memorization of facts and eliminate the need to rely on counting strategies to solve problems. FASTT Math makes it easy for teachers and administrators to monitor students' progress because reports can be generated at the student, class, grade, and school levels.

Microsoft Word, the popular word processing program, can also be used as a "math processor," a program for creating mathematical expressions or equations. Using Microsoft Equation, an object available in Microsoft Office applications (accessed from the Insert menu), students who have difficulty with handwriting but who have good mouse control can create simple or advanced equations in correct mathematical notation. Whereas Microsoft Equation can be used to create equations, completing and showing the intermediary steps used to solve them may be a cumbersome task, especially at more advanced levels. To show their work, students need to use Drawing toolbar items (e.g., line tool and text boxes) in conjunction with Microsoft Equation (Figure 5.7 and Figure 5.8).

Students in advanced math classes may need MathType (Design Science), an expanded, professional-level version of Microsoft Equation. MathType offers additional symbols to create a wider variety of equations and the ability to enhance equations using color-coding. MathType can make advanced math accessible to a broad range of users.

Software Designed Specifically for Students with Disabilities

Some students with disabilities have needs that cannot always be met by software that is targeted at the general public. They need software programs specifically designed to make the general education curriculum accessible to students with disabilities. Chapters 2 and 3 provide extensive discussions about making reading and writing accessible. Many of the assistive technology tools discussed in those chapters (e.g., scan/read systems) can be utilized to make science and social studies content accessible

FIGURE 5–7   Microsoft Equation toolbar

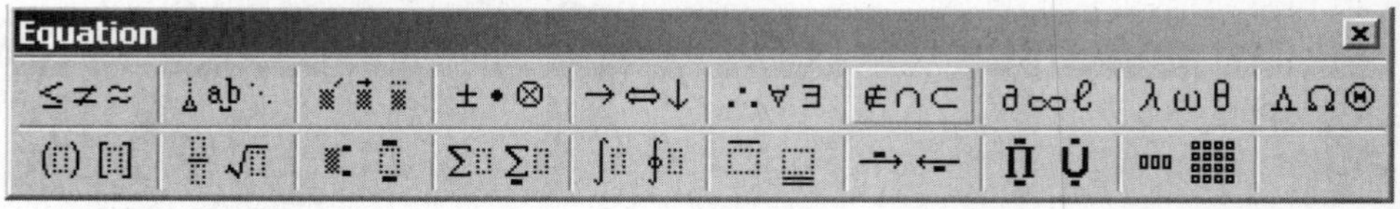

Source: Microsoft product screen shot reprinted with permission from Microsoft Corporation.

FIGURE 5–8   Mathematical expressions and equations typed in Microsoft Word using the Microsoft Equation toolbar

$$\frac{1}{2} + \frac{3}{4} = 1\frac{1}{4} \qquad \sqrt{4} \qquad \frac{3}{10} \div \frac{2}{15} = \frac{1}{15}$$

SIDEBAR

Low-Tech and Mid-Tech Adaptations for Teaching Math

The assistive technology continuum is relevant to the teaching of math, just as it is to the teaching of writing and reading. Manipulatives, which have been standard instructional materials for years, are a good example of low-tech aids. Many other products are available to help students understand and master basic math concepts. Onion Mountain Technology markets fraction rubber stamps, a manipulative number line, laminated addition and multiplication tables, and a special ruler that has multiple transparent overlays to help students understand the relationships between the different units of measure. Large calculators with oversized buttons are useful for students who lack fine motor control. Talking calculators can help students with learning disabilities check their work by reading aloud every keystroke that the student enters. Talking calculators are also needed by students with visual impairments. For students who are learning functional math, easy-to-use mid-tech devices are available. The "coin abacus" and "coin-u-lator" contain keys that are shaped and sized just like coins; they are designed to teach basic money counting. Other calculators offer practical features like automatically calculating tax and tips. Go to http://www.onionmountaintech.com and http://www.pcieducation. com to see these and similar low- to mid-tech math aids.

Courtesy of Onion Mountain Technology.

to students with disabilities. Therefore, this section focuses specifically on making math accessible to students with disabilities. Figure 5.9 provides basic information about the math computation software programs discussed in the following text.

FIGURE 5–9 Math computation software for students with disabilities

Program	Publisher	Level	Description
MathPad	IntelliTools http://www.intellitools.com	Grades K–2	A talking arithmetic worksheet program for basic operations (whole numbers only). Lines up math problems automatically (vertically or horizontally) and prompts students for regrouping.
MathPad Plus	IntelliTools http://www.intellitools.com	Grades 3–8	Extends the features of MathPad to fractions and decimals. Problems can be viewed as pie charts, fraction bars, or decimal grids.
Virtual Pencil Arithmetic	Henter Math http://www.hentermath.com	Elementary	A program for working through basic operations of whole numbers, fractions, and decimals. When paired with screen reading software, it provides speech feedback on positions of digits for students who are blind. Tutorial mode can be turned on or off.
Virtual Pencil Algebra	Henter Math http://www.hentermath.com	Middle and above	Extends the features of VP Arithmetic to algebraic equations. Reads mathematical symbols and describes position of digits within the equations (when used with screen reading software).
MathTalk/ Scientific Notebook	Metroplex Voice Computing, Inc. http://www.mathtalk.com	Middle and above	Must be used with Dragon Naturally-Speaking (voice recognition software). Student speaks math problems at any level—from prealgebra to algebra, trig, calculus, statistics, and graduate-level math. Offers graphing capabilities.

MathPad (IntelliTools) is a talking math worksheet program that enables students to perform arithmetic computations with whole numbers on the computer in much the same way they would using pencil and paper. Students with fine motor difficulties can demonstrate their skill simply by using the keyboard or clicking the mouse, and students with severe disabilities can utilize MathPad's scanning feature. MathPad automatically displays problems so the digits that are supposed to be in each place (e.g., ones place, tens place, hundreds place) are properly aligned, which is helpful for students who have problems lining up arithmetic problems. Customizable speech output can help students with visual impairments and students who are auditory learners; it may also increase the attention of students who are easily distracted. A program feature allows students to easily show regrouping (formerly referred to as borrowing or carrying) when performing calculations so teachers can target the specific levels of addition, subtraction, multiplication, or division at which students need practice (see Figure 5.10). Teacher-generated problem sets can be solved directly on

FIGURE 5–10 MathPad's regrouping feature

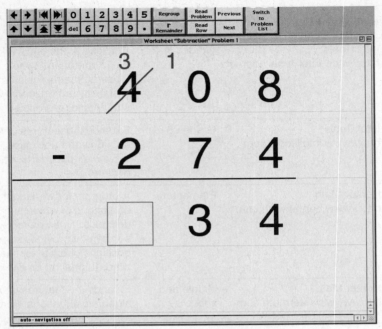

Source: Imagery provided courtesy of InterlliTools®, Inc.

the computer to allow students to receive immediate feedback, or they can be printed out as worksheets. MathPad is beneficial for students who have difficulty working with pencil and paper due to poor fine motor skills, students who need speech output, students who have difficulty setting up problems so digits are aligned properly, students who require immediate feedback, and students who are more motivated and engaged in academic tasks when using the computer.

MathPad Plus (IntelliTools) extends all of the features of MathPad to arithmetic computations with fractions and decimals (Figure 5.11). It provides several additional features to support student success. Students have the option of viewing the problems represented as pie charts, fraction bars, or decimal grids; these representations can increase the students' understanding, especially those who are visual learners. Students' understanding of fractional relations may be enhanced by being able to manipulate problems directly on the screen. This is an especially important feature for students who are unable to use manipulatives as are often used in math instruction.

Virtual Pencil (VP) Arithmetic (Henter Math) is a software tool designed for students who are, in the words of the software publisher, "pencil impaired" (i.e., unable to operate a pencil effectively). Students who are pencil impaired could include those who are blind or have motor impairments or learning disabilities that interfere with writing. VP Arithmetic makes addition, subtraction, multiplication, and division with whole numbers, fractions, and decimals accessible to students with disabilities. Similar to MathPad, VP Arithmetic allows students to solve problems in much the

FIGURE 5–11   MathPad Plus showing a problem in pie charts

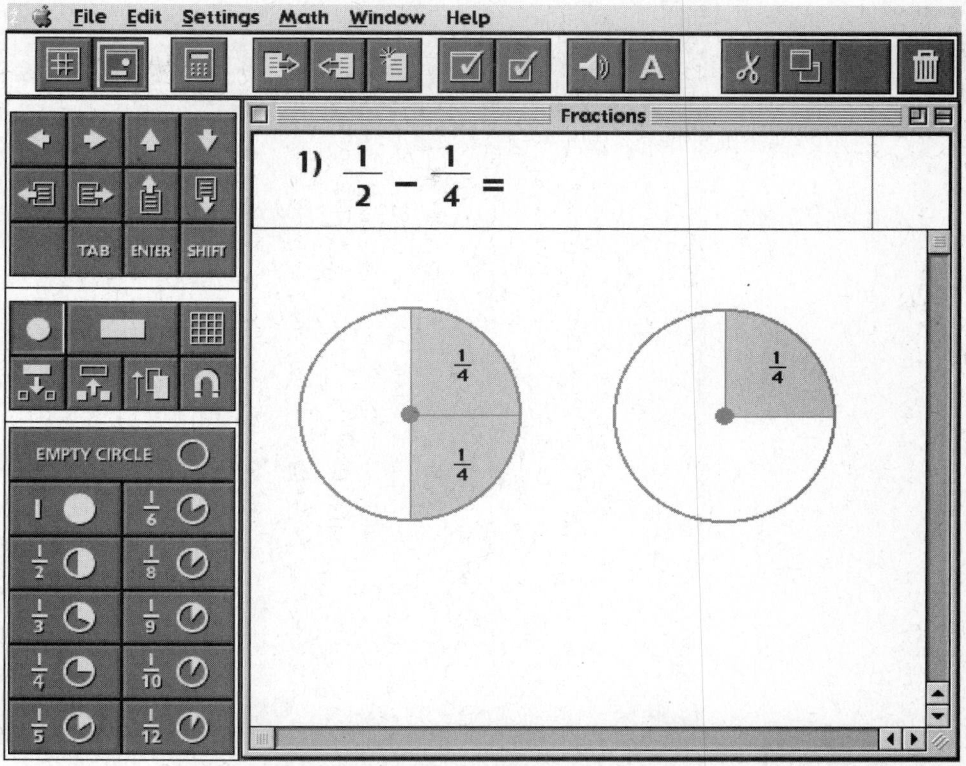

Source: Imagery provided courtesy of IntelliTools®, Inc.

same way they would using pencil and paper, including performing and showing intermediate steps. The program offers speech feedback in a manner that makes it functional for students who are blind. The extensive speech feedback reads problems and provides enough information so students who cannot see the problem can understand the position of digits and can navigate to where they need to be. VP Arithmetic also features a tutorial mode in which "the Tutor tells the student where he is in the problem, what steps need to be done to solve it, and will even do the navigating and provide the answer" (http://hentermath.com/vparithmetic.asp). In test mode teachers can password-protect files, disabling the tutorial features and ensuring that the work produced demonstrates students' knowledge.

Virtual Pencil Algebra extends most of the features of VP Arithmetic so students with disabilities can solve algebraic equations. VP Algebra reads equations using correct math terminology such as *square root of*, *quantity squared*, and *exponent*. Speech feedback allows students to navigate to any point in the equation and provides the information needed to understand their position within the equation. Students can manipulate complicated equations, and can copy and paste portions to be solved separately and then reinserted into the original equation. Password-protecting VP Algebra files prevents them from being altered by students.

FIGURE 5–12 MathTalk/Scientific Notebook (Metroplex) solving a calculus problem

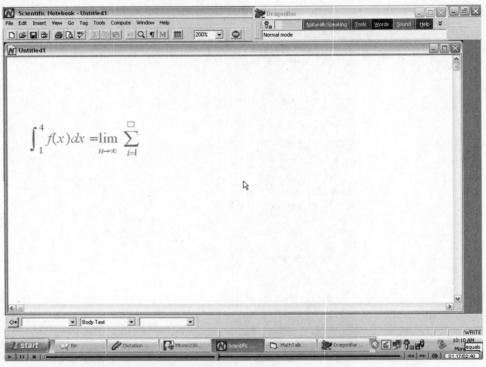

Source: Image courtesy of Metroplex Voice Computing, Inc.

Students with disabilities who rely on speech recognition to operate a computer can perform basic arithmetic and advanced mathematics using MathPad By Voice or MathTalk/Scientific Notebook (Metroplex Voice Computing, Inc.), respectively. Both programs require Dragon Naturally Speaking (Dragon Systems), a voice recognition program. Students can input math calculations into the computer by voice, and then print their work to be handed in just like their peers (see Figure 5.12). These programs are not designed to teach math skills; rather, they provide students who use speech recognition with a way to independently complete math problems at elementary through advanced levels.

FUNCTIONAL SKILLS

The software programs previously mentioned focus on providing access to the standard curriculum. Students with severe disabilities, especially cognitive disabilities, have needs that extend beyond the standard academic curriculum. Often, the goals for these students focus on optimizing independence in areas such as communication, vocation, personal grooming, laundry, dining, meal preparation, housekeeping, leisure activities, and money management (Rocchio, 1995). Collectively, these are known as functional skills.

FIGURE 5–13
Kitchen screen
in My House:
The Language
Activities of
Daily Living
(Barbara Couse
Adams)

Source: Reprinted with permission of Laureate Learning Systems.

Software programs are available to teach functional skills. They provide students with severe disabilities the simple, consistent, repetitive practice needed to master functional skills in risk-free environments. Programs typically focus on low-level content and provide simple, uncluttered presentations. Frequently, options are available to customize both presentation features and content including the ability to

- turn visual and/or auditory prompts on and off
- select specific vocabulary
- set response time limits.

Laureate Learning Systems (http://www.laureatelearning.com) offers over 80 software programs that teach cause and effect, turn-taking, early vocabulary, syntax, cognitive concepts, auditory processing, and early reading. The programs can be accessed using a mouse, switch, or touch screen to accommodate a wide range of physical and cognitive disabilities (see Chapter 7). For example, My House: Language Activities of Daily Living teaches students vocabulary for items in six rooms of a typical home: living room, dining room, kitchen, bedroom, bathroom, and utility room. The teacher can preselect the vocabulary to be presented to match students' ability levels. In the kitchen, for example, students may be learning to identify basic items such as the stove, refrigerator, table, and chair, or they may be at a more advanced level and learning to identify items such as utensils, hot water tap, potholder, and paper towel dispenser (see Figure 5.13).

USING THE INTERNET AS A TEACHING TOOL

The Internet has rapidly become an indispensable vehicle for research and project-based learning activities. Rather than trudging to the library to page through heavy encyclopedia volumes or other reference materials, today's students are more likely

USER PROFILE: Using Yahoo! to Improve Student Achievement

Ms. M. teaches students with intellectual disabilities, ages 14 to 21. The students are enrolled in a high school transitional education program, and instruction focuses on functional academics, communication, social skills, and transition behaviors. Most of the general education students in the high school use the Internet to locate resources for school projects, find directions, communicate with one another, and communicate and socialize with peers in other communities throughout the world. Ms. M. realized that using the Internet independently and accessing Internet resources were important goals for her students as well, and set out to teach them these functional, age-appropriate skills.

Ms. M. selected Yahoo! (http://www.yahoo.com) as their Internet portal because membership is free and because its appearance and functionality are readily customizable using the My Yahoo! feature. She has taught her students to navigate to the Yahoo! website, log in, retrieve and send e-mail, explore specific websites, and engage in assigned Web-based activities. She uses selected Yahoo! services to teach her students specific skills, all of which increase their independence.

For example, the students practice their reading and writing skills, as well as their social and communication skills, when they use e-mail and Yahoo! Greetings to create and send e-cards to classmates, their teachers, and others (http://www.yahoo .americangreetings.com/index.pd). They use Yahoo! Calendar (http://calendar .yahoo.com/) as a time management tool and memory jogger. Students can set event e-mail reminders for upcoming appointments, tasks, special occasions, and assignment due dates, among other things. They use Yahoo! Maps (http://maps .yahoo.com/) to get directions, which provides a real-life example of the importance of learning your address, an opportunity to practice typing their address, and practice in map-reading skills. The students practice functional skills for leisure purposes as well when they use Yahoo! They can view movie trailers and look up show times and locations using the search engine.

Ms. M. evaluates her students' achievement through performance-based assessments, quizzes, direct observations, portfolios of students' e-mails, and students' self-assessments. Using Yahoo! has indeed moved her students closer to their transition goals, and 2 years after integrating Yahoo! into her students' educational programs, she is confident she made the right decision.

to turn to the Internet for information. In fact, the commonly used search engine Google has become a verb in popular lexicon. Use of the Internet expands the amount of information available to all students, and it enhances access to information and opportunities for participation for students with disabilities.

The availability of Internet resources makes it "easy to design, develop and implement differentiated materials and learning opportunities to accommodate the needs of all students" (Smith & Meyen, 2003). A prime example is the inquiry-based activity known as a WebQuest. WebQuests are teacher-designed activities in which most or all of the resources provided for students are available on the World Wide Web. A WebQuest's components, following the same structure as a lesson plan, are introduction, task, process, evaluation, and conclusion. Students are introduced to the overall challenge (objective), given a specific task to complete, provided with instructions for doing so and given specific links to visit, told how their work will be assessed, and asked to reflect on their performance. A distinguishing feature of a WebQuest is that students are presented with a specific challenge to solve using *preselected* Web links. Students are *not* sent on a virtual scavenger hunt where they spend unproductive time searching for information and can become "lost" on the Web or distracted from the task at hand. Rather, the teacher selects appropriate links that he or she knows will provide the information the students need to complete the WebQuest challenge. WebQuests are typically designed to be worked by small, cooperative groups of students, which offers academic support to students with disabilities and provides opportunities for socializing. Because WebQuests are highly customizable (the task, process, evaluation criteria, and resources are set and selected by teachers) they can be created, or modified, to meet specific student needs.

For extensive information about creating and using WebQuests, as well as a searchable database of WebQuests created by others, go to http://webquest.sdsu.edu/.

The Internet provides numerous resources, beyond informational resources for research and inquiry, that offer educational opportunities for all students. Students who need extended practice, visual presentations of concepts, and/or interactive activities can benefit from a wealth of websites. A prime example is Illuminations (http://illuminations.nctm.org/ActivitySearch.aspx), a website maintained by the National Council of Teachers of Mathematics. This site offers numerous online activities that support the development of math concepts for students in Grades K–12. Another excellent example is the National Library of Virtual Manipulatives (http://nlvm.usu.edu/en/nav/vlibrary.html) maintained by Utah State University. Figure 5.14 shows base ten blocks being used to model grouping in addition.

FIGURE 5–14
Virtual Manipulatives website showing base blocks addition

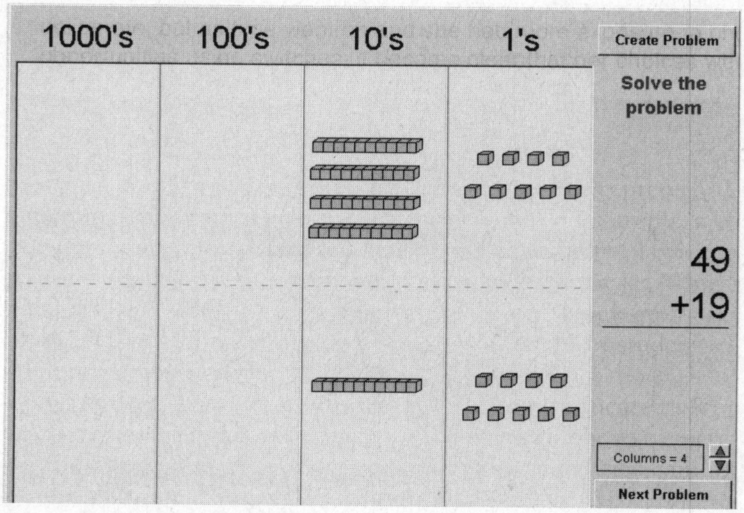

Source: Printed with permission of MATTI Math.

INTERNET ACCESSIBILITY

For students with disabilities to be able to take advantage of the educational opportunities presented by the Internet, they first need to be able to access it. The first step involves access to the computer. Chapters 6, 7, and 8 discuss how to provide computer access for students who have difficulty using the standard keyboard or mouse. This chapter discusses the accessibility options available in Internet browsers, the software used to access and display websites, and the importance of carefully selecting sites for use by students with disabilities. The Internet browsers with which most computers users are familiar are likely to be Internet Explorer, Safari, Firefox, or Opera. All of these browsers offer several features to increase accessibility for individuals with disabilities.

These browsers allow users to override text and background colors specified by Web page designers. Users can designate the text size, font, and background colors that the browsers will use to display Web pages so that students with visual impairments or reading problems can enlarge the font and choose a high-contrast color scheme. Figure 5.15 shows a screenshot of Internet Explorer's zoom feature. Users who are unable to see the graphics and images contained in Web pages can elect to disable the automatic download of these page elements, which will increase speed at which pages load. Selecting the options that best match the needs of students with disabilities increases their ability to access Web pages.

Despite the accessibility features available in popular browsers, barriers to accessing Web page content for students with disabilities remain. Students who are nonreaders or struggling readers will have difficulty accessing the text-based content of most Web pages without appropriate assistive technology. A number of software

FIGURE 5–15 Zoom feature in Internet Explorer

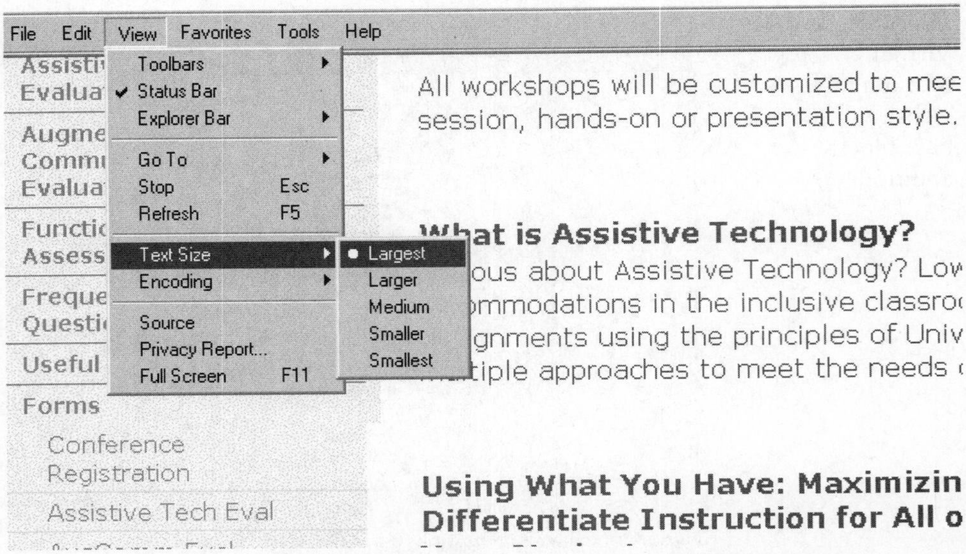

Source: Microsoft product screen shot reprinted with permission from Microsoft Corporation.

netTrekker d.i., an Academic Search Engine for Differentiated Instruction

One obstacle to using Web-based activities in the classroom is the risk that students will digress and end up virtually anywhere. Although school filtering software successfully blocks much unwanted content, it does not screen for age, grade level, or appropriateness, or reduce the volume of results returned when commercial search engines such as Yahoo! or Google are used. For example, a fifth grader searching Google for information on the Revolutionary War will be faced with over 8 million results. To counteract this problem, many school districts subscribe to an academic search engine such as netTrekker d.i (Thinkronize, Inc.). Established and monitored by educators, netTrekker d.i. offers Internet content that is prescreened and organized by five readability levels (see Figure 5.16). Teachers can target their search results to find grade-level content at an appropriate reading level for every child in their class. This means that all children—regardless of their reading level—can read about the topic of study and participate in class discussions and activities. In addition, netTrekker, d.i. offers a read-aloud feature (text-to-speech) for students who need additional reading support. For additional information and a free trial, go to http://www.netTrekker.com.

FIGURE 5–16   netTrekker d.i. Prescreens and organizes search results

Printed with permission of netTrekker.

programs offer text-to-speech functionality so the text on Web pages can be spoken aloud. Some of these programs (e.g., Awesome Talkster, a freeware program) may be designed only for the purpose of providing auditory access to the Web. Other programs (e.g., Kurzweil, WYNN, and TextAloud) offer this as just one of several functions. See Chapter 3 for additional information on reading tools.

Because the World Wide Web is a heavily visual environment, it can be difficult to navigate for students with visual impairments. Web programmers can increase the accessibility of Web pages by providing alternative access to information conveyed by videos or auditory recordings. All videos should be accompanied by an auditory or text-based description for individuals with vision impairments, and captioning should be provided to make audio components accessible to individuals with hearing impairments.

Assistive technology tools such as screen magnification software and screen readers (see Chapter 7) can increase accessibility. Web pages can be enlarged to match users' preferred viewing sizes, and Web page elements such as pictures, text, navigation bars, and tables can be identified via speech output. However, despite utilization of these technology tools, barriers may continue to inhibit Web page access due to the underlying coding of the pages. If a Web page does not conform to recommended accessibility standards, even sophisticated screen readers will not be able to make the page accessible. One method of confirming the accessibility of sites is to determine if they conform to the standards recommended by the World Wide Web Consortium (W3C).

The W3C is an international consortium devoted to leading the World Wide Web to its full potential. To achieve its mission, one of the primary goals of W3C is to make the Web "available to all people, whatever their hardware, software, network infrastructure, native language, culture, geographical location, or physical or mental ability" (http://www.w3.org/Consortium/mission). The W3C develops Web standards and guidelines to assist site developers with the creation of accessible Web pages. (Figure 5.17 provides a brief overview of the W3C guidelines.) When considering websites for use by students with disabilities, teachers should check that the

FIGURE 5–17 Brief overview of the W3C guidelines

The W3C publishes a handy reference titled *Quick Tips to Make Accessible Websites* that offers the following suggestions for accessible Web design:

- **Images and animations.** Use the **alt** attribute to describe the function of each visual.
- **Image maps.** Use the client-side **map** element and text for hotspots.
- **Multimedia.** Provide captioning and transcripts of audio, and descriptions of video.
- **Hypertext links.** Use text that makes sense when read out of context. For example, avoid "click here."
- **Page organization.** Use headings, lists, and consistent structure. Use **CSS** for layout and style where possible.
- **Graphs and charts.** Summarize or use the **longdesc** attribute.
- **Scripts, applets, and plug-ins.** Provide alternative content in case active features are inaccessible or unsupported.
- **Frames.** Use the **noframes** element and meaningful titles.
- **Tables.** Make line-by-line reading sensible. Summarize.
- **Check your work.** Validate. Use tools, checklist, and guidelines at http://www.w3.org/TR/WCAG

Adapted from *Quick Tips to Make Accessible Websites,* by the W3C, 2001. Retrieved from http://www.w3.org/WAI/quicktips/

sites are barrier-free for their students. Several websites and software products are also available to check the accessibility of sites. Watchfire Bobby (http://webxact. watchfire.com/) allows users to check the accessibility of a single Web page simply by typing in the website address. Evaluating entire websites is available for a fee.

An issue related to Internet access is access to information on school district websites. Many school districts post important information such as report card distribution dates, parent–teacher conference dates, and emergency closings on their sites. Increasingly, teachers are making information such as homework assignments and test dates available to students and their families by posting information on their class websites. If school district websites do not conform to the W3C accessibility standards, students with disabilities or their parents or guardians with disabilities may be denied access to the information. We strongly recommend that teachers bring the Internet access needs of students with disabilities and the W3C standards to the attention of their district technology coordinators.

COMPUTER TECHNOLOGY SUPPORTS UNIVERSAL DESIGN FOR LEARNING

As discussed in Chapter 1, Universal Design for Learning (UDL) seeks to make curricular content available to the broadest range of students. It encourages teachers to follow three basic guidelines when planning and delivering instruction:

1. Present information and content in different ways (the "what" of learning)
2. Differentiate the ways that students can express what they know (the "how" of learning)
3. Stimulate interest and motivation for learning (the "why" of learning) (CAST, 2006).

The use of digital media, especially electronic text, makes it easy to present information in different ways. Because electronic text is easily transformed, it is an ideal support for UDL; it makes it possible for students to access important information and content in the manner that best suits their needs. For example, electronic text provides auditory access to information for students who are struggling readers. It can be converted to MP3 format and downloaded so students can access information on their iPods or other MP3 devices. Electronic text is ideally suited to meet the needs of students needing large print as well. Screen magnification (see Chapter 7) programs can be used to display enlarged text on the computer, or a document can be printed in the font size that meets individual needs. Electronic text gives students who are Braille readers the option to print the material in Braille or to access it using a refreshable Braille display (see Chapter 7).

Computer technology is uniquely capable of supporting students with regard to the second guideline of UDL—differentiating the ways that students demonstrate their learning. Although many students can adequately demonstrate their knowledge by handwriting an assignment or report, other students may need access to a word processor, with or without word prediction software (see Chapter 2), in order to demonstrate content mastery. Other students may be more adept at creating PowerPoint or other multimedia presentations to demonstrate their knowledge. In the UDL classroom each of these options is available to students so they can demonstrate their learning and not be hampered by reading and writing disabilities.

The third principle of UDL—stimulating interest and motivation for learning—advocates tapping into learners' interests, offering appropriate challenges, and increasing motivation. These are things that teachers have always sought to do; now, it is much easier to attain these goals by using the computer and the abundance of engaging, interactive, multimedia-rich, and information-rich websites available on the Internet. More academically advanced students can be directed to sites that broaden and deepen their knowledge, whereas other students might be directed to sites that provide exposure to additional information in engaging formats.

For example, middle school students studying prime factorization might watch the *Prime Factorization* video at the BrainPop website (http://www.brainpop.com). After watching the video, students needing additional practice with factoring can use the Factor Tree activity (http://nlvm.usu.edu/en/nav/frames_asid_202_g_3_t_2.html) at the National Library of Virtual Manipulatives website. Those students with greater proficiency can hone their skills playing the Factor Game against a classmate or against the computer at the Illuminations website. Students who have well-developed skills might visit the Nova: Science Now site to learn about the Twin Prime Conjecture described at the website as "a 2,300-year-old mystery surrounding prime numbers" (http://www.pbs.org/wgbh/nova/sciencenow/3302/02.html).

AUTHORING SOFTWARE IN SPECIAL EDUCATION

Authoring software programs are those programs that allow users to add their own content to create customized activities. They are an ideal support for UDL because they can be used to create learning opportunities for students with disabilities for whom a computer is an absolute necessity, as well as those who are simply more engaged and attentive when working on the computer. Authoring programs expand learning opportunities for students who need auditory output, students who are unable to use handwriting to practice skills and demonstrate knowledge, students who are unable to manipulate materials (e.g., arranging objects into arrays as an introduction to multiplication), and students who rely on the computer for access to the curriculum but whose needs cannot be met with "out-of-the-box" software programs. With the appropriate authoring program teachers can create learning activities that are engaging, correlate to the general education curriculum, and support the success of all students.

Authoring programs vary in complexity. Programs like Macromedia's Flash that are targeted for Web page developers and for other commercial users require computer skills beyond those possessed by most classroom teachers. Other authoring programs are designed to be used by teachers to create curricular activities that are accessible using a variety of alternate input methods. Programs fitting into this last category will be the focus of the following discussion.

Software for Creating Curriculum-Related Activities

Authoring programs can be used to create learning activities in any curricular area—science, mathematics, social studies, language arts, and so on—to be accessible to students with disabilities. Some authoring programs allow only a specific type of activity to be created. For example, My Own BookShelf (SoftTouch, Inc.) allows

FIGURE 5–18 My Own BookShelf offers teachers the option of designing books to meet their students' specific interests and needs.

Source: Image courtesy of SoftTouch, Inc.

users to create customized, accessible electronic storybooks (see Figure 5.18). Teachers can import pictures of their students to create personalized social stories, create stories on topics that appeal to individual students, create stories with controlled vocabulary, or any other type of story. Any story created with My Own BookShelf is accessible using the standard keyboard or mouse, an adapted keyboard or mouse, or with the built-in scanning feature that makes it switch-accessible.

ClozePro (Crick Software) is another example of an authoring program that creates a single type of activity (Figure 5.19). Using ClozePro, teachers can easily create cloze (fill-in-the-blank) activities to match students' individual needs, including their reading levels, curricular content, visual presentation requirements, need for picture cues, and need for auditory output. ClozePro is also switch-accessible. Authoring programs that create one type of activity are valuable, versatile tools, and they are often the easiest to learn to use.

Other authoring programs allow for the creation of a wider range of activities. As an example, Clicker 5 (Crick Software) provides teachers with the ability to create what Crick Software calls "hit and happen" activities; these are also known as cause-and-effect activities in which users simply execute a mouse click using a standard mouse, mouse emulator, or switch (see Chapter 7) to cause "something" to happen on the computer. The something can be a visual display, auditory output, or a combination of the two, and can be customized to be meaningful, interesting,

FIGURE 5–19
ClozePro's fill-in-
the-blank activities

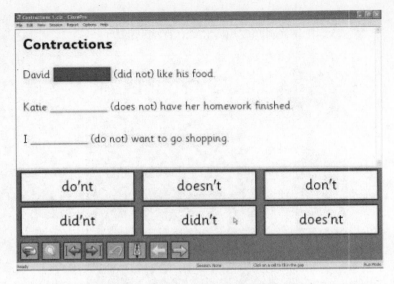

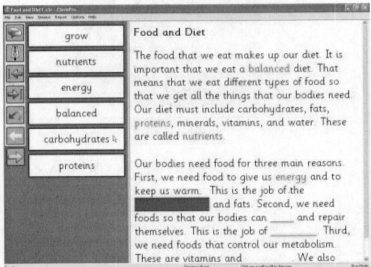

Source: Printed with permission of Crick Software, Inc.

and/or motivating according to students' individual needs. Clicker 5 also functions as a talking word processor that affords teachers the opportunity to create grids containing letters, words, phrases, sentences, numbers, pictures, or any combination of these that students can insert into a document with the click of a mouse. This flexibility allows teachers to create learning activities for virtually any curricular area.

Classroom Suite (IntelliTools) is another authoring program that teachers can use to create numerous types of accessible learning activities. IntelliTalk, IntelliMathics, and IntelliPics, the three components of Classroom Suite, can each be used to create a variety of original learning activities to meet the individual needs of students with disabili-

Student reading and completing a worksheet using IntelliTools' IntelliTalk software
Photos by Elaine Wolkoff

ties. Together, these three components offer possibilities for creating customized, accessible activities that address a wide range of concepts in any curricular area. In addition to authoring capabilities, Classroom Suite offers an extensive set of premade activities and a template library of activities for Grades K–8. The templates can be used as is or modified to meet individual needs. Figure 5.20 shows an IntelliMathics template.

FIGURE 5–20 IntelliMathics template for illustrating single digit multiplication

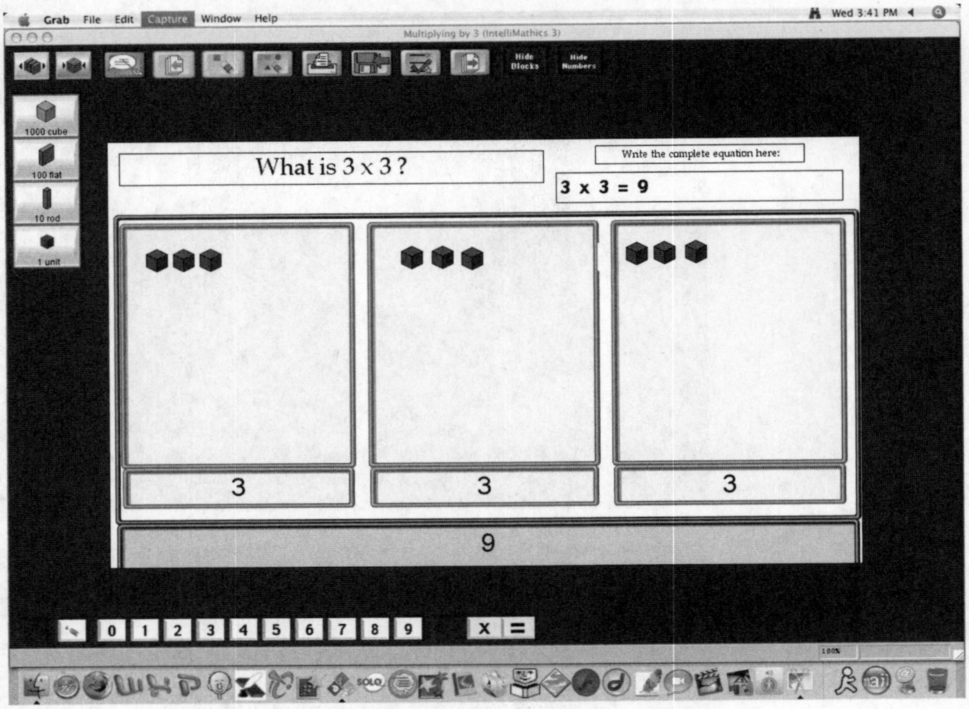

Source: Imagery provided courtesy of IntelliTools®, Inc.

The use of authoring programs may require developing some new technical skills; however, these skills can usually be easily mastered by teachers with general computer proficiency, and most authoring programs provide detailed tutorials that are invaluable for novice users. Of course, mastering any new skill takes time and practice, and teachers will find that the longer they work with a specific authoring program the quicker they become at creating activities. Clicker 5 and IntelliTool's Classroom Suite also provide a helpful venue for sharing teacher-created materials. Rather than always having to always design original activities, teachers can search Crick Software's Learning Grids website (http://www.learninggrids.com) or IntelliTools's Classroom Activity Exchange (go to http://www.intellitools.com/ and click on Activity Exchange) to see if someone else has created an activity that can be used as is or modified to meet the needs of their own students.

SUMMARY

- Myriad popular software programs, interactive Web-based activities, and software specially designed for students with disabilities offer opportunities to make the general education curriculum accessible to students with a wide range of disabilities.

- The computer can be a patient tutor, providing instruction or repetitive practice in an engaging and motivating manner.

- With the proper software program or Web-based activity, students who cannot use pencil and paper effectively can use the computer to acquire skills and demonstrate their knowledge. They can even use the computer to perform math computation and calculations at a basic or an advanced level.

- In order for the computer to be an effective instructional tool, teachers need to carefully select software and websites for student use. They need to be certain that the computer activities they choose, whether software or Web based, align with the curriculum and move students toward meeting their educational goals. That is, the activities should not be merely fun and engaging, but meaningful and educationally relevant.

- Teachers need to ensure that the computer activities provide the flexibility to meet the needs of students with disabilities. Specifically, they need to check that students' individual needs can be accommodated with respect to the visual display, auditory feedback, academic level, content, response time, and need for accessibility with any alternate input devices students may be using.

- The computer's capacity to transform digital text into a format that meets the needs of students with disabilities supports universal design for learning (UDL), which emphasizes providing multiple, flexible means of presentation, expression, and engagement. Once text is in digital format it can be made accessible to students regardless of their individual needs. With the appropriate software the computer can easily convert text to MP3 or other formats so students can hear the information spoken aloud; the font, size, and style of the text can be adjusted; and it can be outputted as Braille.

- Authoring software designed to meet the needs of students with disabilities is an especially valuable UDL support; it affords teachers an opportunity to create activities with customized content that are accessible using the standard keyboard and mouse or built-in accessibility features.

- Regardless of whether they are used to create one type of activity or many types, authoring software programs are powerful tools for teachers, increasing students' independence and participation, and making the curriculum accessible to students with a wide range of disabilities.

WEB RESOURCES

For additional information on the topics listed, go to the following websites:

Enhancing Instruction with Computers

Kathy Schrock's Guide for Educators
http://school.discovery.com/schrockguide

Eduscapes
http://eduscapes.com/

Software Reviews

http://www.superkids.com
http://www.education-world.com/a_tech/archives/edurate.shtml
http://www.learningvillage.com

Technology for Math

Riverdeep's Mighty Math series
http://www.riverdeep.com
FASTT Math
http://www.tomsnyder.com
MathType
http://www.dessci.com/en/products/mathtype
Math Matrix
http://www.citeducation.org/mathmatgrix/#
A+ Math
http://www.aplusmath.com
Visual Fractions
http://www.visualfractions.com
Mrs. Glosser's Math Goodies
http://www.mathgoodies.com

Web-Based Activities: All Subjects

Digital Frog
http://www.digitalfrog.com
The WebQuest Page
http://webquest.sdsu.edu
PBS Kids
http://www.pbskids.org
Funbrain by Pearson Education
http://www.funbrain.com

Web Accessibility

Microsoft
http://www.microsoft.com/enable/training/ie6/default.aspx
Awesome Talkster (free download)
http://www.awesomelibrary.org/Awesome_Talking_Library.html
World Wide Web Consortium (W3C)
http://www.w3.org
http://webxact.watchfire.com
Web accessibility evaluation tools
http://www.w3.org/WAI/ER/tools/complete

Creating Curriculum-Related Activities

My Own BookShelf
http://www.softtouch.com
ClozePro
http://www.cricksoft.com/uk/products/clozepro
DeafBlind Online
http://www.deafblindonline.org.uk/software.html
Clicker 5
http://www.cricksoft.com/uk/products/clicker
Classroom Suite
http://www.intellitools.com

SUGGESTED ACTIVITIES

1. *Review a software program or Web-based activity.* Choose one of the sites listed above under Technology for Math or Web-Based Activities. Learn the program thoroughly—this means you need to use it several times, change the settings/preferences/options, deliberately make errors, and so on. Write a review of the program or activity using Figure 5.1 as a guide. Use the following headings: Title, Publisher, website address, Cost, Notable system requirements, Purpose (Goals), Structure, Special features, Strengths, Weaknesses, and Summary. Share these in class or on a class discussion board.

2. *Explore an accessible Web-based activity.* Go to http://www.digitalfrog.com/products/rainforest.html and download a demo version of the Digital Trip to the Rainforest–AT Edition. Explore the activity in detail. What features make it accessible to students with disabilities? How could this Web-based activity be integrated into a classroom to enhance students' learning of the subject matter?

3. *Evaluate WebQuests.* Bernie Dodge has developed a WebQuest to introduce teachers to this instructional model. Go to http://webquest.sdsu.edu/materials.htm and select the appropriate version under the heading "A Webquest about Webquests." In a small group, evaluate each WebQuest listed according to the roles described in the posted instructions. Discuss criteria for a good WebQuest based on your evaluation.

4. *Create with IntelliTalk.* Go to IntelliTools's Classroom Suite at http://www.intellitools.com/classroom_suite/download.aspx?site=itc and download the 90-day trial version. Then access the QuickStart IntelliTalk 3 tutorial by clicking on the link at http://www.intellitools.com/classroom_suite/documentation_tutorials.aspx. Follow the directions for "Creating an Activity" (pp. 24–33). When you have finished creating the activity, complete the activity and check your work. Print your work, including the checked answers, and submit it to your instructor.

5. *Add to your portfolio.* Use a search engine (e.g., Google [http://www.google.com] or Yahoo [http://www.yahoo.com]) to locate educational resources and interactive activities. Conduct searches using phrases such as "websites for teachers"

and "interactive educational activities." Explore the sites identified by your search. Then add a selection of resources that are most relevant to your area of professional practice to your portfolio.

REFERENCES

Ayres, K., & Langone, J. (2005). Evaluation of software for functional skills instruction: Blending best practice with technology. *Technology in Action, Technology and Media Division, 1*(5), 1–8.

Brown, A., Miller, D., & Robinson, L. (2003). Teacher-directed software design: The development of learning objects for students with special needs in the elementary classroom. *Information Technology in Childhood Education*, No.1, 173–186.

Center for Applied Special Technology. (2006). *Research and development in universal design for learning.* Questions and answers retrieved April 11, 2007, from http://www.cast.org/research/faq/index.html

Geary, D. C. (1999). *Mathematical disabilities: What we know and don't know.* Retrieved from the Learning Disabilities Online website: http://www.ldonline.org/article/5881

Hasselbring, T. S., Lott, A. C., & Zydney, J. M. (n.d.). *Technology-supported math instruction for students with disabilities: Two decades of research and development.* Retrieved November 20, 2006, from the Center for Implementing Technology in Education website: http://www.cited.org/library/resourcedocs/Tech-SupportedMathInstruction-FinalPaper_early.pdf

Hickson, L., Blackman, L. S., & Reis, E. M. (1995). *Mental retardation: Foundations of educational programming.* Boston: Allyn & Bacon.

Meyer, A., & Rose, D. (1998). *Learning to read in the computer age.* Newton, MA: Brookline Books.

National Council of Teachers of Mathematics. (2000). *Principles and standards of school mathematics.* Reston, VA: National Council of Teachers of Mathematics.

National Council of Teachers of Mathematics. (2004). *Principles and standards of school mathematics* (Appendix: Table of Standards and expectations). Retrieved from http://standards.nctm.org/document/appendix/numb.htm

Newton, D.A., Dell, A. G., & Disdier, A. M. (1998). Content software makes the grade. *Exceptional Parent, (28)* 12.

Rocchio, L. (1995). The LIFE program—Living Innovations in Functional Environments—Deaf-blindness. *American Rehabilitation.* Retrieved July 9, 2005, from http://www.findarticles.com/p/articles/mi_m0842/is_n2_v21/ai_17986026

Rose, D., & Meyer, A. (2002). *Teaching every student in the digital age: Universal design for learning.* Alexandria, VA: Association for Supervision and Curriculum Development.

Smith, S., & Meyen, E. (2003). Application of online instruction: An overview for teachers, students with mild disabilities, and their parents. *Focus on Exceptional Children, 35*(6), 1–16.

Wehmeyer, M., Smith, S., Palmer, S., & Davies, D. (2004). Technology use by students with intellectual disabilities: An overview. *Journal of Special Education Technology, 19*(4), 7–21.

CHAPTER 6

Providing Access to Computers: Using What You Have

FOCUS QUESTIONS

1. What universal design features facilitate computer access for students with disabilities? What are the characteristics of students for whom the specific features may be appropriate?

2. What additional operating system features are provided for users with disabilities, and what are the characteristics of students for whom these specific features may be appropriate?

INTRODUCTION

In Chapters 1 through 5 you read about how computers have the capacity to help students with disabilities participate in educational, social, and leisure activities. In order to participate in these activities students must be able to use a computer. Many students with disabilities will be able to use a computer effectively simply by taking advantage of adjustments and settings readily available within the computer operating system.

This chapter focuses on universal design features that are relevant for students with disabilities and other operating system accessibility features. Not every feature is applicable to every student, nor is a particular feature appropriate for every student with a particular disability; computer access solutions must be decided on a case-by-case basis according to each student's specific needs and preferences (see Chapter 8). Thus, as we discuss features in this chapter, we match them with the characteristics of students for whom they might be appropriate, rather than with disability categories.

The computer operating systems that dominate P–12 educational environments are Macintosh OS and Microsoft Windows; consequently, discussion focuses on these two systems. Operating systems are continually updated, which has lead to an inconsistency in versions that are installed on computers in schools. Because it is not possible to address each operating system version, only Macintosh OS X and Microsoft Windows XP are referenced in the sections that follow.

UNIVERSAL DESIGN

As explained in Chapter 1, the computer industry has adopted the concept of universal design that was first introduced in the fields of architecture and design. Wanting to sell as many computers as possible, the industry recognized the commercial value of designing operating systems that are usable by as many people as possible. This means people who are new to computers, as well as expert users; people who use computers for enjoyment at home, and those who use them in the workplace; young people who have good eyesight, and people over 40 who need reading glasses. In this section, we discuss how the second principle of universal design, flexibility in use, has been incorporated in operating systems and how this benefits students with disabilities.

Flexibility in Use

The first guideline for the principle of flexibility in use encourages designers to make products that provide choice in methods of use. The developers of the most recent computer operating systems have adhered to this guideline, and it is manifested in

SIDEBAR

Windows Vista

Windows Vista, which became available in 2007, is the latest version of Microsoft's Windows operating system. Improvements in accessibility features in Windows Vista include the following:

- The Ease of Access Center, providing a centralized place to manage accessibility programs and adjust accessibility settings. This replaces the Accessibility Wizard and utility manager in previous Window versions.
- Expanded magnification capabilities to a maximum magnification of 16 times the original image
- Newly added speech recognition enabling users to enter text into documents such as e-mail and Web forms, as well as control applications and the operating system

One feature included in previous Windows versions that will no longer be available with the release of Vista is SerialKeys. SerialKeys allows alternative devices (e.g., augmentative communication devices) to be connected through the computer's serial port and to be used to access keyboard and mouse features. With Windows Vista, additional software will need to be installed in order to use alternative devices through the serial port.

having the choice of using either the mouse or the keyboard to control the computer. Being able to operate a computer solely using the keyboard may be surprising to many. Using the mouse to control and navigate computers is so common, comfortable, and familiar that many people assume it is the *only* option. However, both Macintosh and Windows operating systems offer keyboard shortcuts that provide access to all functions directly from the keyboard. For example, in Windows XP an item can be permanently deleted by pressing Shift + Delete, rather than by using the mouse to drag the item to the Recycle Bin.

Having the option to use the keyboard instead of the mouse provides computer access for users who find it difficult or impossible to control a mouse. This includes students with fine motor control difficulties, limited range of motion, or visual impairments that interfere with seeing or tracking the mouse pointer on the computer screen. An important consideration for students who use keyboard shortcuts is that this method places a considerable cognitive load on the students. They must remember a large number of keyboard shortcuts, and they must be able to read and understand a keyboard shortcut reference list so they can locate seldom used or forgotten commands.

The second guideline for the principle of flexibility in use calls for designers to accommodate left- and right-handed users. Both the Macintosh one-button mouse and the Microsoft two-button mouse are suitable for this purpose. Because Macintosh computers use a one-button mouse, a student can simply position the mouse on the side of the keyboard that is most convenient. At first glance the Microsoft two-button mouse may not seem to be designed for left-handed users because the left button controls the major mouse functions, a design suited for right-handed users. However, the functions of the two buttons can be switched using the Mouse Properties Control Panel in the Windows XP operating system (see

By making laptop computers available in a range of sizes, computer manufacturers adhere to the principles of universal design.

Photo by Ellen C. Farr

Figure 6.1). When the mouse is positioned to the left side of the computer the students can use their left index fingers because the right button now controls the major mouse functions. Thus, both the one-button mouse and the two-button mouse accommodate left- and right-handed users, and both mice meet the needs of students who may have only a left hand or who can control only left-hand movements well enough to use the mouse.

The third guideline of the principle of flexibility in use suggests designers take into account variations among the precision and accuracy of computer users. Both the Macintosh OS X and Windows XP operating systems incorporate this guideline by providing the means to enlarge the size of icons and slow down the speed of the mouse. Larger icons combined with a slower mouse speed make it possible for some students with disabilities to use a computer without the need to add specialized devices. For students who have hand-eye coordination problems, visual impairments, hand tremors, or cognitive disabilities, these two options are especially helpful.

The final flexibility-in-use guideline advises designers to provide adaptability to the user's pace. This has been incorporated in computer operating systems in a variety of ways and is exemplified in the control users have over certain mouse

FIGURE 6–1

Mouse properties control panel in Microsoft Windows XP

Source: Microsoft product screen shot reprinted with permission from Microsoft Corporation.

and keyboard features. In both operating systems users can adjust how fast the mouse pointer moves and the speed at which the button must be pressed to register a double-click. Slowing the mouse pointer speed may assist students who have difficulty with visual tracking; students who find it difficult to execute small, precise mouse movements; and students who need to look at the mouse while they move it and then need time to look up to the monitor to see where the mouse pointer is located. Increasing the speed at which the mouse pointer moves may benefit those with a limited range of motion as the mouse pointer will move a greater distance with each movement. Students who control the mouse pointer through the use of mouse emulators (alternative devices used to perform mouse functions) benefit from being able to select the mouse pointer speed that best meets their needs. Slowing down the double-click speed (i.e., increasing the amount of time between the two mouse clicks) may be helpful for students who have fine motor control issues.

Being able to make adjustments to the keyboard repeat rate is another illustration of adaptability to a user's pace. Users can adjust the delay before a key will start repeating and how fast it repeats once it starts. Increasing the delay before a key begins to repeat makes the computer more accessible for students who have fine motor control or other issues making it difficult to release a key after it has been selected. Slower repeat rates also benefit students who need to look at the keyboard as they type and have difficulty raising their heads to verify typing accuracy.

Table 6.1 provides a summary of the guidelines associated with the principle of flexibility in use, features, and the characteristics of students for whom the features may be beneficial. Remember that no operating system feature can meet the needs of every student with the characteristics listed in Table 6.1, and that these features may also benefit students with characteristics not mentioned.

Each of the four guidelines of the flexibility-in-use principle has resulted in operating system features that positively impact computer access for students with disabilities. These features were developed to increase usability and meet the needs of the general public, not just users with disabilities. However, there are certain features that are incorporated into operating systems especially to enable people with disabilities to use the computer; these are discussed in the following section.

ACCESSIBILITY FEATURES FOR USERS WITH DISABILITIES

The accessibility statements of Apple Inc. and Microsoft Corporation indicate that these producers of the two major computer operating systems are committed to promoting computer access for individuals with disabilities (Apple Inc., n.d.; Microsoft, n.d.). Both companies provide a variety of special features in their operating systems specifically to increase the usability of their products by people with physical disabilities, vision impairments or blindness, and hearing impairments or deafness. Most, but not all, of the accessibility features are found in what Macintosh OS X refers to as Universal Access and Windows XP refers to as Accessibility Options (see Figures 6.2 and 6.3). There are many similar features in both operating systems; however, the way they actually operate may differ. For example, both operating

TABLE 6–1   Operating system features adhering to flexibility-in-use principle

Flexibility-in-Use Guideline	Operating System Features	Student Characteristics
Provide choice in method of use	Control computer with mouse or keyboard	Keyboard use supports students who have • Poor fine motor control • Limited range of motion • Difficulty in visually tracking mouse pointer
Accommodate left- and right-handed users	One-button mouse; functions of the two-button mouse can be switched	Able to use only one hand
Take into account variations in precision and accuracy of mouse use	Enlarged icons	Low vision Visual perceptual issues Hand-eye coordination problems Hand tremors Poor fine motor control Cognitive deficits
Adaptability to user's pace	Set speed of mouse travel Set timing for double-click Set keyboard repeat delay Set keyboard repeat speed	**Increase** mouse speed for students with limited range of motion **Decrease** mouse speed for students with • Visual tracking difficulty • Poor fine motor control • Difficulty raising head to monitor the movement of the mouse pointer **Increase** repeat delay for students with • Poor fine motor control • Difficulty raising head to check for typing accuracy

systems provide screen magnification, but OS X magnifies the entire image on the screen whereas XP provides a small adjustable pane at the top of the screen where the image under the mouse cursor or the text near the insert cursor is magnified. The insert cursor is the blinking line that shows where text will be entered when the keyboard is used.

Keyboard Modifications and Mouse Control

Readily available keyboard modifications, used alone or in various combinations, can increase students' productivity and eliminate much of the frustration associated with using the standard keyboard and mouse. These modifications may eliminate the expense of purchasing specialized equipment and avoid drawing undue attention to students' disabilities through the use of that equipment. Many students with disabilities will be able to engage in computer-based activities using the same computer components as their typical peers.

FIGURE 6–2   Universal Access in Macintosh OS X

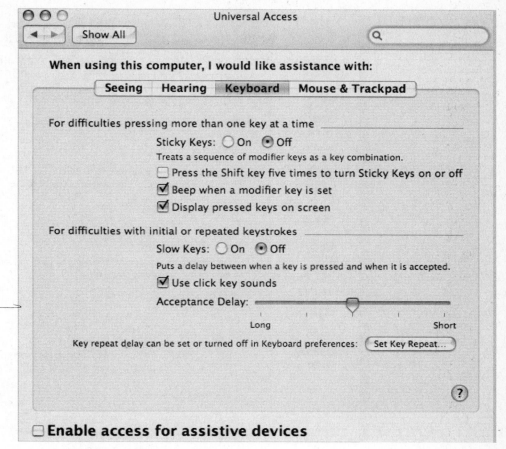

Source: Printed with permission of Apple Inc.

StickyKeys. StickyKeys allows students to press keys sequentially to execute functions that typically require pressing the keys simultaneously. With StickyKeys activated, the modifier keys (Shift, Control, Alt) respond as if they are held down until the next nonmodifier key is pressed. Students who are able to press only one key at a time can use keyboard shortcuts (e.g., Control + S to save, Control + C to copy) to access software program and operating system functions. This is enormously empowering because keyboard shortcuts can eliminate the need to use the mouse, which can be problematic for some students with disabilities.

Slow Keys. Slow Keys increases the amount of time a key must be depressed before registering a keystroke so that brief keystrokes will be ignored. This facilitates effective keyboarding for students who have difficulty releasing a key once they have applied pressure or students who may unintentionally put pressure on keys as their hands travel from one key to the next. Slow Keys is especially useful in increasing productivity by

FIGURE 6–3 Accessibility Options control panel in Microsoft Windows XP

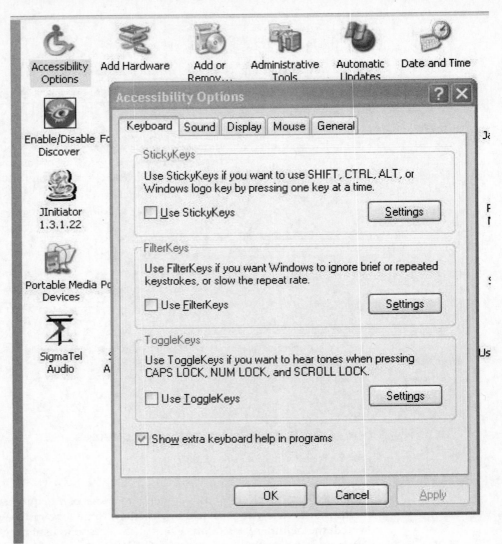

Source: Microsoft product screen shot reprinted with permission from Microsoft Corporation.

eliminating the frustrating sequence of typing too many letters, unintentionally erasing too many letters while trying to correct the original mistake, then retyping the desired letter. Students who may benefit from activating Slow Keys include those with hand tremors, muscle weakness or fatigue, and poor fine or gross motor control.

MouseKeys. MouseKeys is an accessibility feature that allows users to direct the mouse pointer and execute all mouse functions using the numeric keypad on the

FIGURE 6–4 MouseKeys

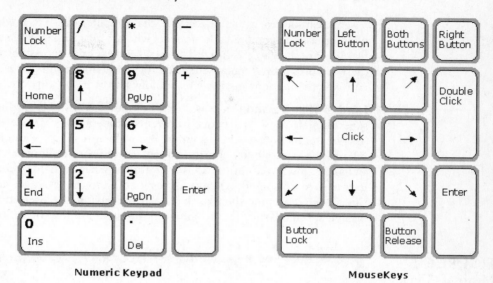

keyboard (Figure 6.4). Both the speed at which the mouse pointer travels and accelerates are adjustable to meet individual needs. MouseKeys gives students who can use a keyboard successfully, but not a mouse, the ability to direct the mouse pointer, click, double-click, and drag directly from the keyboard. They do not ever have to move the mouse.

Keyboard modifications and mouse control that are enabled via Universal Access or Accessibility Options enhance computer accessibility alone or in combination with keyboard adjustments made through the keyboard and mouse control panels. Considering the possible combinations of keyboard and mouse modifications and adjustments, it is easy to see that the needs of many students may be met by determining the appropriate configuration of features provided by computer operating systems.

Despite employing the modifications and adjustments already discussed, some students may continue to experience difficulty using the standard keyboard. If these students are able to use a mouse efficiently they may be able to utilize the On-Screen Keyboard available in the Windows operating system. The On-Screen Keyboard allows students to select a key simply by pointing and clicking on it. Those students who are unable to use a mouse may still be able to utilize the On-Screen Keyboard by setting the Typing mode to "Joystick or key to select." In this mode, pressing the spacebar activates scanning, which highlights each row in sequence. When the row with the desired key is highlighted the student presses the spacebar to select the row. Then each key in the row highlights in sequence, and the student presses the spacebar to select the key. The On-Screen Keyboard offers another option for computer accessibility for students with disabilities.

Modifications for Students with Sensory Impairments

Several features are available to make the computer easier to use for students who are blind or visually impaired and students who are deaf or hard of hearing. Many of these features are available through Universal Access and Accessibility Options. Utilizing these features may eliminate the need for or enhance computer accessibility in combination with additional assistive technology hardware or software (see Chapter 7).

Hard of Hearing and Deafness. The computer emits beeps, tones, and voiced messages to alert users to a variety of events; students who are hard of hearing or deaf may be unable to hear these sounds. Both Macintosh OS X and Microsoft Windows XP provide accessibility controls to replace auditory prompts and signals with visual signals, icons, or captions. So, for example, when a dialog box is displayed and a user tries to do something without responding to the message, rather than just emitting a beep to remind the user that he or she must make a selection, there would also be a visual signal such as a flashing caption bar, window, or desktop (see Figure 6.5).

FIGURE 6–5

Microsoft Windows XP Accessibility Options dialog box with Sound tab displayed

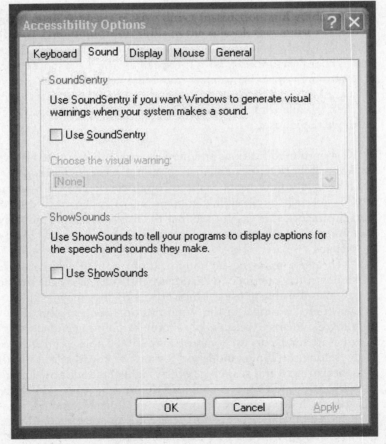

Source: Microsoft product screen shot reprinted with permission from Microsoft Corporation.

Visual Impairments or Blindness. Students with visual impairments often require a higher visual contrast and font size than the standard computer display provides in order to make text clearly discernible. This situation can be remedied using Universal Access or Accessibility Options to apply a high-contrast color scheme, black background with white lettering, or white background with black lettering. Selecting the high-contrast display option presents file, folder, program names, and menu bar items with a large font in the selected color scheme. The display settings apply not only to the desktop, but to programs as well. So, for example, if a student chooses a black background and white text, the menu bars of every program will use that high-contrast color scheme.

Both operating systems provide screen magnification for users with low vision. OS X magnifies the entire image on the screen from 2 to 16 times (see Figure 6.6). XP provides a small pane at the top of the screen where the image under the cursor is magnified from 2 to 9 times, whereas the rest of the screen image remains unchanged. These magnification ranges may meet the size enlargement needs of many students with vision impairments; however, remember that as the magnification is increased a smaller portion of the whole image is visible at one time. This may not interfere with understanding text-based items, but may make it difficult to comprehend graphic images.

Auditory signals can make the computer more user-friendly for students with visual impairments or blindness. Signals can be enabled by pressing the Caps Lock, Num Lock, and Scroll Lock keys. Slow Keys (discussed previously) can be set to give

FIGURE 6–6
Magnification in
Macintosh OS X

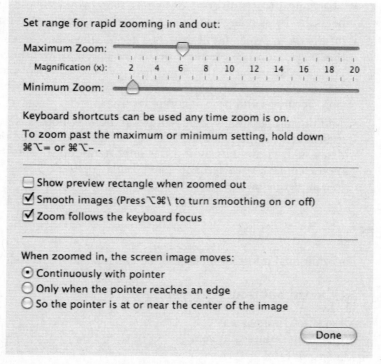

Source: Printed with permission of Apple Inc.

an auditory tone indicating a keystroke has been accepted. A StickyKeys (discussed previously) option provides an auditory tone whenever a modifier key (Shift, Alt, Ctrl) is pressed. The auditory signals help increase the accuracy of students' computer work and confidence in their accuracy.

Both Macintosh OS X and Windows XP provide voiced feedback to help students who have visual impairments or blindness utilize the computer. The voice feedback can read menu bars and menu items, inform users about the content of dialog boxes, and read text. Although both systems provide voiced feedback, just as with other accessibility items, the manner in which the voiced feedback is provided is different from one system to the other.

Finding the appropriate combination of general operating system and accessibility features is an important step in providing access to computer-based educational, recreational, and leisure activities. These features alone may be enough to meet the computer access needs of students with disabilities; however, they may need to be combined with assistive technology devices. Keep in mind the operating system features presented in this chapter as you read Chapter 7; the success of assistive technology devices often depends on the proper adjustments of the system features.

SUMMARY

- The concept of universal design is that products and environments should be usable by as many people as possible without the need for special adaptations.
- Of the seven principles of universal design, flexibility in use is most applicable to this discussion of computer design as it relates to students with disabilities. Programs adhering to this principle provide a variety of methods of use, accommodate right- and left-handed users, and provide for flexibility among the precision, accuracy, and pace of computer users.
- Additional operating system features in both Windows XP and Macintosh OS X that adhere to the flexibility-in-use principle provide additional support for students with disabilities. Both offer important adjustments such as keyboard and mouse control, voice feedback, and display options to assist users with disabilities in completing tasks more easily.

WEB RESOURCES

For additional information on the topics listed, go to the following websites:

Keyboard Shortcuts

Microsoft Windows XP
http://support.microsoft.com
Macintosh OSX
http://docs.info.apple.com/article.html?artnum=75459

Accessibility Options

Windows XP Accessibility Tutorials
http://www.microsoft.com/enable/training/windowsxp/default.aspx
Windows Vista Accessibility Improvements
http://www.microsoft.com/windows/products/windowsvista/features/details/
accessibility.mspx
Macintosh Universal Access
http://www.apple.com/macosx/features/universalaccess/

SUGGESTED ACTIVITIES

1. *Add to Your Portfolio.* Visit the Microsoft website (www.microsoft.com) and enter the phrase "accessibility options" in the search box. Review the resources located, then select relevant resources to add to your portfolio. Next, visit the Apple Inc. website (www.apple.com) and enter the phrase "universal access" in the search box. Review the resources identified and then select relevant resources to add to your portfolio.

2. *Use MouseKeys.* Log in to a desktop computer running a Windows or Macintosh operating system. Turn on MouseKeys through the Accessibility Control Panel (Windows 2000 or XP), Ease of Access Center (Windows Vista), or Universal Access in System Preferences (Macintosh OSX). Set aside the mouse, and use the numeric keypad instead to control the mouse. (Refer to Figure 6.4 for information on which keys correspond to specific mouse movements.) Open a browser, use MouseKeys to navigate to Favorites or Bookmarks, and select a website. Explore the site by using MouseKeys to follow links. If you prefer, navigate to the address bar and enter a URL. Open the Mouse Control Panel to change the speed of the mouse, and experiment with different mouse speeds. After a minimum of 10 minutes, turn off MouseKeys and write a two-page paper describing your experience with this feature and the insights you gained from this activity.

3. *Use High Contrast.* Log in to a computer running a Windows operating system. Locate the Accessibility Options through the Accessibility Control Panel (Windows 2000 or XP) or Ease of Access Center (Windows Vista). Explore the various High Contrast settings by selecting different settings and clicking Apply to activate them. Create a table detailing the features of the various high contrast appearance schemes.

4. *Explore Universal Design.* Explore the universal design publication list of the Center for Universal Design at North Carolina State University, http://www .design.ncsu.edu/cud/pubs_p/pud.htm. Read at least four of the case studies in the section titled "Case Studies on Universal Design." Then write a two-page paper identifying the case studies you read and discussing the impact universal design has on people with disabilities and others.

5. *Use the Accessibility Wizard.* Use the Microsoft Windows Accessibility Wizard to see how to configure the computer to meet individual user needs. From the Start

menu, select Programs; select Accessories, then Accessibility, and finally Accessibility Wizard. Read the information and answer the questions in each dialog box. Keep a written record of the questions, and your answer choices. When you have answered all the questions, the Accessibility Wizard dialog box displays the changes that have been made to the system. Record the list of changes. Repeat this procedure at least two more times. When you have finished experimenting with the Accessibility Wizard, write a two-page paper discussing your experience, the pros and cons of using the Accessibility Wizard versus setting individual accessibility options through the control panel, and what individuals might find the Accessibility Wizard most helpful. Submit the narrative along with your written records of questions, answers, and changes that were made.

REFERENCES

Apple Inc. (n.d.). *Accessibility statement.* Retrieved from http://www.apple.com/accessibility

Center for Universal Design. (1997). *About universal design.* Retrieved from http://www.design.ncsu.edu/cud/about_ud/about_ud.htm

Microsoft. (n.d.). *Accessibility statement.* Retrieved from http://www.microsoft.com/enable/

CHAPTER **7**

Assistive Technology for Computer Access

FOCUS QUESTIONS

1. What is the assistive technology continuum, and what is its significance?

2. What are the major types of alternative keyboards, and what are the characteristics of students for whom each type would be appropriate?

3. What are the major types of mouse emulators, and what are the characteristics of students for whom each type would be appropriate?

4. How can alternative input and output devices make the computer accessible for students with vision impairments and blindness?

INTRODUCTION

Chapter 6 presented operating system features that help provide computer access to students with disabilities; however, some students require additional adaptations to be successful computer users. As stated in Chapter 1, the assistive technology that facilitates computer access for these students exists on a continuum from low tech to high tech (Blackhurst, 1997). This chapter presents technology covering the full range of the assistive technology continuum beginning with the low-tech end. This is the point at which technology consideration should begin, progressing to mid-tech and high-tech solutions only if student needs remain unmet. This chapter describes only suggestions or guidelines. With assistive technology there are no hard and fast rules; the most appropriate device must be determined through careful evaluation and actual usage. Principles guiding the selection process are discussed in Chapter 8.

LOW-TECH ADAPTATIONS FOR COMPUTER USE

Low-tech adaptations use no electronic components and are relatively low-cost items. Universal design features and accessibility features discussed in Chapter 6 have increased computer accessibility and have replaced the need for some low-tech adaptations such as devices to physically hold down the Shift or other modifier keys. However, low-tech assistive technology devices such as keyboard labels, selecting/pointing

TABLE 7–1 Low-tech adaptations

Low-Tech Adaptations	Types	Student Characteristics
Keyboard labels	Larger letters High-contrast colors Braille Blank	Have visual/perceptual issues Have low vision Read Braille Have cognitive deficits Have visual/perceptual issues Have attention issues
Selecting/Pointing devices	Handheld Mouthsticks Chinsticks Headsticks	Can control upper extremities but are unable to isolate finger Cannot use hands but have good head control
Keyguards	Acrylic Metal	Need targeting assistance Use selecting/pointing device Need hand support
Moisture guards	Transparent—long-term use Transparent—disposable Printed with key labels	Have a tendency to spill and/or drool Have a tendency to spill and/or drool Have visual/perceptual issues Have low vision

devices, keyguards, moisture guards, magnifying lenses, and equipment to position computer components still play a vital role in providing computer access for individuals with disabilities. Table 7.1 lists low-tech adaptations, features, and the characteristics of students for whom the devices may be beneficial.

Keyboard Labels

Some students have difficulty using the standard keyboard because they cannot see the letters, numbers, and symbols on the keys. The standard keyboard can be customized to meet individual needs by affixing a variety of self-adhesive keyboard labels. Labels with larger letters and higher contrast (e.g., white letters on a black background) may meet the needs of students with visual-perceptual difficulties or those with low vision. Tactile labels with Braille markings make the computer keyboard accessible for students who are Braille readers. Blank keyboard labels can be used to cover nonessential keys, making the keyboard less confusing and visually distracting. Blank labels may make the keyboard more accessible for students with cognitive deficits and those with visual-perceptual or attention issues.

Selecting/Pointing Devices

Some students who have physical disabilities cannot isolate a finger or use their hand at all to press a single key on the standard keyboard. Selecting/pointing devices make that possible. These devices may be controlled by hand movement or movement of the

USER PROFILE: Jade

Jade is a 9-year-old girl with cerebral palsy. An assistive technology evaluation was requested by her school district. Reports indicated that a variety of assistive devices had already been tried, but nothing worked. When Jade tried to use an alternative keyboard she hit more than one key. She could isolate and point her index finger to some degree, but when she selected a letter her other fingers invariably pressed other keys as well. She was unable to curl her other fingers tightly enough to avoid the unintentional keystroke. When Jade grasped an ordinary marker in a loose fist she was able to select only one letter at a time. This was the first part of her computer access solution; however, she could not consistently select the key she wanted. When a keyguard was affixed to the keyboard, Jade's accuracy increased significantly. The combination of a keyguard with a pointing/selecting device gave Jade a reliable method of accessing the computer, and therefore, access to a wealth of educational opportunities.

Person typing with a low-tech dowel and keyguard
Photo by Tammy Cordwell

head. Mouthsticks, headsticks, and chinsticks are controlled with head movement. Both headsticks and chinsticks require a headpiece to hold the selecting/pointing device in position. These devices may be purchased from commercial vendors, but are often homemade using dowel rods of varying lengths and diameters with pencil erasers affixed to the end. Items such as a thick marker or pencil may be used as a handheld selecting/pointing device. Students who benefit from selecting/pointing devices are those who can control their upper extremities, but are unable to point a finger to select a key, or students who have good head control, but limited ability to use their upper extremities. Sometimes a selecting/pointing device is the only assistive technology needed, but it may be just one part of a computer access solution.

Keyguards

Keyguards are acrylic or metal covers with holes for each of the keys that are placed atop the computer keyboard. Keyguards are available ready-made for many keyboards and can be custom-made to fit any keyboard. Keyguards increase typing accuracy because the holes allow only one key at a time to be pressed. Students using a selecting/pointing device or those with poor fine motor control find it easier to target specific, individual keys. Students who experience hand or arm fatigue can rest their hand on the keyguard when selecting keys, and if necessary, slide their hands across the keyguard to get from one key to the next. The keyguard prevents unintended keystrokes from registering.

Moisture Guards

Moisture guards, also known as keyboard protectors or keyboard skins, are flexible, polyurethane covers that fit over the keyboard to protect it from moisture, dirt, dust, or other damaging substances. Moisture guards can be completely transparent allowing the lettering on the keys to show through, or they may incorporate large-print, high-contrast key labels. Most moisture guards are designed for long-term use, but disposable moisture guards are available as well. Students who drool or have a tendency to spill or drop things may require a moisture guard to facilitate successful computer use. The type of moisture guard that is most appropriate will depend on the specific characteristics of the student and whether the keyboard is used by multiple users. For example, a moisture guard with high-contrast key labels would be appropriate for a student who drools and has low vision. However, if the keyboard is frequently shared with other students then it may be more appropriate to put high-contrast labels directly on the keys and use a transparent, disposable keyboard skin.

ALTERNATE INPUT DEVICES

Mouse Alternatives

Macintosh OSX, Windows XP, and Windows Vista feature a graphical user interface (GUI). With the introduction of GUI operating systems, computer use became easier for the general public. No longer did users have to memorize and type in commands; they could simply position the mouse pointer on what they desired and double-click. For computer users with physical disabilities or vision impairments, however, a GUI often presents a challenge—controlling the mouse pointer. As discussed in Chapter 6, one possible solution to accessing operating system features is to use keyboard shortcuts in place of a mouse.

However, there are many reasons why keyboard shortcuts, or keyboard shortcuts alone, will not meet the needs of all students: (1) Remembering operating system shortcuts can be extremely challenging or impossible for many students. (2) Once students have accessed the software program that they want to work with, they may discover that the program does not respond to keyboard shortcuts or only certain features are available with keyboard shortcuts. (3) Students who use a wide variety of software programs face the difficult task of recalling the keyboard shortcuts specific to each program. (4) Keyboard shortcuts fail to serve the needs of students who cannot use a keyboard or who cannot clearly see images on the monitor. This section discusses mouse alternatives, also called mouse emulators, that enable students with physical disabilities to use their most reliable, controllable movements to direct the mouse pointer. (Special software designed to meet the needs of students with vision impairments and blindness is discussed in the sections on screen magnification and screen readers.)

Trackballs

It is helpful to think of a trackball as a mouse lying on its back. The base of the trackball remains in one place; to move the mouse pointer, the ball is rotated with a thumb, fingers, the palm of the hand, a foot, or other body part. Trackballs usually have one to three buttons positioned near the ball that function just like mouse buttons (Webopedia, 2001). A variety of trackballs are available to meet a wide range of individual needs. Most are designed for the general public to make computing tasks faster or more convenient, but they may also be appropriate for individuals with disabilities. Other trackballs are designed *especially* for individuals with disabilities, and these are the focus of this discussion.

Although each feature of a trackball is important in determining its appropriateness for students with disabilities, the size of the roller ball and the position or protection of the buttons are foremost concerns. Trackballs can be divided into three categories according to their size: (1) mini-trackballs, (2) standard trackballs, and (3) large trackballs. Mini-trackballs work well for users with very good fine motor control and for those who have a very limited range of motion (e.g., a student with muscular dystrophy). The Mini-Trackball (IBS Electronics) is a good example; the entire trackball measures just 1 inch by 2 inches so the roller ball itself is quite small and can be manipulated with the movement of a single finger or very slight hand movement. Standard trackballs are useful for students with a wide range of fine motor control. They require a greater range of motion than a mini-trackball but can be operated with a whole hand, a fist, a single finger, or a selecting/pointing device such as a headstick. Large trackballs, such as BIGtrack (Keytools) with a three-inch roller ball, may be appropriate for younger students, those with poor fine motor control in their upper extremities, and those who use a foot to operate the trackball.

The position of the buttons on the trackball makes a trackball accessible or inaccessible to students with disabilities. The buttons must be positioned so the student can easily reach and press them, but not in a position that subjects them to unintentional presses. In fact, as you will see in the following discussion, accessibility and protection of the buttons are key features that distinguish trackballs designed for users with disabilities from those designed for the general public.

We stated that keyguards are useful for students who experience hand or arm fatigue because they can rest their hand on the keyguard when selecting keys without initiating unintentional keypresses. The same solution can be applied to protecting the buttons of a trackball: a keyguard (which may also be referred to as a handguard or fingerguard) is positioned on the trackball. Holes cut in the acrylic allow students to rotate the ball and to access the buttons when they are ready to press them. To use a trackball with a handguard, such as the Penny & Giles Trackball, students need to have an appropriate range of motion and be able to isolate a finger or use a selecting/pointing device to reach into the holes and press the buttons.

A variety of switch-adapted trackballs are available to address difficulty students may have with pressing the buttons to execute mouse functions. Sometimes the buttons are too small, sometimes they are not in a position that students can reach, or students may not be able to hold down the button and move the ball at the same time

This adapted trackball has a keyguard and separate buttons for click, double click, click and drag.

Reprinted with permission from Traxsys Input Products.

to be able to drag. Switch-adapted trackballs have receptacles into which switches can be connected. Once connected, the switches are positioned so they are easy to press with either the same body part that is used to move the roller ball or another body part. Each switch executes a different mouse function (i.e., right-click, left-click, double-click, or drag-lock). The buttons on some of the switch-adapted trackballs remain active when the switches are connected, whereas in others the buttons are deactivated when the switches are connected. Deactivating the buttons eliminates unintentional presses and may be helpful when trying to teach trackball skills; the switches can be presented only when the mouse pointer has reached the desired position. This may be especially valuable when working with students who have cognitive impairments, students who might perseverate on pressing buttons, or students with attention issues.

Joysticks

Joysticks are similar to trackballs in that they provide a stationary base; however, in place of a ball set into the base, joysticks offer a moveable handle that is perpendicular (or almost perpendicular) to the base. Joystick handles do not need to be moved very far to direct the mouse pointer to any spot on the computer monitor, so they may be a good solution for students who have a limited range of motion.

The accessibility and protection of the buttons are key to usability of joysticks, just as they are for trackballs. Buttons must be positioned so they are not accidentally pressed while moving the joystick handle but are still within reach of the student. A keyguard can facilitate joystick use by making it possible for students to rest their hands on the base without activating any of the buttons.

Several joysticks—such as SAM (Switch-Adapted Mouse) Joystick (RJ Cooper & Associates) and Penny & Giles Joystick—offer features geared toward enabling students with disabilities to control the mouse pointer. Adapted joysticks may include one or more of the following features: special handles to accommodate different grasping abilities, keyguards (as mentioned previously) to prevent accidental clicking, a drag-lock button so the button does not need to be held down while moving the handle, and switch receptacles that provide switch access to button functions. Adapted joysticks may be plug-and-play (simply plug them in and they are ready to go) or software may need to be installed so the computer will translate the joystick movements and button presses into mouse movements and button clicks.

Touch Screens

Touch screens, also called touch windows, provide computer input by a direct touch to the computer monitor. These are commonplace in today's society; they are often used at information kiosks and to complete transactions at automated teller machines (ATMs). Whereas the touch screens we see in the community are integrated into the computer display, there are also touch screens that can easily be

Student accessing a computer with an adapted joystick

Photo by Deborah A. Newton

added to existing monitors. The TouchWindow by Riverdeep is an add-on touch screen available to fit either 15-inch or 17-inch monitors. They are a very direct, almost intuitive way to interact with the computer—you reach out and touch what you want to select. It is the directness and intuitiveness of touch screens that make them an appropriate computer input device for many young children, students with severe disabilities, and students with autism. They are often used to establish cause and effect; that is, to teach students that what they do has a direct result: A point causes the computer to react.

Head Pointing Systems

Just as head-controlled pointing devices (e.g., headsticks and mouthsticks) can provide access to the standard keyboard, head-controlled devices can be used to position the mouse pointer and access all mouse functions. For mouse control, however, the devices are high tech—the opposite end of the assistive technology continuum. They are sophisticated electronic devices that are relatively expensive.

Head pointing systems are available for both desktop and laptop computers. Typically, one component of the system sits on top of the computer monitor, and the student wears the other component. The location of the wearable component depends on the specific system. The device on top of the monitor tracks the movement of the student's head from the signals it receives from the wearable component. The wearable component may be a type of headset or a piece of special reflective material (usually a dot) placed on the forehead, the rim of eyeglasses, or the brim of a hat. Infrared or optical sensors detect the position and movement of the reflective material.

A head pointing system, like a standard mouse, requires the student to execute a left-click, right-click, and/or double-click. The mouse clicks can be accomplished by activating a switch with some part of the body or with special software that interprets dwelling (remaining at a certain spot for a specified length of time) as a click. Students using a head pointing system would be likely to use an on-screen keyboard for word processing. On-screen keyboard programs are available with dwell selection options; users select letters by holding the mouse pointer on the letters for a predetermined amount of time.

Head pointing systems are an option for students who cannot use their hands for operating the mouse, including students with cerebral palsy, muscular dystrophy, and spinal cord injuries, among others. Being able to see and follow the movement of the mouse pointer on the monitor and having good head control are prerequisites for using a head pointing system. Students must be capable of moving their heads in small increments for precise positioning and keeping their heads still when necessary. Students also must be able to manage multiple programs simultaneously, including combinations of dwell-clicking software, on-screen keyboard programs, and computer applications such as word processing programs or Internet browsers.

Eye-Gaze Systems

Eye-gaze systems utilize the movements of students' eyes to direct the mouse pointer. Eye-gaze systems use an infrared-sensitive video camera, or several, to determine where a student is looking and then position the mouse pointer at that spot. Most systems provide on-screen grids or on-screen keyboards that the user looks at to select letters, words, or computer functions. Some systems position the devices(s) on the computer monitor, whereas others mount the eye tracking devices on eyeglasses or goggles. Depending on the eye-gaze system, clicking is accomplished by using a switch, dwelling, or blinking the eye.

Using the eye movement to direct the mouse pointer may provide computer access for people who have no reliable muscle movements but good voluntary control over their eyes. Students who have muscular dystrophy, spinal muscular atrophy, high-level spinal cord injuries, or brainstem strokes (which can result in "locked-in syndrome") may be candidates for this access method. To be successful with an eye gaze system, students must have adequate vision and must be able to control their eye movements, including moving them in small increments and focusing on one spot; they cannot have continuous, uncontrolled head movement. Eye-gaze system users must be able to understand and manage the system and the computer applications they are using simultaneously.

Table 7.2 lists mouse alternatives, features, and the characteristics of students for whom the devices may be beneficial.

TABLE 7–2   Mid-tech to high-tech mouse alternatives

Mouse Alternatives	Types	Student Characteristics
Trackballs	Mini-trackballs	Have good fine motor control but have a limited range of motion
	Standard trackballs	Have a greater range of motion
		Have moderate fine motor skills
		Have good gross motor skills
	Large trackballs	Are young
		Have poor fine motor skills
		Operate the trackball with feet
	Adapted trackballs	Have poor fine motor skills
		Need to rest wrist on a keyguard
Joysticks	Software that converts game joystick input to mouse control	Can control a standard, game joystick
	Adapted joysticks	Need to use switches to click
		Need a keyguard
		Need to operate the joystick with a body part other than hand
Touch screens	Integrated touch screens	Are young
	Add-on touch screens	Need to learn cause and effect
		Need a direct, intuitive interface
Head pointing systems	Headset and reflective dot	Cannot use hands
		Can see and follow the movement of the mouse pointer
		Have good head control
Eye-gaze systems	Camera(s) on monitor and eyeglasses or goggles	Cannot use hands or head
		Can control eye movements

Alternative Keyboards

Many times the word *keyboard* invokes an image of the standard computer keyboard with the keys approximately one-half-inch square and a QWERTY (named for the first six letters of the top row of letters) arrangement. The standard QWERTY keyboard works well for most students; however, many students with disabilities are unable to use the standard keyboard and alternatives must be found. There are a wide variety of alternative keyboards that make the computer accessible to almost every student. These keyboards fall into the major categories of expanded keyboards, mini-keyboards, one-handed keyboards, and on-screen keyboards. Each of these categories is discussed in detail in the following text, including the students for whom each type of keyboard is most appropriate.

Expanded Keyboards

Expanded keyboards, also referred to as enlarged or oversized keyboards, are exactly what they sound like—keyboards that offer a larger surface area than the standard keyboard. They are beneficial to students with poor fine motor control who need a large target area to execute an accurate keystroke whether they are using their hand, foot, or typing aid. To be successful with expanded keyboards students must have a range of motion sufficient to access all the keys. Students with vision impairments who cannot learn to touch-type and who require large key labels to assist with identifying specific keys may also benefit from expanded keyboards.

Expanded keyboards differ from one another in overall size, key size, keyboard layout, and functionality. Despite variations in the overall size of expanded keyboards, as well as the size of the keys, they are all larger and offer keys that are larger than the standard keyboard. Some expanded keyboards provide the QWERTY arrangement, whereas others use an alphabetical layout. Other expanded keyboards come with sets of overlays, which are preprinted keyboard layouts that can be easily substituted for the standard QWERTY overlay. IntelliKeys (IntelliTools) is a popular expanded keyboard that uses overlays (see Figure 7.1). Students can use the overlay that most closely meets their needs. Selection of the optimal layout depends on many factors including the cognitive ability, prior familiarity with the QWERTY layout, programs being used, and students' desire to use keyboards similar to their typical peers.

FIGURE 7–1
IntelliKeys with
ABC overlay

Source: Imagery provided courtesy of IntelliTools®, Inc.

One difference in keyboard functionality is the tactile and/or auditory feedback that a student receives when making a keystroke. An expanded keyboard may function similarly to a standard keyboard, and students will be able to feel the key move downward when they press on it. This provides tactile feedback indicating a key has been selected. Other expanded keyboards feature a flat membrane surface. Pressure on the key registers a keystroke but there is no movement of the key, so no tactile feedback is received. Students must depend on auditory feedback to be sure a keystroke has registered. We discuss other differences in functionality in the section on customizable keyboards.

Mini-Keyboards

Mini-keyboards, as the name implies, are keyboards that are substantially smaller than the standard keyboard. In general, mini-keyboards are beneficial for students with motor impairments that (1) restrict range of motion, making it difficult or impossible to access all the keys on the standard keyboard; and (2) have good accuracy within a narrow range of motion. This applies to students who are using their fingers as well as to students who are using selecting/pointing devices such as mouthsticks or headsticks. Mini-keyboards may also be effective computer input devices for students who have use of only one hand (see the section One-Handed Keyboards).

These keyboards differ from one another in overall size of the keyboard, key size, keyboard layout, and functionality. In comparison to the standard QWERTY keyboard, mini-keyboards are smaller in both overall size and the size of the keys. They

Tash USB Mini-Keyboard
Courtesy of Tash, Inc.

are available in the QWERTY layout and also in frequency-of-use layouts, which place the letters used most often toward the center of the keyboard. Selection of the appropriate layout must be made on a case-by-case basis depending on the needs of the individual student. Students already familiar with the QWERTY layout may prefer to continue to use it. However, students who are just learning to keyboard may have no preference and would be open to a frequency-of-use layout that increases the speed of text entry or reduces fatigue.

Some mini-keyboards function in the same way as a standard keyboard—that is, keys must be physically depressed. Other mini-keyboards offer a pressure-sensitive membrane surface that responds to very light pressure. There is even a mini-keyboard that requires no pressure at all; to operate the Magic Wand Keyboard (In Touch Systems) students touch the keyboard with the accompanying hand wand or mouth wand. Tactile and auditory feedback varies from one mini-keyboard to the next. Those that do not require physically depressing a key will usually provide an auditory tone that signals a keystroke has registered.

One-Handed Keyboards

A variety of keyboard options are available for those who have good finger dexterity and use of one hand. As previously mentioned, a mini-keyboard is one option; other one-handed keyboarding options include half-QWERTY keyboards, one-handed Dvorak keyboards, and chorded keyboards. Each type of keyboard provides full keyboard functionality and permits students to type without having to look at the keyboard. To use a half-QWERTY keyboard students must have good dexterity in one hand. They place this hand on the home row keys just as they would if they were going to touch-type in the traditional manner. The letters that are typically typed with that hand are typed as usual. To type the letters that are typed with the other hand, the student holds down the spacebar and the keyboard responds as if the other hand is being used. Each key on the keyboard is capable of entering two different letters, one when the key is pressed alone and another when it is pressed in conjunction with the spacebar. For example, a student using his or her right hand would use the right index finger in the home row position to type a "j." To type an "f" the student would hold down the spacebar with the thumb and use the index finger on the j key because the f key is pressed with the index finger of the left hand.

Half-QWERTY keyboards can have the physical appearance of a standard keyboard and serve the needs of both left-handed and right-handed typists; the student simply uses the appropriate side of the keyboard. Half-QWERTY keyboards are also available that are just the half of the keyboard that the user requires. In the classroom setting, for a computer that is shared among all the students, the full keyboard may be the better option because it can be used by two-handed typists as well as students who keyboard with one hand. Aside from being able to share the computer more easily, the keyboard has a more typical appearance, which is important to many students.

Access to a Dvorak keyboard layout can be provided in a variety of ways (see Figure 7.2). First, there are Dvorak keyboards that are hardwired and replace the

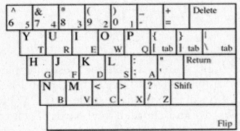 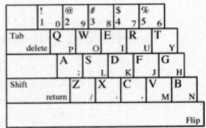

Half-QWERTY Keyboard

Used with permission from Matias (http://half-qwerty.com/).

standard keyboard; no software is needed. A hardwired keyboard is a good solution for students needing to use computers in more than one location. Students can bring their keyboards with them, plug them in, and be ready to go. Next, there are keyboards with keys labeled to represent the Dvorak layout that require installing software in order for the keyboard to function. The least costly option for one-handed typists is using one of the Dvorak keyboard layouts that are available free of charge from Microsoft and Apple Inc. There are Dvorak keyboard layouts for typists who use only the left hand and for typists who use only the right hand. In both layouts, the keys are arranged to facilitate touch-typing. If this method is selected the keys will need to be relabeled, perhaps by using stick-on key labels.

Chorded keyboards have an appearance that is markedly different from standard keyboards. Rather than presenting the array of keys found on a typical keyboard, a chorded keyboard has very few keys. Chorded keyboards are available for either the left hand or right hand. Students place a finger on each of the keys on the keyboard, and their fingers remain in the same position, except for the thumb. The thumb is used to press several different keys. All of the functions of the standard keyboard are available from the chorded keyboard by pressing the keys in various combinations, analogous to playing musical chords. Each letter is formed by pressing the correct

FIGURE 7–2 Dvorak keyboard

combination of keys. Good dexterity is needed for chorded keyboarding as well as good memory skills because the user must remember the various key combinations.

On-Screen Keyboards

On-screen keyboards, such as the Discover:Screen 2.0 (Madentec Limited), place an image of the keyboard on the computer monitor. Letters and functions are selected by clicking on them with a mouse or any of the mouse emulators (mouse alternatives) discussed previously. Once students position the mouse pointer on the key they want, they simply click the mouse to select it. If they are unable to click a mouse, a dwell selection is frequently an option. When the mouse pointer is positioned on a letter and allowed to remain, or dwell, on the key for a user-defined amount of time, a keystroke registers.

On-screen keyboards provide computer access for students who do not have the motor skills necessary to utilize the keyboard but can control a mouse emulator such as a joystick, trackball, or a head-controlled mouse (see mouse alternatives

USER PROFILE: Danny

Danny, a high school student, provides a good example of this last scenario. His right hand was severely burned in a fire. During the healing process he was wearing a pressure bandage to help reduce scarring, and because he was right-handed he was unable to write. Although this was a temporary problem, Danny needed a way to take notes and keep up with his schoolwork until he could use his right hand again. During an assistive technology assessment, Danny tried various standard and alternative keyboards but had a great deal of difficulty locating the letters he wanted. This made typing with his left hand slow and arduous. An on-screen keyboard was presented during the assessment, and Danny was quickly able to locate the keys he wanted. Despite the pressure bandage, he was able to control a mouse with his right hand and could quickly and easily navigate from key to key. An on-screen keyboard was just what he needed.

already discussed). They also help students who have difficulty visually refocusing when they transfer their attention from the monitor to the keyboard.

Customizable Keyboards

Customizable or programmable keyboards can be configured to meet students' individual needs; that is, the keyboard can be told what text to enter or what commands to execute when keys are pressed. So, for example, a single key could be programmed to enter a letter, word, phrase, or sentence with one stroke. It could enter the closing to a letter, leave space for a signature, and send the letter for printing—all with a single keystroke. There are three basic types of customizable keyboards: (1) standard QWERTY-type keyboards with additional programmable keys, (2) customizable keyboards utilizing interchangeable overlays, and (3) customizable on-screen keyboards.

Just like the standard QWERTY keyboard, standard customizable keyboards come with a fixed number and placement of keys. These keyboards vary in the number of keys that can be programmed and in the placement of the programmable keys. To register keystrokes students must be able to depress the keys.

Customizable keyboards that employ interchangeable keyboard layouts (e.g., IntelliKeys) will usually come with a variety of preprinted, preprogrammed overlays (see Figures 7.1 and 7.3). If one of the supplied overlays is appropriate for a student, the overlay is simply placed on the keyboard. Special coding on the overlay may allow it to automatically be recognized or the user may have to let the keyboard know which overlay is being used. (The manner in which this is done depends on the specific keyboard.) Companion software empowers users to create their own layouts that can be configured precisely to meet their needs. In addition to being able to specify what happens when a key is pressed, the number, size, spacing, and position of the keys are customizable as well.

On-screen customizable keyboards are simply on-screen keyboards (as already discussed) that can be adapted to the needs of individual students. The degree to which these keyboards can be customized varies greatly. Most on-screen keyboards are customizable to some degree, providing the flexibility to change such things as the key size, color, and font. Many offer a variety of on-screen layouts from which to choose and the ability to tailor those to student needs. The most customizable provide the option of changing the size, color, font, number, function, placement, and auditory feedback of the keys; they also provide the option of creating a custom keyboard from scratch. As with programmable keyboards, the keys of some on-screen keyboard arrays can contain words, phrases, sentences, or computer commands.

Students who can use a standard keyboard—but need to be able to do a limited number of tasks or enter a limited number of selected words, phrases, or sentences with a single keystroke—might find a standard-type programmable keyboard suits their needs. Students for whom an expanded keyboard may work with just a few alterations are good candidates for keyboards with interchangeable, customizable overlays. These keyboards are also appropriate for students with cognitive deficits who might benefit from using a keyboard featuring only the keys they

FIGURE 7–3
IntelliKeys with
math overlay

need to operate a particular program (e.g., the numbers in order from 1 to 10). Students with learning disabilities who find the standard keyboard too visually confusing or distracting may be more successful with an overlay that eliminates keys they would seldom, if ever, use (e.g., the F keys, Print Screen, Scroll Lock, Pause/Break).

There are several advantages to having a keyboard with a broad range of customizable features. Most important, it is possible to tailor the keyboard to a student's individual needs. In classrooms where students have differing computer access needs, a customizable keyboard may be able to meet the needs of a number of students.

Several points must be considered when choosing a customizable keyboard. First, the students are the users of the finished product. Most likely a teacher, therapist, parent, or other person will need to customize the keyboard for the student, so time must be devoted to learning how to make the modifications. The second consideration is that finding just the right settings requires time and patience, both the teacher's and the student's. The adage, "If at first you don't succeed, try, try again," is fitting. It may take many adjustments and much fine-tuning to get things just right. Table 7.3 lists alternative keyboards, features, and the characteristics of students for whom the devices may be beneficial.

TABLE 7–3 Mid-tech to high-tech alternative keyboards

Alternative Keyboard	Types	Student Characteristics
Expanded keyboards	QWERTY layout	Have poor fine motor control Need a large target area Are familiar with the QWERTY layout Want a layout similar to typical peers
	Alphabetical layout	Have poor fine motor control Need a large target area Are young Have cognitive deficits
	Overlays	Have poor fine motor control Need a large target area Require nonstandard layout (e.g., numbers overlay) Share a keyboard with students who have different needs
Mini-keyboards	QWERTY layout	Have restricted range of motion Can use only one hand Have good targeting skills Are familiar with the QWERTY layout Want a layout similar to typical peers
	Frequency-of-use layout	Have restricted range of motion Can use only one hand Have good targeting skills Need to increase keyboarding speed Are willing to learn frequency-of-use layout
One-handed keyboards	Half-QWERTY	Have good dexterity in one hand Are familiar with the QWERTY layout
	One-handed Dvorak	Have good dexterity in one hand Are willing to learn Dvorak layout
	Chorded keyboards	Have good dexterity in one hand Have no, or almost no, range of motion Can remember the chords
On-screen keyboards		Cannot use a keyboard Can control a mouse or mouse emulator Find it easier to locate keys on-screen than on a keyboard
Customizable keyboards	QWERTY keyboards with programmable keys Customizable-interchangeable overlays	Can use a standard keyboard Need access to a limited number of customized tasks or commands Need modifications to standard overlays Have cognitive deficits Find the standard keyboard too confusing or distracting
	Customizable on-screen keyboards	Cannot use a keyboard Can control a mouse or mouse emulator Find it easier to locate keys on-screen than on a keyboard Need modifications to provided layouts Have cognitive deficits Find the standard keyboard too confusing or distracting

Single Switches for Scanning and Morse Code

Some students who have severe physical disabilities do not have enough motor control to use any of the access methods discussed previously. If, however, they can reliably control a single movement such as flexing a fist, turning a head to one side, or pressing a foot, they may be able to access a computer using a single switch with scanning. To understand single-switch scanning it is necessary to understand how the terms *switch* and *scanning* are used in this context.

Single switches are hardware devices that send signals to the computer to emulate various computer inputs such as a mouse click or an Enter command. Switches come in a wide variety of shapes and sizes and can be activated by almost any deliberate action. Many switches are activated by being pressed with hands, feet, elbows, heads, or other body parts. Other switches are activated in a variety of ways including pulling, squeezing, blinking an eye, or sipping and puffing.

Scanning refers to a selection method in which a highlighter moves from item to item in an on-screen array provided by a software program. Figure 7.4 shows an on-screen array in Discover Envoy (Madentec Limited). The student monitors the highlighter as it moves from item to item. When the highlighter is on the item that the student desires, the student activates the switch to select the item. The computer then performs as if it received conventional input (i.e., as if the keyboard or mouse had been used). On-screen arrays can be used to do anything a keyboard or mouse can do—access operating system functions, surf the Internet, and enter text into word processing or other software programs.

An interface device of some type is needed to connect the switch to the computer. The device may be designed solely for the purpose of accommodating use of a

Sample switches from AbleNet, Inc.

Courtesy of AbleNet, Inc.

FIGURE 7–4
The Discover Envoy (Madentec) scanning array. First groups of letters are highlighted. After the user selects a letter group, the program scans each individual letter.

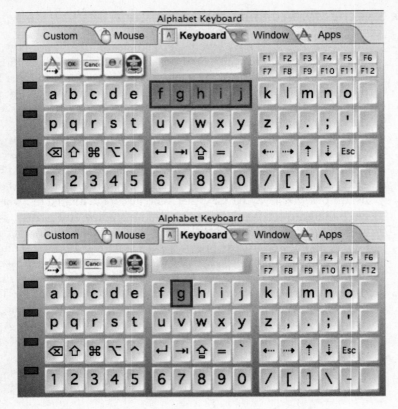

Source: Courtesy of Madentec Limited.

switch or may be a mouse, joystick, or other item through which a switch may be connected. The interface device, along with the software providing the on-screen array, determines the way the computer responds to switch activations. For example, switch activation may cause the computer to respond as if the mouse button had been clicked, the Return key had been pressed, a letter key had been pressed, or a sequence of keys had been pressed to enter a computer command or string of text, or a variety of other responses.

There are several software programs that are programmed to support single-switch scanning and provide on-screen scanning arrays. Many on-screen keyboards (discussed previously) have a scanning option. All these programs come with at least one premade array, usually a representation of the standard QWERTY keyboard, and many come with multiple arrays. Some programs allow for extensive modifications to premade arrays, whereas others allow none, or only minor modifications. Programs offering the most flexibility provide the means to create completely original, custom arrays.

Speech output is offered by some scanning programs so students' selections can be confirmed or they can receive auditory cues. In auditory scanning, the item name or another cue is spoken aloud as it is highlighted to inform the user of the content before he or she makes a selection. Auditory scanning may be beneficial to students who have vision impairments, reading problems, or cognitive issues, along with severe physical disabilities.

Other features also vary from program to program. One is the way in which an array is scanned. Some programs allow the user to control whether the program scans (highlights) column-by-column, row-by-row, item-by-item, or some combination of these. Although most programs allow some control of the speed at which the program scans, the degree of control of response time varies. Many programs offer a choice between automatic and step scanning. Automatic scanning mode moves the highlighter from item to item with a single switch activation. Step scanning requires the user to activate the switch to advance the highlighter.

As with other alternative computer access devices, it is a student's individual characteristics and needs that determine which switch and software program(s) are most appropriate. For example, a student who is unable to use his or her hands reliably might have better head control. Capitalizing on this strength, a switch could be positioned for activation by tilting the head to the side, tipping the head back, or tipping the head forward—whatever motion is most accurate and easiest to accomplish. If this student has good vision and good response time, a program with premade arrays allowing minimal modifications might meet the student's needs. However, if he or she has a vision impairment, the on-screen scanning software would need to offer auditory scanning and/or an enlarged array.

Most on-screen scanning software programs are used in conjunction with another computer application. To word process a report, a student could use the on-screen scanning array to select letters that are then entered into whatever word processing program the student is using. The word processing program responds just as if the text had been entered from the keyboard. Students who use scanning often increase their rate of text entry by using word prediction, discussed in Chapter 2.

USER PROFILE: Pintoo

Clear, bright, dark eyes peer at the cursor as it moves across the computer screen in highly selective and controlled increments. Noticing me, the young man pauses, smiles, and says, "Hello, I'm Pintoo. I'm happy to see you." I introduce myself and glance at the journal entry on the screen; it tells of my anticipated arrival and our interview.

Although he has difficulty moving due to athetoid cerebral palsy, Pintoo turns toward me by maneuvering his lean frame with a wriggling kind of motion. He explains that he and his speech therapist are refining the settings on his new computer. "I like this a lot," he says. He accesses the computer using a sip and puff switch. Used in connection with an interface called Discover:Switch (originally by Don Johnston Inc., now marketed as DiscoverPro by Madentec Limited), it enables Pintoo to input into his computer with single-switch scanning, in lieu of a keyboard.

First School Experience at Age 9

Pintoo has come a long way in his short time at this school. Born in India, he spent his first 8 years at home with his family, whose dominant language is Gujarati, a dialect of Hindi. Pintoo credits watching TV for his fluency in English. He speaks Gujarati as well. Attending school for the first time when his family moved to the

United States, he has demonstrated incredible academic achievement. In only 1 year's time he has advanced to second-grade levels in math and reading.

Single-Switch Scanning with Write:OutLoud and Co:Writer

Pintoo's computer enables him to complete his schoolwork with relative ease. His teacher and speech-language therapist have taught him to use Co:Writer (Don Johnston Inc.) the word prediction program, with Write:OutLoud (Don Johnston Inc.), the talking word processing program. Using his sip and puff switch (a switch that is activated by either a sip or puff into a tube positioned by the user's mouth) and a scanning array from Discover:Switch (currently DiscoverPro by Madentec Limited), he activates the switch by puffing when the desired letter is highlighted. When scanning is used in conjunction with Co:Writer, selecting the letter *P*, for example, presents a list of predetermined words beginning with that letter. Co:Writer then scans the list of words. When the scan reaches the word he wants, Pintoo puffs the switch again, and the word is entered into the word processing document. To speed things up, Pintoo and his teachers or therapists have added custom lists of frequently used words and expressions to the Co:Writer dictionary.

When working to determine Pintoo's best access method, his teacher and therapist found that he utilizes a sip and puff switch better than voice-activated software. He speaks clearly and is able to use voice commands with the computer, but his voice is not strong enough for extended work on the computer, and using speech recognition tired him quickly. Although his current setup is adequate, he is always on the lookout for new and better access tools. Reflecting on his many experiments with various computer input devices, he explains, "You have to try everything."

Technology Offers Power and Control

Pintoo's teacher shares that he is strong in math and written expression. Pintoo beams with pride as he tells me that he uses Big:Calc (Don Johnston Inc.) for math. They are awaiting the more advanced Access to Math (Don Johnston Inc.) so that Pintoo can make up math worksheets for himself and other students in the class. Pintoo adds, "I take things home that I've done at school during the day, too." A quick glance at his computer's directory indicates sizable files. Pintoo also enjoys current events. He explains, "I want to read the news online. I'm getting a modem so I can get online. I want to send e-mail to the president, governor, and others who can help people." What is the impact of this assistive technology on Pintoo? "The computer gives me a feeling of power and control over what I'm doing. I want to go to college and be a doctor."

Source: From "Assistive Technology Promotes Rapid Academic Advances," by G. Quinn, 1998, *TECH-NJ, 9*(1), 3–6.

Single-switch scanning is an important access method because it is often the *only* means of computer access available to individuals with severe physical disabilities. However, it is extremely slow. For students whose physical disabilities limit them to use of a single switch but who have high cognitive abilities and good memories, a faster option may be Morse code. Some switch interface devices allow users to enter text and computer commands using Morse code. Usually a software program is

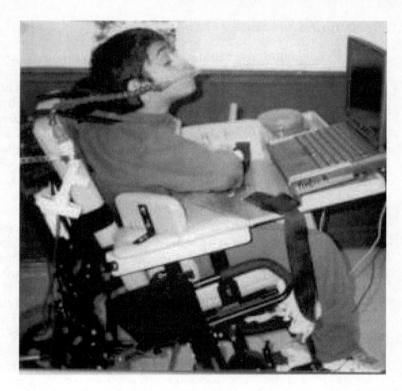

Pintoo, who has quadriplegia cerebral palsy, operates his computer using single-switch scanning and a sip and puff switch

Reprinted with permission from TECH-NJ.

needed to translate the code into computer input, but a device such as the Darci USB (WesTest Engineering) is a plug-and-play Morse code computer access device—no software needed. All Morse code software programs accept input from just one switch that is used to enter both dots and dashes; the amount of time the switch is activated determines whether a dot or dash is entered. Some software programs will accept input from two, or even three switches, which is beneficial for students who cannot control the timing of switch presses to enter dots and dashes from just one switch. With two switches, one switch is used to enter dots and the second to enter dashes. After a prescribed amount of time, if no additional dots or dashes are entered, the code is considered complete and sent to the computer. Using three switches eliminates timing as a requirement for successful use of Morse code; the third switch is used to signal that the code is complete and should be sent to the computer.

Not all students who can use switches can use Morse code for access to the computer. There is a heavy cognitive demand for Morse code users; they must be able to remember the codes for all of the computer commands, as well as the entire alphabet. If a student is unable to control the timing of switch activations and needs to use two or three switches, then he or she must be able to reliably activate each switch, a difficult (or impossible) task for many switch users.

Speech Recognition

Speech recognition, also called voice recognition, technology permits a user to speak into a microphone to operate the computer or to create text. Speech recognition software must be installed on the computer so spoken words can be translated into computer commands or text. The emphasis in this chapter is on using speech recognition to provide access to the computer and computer applications for people with disabilities. Chapter 2 addressed the use of speech recognition programs to help with written expression. Although there is repetition of some information, readers who desire a thorough understanding of the applications of speech recognition technology for students with disabilities need to read both chapters.

Students who are unable to use a computer with their hands, for reasons such as muscular dystrophy, cerebral palsy, or spinal cord injuries, but are able to speak, may find speech recognition technology an option for computer access. One way of classifying speech recognition systems is based on the way the user speaks, with a pause between each word or with a natural speech pattern. These programs are termed **discrete speech programs** and **continuous speech programs,** respectively. Discrete speech programs require the user to pause briefly, approximately one tenth of a second, between each word. Continuous speech requires users to produce a steady stream of words, pausing only between phrases or sentences. The needs of the individual student determine which type of program is most appropriate.

The earliest speech recognition programs utilized discrete speech, but discrete speech programs are increasingly hard to find. They are usually the better choice for hands-free computer operation so when control over the operating system is a priority, a discrete speech program, such as DragonDictate Power Edition (Dragon Systems) may be required. DragonDictate can launch and close programs, access menus, select items in dialog boxes, control the mouse, and execute most computer functions without ever having to use the mouse or keyboard (see Figure 7.5).

Discrete speech programs are more accurate than continuous speech programs for students whose articulation of words varies from the standard (Alliance for Technology Access [ATA], 2000), and for those who are able to speak only one word at a time; consistency in pronunciation is more important than precise articulation. The speech recognition program can be trained to recognize words the way students say them, but they must say the word the same way every time.

Continuous speech programs focus more on speed and accuracy of text entry than total hands-free computer use (ATA, 2000). They are a good choice when increased text output is a priority and students are capable of speaking continuous streams of words, because word processing rates using continuous speech programs surpass those of discrete speech programs. Many continuous speech programs also provide some degree of control over Windows-based applications and may provide mouse control as well. Higher end programs, such as Dragon NaturallySpeaking Preferred or Dragon NaturallySpeaking Professional, also provide access to additional operating system features.

Although continuous speech programs offer increased speed and accuracy for typical computer users, they work against students who must speak one word at a time. The initial training requires students to speak phrases or sentences so the students' voices can be matched to the voice models on which the speech recognition is

FIGURE 7–5 Mouse navigation in Dragon NaturallySpeaking

To use MouseGrid:

1 Say *"MouseGrid"* to place the MouseGrid™ over the full screen (as in this example) or say *"MouseGrid Window"* to place it over the active window.

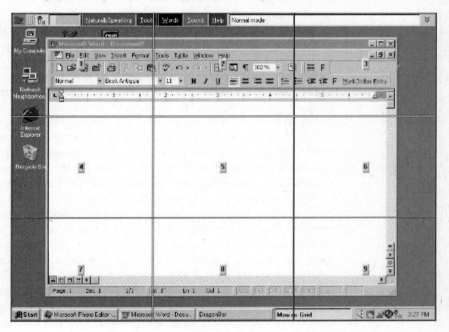

The mouse motion commands

Here is a summary of the available mouse motion commands.

SAY	THEN A DIRECTION	THEN A SPEED (OPTIONAL)
Move Mouse	Up	Fast
Mouse Move	Down	Faster
Drag Mouse	Right	Much Faster
Mouse Drag	Left	Very Fast
	Upper Left	Slow
	Lower Left	Slower
	Upper Right	Much Slower
	Lower Right	Very Slow

Source: Reprinted with permission from *TECH-NJ*.

based. This is impossible for some students with disabilities. Speaking continuous streams of text increases accuracy because the program can analyze the context in which a word is spoken. For example, the words *possible* and *passable* might be confused if spoken alone. When spoken in the phrase "as soon as possible," the program would analyze the other words in the phrase and know that the speaker mostly likely said *possible*. Students who can speak only one word at a time are at a disadvantage with such programs.

Another way in which speech recognition programs are categorized is speaker-dependent and speaker-independent. Speaker-dependent programs are designed for a single user who proceeds through a process to train the voice files, which continue to develop as the programs are used. This type of program can be advantageous for users who have speech differences because it will adjust to the way in which a particular user says the words. Speaker-independent programs, on the other hand, are designed to be used by many different people. There are many voice models against which their voices will be compared. There may be no training process or only an abbreviated one. Drawbacks to speaker-independent systems are that there may be smaller vocabulary sets from which to draw, and they are less likely to accurately recognize words spoken by students with speech differences.

Many factors must be considered when deciding to use a speech recognition program. The programs typically require fast computer processing speeds and lots of memory (both RAM and ROM). This means they will not run smoothly on older computers. However, human resources, more than technical issues, will ultimately determine whether speech recognition is a successful access solution. Students and school personnel must make a commitment to training the voice files and working with the program in an appropriate way. They need to correct errors in the prescribed manner to build the voice file because uncorrected errors and errors improperly corrected can degrade the voice file resulting in decreased accuracy. Students must be patient and able to handle frustration. They will need to interrupt their work in other applications (e.g., word processing) to do necessary training and correcting, and interruptions may be frequent, at least initially. Students also must be able to work with the computer operating system, the speech recognition program, and other applications simultaneously. For example, when using speech recognition to work with a word processing application, students need to understand and manage the functioning of both programs. They need to know what the word processing program is capable of doing and the commands they must speak to get the program to do what they want (e.g., select sections of text, apply styles and formats, or create tables). Simultaneously, they need to work with the speech recognition program and when errors occur, be able to determine whether they are due to what they said (e.g., having spoken the wrong command) or inaccurate recognition of what they said. This determines the approach to resolving the problem.

Environmental factors impact success with speech recognition and must be given careful consideration. Obviously, students must speak aloud to utilize speech recognition technology. This may cause distractions to others in a classroom setting. It may also make it impossible for students to keep their work private until they are ready to share, to record confidential information such as journal or diary entries, or to answer questions during class assessments such as tests and quizzes.

The noise produced by other students engaged in typical classroom activities may interfere with the accuracy of recognition. Using a noise-filtering microphone or placing students away from the noisiest locations in the classroom can help increase accuracy; however, students will achieve optimal accuracy when using speech recognition in a quiet environment. Note that separating students from their peers to increase the accuracy of recognition runs counter to principles for inclusive education.

USER PROFILE: Megan, Part 2

In Chapter 2 you were introduced to Megan M., who has no use of her hands and who taught herself how to use speech recognition for writing. Megan also uses Dragon NaturallySpeaking for accessing her computer. She speaks keyboard equivalents for typing, tabbing, and entering and deleting text, as well as for opening and closing programs and files. For example, when capitalizing a letter, instead of hitting the Shift key with the corresponding letter, Megan says "Shift key" and then the corresponding alpha character to capitalize. Essentially any key on the keyboard can be spoken and understood by Dragon as a keyboard function.

Most people are familiar with this dictation ability of voice recognition technology, but many are unaware of the power voice recognition holds for navigating around the computer screen by emulating mouse commands. Megan controls her mouse using a function within Dragon called MouseGrid. MouseGrid enables her to separate the screen into nine quadrants. As each quadrant is selected, it becomes a smaller quadrant, making the movement of the mouse extremely precise. As Megan fires out numbers, she is essentially breaking down the computer screen into mini-quadrants so she can target her mouse click accurately.

An important part of Megan's speech recognition setup is the microphone she has chosen to use. It is called an array microphone and it offers two important advantages. It has a noise canceling feature that allows background noise not to interfere with the dictation. Megan finds this feature essential because she constantly listens to music through her computer while working. Another benefit of an array microphone is its position. Instead of requiring a headset, an array microphone sits below the computer monitor and sends a listening beam. This enables Megan to work on her computer at any time without having to rely on an assistant to place the headset on her head. With this combination of assistive technology—speech recognition and an array microphone—the only assistance Megan needs is someone to turn on her computer at the beginning of the day.

Megan explains the impact of the technology on her life: "Assistive technology helps me communicate and function independently through several different mediums: instant messaging, text messaging, writing, e-mail, live chats, etc. It has given me control in many areas of my life. Ultimately, voice recognition software will contribute greatly towards my obtaining a successful career in the future. This technology enables me to accomplish things that would be virtually impossible to accomplish on my own. There is no way I would have all the success I've had, and will continue to have, without this technology."

Source: Adapted from Schindler (2005).

ALTERNATIVE OUTPUT OPTIONS

Screen Magnification

It is common educational practice for students who are blind or visually impaired to be taught to touch-type in the early grades. This eliminates the need to see the keyboard when typing. However, students who have visual impairments may not be able to see the computer monitor clearly enough to be able to read text, menus, icons, and so on. These students will likely benefit from screen magnification. As the name implies, screen magnification provides an enlarged view of text, images, and the entire desktop on the computer monitor. There are various ways to accomplish screen magnification. This section discusses the two most common methods—physical magnifying lenses and screen magnification software.

Low magnification powers, from just over 1X up to 3X, can be achieved with physical magnifying lenses. Magnification lenses are available in a variety of sizes to accommodate the most common computer monitor sizes. Depending on the particular product, lenses attach directly to the computer monitor or are freestanding, positioned just in front of the monitor.

For students who need greater magnification, physical magnifying lenses are not adequate. Instead, screen magnification software can provide up to 32X magnification power. Screen magnification software programs feature varied option and display modes. Some programs magnify the full-screen image so only a portion of the original, unmagnified view is visible at any time. To view more of the image the student needs to move the mouse or use keyboard commands to bring another section of the image into view. Other programs show the unmagnified view at all times, but magnify the area directly under the cursor or mouse pointer. Again, the student needs to move the cursor or mouse pointer to get a magnified view of another part of the screen. More full-featured programs provide a range of options that may include inverting or changing colors to provide high contrast, adjustable size or placement of the magnification area, larger mouse pointers, cursor and/or pointer locator features, options for controlling the way in which the magnified area is brought into view, and screen reading (voice output), which is discussed in the following text. Figure 7.6 shows toolbar controls in ZoomText (Ai Squared).

The higher contrast and larger text and graphics that screen magnification technology provides promotes successful computer access for students with low vision. Screen magnification may also be helpful to some students with learning disabilities. Enlarged text is frequently an adaptation for students with perceptual impairments, so screen magnification may help them work more successfully with the computer. Each student's unique characteristics and needs must be considered when selecting screen magnification technology, either lenses or software. When selecting screen magnification software, ample time must be devoted to finding the optimal settings for color, magnification power, and speech output, if required.

FIGURE 7–6   ZoomText window: The Magnifier tab in ZoomText displays toolbar controls for the program's magnification features.

Source: Printed with permission of Ai Squared.

Screen Readers

Screen-reading software programs provide auditory output for some or all of the elements that are visible on a computer monitor. Full-featured screen readers speak the contents of dialog boxes and menus, identify toolbar buttons and the presence of graphic images, alert users to new windows, and speak the text found in word processing documents and other applications. In addition to spoken output, some screen-reading programs provide Braille output (discussed in the next section) and/or screen magnification. These various output options help meet the needs of students with vision impairments ranging from low vision to total blindness.

Screen-reading programs utilize the operating system keyboard commands discussed in Chapter 6, as well as commands specific to the screen-reading programs themselves. For example, program-specific commands direct the screen reader to begin speaking, stop speaking, speak toolbar buttons, or speak the names of desktop icons. These commands enable students to navigate through documents and control the screen-reading program, other programs, and the operating system.

Screen readers are customizable to meet individual needs. Customizable speech output features allow adjustments to such things as the rate, pitch, amount of text spoken when commanded to read, and the way the program speaks while a student is typing. In some programs, specific commands can be created to execute user-specified functions to make computer use more convenient or to work with nonstandard computer applications. Programs that offer customizable features are useful for meeting the changing needs of a single student or meeting the needs of more than one student.

As previously mentioned, students with a broad array of vision impairments may benefit from the auditory output provided by screen-reading programs, used alone or in conjunction with other assistive technology. However, students with vision impairments are not the only ones that can benefit from screen readers. Students who have reading difficulties, visual-perceptual problems, or those who benefit from simultaneous visual and auditory access to information may also find screen-reading software promotes successful computer use.

Refreshable Braille

Refreshable Braille is one of the ways that some screen-reading programs output information about what appears on the computer monitor. A refreshable Braille display (RBD) is a separate device that sits in front of the keyboard. Refreshable Braille is similar to traditional Braille embossed on paper in that it uses raised dots to indicate letters, contractions, punctuation, and other elements of writing, and students read it the same way—by moving their fingers across the lines. However, there are two important differences: Traditional Braille uses six-dot cells to produce a character, whereas refreshable Braille uses 8-dot cells. The extra dots are specific to the computer, indicating such things as cursor location or special formatting. The most important difference is that refreshable Braille is dynamic rather than static. A series of pins raise and lower in response to electronic signals to form the dot pattern in each cell of the RBD. As the student moves through a document, either adding new text or reading existing text, the pins reconfigure, or refresh, to reflect the new information. For example, an RBD device might show the Braille characters for the first line of text from a page in an electronic book. After the student reads the first line, she advances the cursor and the pins refresh to display the Braille equivalent for the next line.

Various manufacturers produce RBDs for use with laptop or desktop computers. The size of the display varies with price. An 80-cell RBD is capable of displaying the Braille translation for one line of computer text. Forty-cell RBDs need to refresh twice to display one line of computer text, and 20-cell RBDs need to refresh four times. Regardless of the number of cells, most RBDs are positioned under the keyboard with only the part that the user "reads" sitting directly in front of the keyboard.

RBDs are incorporated into many Braille notetaking devices. Notetakers are similar to handheld computers; they are small, portable, lightweight devices with either a Braille or QWERTY keyboard. Depending on the model, students can monitor and review their work through speech output, refreshable Braille, or both. When connected to computers that have screen-reading programs, notetakers with refreshable Braille will function as RBDs for the computer.

RBDs can facilitate successful computer use for students with vision impairments or blindness who read Braille. Depending on the needs of the students, RBDs may be used alone or in conjunction with speech output from a screen-reading program.

Students with vision impairment or blindness may benefit from simultaneously listening to and reading the material, just like their sighted peers.

Braille Embossers

Braille printers, known as Braille embossers, make the output from word processing and data entry efforts accessible in hard copy format to students who read Braille. Depending on the model of Braille embosser, students can produce hard copy that displays standard-sized print or large print along with the Braille. Using a Braille embosser, students can produce a hard copy of their work for themselves or for sharing with others; they can also use the embossed copy to check the accuracy of their work. However, having access to a Braille embosser is not comparable to having an RBD that provides real-time access to information. Refreshable Braille gives students feedback while they are creating text, whereas Braille embossers provide a hard copy of the finished product.

Whether students need alternative or adapted computer input, output, or both, the search for solutions to access issues begins at the low-tech end of the assistive technology continuum and capitalizes on what students are able to do. The focus is on students' strengths, not their weaknesses. Some issues for consideration were presented in the previous discussion, along with suggestions for whom various input and output solutions might be appropriate. However, the match between student needs and assistive technology must be made on a case-by-case basis. Each student's needs must be considered individually and a decision made only after the student has had an opportunity to use the assistive technology in his or her natural environment. The following chapter provides information that will help guide this decision-making process.

SUMMARY

- Assistive technology that facilitates computer access for students with disabilities exists on a continuum from low tech to high tech. Low-tech solutions include keyboard labels, selecting/pointing devices, keyguards, and moisture guards.
- Alternatives to navigating with a mouse for students who do not have the fine motor dexterity needed to use a mouse include keyboard shortcuts, trackballs, joysticks, touch screens, head pointing systems, and eye-gaze systems.
- Alternatives to regular keyboards for students who do not have the fine motor dexterity needed to use them include expanded keyboards, mini-keyboards, one-handed keyboards, on-screen keyboards, customizable keyboards, single-switch scanning, Morse code, and speech recognition.
- Alternatives to the traditional visual output (i.e., computer screen) are needed for students who are blind or visually impaired. These alternatives include screen magnification, screen readers, refreshable Braille displays, and Braille embossers.
- There are advantages and disadvantages to each of these input and output methods. The match between students' needs and assistive technology solutions must be carefully considered. This decision-making process is presented in the next chapter.

WEB RESOURCES

For additional information on the topics listed, go to the following websites:

Low-Tech Adaptations for Access

Hooleon Corporation
http://www.hooleon.com/menu-vision.htm

Mouse Alternatives

Ability Hub
http://www.abilityhub.com/mouse/index.htm
Assistive Technology Training Online Project (ATTO)
http://atto.buffalo.edu/registered/ATBasics/AdaptingComputers/MouseOptions/
index.php
SmartNav
http://www.naturalpoint.com/smartnav/TrackerPro
TrackerPro
http://www.madentec.com/products/tracker-pro.php
Eye Gaze Tracking System
http://www.eyetechds.com

Alternate Keyboards

Adaptive Technology Resource Centre: University of Toronto
http://www.utoronto.ca/atrc/reference/tech/altkey.html

On-Screen Keyboards

DiscoverPro, Discover Screen, Discover Envoy
http://www.madentec.com
IntelliKeys
http://store.cambiumlearning.com/resource.aspx?page=ProgramOverview&site=itc
&parentId=074003405

Dvorak Keyboard Layout

http://www.dvorak-keyboard.com

Switches

Tash, Inc.
http://www.tashinc.com/catalog/s_index.html

Senswitcher: Developing Switch Skills
http://www.northerngrid.org/sen/Skills.htm
Darci USB: Morse Code Computer Access
http://www.westest.com/darci/usbindex.html

Speech Recognition

Adaptive Technology Resource Centre: University of Toronto
http://www.utoronto.ca/atrc/reference/tech/voicerecog.html#points
CALL Centre, University of Edinburgh: Introduction to Speech Recognition
http://www.callcentrescotland.org.uk/Research/Speech_Recog_PRA/IntroSR_PRB/
introsr_prb.html

Assistive Technology for Students with Visual Impairments

National Federation of the Blind's Technology Resource List
http://www.nfb.org/nfb/Technology_Resource_List1.asp?SnID=887575
The Screen Magnification Home Page
http://www.magnifiers.org/index.shtml
Texas School for the Blind and Visually Impaired
http://www.tsbvi.edu/technology/at-overview.htm

Braille and Braille Technology

American Foundation for the Blind
http://www.afb.org/braillebug/braille.asp

SUGGESTED ACTIVITIES

1. *Add to Your Portfolio.* Use a search engine (e.g., Google or Yahoo!) to locate websites related to assistive technology for computer access. Explore the sites and add to your portfolio the sites you feel will be most valuable.

2. *Create a Computer User Profile.* In Chapter 1 you were asked to observe or interview a person with a disability and to write a short paper discussing the benefits of assistive technology for this person. Conduct a follow-up observation or interview with this individual, this time focusing on the technical details of the assistive technology.

   a. *Means of Access:* What movements does the person use to access the computer?

   b. *Software:* List the titles of software programs used. Provide a brief description of each program and how it is used.

   c. *Hardware:* Describe the hardware used. Include the brand of computer, peripherals, adaptive inputs, and adaptive outputs. Include clear descriptions of what the assistive devices do.

d. *SetUp:* If relevant, describe how the person is positioned to use the computer. (What kind of seating is used? Where is the equipment placed? etc.)

e. *Effectiveness:* How effective are the person's attempts at using the computer? Is the person accomplishing his or her goals?

3. *Use Single-Switch Scanning as an Access Method.* Write a three-or four-sentence "autobiography" using both hands on a regular keyboard. Then type the same paragraph using single-switch scanning with an array of your choice. If using the on-screen keyboard in Windows, from the Settings menu set the Typing mode to "Joystick or key to select" to enable scanning using the spacebar. If using IntelliTalk you can choose a QWERTY, ABC, or Frequency on-screen keyboard and you can set the program to use the mouse for "dedicated scanning." How did the two input methods compare? Discuss the benefits and drawbacks to single-switch scanning. What features affect speed and accuracy? What are the implications for training? If you could, how would you modify the scanning array to meet your students' needs?

4. *Simulate Visual Impairment.* Download and install the Visual Impairment Simulator (VIS) available at http://www.cita.uiuc.edu/software/vis/ on a computer running Windows. Launch VIS and read the Help file before beginning. Select an item under Impairment and use the mouse to access the Start menu, launch a program of your choice, and use the program for a couple of minutes. Exit the program, and then select the next Impairment. When you have experienced each condition in the Impairment list, write a three-page reflection about the experience. Be sure to comment about the most challenging aspects of using the computer with the simulated visual impairments, any solutions you discovered to make computer use easier, and the emotions you experienced. In addition to the narrative, create a document (e.g., table or bulleted lists) identifying each of the simulated visual impairments in VIS and suggestions for assistive technology that might make computer use easier for students with visual impairments.

REFERENCES

Alliance for Technology Access. (2000). *Computer and web resources for people with disabilities* (3rd ed.). Alameda, CA: Hunter House.

Blackhurst, A. E. (1997). Perspectives on technology in special education. *Teaching Exceptional Children, 29*(5), 41–48.

Quinn, G. (1998). Assistive technology promotes rapid academic advances, *TECH-NJ, 9*(1), 3–6.

Schindler, C. (2005). Voice recognition provides independence for Ramapo College student. *TECH-NJ, 6*(1), Retrieved April 12, 2007, from http://www.tcnj.edu/~technj/2005/ramapo.htm.

Webopedia. (August 30, 2001). *Trackball.* Retrieved January 30, 2004, from http://www.webopedia.com/TERM/t/trackball.html

CHAPTER 8

Issues in Selection of Access Method(s)

FOCUS QUESTIONS

1. What are the seven hallmarks of exemplary assistive technology assessment?
2. What are the essential factors of each hallmark?
3. What are some of the most common assistive technology decision-making guides?

INTRODUCTION

Chapter 7 presented an extensive array of assistive technology options that make computers accessible to students with a broad range of disabilities. These options have expanded greatly in the past 10 years and continue to grow and improve; new products are developed and existing products enhanced each year. Although it is easy to be captivated by the latest technology, impressed by perceived potential, and carried away with visions of student success, it is essential to remember that it is not the technology itself, but the student himself or herself that must be the focus of any attempt to identify appropriate assistive technology.

> The overarching objective during the assessment process is to keep the learner's strengths and abilities squarely at the forefront of the assessment and to use these to ameliorate potential difficulties in the classroom. If the assessor loses sight of the learner and becomes too enamored of "gee-whiz" technology . . . then the learner . . . may not find much of a functional use for the assistive technology device. (Beigel, 2000, *Learner Focus During Assessment*)

This chapter on assistive technology decision making is based on this fundamental concept: It is imperative to match the technology to the student, not the other way around.

ASSISTIVE TECHNOLOGY DECISION MAKING

The Individuals with Disabilities Education Act (IDEA) mandates that teams responsible for developing the IEP for students with disabilities consider each student's need for assistive technology devices and services. However, there is no clear-cut definition of *consider*, and the process varies greatly from state to state, district to district, and sometimes even school to school. Ideally, the student's goals and objectives are

191

reviewed by the team, and a discussion ensues regarding the need for assistive technology to help meet these goals. The effectiveness of this discussion directly relates to the assistive technology expertise of those involved in the process; to adequately consider assistive technology needs, the IEP team must be aware of the wide range of options along the entire assistive technology continuum (low tech to high tech). If the IEP team recognizes that adequate consideration of the student's needs exceeds their knowledge and skills, then a formal assistive technology assessment is vital.

Assessment is one of the assistive technology services to which students are entitled under the IDEA. Decision making related to computer access, as well as other assistive technology needs, may occur during the consideration process, but a formal assessment may be required before appropriate decisions can be made. Reed (2004) notes that the major differences between "consideration" and "assessment" are in the duration, complexity, and need for new information. We would add that the assistive technology expertise of the professionals involved in these processes is another important difference.

HALLMARKS OF EXEMPLARY ASSISTIVE TECHNOLOGY DECISION MAKING AND ASSESSMENT

Just as with assistive technology consideration, assistive technology assessment is not a uniform and clearly defined process. However, the field is enriched by the development of several models that guide assessment. Utilizing one of the assessment or decision-making guides discussed later in the chapter is not essential for successful assistive technology assessment. What is essential is that decision making or assessment include seven elements that are the hallmarks of an exemplary assistive technology assessment:

1. Use of a team approach
2. Focus on student needs and abilities
3. Examination of tasks to be completed
4. Consideration of relevant environmental issues
5. Trial use of assistive technology
6. Providing of necessary supports
7. Viewing of assessment as an ongoing process

Each of these elements is discussed in detail in the following sections.

Use of a Team Approach in Assistive Technology Assessment

Assistive technology can benefit students with disabilities in a number of different ways, including enhancing speech and communication, mobility, ability to perform activities of daily living, and access to educational and vocational opportunities. No individual can be expected to single-handedly meet students' needs in all areas because of the unique skill set each area requires. Indeed, simply keeping abreast of new technology in some areas is a daunting task. Utilizing a team approach to assistive technology assessment, however, mitigates the need for one person to know everything—a virtually unattainable goal.

Occupational therapists, physical therapists, and speech language pathologists often have a wealth of assistive technology information and expertise as it relates to their individual fields. Working together they are more likely to meet a student's assistive technology needs. Occupational therapists, whose expertise includes fine motor skills, may be the most knowledgeable about technology that assists students who struggle with the mechanics of handwriting. Physical therapists, who specialize in posture and mobility, may be most skilled at identifying technology for mobility-related issues, such as power wheelchairs. Speech-language pathologists are the professionals most likely to be aware of technology that aids expressive and receptive communication.

Some schools or districts include an assistive technology specialist on the team. The specialist may have the broadest assistive technology knowledge base, perhaps encompassing the technology in each of the other disciplines. However, this does not diminish the significance of contributions from other team members. The insights they provide pertaining to discipline-specific issues can be invaluable. For example, if an alternative keyboard is suggested for trial by a student, the occupational therapist on the team can help determine the optimal positioning so the keyboard can be accessed in a manner that is least likely to cause problems from stress or strain. If that keyboard will be used to access a computer-based augmentative communication system, then the team's speech-language pathologist can offer valuable insights regarding vocabulary selection and arrangement of items.

Other essential members of the team are the parent(s) and the student (Wahl & Haugen, 2005). Family members are the ones with the most intimate knowledge of the student, in addition to being the ones most vested in the student's future success. They may have priorities that differ from, yet are equally as important as, those of educational personnel. It may be necessary for family members to support the use of assistive technology outside the school environment. They will be willing to do so only if they are in agreement with the purpose for and the choice of technology; there must be no conflict with family values and culture (Parette & McMahan, 2002). (See Chapter 12 for a discussion of cultural issues in assistive technology selection and use.) Likewise, students' opinions and feelings about the technology must be solicited; these are key to acceptance and use. If the technology does not appear to offer benefits desired by the student, or the student has not been involved in the selection process, there is an increased risk of technology abandonment (Riemer-Reiss & Wacker, 2000). If the technology makes the student feel stigmatized, self-conscious, or otherwise socially ill-at-ease, it is likely to be used very little or abandoned entirely (Newton & Petroff, 2005). Including students in the decision-making process can prevent such negative outcomes.

A student's teacher or teachers should also be considered part of the team. Teachers have a considerable amount of information about the student that other team members may lack. Within the school environment, they may be most familiar with the student's work habits and behavioral characteristics, tasks that need to be completed, activities in which the student needs to participate, and environments in which the student functions. These pieces of information contribute substantially to a successful assessment; indeed, they are among the hallmarks of exemplary assistive technology decision making/assessment and are discussed in more detail in the following text.

Focus on Student Needs and Abilities

An assistive technology assessment must always be student centered, identifying the technology to meet students' individual needs; never should the available technology drive the assessment. Accordingly, the goals for the technology assessment derive from the general tasks the student needs to perform in school; for example, reading for information in the content area, accessing information from the Internet, completing expository or creative writing assignments, or finding a way to use the computer (Chambers, 1997; Lueck, Dote-Kwan, Senge, & Clarke, 2001; Reed, 2004).

Once goals, based on student need, have been identified, the student's current abilities must be explored. It is important to base assistive technology solutions on

---

USER PROFILE: Marshall

Marshall is a ninth-grade student who struggles with reading. He is able to decode many words, but his efforts at decoding are so resource intensive that he has little left over to make sense of what he reads. Marshall needs an assistive technology solution to help him comprehend printed material so he can be successful in his classes. Certainly this entails making meaning from his textbooks, but it could also mean being able to understand what is printed in reference books and on worksheets, handouts, and tests. Beyond paper-based materials, Marshall also needs to be able to access and comprehend Internet resources.

Marshall continues to receive reading instruction. When classroom instruction focuses on word recognition, phonics, or word attack skills, Marshall does not need text-to-speech software because the goal is to improve his decoding skills, not read for meaning. He says he does not need to have a text-to-speech program or scan/read system available during reading class as the material is read aloud by the teacher or classmates. At home, however, when he needs to read and understand a novel, read in the content areas, or research topics on the Internet, he needs assistive technology to be independent and successful. A scan/read system was recommended to provide auditory access to print-based materials. A system that reads Web pages was recommended so Marshall has access to the same wealth of information that is available to his typical peers.

Marshall attends his local high school for part of the school day and participates in three academic classes. He spends his afternoons at a vocational-technical school. In each location Marshall needs to be able to take notes and complete written assignments. A portable word processing device (e.g., Neo or Dana [AlphaSmart]) is a good choice for him. He will be able to easily transport this device from school to school. He will also be able to get through the school day without having to worry about dead batteries or being able to replace the batteries as needed with standard, reasonably-priced batteries.

student strengths—what students *can* do rather than simply on what they are unable to do. Among the questions you might ask are the following:

- Is the student an auditory, visual, or kinesthetic learner?
- Does the student have good phonetic and/or decoding skills?
- Is the student able to remember numerous keyboard shortcuts?
- Can the student control a mouse?
- Does the student have good control of at least one body part, and if so, which one?

Remember, it is important to build on strengths to minimize or overcome deficits.

Examination of Tasks to Be Completed

The focus on the student looks at the general tasks the student needs to complete, such as reading textbooks or writing papers. Examination of tasks to be completed looks more closely at the specifics of the tasks, at all of the steps involved in completing a certain task. Reading a book, for example, involves more than simply decoding the words. At a minimum, it also involves turning the pages and using reading comprehension skills, those skills necessary to make sense of the words that have been decoded. Using a computer involves more than being able to accurately hit the keys on a keyboard and target items with a mouse. The user must also be able to launch programs and remember the commands for specific software programs, among other things.

USER PROFILE: Meredith

Meredith is a seventh-grade student who has some gross motor movement in her right arm and hand, and good fine motor control in her left hand. She is unable to write legibly to demonstrate her knowledge or to participate in classroom activities such as creative writing and notetaking. Being able to produce legible written text is the general task that needs to be accomplished.

Word processing is an obvious solution for producing legible written work. However, the word processing task has to be carefully analyzed. In addition to simply being able to accurately target and select specific keys, Meredith needs to be able to type capital letters, punctuation marks, and the symbols above the number keys. Many of these require the use of two hands—one to hold down the Shift key and the other to press the key with the desired character. Using a computer program for word processing requires Meredith to be able to use the mouse to select menu items or use keyboard shortcuts (which typically require pressing at least two keys simultaneously) to access important functions such as formatting, saving, and printing. For many students the component tasks of word processing must be taken into account, but they generally do not pose a problem; however, because Meredith can use only one hand for keyboarding, each component task may present a challenge.

Considering Meredith's abilities and needs, and the identified task, it is apparent that at least part of the technology solution involves StickyKeys or MouseKeys.

Consideration of Relevant Environmental Issues

The environments in which a student functions must be carefully examined. One significant issue is the variety of locations the student frequents during the school day and whether the student engages in educational tasks at home. There are several options for meeting a student's needs in multiple locations. One option is to provide a portable device such as a laptop computer that can travel with the student from location to location. Another option is to have duplicate technology available in each location in which it is needed; for example, a student with a visual impairment might be provided with a video magnifier in school as well as at home. Students might have a variety of assistive technology solutions that meet their needs in different locations. A student who depends on augmentative communication, for example, may use a computer-based system such as Speaking Dynamically Pro (Mayer-Johnson) in the classroom, a portable voice output device such as a MessageMate (Words+, Inc.) in the cafeteria or on community outings, and a communication wallet in physical education class.

Mid- and high-tech assistive technology usually requires a power source. Extra batteries need to be stored or recharged in a convenient location so that fresh batteries are readily accessible when needed. Assistive technology that must be plugged into an electrical outlet impacts where a student must be situated (i.e., in close proximity to the outlet). Electrical outlets positioned on walls necessitate students being placed on the periphery of the classroom. Should this be the case, there are three priorities when arranging the furniture in the classroom: (1) Students must be able to easily navigate to the specific location; (2) access to the electrical outlet should be unobstructed; and (3) the placement should not isolate students from their peers. If a student's classroom does not have accessible power outlets, then the technology chosen needs to run adequately on batteries.

In addition to physical environments, the decision-making process must also consider attitudinal environments. The attitudinal environments in which students function significantly impact the success or failure of assistive technology implementation. Teachers, therapists, family members, caregivers, and others must encourage and support the use of the technology as a tool that facilitates student success in achieving educational goals. It is not meant to and does not provide an "unfair advantage" over typical peers. Rather, assistive technology provides students with a means of accessing curriculum content, engaging in learning opportunities, and expressing what they know in a manner that capitalizes on their strengths.

Collaborative and collegial attitudes among educational professionals support successful assistive technology implementation. Research demonstrates that learning from knowledgeable colleagues is an important source of technology knowledge-building (Lewis, 1997). Educational professionals must also support and collaborate with family members. Sharing information about positive assistive technology experiences, problems encountered, problem resolution, and other related questions and concerns among all stakeholders opens important lines of communication. Sharing information about assistive technology use in school and at home develops a collective body of knowledge that is more likely to support the student's technology use. Collaborative and collegial attitudes ensure that no one needs to feel isolated and unsupported or needs to reinvent the wheel when problems arise. When education professionals and family members support one another they are better able to meet the needs of the assistive technology user.

Trial Use of Assistive Technology

When only written documentation is considered, many students and their technology needs may appear to be similar. It is easy to fall into the trap of assuming that assistive technology that is beneficial for one student will be beneficial for all students. However, there is no way to know if specific technology will meet a student's needs until that student has an opportunity to try it. "Trial use" refers to a time period in which a student experiments with the recommended technology, preferably in his or her natural environment(s). Sometimes it is immediately obvious that technology solution is effective, whereas other times an extended trial period of 6 to 8 weeks or longer may be necessary. The length of the trial period depends on many factors, including the complexity of the technology and the extent of training required for the student and those who support the student in using the technology, based in part on entering knowledge or skill levels and student characteristics (Chambers, 1997).

It may be necessary to develop prerequisite skills before it is possible to determine if the assistive technology will be beneficial. If computer-based technology seems to be a likely solution and the student has no computer skills, time and training need to be devoted to developing basic computer competency before determining if the technology can be used successfully. A student may need to develop keyboarding skills before it is possible to determine if assistive technology will be beneficial. For students whose handwriting is slow and laborious, using a computer-based word processing program or portable word processing device can ease the burden and increase the rate of text entry. An initial assessment may determine whether these students can use the computer or a portable device as well as whether they are open to the idea of word processing. However, until they have sufficiently developed their keyboarding skills it is impossible to make a meaningful comparison between handwriting speed and keyboarding speed.

Another purpose for an extended trial is determining the feasibility of actually using assistive technology in the student's natural environment. There are numerous reasons why technology that may appear to meet students' needs during a brief trial in an assessment may not work as well for students in their "real lives" in classrooms. Time constraints and other organizational issues may cause insurmountable problems. Students may be reluctant to use the technology in all environments, at times because of the presence of peers. They may be reluctant to use it when they feel it segregates them from peers or is intrusive and labels them as "special education" students. Newton (2002) found students may refuse to use technology that is made available only to special education students, but may enthusiastically embrace the same technology when it is available to all students. Newton and Petroff (2005) report that students may reject using assistive technology in the classroom solely because they do not consider it to be age appropriate.

Providing of Necessary Supports

Deciding on the appropriate technology is just the beginning of the process for utilizing assistive technology for accessing educational opportunities. Technical support and training have been identified as major barriers to technology implementation by numerous researchers (Gruner et al., 2000; McGregor & Pachuski, 1996; Wessels, Dijcks, Soede, & DeWitte 2003). Therefore, it is critical that training and technical support receive due attention. Educational professionals cannot integrate and support the use of assistive technology if they are unfamiliar with what it does, how it works, or how to troubleshoot basic problems.

Technical problems are not unusual. Reported technical problems include software conflicts, especially with programs that require speech engines for voice output; hardware and software conflicts; and computers not meeting the minimum system requirements for software to run effectively (Newton, 2002; Newton & Petroff, 2005). Assistive technology, like all technology, will need repairs and maintenance from time to time. Technical support needs to be readily available to resolve problems and maintenance issues quickly. Students must have ready access to functioning assistive technology to make progress toward meeting their IEP goals and objectives.

The successful use of assistive technology requires appropriate training for students and those who support their use of it. Students must learn to use the technology fluently before they can be expected to use it to support their academic achievement. Many teachers and educational professionals report feeling they have not received enough training to adequately meet the technology needs of their students (McInerney, Osher, & Kane, 1997; Office of Special Education Programs, 2000). Often, parents and family members have no training or experience with recommended technology. Training that builds competence and confidence of students, family members, and educational professionals is essential.

At times, the supports necessary for successful assistive technology use are a matter of logistics. This includes making sure that the technology is available when and where it is needed. Arrangements may need to be made for transporting the device

SIDEBAR

Sample Assistive Technology Implementation Plans

Sample assistive technology implementation plans can be found at the following websites:

Oregon Technology Access Program
http://www.otap-oregon.org/ATForms.htm

Minnesota Assistive Technology Manual
http://education.state.mn.us/mdeprod/groups/SpecialEd/documents/Manual/001089.pdf

from classroom to classroom or from home to school and vice versa if the student cannot transport it independently. Logistical issues must be addressed when using scan/read systems or obtaining accessible materials from organizations such as Recordings for the Blind and Dyslexic (RFB&D) or Bookshare.org. The materials students need must be scanned or ordered in advance of when they are scheduled to be used; materials must be readily available in accessible format when they are needed. These implementation issues are discussed in more detail in Chapter 12.

Technical support, training, and logistical issues must be carefully considered. Best practice calls for using an assistive technology implementation plan to focus attention on all aspects of technology support. As part of the implementation plan "it is important to identify who is responsible for monitoring each aspect of the implementation of an assistive technology plan" (Bowser, 1991, as cited in Bauder, Lewis, Gobert, & Bearden, 1997, p. 33). Specifying responsible parties helps everyone involved know what they are accountable for and increases the chances that the plan will be successfully implemented.

Viewing of Assessment as an Ongoing Process

An assistive technology assessment is not an end point; rather, it should be viewed as the beginning of a new cycle. Once the technology has been decided on, provided, and supported, the adequacy of the technology must be continually monitored. It is important to periodically reexamine the student's characteristics, tasks to be accomplished, and environments in which the student functions because these may change over time. The assistive technology solutions that initially met a student's needs may become inadequate or inappropriate.

Technological advances and innovations continuously provide new and improved assistive technology solutions. The technology that most effectively met a student's needs at one point in time may be supplanted by newly available technology, which may provide greater independence, ease of use, or more flexibility. Students for whom no assistive technology solutions can be identified initially may realize even greater benefits from technological advances and innovations; the technology necessary to meet their needs may become available over time. When assessment is an ongoing process, follow-up services ensure that assistive technology keeps pace with students' changing needs and that they benefit from the most recent developments.

RESOURCES TO GUIDE ASSISTIVE TECHNOLOGY CONSIDERATION AND ASSESSMENT

A major obstacle to effective assistive technology implementation has been educational professionals' lack of knowledge about the technology (Gruner et al., 2000). Responding to this situation, some states have established assistive technology resource centers that provide technical support and training to local education agencies and clear guidelines for technology assessments. The Wisconsin Assistive Technology Initiative (WATI), the Georgia Project for Assistive Technology (GPAT), and the Oregon Technology Access Program (OTAP) are notable examples.

Resources for Assistive Technology Assessments

Many schools and districts have their own assistive technology teams. If your district does not, the following resources may help you locate a qualified professional for assistive technology assessments.

Alliance for Technology Access (ATA) Centers
http://www.ataccess.org
Services vary by center

RESNA Credentialed Assistive Technology Service Providers
http://www.resna.org/PracInAT/CertifiedPractice/Directory/Practitioners.html

State Tech Act Programs
http://www.resna.org/taproject/at/statecontacts.html
Projects funded under the Assistive Technology Act of 2004

State Occupational Therapy Associations
http://www.aota.org/featured/area6/links/LINK03.asp

American Speech-Language-Hearing Association
http://asha.org/proserv/
Searchable online directory of service providers—lists areas of expertise

Some states, such as Kentucky and Minnesota, provide assistive technology manuals that include assessment guidelines. Other models, frameworks, and best practice guidelines for technology decision making have been developed by various organizations and individuals for use during technology consideration or assessment.

In this textbook we refer to decision-making and assessment guidelines, models, and/or frameworks collectively as assistive technology decision-making guides. Decision-making guides that have frequently appeared in the literature and are among the most widely known are:

- Quality Indicators for Assessment of Assistive Technology Needs
- Education Tech Points for Assistive Technology Planning
- SETT Framework

These guides were developed by collaborative teams of experienced assistive technology specialists and reflect best practices at the time of this writing. Analysis of these guides reveals important commonalities—each one incorporates the seven hallmarks of exemplary assistive technology assessment discussed previously. A brief discussion of each of the three decision-making guides follows.

Quality Indicators for Assessment of Assistive Technology Needs

The QIAT (pronounced "quiet," an acronym for Quality Indicators for Assistive Technology) Consortium, comprised of assistive technology professionals and other stakeholders throughout the country, has established sets of quality indicators to ensure the delivery of effective assistive technology services. Assistive technology assessments, as mentioned previously, are required when the members of the IEP team do not have a sufficient level of technology knowledge and skills to adequately consider a student's needs. An assistive technology assessment is also called for when it is believed that the assessment will provide additional information that the IEP team needs to make a decision regarding appropriate technology.

Figure 8.1 presents the indicators for assessment of assistive technology needs developed by the QIAT Consortium. These indicators do not recommend or endorse a specific assessment procedure. Instead, they advocate that educational agencies clearly articulate an assessment process and use it consistently. Regardless of the specific process, assessments are to be conducted by multidisciplinary teams that seek input from students and families. The assessments are to take place in students' customary environments and focus on the tasks students need to complete in those environments. Assessment is viewed as an ongoing process because needs, environments, and the students themselves change over time.

Education Tech Points for Assistive Technology Planning

Rather than presenting an assessment protocol, Figure 8.2 defines six points at which assistive technology needs to be considered (Bowser & Reed, 1995). Education Tech Points 1 and 2 occur during the processes of referring and evaluating students for eligibility for special education services. The major question at the

FIGURE 8–1 Quality Indicators for Assessment of Assistive Technology

---

1. Assistive technology assessment procedures are clearly defined and consistently used.
2. Assistive technology assessments are conducted by a multidisciplinary team that actively involves the student and family or caregivers.
3. Assistive technology assessments are conducted in the student's customary environments.
4. Assistive technology assessments, including needed trials, are completed within reasonable timelines.
5. Recommendations from assistive technology assessments are based on data about the student, environments, and tasks.
6. The assessment provides the IEP team with documented recommendations about assistive technology devices and services.
7. Assistive technology needs are reassessed by request or as needed based on changes in the student, environments, and/or tasks.

Source: QIAT Consortium (2005). Quality Indicators for Assistive Technology Services: Research-Based Update. Retrieved April 16, 2007 from http://www.qiat.org

FIGURE 8–2 Education Tech Points for assistive technology planning

Education Tech Point 1—Initial Referral Questions Assistive technology questions at the referral stage center around the specific problem that the student is experiencing and whether simple, readily available assistive technology utilized in the classroom might provide enough support that referral to special education would not be necessary.

Education Tech Point 2—Evaluation Questions Questions for the evaluation team include whether the student can be evaluated accurately without assistive technology and what types of assistive technology might enhance the student's performance on the evaluation.

Education Tech Point 3—Extended Assessment Questions Generally understood to mean a trial period, questions to be addressed relate to what specific tasks the student needs to be able to do and what, if any, assistive technology could possibly help. Needs to incorporate a focus on the specific environments in which the student functions.

Education Tech Point 4—IEP Plan Development Questions The school district must determine if assistive technology is needed for the child to receive a free appropriate public education (FAPE).

Education Tech Point 5—Implementation Questions Implementation questions focus on responsibility for day-to-day operations. This includes questions such as who will make sure the equipment is up and running, what will happen when it needs repair, and what the district will provide in the interim if they are going to seek outside funding to purchase a device (Bowser, 1995).

Education Tech Point 6—Periodic Review Questions IDEA requires the periodic review of each student's IEP. This review should include evaluation of the effectiveness of the assistive technology solutions in the child's plan.

Source: From "Education Tech Points for Assistive Technology Planning," by G. Bowser and P. Reed, 1995, *Journal of Special Education Technology, 12*(4), 325–338.

referral stage is whether the provision of appropriate assistive technology might negate the need for special education evaluation and possible classification. At the evaluation stage the basic question is whether technology is needed to obtain accurate evaluation results.

Education Tech Point 3 focuses on identifying appropriate assistive technology through extended trial use. Points 4 through 6 center on providing the supports necessary for student success. The first support component, Education Tech Point 4, occurs during the development of the IEP. It is at this point that needed assistive technology devices and services are incorporated into the IEP and education agencies become legally bound to supply them. Education Tech Points 5 and 6 relate to short- and long-term follow-up, respectively. These are especially important because "merely prescribing a specific device or piece of equipment does not necessarily enhance or enable an individual to perform basic life skills" (Lueck et al., 2001, p. 22). The devices must be used and supported. Relatively soon after a student is provided with assistive technology, implementation problems, such as technical difficulties and additional training needs, must be identified and resolved. The tasks students need to perform change over time, as do their environments. Therefore, students' assistive technology needs must be periodically reviewed to ensure they continue to receive the free appropriate public education (FAPE) to which they are entitled.

SETT Framework

The SETT Framework, shown in Figure 8.3, is the work of Joy Zabala, an independent developer and consultant in assistive technology. The framework is not an assessment protocol; rather, it provides a general structure for exploring four major areas of concern regarding the provision of assistive technology:

1. the student
2. the environments

FIGURE 8–3 SETT Framework

Questions under each section are expected to guide discussion rather than be complete and comprehensive in and of themselves.

The Student

- What is the functional area(s) of concern? What does the student need to be able to do that is difficult or impossible to do independently at this time?
- Special needs (related to area of concern)
- Current abilities (related to area of concern)

The Environments

- Arrangement (instructional, physical)
- Support (available to both the student and the staff)
- Materials and equipment (commonly used by others in the environments)
- Access issues (technological, physical, instructional)
- Attitudes and expectations (of staff, family, others)

The Tasks

- What *specific* tasks occur in the student's natural environments that enable progress toward mastery of IEP goals and objectives?
- What *specific* tasks are required for active involvement in identified environments?

Analyze the information gathered on the student, the environments, and the tasks to address the following questions and activities:

The Tools

- Is it expected that the student will not be able to make reasonable progress toward educational goals without assistive technology devices and services?
- If yes, describe what a useful system of assistive technology devices and services for the student would be like.
- Brainstorm tools that could be included in a system that addresses student needs.
- Select the most promising tools for trials in the natural environments.
- Plan the specifics of the trial (expected changes, when and how tools will be used, cues, etc.).
- Collect data on effectiveness.

Revisit the SETT Framework information periodically to determine if the information that is guiding decision making and implementation is accurate, up-to-date, and clearly reflects the shared knowledge of all involved.

Source: Zabala, J. S. (2002). A brief updated introduction to the SETT framework. Retrieved April 16, 2007 from http://sweb.uky.edu/~jszaba0/SETTupdate2002.html

3. the tasks

4. the tools

Within each area, specific guiding questions are provided or issues are raised to assist those who are charged with considering students' assistive technology needs. The SETT Framework intentionally puts tools (assistive technology) last, emphasizing the importance of keeping the focus on the student, where the student functions, and the tasks the student needs to accomplish. It is only after these three elements have been given due attention that Zabala recommends thinking about assistive technology. In this manner, technology decisions remain student focused; meeting a student's needs, not the technology, is predominant. The SETT Framework is an iterative process; the student's characteristics, environments, and tasks need to be periodically revisited to ensure previously identified technology remains appropriate and additional technology is provided as needed.

SUMMARY

- A plethora of assistive technology options exist, yet selection must be based on student needs, not availability of technology.
- Federal law mandates that IEP teams consider whether a student would benefit from assistive technology. In order for this consideration to be effective, teams should employ a method that includes the seven elements that are hallmarks of exemplary assistive technology decision-making and assessment:

1. A team approach should be used. Occupational therapists, physical therapists, speech-language pathologists, assistive technology specialists, teachers, parents, and the student all contribute their expertise and unique perspectives. Working together, assistive technology solutions are apt to be more appropriate than solutions developed with less input.

2. The focus should be on students' needs and abilities. The selection of assistive technology should address specific goals and be based on a student's strengths.

3. The tasks a student needs to complete should be considered in detail and assistive technology selected that would enhance the student's ability to successfully complete the task.

4. Consideration should be given to relevant environmental issues such as portability and whether or not access to a power supply is required. The attitudinal environment must also be considered. Assistive technology use will be more successful when those supporting the student understand and appreciate that the technology is a tool that facilitates student success in achieving educational goals.

5. A trial use of assistive technology is necessary to determine if the assistive technology is appropriate. At times, an extended trial may be needed. Time and consideration must be given to a potential learning curve when introducing new technology.

6. Sufficient technical support and training must be provided for students and all persons involved in supporting students' use of the technology.

7. Assistive technology assessment should be considered an ongoing process to address students' changing needs, abilities, and environments and ensure that they benefit from advances in technology.

- Assistive technology resource centers can provide training and technical support and offer guidelines to support technology assessments.
- There are a variety of assistive technology decision-making guides. Among the most widely known are Quality Indicators for Assessment of Assistive Technology Needs, Educational Tech Points for Assistive Technology Planning, and the SETT Framework. Each includes the seven hallmarks of exemplary assistive technology assessment.

WEB RESOURCES

For additional information on the topics listed, go to the following websites:

Assistive Technology Teams

National Assistive Technology in Education Network (NATE Network)
Assistive Technology Teams: Many Ways to Do It Well
http://natenetwork.buffalo.edu

Assistive Technology Assessment

Alliance for Technology Access: Assessment Resources
http://www.ataccess.org/resources/atk12/assessment.html
Special Education Technology British Columbia: Alternate Access Technologies: A Guide for School-Based Teams. Download PDF from:
http://www.setbc.org/Download/LearningCentre/Access/alt_acc_tech.pdf

Trial Use of Assistive Technology

NATE Network: Data Collection Forms
http://natenetwork.buffalo.edu/products.htm
WATI: Extended Assessment of Assistive Technology Needs
http://www.wati.org/AT_Services/extendedassess.html

Assistive Technology Decision-Making Guides

Quality Indicators for Assessment of Assistive Technology Needs
http://QIAT.org
Education Tech Points
http://www.wati.org/AT_Services/edutech.html
SETT Framework
http://sweb.uky.edu/~jszaba0/SETTupdate2002.html

SUGGESTED ACTIVITIES

1. *Add to Your Portfolio.* Visit the QIAT website (http://www.qiat.org). Review the Quality Indicators for Assistive Technology Services by clicking on the link "Quality Indicators." Add a copy of the Quality Indicators to your portfolio.

2. *Use the SETT Framework.* Using a SETT form like the one below, complete the section on technology tools for the following student.

Student: Bradley is a 6-year-old boy in first grade. He is nonverbal, cannot use a pencil or other writing tools, and is unable to use a standard keyboard or mouse. Bradley controls his wheelchair by using a joystick with his right hand. He has a delightful personality, no visual or perceptual impairments, and at least average cognitive ability.

Environment: Bradley is included in a general education first-grade classroom in his neighborhood school.

Tasks: Bradley needs a means of completing daily assignments and demonstrating his knowledge related to early reading and writing.

SETT Framework for Assistive Technology Decision-Making

Student	Environment(s)	Tasks	Tech Tools
Bradley 6 years old, in first grade, non-speaking, cannot use a pencil or other writing tool, not able to use a standard keyboard or mouse, controls his wheelchair with a joystick with his right hand, has a delightful personality, no visual or perceptual impairments, at least average cognitive ability.	Is included in a general education first grade classroom in his neighborhood school.	Needs a means of completing daily assignments and demonstrating his knowledge related to early reading and writing.	

3. *Conduct a Parent Interview.* Interview the parent(s) of a student who uses assistive technology for computer access. After you have completed the interview, compare the answers with the information provided in this chapter regarding the role of the parent and trial use of assistive technology. Prepare a three to five page paper that summarizes the parental responses and your comparison. Ask the following questions as well as questions that have been approved by your instructor:
   a. What professionals were involved in making the decision regarding the assistive technology that was appropriate for your child?
   b. Did your child get to try the assistive technology before a final decision was made? If so, how long did he or she use it before the final decision?
   c. Were you involved in the decision-making process? If so, in what ways were you involved?

REFERENCES

Beigel, A. R. (2000). Assistive technology assessment: More than the device. *Intervention in School and Clinic, 35*(4), 237–243.

Bauder, D., Lewis, P., Gobert, C., & Bearden, C. (1997). *Assistive technology guidelines for Kentucky schools.* Frankfort, KY: Kentucky Department of Education. Retrieved January 29, 2005, from http://kysig.louisville.edu/pdf/atguide.pdf

Bowser, G., & Reed, P. (1995). Education TECH points for assistive technology planning. *Journal of Special Education Technology, 12*(4), 325–338.

Chambers, A. (1997, October/November). Consideration: A detailed look . . . Has technology been considered? *Closing the Gap, 17*(4).

Gruner, A., Fleming, E., Carl, B., Diamond, C. M., Ruedel, K. L. A., Saunders, J., et al. (2000). *Synthesis on the selection and use of assistive technology* (Final report). Washington, DC: U.S. Department of Education.

Lewis, R. B. (1997). Changes in technology use in California's special education programs. *Remedial and Special Education, 18*(4), 233–234.

Lueck, A. H., Dote-Kwan, J., Senge, J. C., & Clarke, L. (2001). Selecting assistive technology for greater independence. *RE:view, 33*(1), 21–33.

McGregor, G., & Pachuski, P. (1996). Assistive technology in schools: Are teachers ready, able, and supported? *Journal of Special Education Technology, 13*(1), 4–15.

McInerney, M., Osher, D., & Kane, M. (1997). *Improving the availability and use of technology for children with disabilities* (Final Report). Washington, DC: Chesapeake Institute of the American Institutes for Research.

Newton, D. (2002). *The impact of a local assistive technology team on the implementation of assistive technology in a school setting.* Unpublished doctoral dissertation, University of Cincinnati.

Newton, D., & Petroff, J. (2005, January). *What happens after the evaluation?* Paper presented at the Assistive Technology Industry Association Conference, Orlando, FL.

Office of Special Education Programs. (2000). *Promising practices in technology: Supporting access to, and progress in, the general curriculum.* Washington, DC: U.S. Department of Education.

Parette, P., & McMahan, G. A. (2002). What should we expect of assistive technology? Being sensitive to family goals. *Teaching Exceptional Children, 35*(1), 56–61.

QIAT Consortium (2005). Quality Indicators for Assistive Technology services: Research-based update. Retrieved April 16, 2007, from http://www.qiat.org

Reed, P. (2004). *The W.A.T.I. assessment package: Assistive technology assessment.* Oshkosh, WI: Wisconsin Assistive Technology Initiative.

Riemer-Reiss, M., & Wacker, R. (2000). Factors associated with assistive technology discontinuance among individuals with disabilities. *Journal of Rehabilitation, 66*(3), 44–50.

Wahl, L., & Haugen, K. (2005). Selecting technology: What products are best for me? In Alliance for Technology Access (Ed.), *Computer resources for people with disabilities: A guide to assistive technologies, tools and resources for people of all ages* (4th ed., pp. 58–89). Alameda, CA: Hunter House.

Wessels, R., Dijcks, B., Soede, M., & DeWitte, L. (2003). Non-use of provided assistive technology devices, a literature overview. *Technology and Disability, 15*, 231–238.

Zabala, J. S. (2002). A brief updated introduction to the SETT framework. Retrieved November 11, 2004, from http://sweb.uky.edu/~jszaba0/SETTupdate2002.html.

PART **III**

Augmentative Communication

CHAPTER 9
Selecting and Designing a Student's Augmentative
Communication System

CHAPTER 10
Low-Tech Approaches to Teaching Early Communication
and Emergent Literacy

CHAPTER 11
Integrating Augmentative Communication in the Classroom,
Home, and Community

Selecting and Designing a Student's Augmentative Communication System

FOCUS QUESTIONS

1. Are there any prerequisites to augmentative communication?
2. What are the myths and realities surrounding augmentative communication?
3. Who must be involved in the selection and design of a student's augmentative communication system?
4. What are the primary considerations involved in selecting and designing a student's augmentative communication system?
5. What are the three major components of an augmentative communication system that must be determined during the selection process?

INTRODUCTION

Over the past several decades, the use of augmentative or alternative communication systems (referred to as augmentative communication in this text) increasingly has become a solution for many people with disabilities who in the past would not have been able to participate fully in school, the workplace, or the community (Downey & Hurtig, 2003). Students who are nonspeaking or unable to express themselves effectively through spoken language are candidates for augmentative communication systems. As defined in Chapter 5, *augmentative communication* is a term used to describe a wide range of solutions to difficulties in communication. These solutions are considered "aided" when they include the use of a device such as a language board or talking computer, or "unaided" when they involve the use of pointing, facial expressions, or sign language. Augmentative communication systems may be based on low-, mid-, or high-tech solutions, or a combination of all three, but it is essential to include the individual's personal approach to expressing himself or herself in the system. For example, some people who have difficult-to-understand speech may use a voice output computerized device for communicating complex messages, but use facial expressions, a nod, or single word approximations for simple responses to questions. Other people may use a language board to point to specific pictures that represent words or ideas, but also respond to yes/no questions using gestures. The sidebar presents the perspective of an adult augmentative communication user on the benefits of combining low-, mid-, and high-tech approaches.

SIDEBAR

Confessions of a Multimodal Man

Call me fickle, I've never been loyal to one communication mode. I'll use anything that seems most efficient in a given situation. Like when I am going to the movies, I know I'm not going to spend a lot of time chatting up the ticket seller, so before I leave home I use my computer to print up a sign that says what movie I want a ticket for. I flash that at the ticket seller when I get to the theatre. It's just a whole lot quicker.

Becoming a parent has forced me into situations I never dreamt I'd be in. Who knew I'd be going to PTA meetings, parent-teacher conferences, or having to deal with such things as play dates?

Then there's the whole youth culture thing. My son, who's grown now, exposed me to the wonderful world of Eminem and Snoop Dogg. Now with my daughter, I'm having to deal with such people as Brittany Spears and those tycoons, Mary-Kate and Ashley. I would never choose any of these people to be in my social network. It's been quite an experience for a guy who grew up listening to the music of the 30s and 40s.

My favorite communication mode is e-mail. E-mail really levels the social playing field for me. It lets me present who I really am without all the annoying visual distractions of the in-person Michael Williams. I use e-mail to conduct business, negotiate contracts, make dates with friends, and foment cultural mischief. I find e-mail much more comfortable than the telephone, which I find extremely slow and frustrating.

Michael Williams with his Liberator (Prentke Romich).
Courtesy of Attainment Company

I use the Liberator, LightWRITER, and a printed letterboard every day at various times during the day. Why do I need three devices? Isn't one sufficient? In a word, no.

If I didn't have the Liberator, I wouldn't be here talking with you today. However, you'll notice the Lib is big and awkward, and if you could lift it, you'd discover it has a considerable weight factor to it. I carry the Lib on my lap, and it's very hard on my knees. I can feel your puzzled eyes boring through this page. You want to know why I don't mount the Liberator on my damn wheelchair. The short answer to this question is, I don't want to mount the Liberator on my damn wheelchair! Okay? Call me silly, but I don't want tons of assistive technology dripping off my chair. Its scares people off to see all that technological firepower coming at them. You think I'm kidding about this? I'm deadly serious about this.

There's a more important reason I don't mount the Lib on my wheelchair. Sitting here, I may look very disabled, but actually I have quite a bit of functionality in my body. I can transfer in and out of my wheelchair by myself fairly easily. This allows me to do some very important personal things without the help of other people. Things like go to the bathroom. Have you tried to negotiate your way into a public bathroom stall with a big, old communication device mounted on a wheelchair? You may get in the stall, but how do you get from your wheelchair onto the throne without falling on your ass as you hold onto the grab bar and gingerly attempt to swing past your communication device and lower yourself onto the seat? And that is why I don't mount the Liberator on my wheelchair!

Here's another thing to ponder: Observe the size of the Liberator. Notice its rather large footprint. Now imagine you have a really hot date and you want to book a table at a swank restaurant. How big a table do you book? If you book a table for two, one of you ain't gonna eat, or one of you ain't gonna talk, because the Liberator soaks up too much table space. If you book a table for three, you risk igniting the ire of the maitre d'. Either way, your evening is a bust, and your budding relationship is down the tubes.

I can feel your puzzled eyes boring through the page again. You're asking yourselves, What would Michael Williams do at a critical time like this? Well, I'll tell you what I'd do. I'd use either one of these handy-dandy augmentative communication tools. The letterboard lies nicely next to you on the table. Its basic black contributes an additional touch of suaveness to an already elegant dining ambiance. The letterboard, however, also provides a slightly more intense conversational experience. Your partner watches intently as your hand glides slowly across the smooth surface of the letterboard. Your long, lean finger languishes lovingly over each letter as it slowly constructs linguistic meaning out of chaos.

Don't care for such intensity? Try this LightWRITER. It's small, it's simple, it's elegant. And yes, ladies and gentlemen, it provides the perfect atmosphere for

(continued)

a conversation while dining. It sits primly on the corner of the table. Your partner need only flick a glance to the screen now and then to see what you are saying. And you have the added assurance that if your partner misses something, you need only push the talk button at the end of your thought and the LightWRITER will say it for you. And that, ladies and gentlemen, is why I use more than one communication device.

From *Why I Use More than One Communication Device,* by Michael B. Williams, presentation at California State University–Northridge's 20th Annual International Conference "Technology and persons with Disabilities," March 16, 2005, Los Angeles, CA. Reprinted with permission.

In order to realize success for an individual who is nonspeaking, an augmentative communication system must be carefully designed for use within the student's natural environments. Therefore, this chapter presents the critical issues in the decision-making process of selecting the appropriate components of a student's augmentative communication system, the implications for implementation, and the importance of ongoing evaluation and system modification. In addition, the roles of educational personnel, students' families, and the students themselves are presented within a structure of collaborative teaming for assessment and implementation.

An augmentative communication system must reflect the basic features of any traditional method of communication. That is, it must provide the user with the ability

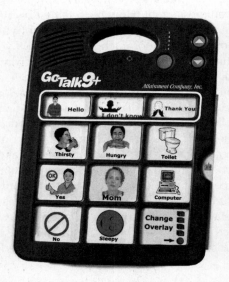

Sample mid-tech augmentative communication devices.
Courtesy of Attainment Company

Student using an augmentative communication system while doing school work.
Kevin J. Cohen. Used with permission.

to (1) construct a message using symbols, (2) deliver that message to another person (receiver), and (3) further respond to the receiver in a timely manner. In other words, an augmentative communication system must enable the user to initiate or sustain a conversation with another person. The following profiles of augmentative communication users illustrate the variability in systems while showing the consistency in the basic components of any model. (The technical features mentioned in these profiles are explained in more detail later in this chapter.)

Each of these students effectively and efficiently incorporates their innate abilities to communicate within a system of aided and unaided augmentative communication solutions. They have systems that are well constructed to meet their individualized

USER PROFILE: Julie

Julie is a fourth-grade student in a general education classroom who receives special education supports and services. She was born with a congenital condition, uses a motorized wheelchair, and is nonspeaking. Julie uses an augmentative communication system that consists of three methods of communication: (1) unaided; (2) aided, low-tech; and (3) aided, high-tech. Her unaided methods include a yes/no gesture and some intelligible single-word responses; the aided, low-tech method she uses is a simple call button that enables her to get people's attention; and the aided, high-tech method she uses is a computerized voice output device that she accesses with a stylus that she grasps in her fist. The voice output device uses an encoded symbol system that is capable of producing any word or phase with a reduced number of keystrokes.

USER PROFILE: Tim

Tim is a 12th-grade student who attends a program at his local high school that provides community-based vocational instruction. He has been sampling jobs in the community for the past 3 years and currently is working full time with supervision at the local video rental store. Tim has Down syndrome and has significant speech production difficulties. In addition, Tim has a moderate bilateral mixed hearing loss that compounds his verbal intelligibility and receptive language skills. To help him communicate on the job, Tim's augmentative communication system consists of facial expressions and simple gestures, and four aided components: (1) a handheld electronic device with a QWERTY keyboard that produces a visual display and printed message; (2) a small voice output device with 16 messages; (3) a white board to write messages; and (4) an FM amplification system to enhance specific listening circumstances such as work meetings and school functions.

needs. How were these systems designed? What factors were considered? The next section presents a recommended protocol for the process of selecting and designing augmentative communication systems.

CONSIDERATIONS IN SYSTEM SELECTION AND DESIGN

The initial steps in the selection and design of an augmentative communication system begin with a recognition that an individual requires and can benefit from enhanced methods of communication. Although professional dogma in the past declared that only certain people were candidates for augmentative communication systems, it is now believed that regardless of an individual's disability or the severity of that disability, *all* people with communication difficulties can achieve enhanced communication abilities through the use of augmentative communication (Hourcade, Everhart-Pilotte, West, & Parette, 2004; Kroth & Bolson, 1996). Individual differences and abilities inform the selection and design process, especially as it relates to the complexity of some devices, but *all* nonspeaking individuals should be given the benefit of augmentative communication consideration. Current practice reflects the position that the only prerequisite to communication is opportunity. In other words, every individual who is nonspeaking or presents difficulty in using speech that cannot be easily remediated is a candidate for consideration.

Myths and Realities

Waiting for so-called prerequisites to develop is only one of many misconceptions that have negatively affected services to students with disabilities who are nonspeaking. Table 9.1 lists other common myths and provides accurate information to counter these myths. Teachers need to be aware of these realities so that they can

TABLE 9–1   Myths and realities about augmentative communication

Myth	Reality	Reference
Augmentative communication will inhibit further development of speech and therefore must be used only as a last resort.	Augmentative communication does not inhibit an individual's further development of speech and, in some cases, may actually enhance speech development.	Daniels, 1994; Finch & Romski, 2004; Schlosser, 2003
Specific levels of cognitive abilities are required prior to using augmentative communication devices.	There are no readiness criteria for teaching communication. Waiting for students to be "ready" only prevents the further development of needed communication skills.	Kangas & Lloyd, 1988; Van Tatenhove, 1987
A student must present specific adaptive behavior skills such as eye contact and a well-defined point before augmentative communication may be considered.	Readiness criteria based on behavioral characteristics are unsupported by the research and should not apply to the augmentative communication consideration process.	Beukelman & Mirenda, 2005 (p. 134)
Augmentative communication requires some level of literacy skill prior to consideration.	Augmentative communication devices can be used as a source of support or scaffolding in the educational process and can provide a means to further develop literacy skills.	Hetzroni, 2004; Erickson, 2000; Musselwhite & King-DeBaun, 1997

provide appropriate supports for students who are—or soon will be—augmentative communication users in their classes.

Who Should Assess? Collaborative Team Assessment Approach

The process for selecting and designing an augmentative communication system for a student involves the coordinated efforts of a team of professionals, parents, and the student. It is critical that decisions regarding system selection and design use a broad range of information (Beukelman & Mirenda, 2005). Therefore, a team that represents a variety of relevant disciplines and has knowledge of the student must be convened. The team members may vary depending on the needs of the specific student. For example, in the two profiles presented earlier, Julie's team includes an occupational therapist to help with fine motor issues related to her accessing the call button and the high-tech device with a stylus. In contrast, Tim's augmentative communication system does not need the input of an occupational therapist; rather, his team includes the job coach from his community-based vocational program.

In addition to these individualized team members, all augmentative communication assessment teams must include the following: (1) a professional, such as a speech-language therapist, who is trained and experienced in augmentative communication assessment and applications; (2) the student; (3) his or her parent(s) or family members; and (4) the teacher(s) or other professionals involved in the student's everyday school, community, or work environment. These four core categories are essential to ensure the identification of a successful augmentative communication

USER PROFILE: John

John is a 7-year-old boy with cerebral palsy who is nonspeaking. His parents arranged to have him evaluated for augmentative communication at a hospital-based assistive technology assessment center. Although they accompanied him to the evaluation, no one from John's school program attended the evaluation. The assessment results recommended a complex augmentative communication system that used auditory scanning and a head switch for activation. Unfortunately, when the recommendation was provided to the school, several problems were apparent. First, the auditory scan feature was loud and disruptive to the other students in John's general education classroom, and there was no option for using headphones. Second, John's head switch was in a position that may have seemed appropriate at the assessment center but was incongruent and in opposition to his physical therapist's goals for positioning.

system; other members may be added to the team if they have specialized knowledge or expertise related to the specific student. Without the participation of these team members, the resulting system will be poorly designed and difficult or impossible to implement. The following user profile illustrates the problems that can arise when appropriate team members are not included in the assessment process.

When teachers or other professionals familiar with the student are not included in the decision-making process, it is more likely that the augmentative communication system will not be appropriate to the school setting and that school personnel will not have an understanding of the implementation features of the system. A comparable situation occurs when school staff does not adequately involve the parent(s) or family in the assessment process. This often results in the development of communication systems that may not transfer well to the home environment, the one in which the student spends most of his or her time. Further, when the student's ideas and preferences are not considered in the assessment process, the result may be technology abandonment (Grady, Kovach, Lange, & Shannon, 1993). In this case, the student abandons the use of the devices and resorts to more familiar but less effective forms of communication. Therefore, it is critical to recognize that the selection and design of an augmentative communication system must reflect a collaborative team approach and must include the student and people who are familiar with the student. Table 9.2 lists possible collaborative team members and their functions.

A collaborative team is characterized by people working in concert to achieve a common goal, using an interdependent process in which there is parity, shared resources, and respect for each other's disciplines (Snell & Janney, 2000). This form of teaming represents a transdisciplinary approach in which members contribute and integrate their knowledge to select and design an individualized augmentative communication system. It allows for role differentiation between disciplines that are defined by the situation, rather than by discipline-specific characteristics (Bruder, 1994). For example, although the speech-language therapist is the expert in communication, it is the teacher who implements the augmentative communication system routinely in the classroom, so the team may decide that the teacher will be the person to introduce the new system and its new vocabulary to the student. The

TABLE 9–2 Possible collaborative team members

Augmentative Communication Team Member	Function
Student	Provides input regarding successful existing methods of communication, personal preferences, and ease of use.
Teachers	Provide input regarding classroom environment, daily schedules, and communication needs in the curriculum.
Parent(s) and family members	Provide input regarding home environment, family activities, and communication needs at home and in the community.
Professional who is trained and experienced in augmentative communication assessment and applications	Provides input regarding the student's communicative status and function; knowledgeable about augmentative communication systems and features.
Occupational therapist	Provides input regarding the student's fine motor abilities and sensory challenges.
Physical therapist	Provides assistance and support for the gross motor and seating or positioning needs of the student.
Information technology support person	Provides advice about and technical assistance in connecting augmentative communication devices to computers, the school's network, and the Internet and serves as a troubleshooter for implementation.
Peer of the student	Provides input to the appropriateness and function of an augmentative communication system from an age-appropriate perspective

speech-language therapist remains an important team member but releases his or her direct service role to the teacher.

Other characteristics of the augmentative communication team are that the assessment process must be viewed as ongoing and team members must communicate regularly with each other. Last, the collaborative assessment team must place the student in a central and active role in decision making. Regardless of the student's abilities or challenges, the student must be involved in every step of the process and must be a major contributor to all decisions.

How Should the Team Assess? Features of the Collaborative Assessment Process

The approach to augmentative communication assessment has evolved over the past several decades. Currently, students are assessed by teams who work in collaboration from the early stages of selection and design, through implementation, and finally to

TABLE 9–3   Participation model for collaborative team assessment

- Assessment of a student's current communication patterns
- Assessment of a student's needs across daily routines
- Identification of access barriers within the natural environment
- Determination of future communication needs in these environments
- Selection and design of an augmentative communication system
- Evaluation of the efficiency and effectiveness of the augmentative communication system (ongoing)

Source: Adapted from *Augmentative and Alternative Communication* (3rd ed.), by D. R. Beukelman and P. Mirenda, 2005, Baltimore: Paul Brookes Publishing.

evaluation of the efficiency and effectiveness of the system. The **communication needs model** developed by Beukelman, Yorkston, and Dowden (1985) has been refined to reflect a systematic collaborative process, which they refer to as the **participation model** (Beukelman & Mirenda, 2005). The participation model is a collaborative assessment approach that requires a multiphase assessment process, as outlined in Table 9.3, and uses consensus building as a central feature of the process. It begins with the assessment of a student's current communication patterns and needs across daily routines, and it continues with the identification of access barriers within the natural environment. Next, future communication needs are discussed; only then is the

TABLE 9–4   Factors to consider during collaborative augmentative communication assessments

Considerations in Augmentative Communication Assessment	Questions to Ask
Developmental status	What are the student's abilities and challenges in related developmental domains such as fine motor skills and problem-solving skills?
Communication status	What are the student's current communication methods? Are they effective and efficient in the current environment? Will they be sufficient in the student's future environments?
Attributes of the environment	What are the communicative demands of the student's current and future environments? What barriers to communication exist in the student's environments?
Communication needs	What communication needs of the student are not being met efficiently and effectively through his or her current forms of communication?
Augmentative communication solutions	What augmentative communication solutions can be implemented to reduce the unmet needs?
Effectiveness of augmentative communication solution	Is the selected system effectively meeting the student's communication needs in all environments?

From *Augmentative and Alternative Communication* (3rd ed.), by D. R. Beukelman and P. Mirenda, 2005, Baltimore: Paul Brookes Publishing.

selection and design of a system undertaken. This is followed by the team's ongoing evaluation of the efficiency and effectiveness of the system.

The use of a collaborative team approach that is future oriented prevents the static nature of some augmentative communication systems. There must be ongoing recognition that students' communication needs change and evolve to meet the demands of new environments. As students grow, their augmentative communication systems need to transform to meet new challenges and situations. Table 9.4 summarizes Beukelman and Mirenda's (2005) recommendations for factors to consider during collaborative augmentative communication assessments.

What Components Must Be Identified?
Symbols, Vocabulary, and Access Method

In determining the best augmentative communication solution, the collaborative team must determine the most appropriate components of the student's system. This section focuses on three major decisions that need to be made at this point in the assessment: the **symbol system** to be used to represent vocabulary, the specific **vocabulary**—or messages—the student will express with the system, and the method by which the student will **access** the system. Decisions regarding these three components are guided by the following questions:

- To what extent can the student access symbolic language? What kind of symbols are most understandable to the student?

- What messages would the student most likely need and want to express to others?

- What parameters and challenges does the student present regarding access to the use of augmentative communication devices? Which access method would be most effective at this time?

How Are Symbol Systems Selected? A symbol is "something that stands for or represents something else" (Vanderheiden & Yoder, 1986, p. 15). More specifically, it is an arbitrary representation of a concept that speakers of a language agree has a specific meaning. Symbols can be spoken as in speech, graphically represented as in written language, or formed through hand shapes, as in sign language. Symbols are arbitrary because there does not need to be any clear relationship between the symbol and the concept. For example, all English-speaking people recognize that the graphic symbols "D," "O," and "G" represent specific sounds that when put together refer to a class of animals that have four legs and fur, bark, and are kept as pets. The symbol "dog" and the spoken word *dog* do not look or sound anything like the object to which they refer.

Selecting a symbol system is a major part of an augmentative communication assessment. A symbol system can range from abstract symbols, such as the alphabet and words, to concrete systems such as real objects. In between these two points on the continuum are symbol systems comprised of line drawings, icons, pictures, and photographs. Symbol systems are classified according to their degree of **iconicity**, that is, the clarity of their meanings in isolation (Beukelman & Mirenda, 2005).

Photographs and real objects are said to be **transparent** because their meaning is clear without any additional information. Written words are considered **opaque** because they can be understood only by people who can read. In between, symbol sets are said to be **translucent** because the meanings of some of the symbols are obvious, but other symbols are more abstract; translucent symbol sets are usually comprised of line drawings. "Much of the magic of augmentative communication lies in the vast array of symbols, . . . other than those used in speech, that people can employ to send messages. Especially for individuals who cannot read or write, the ability to represent messages and concepts in alternative ways is central to communication" (Beukelman & Mirenda, 2005, p. 40).

Boardmaker (Mayer-Johnson) is a widely used software program that is based on a system of line drawings called the Picture Communication Symbols. Many of the symbols for common nouns and verbs are easily understood and are considered transparent. Other symbols require some shared knowledge to understand; these are not as obvious and are considered translucent (see Figure 9.1 for examples of Boardmaker symbols). In designing an augmentative communication system, the team could choose to use either or both of these kinds of symbols.

Some augmentative communication users are able to use the alphabet and the written word, and prefer a text-based system as their symbol system. The advantage to a spelling system is that *any* idea or thought can be expressed. However, spelling out entire sentences is extremely time-consuming and does not lend itself to spontaneous conversation. In addition, it requires high levels of literacy. Children and young adults who read below grade level do not have the necessary reading and spelling skills to use text-based symbol systems effectively. The slow rate at which complex messages can be constructed using alphabet and word boards has led many augmentative users to prefer alternatives to text-based systems.

One popular alternative is the pictorial language system called Minspeak (Semantic Compaction Systems), which forms the basis for the Unity system used in augmentative communication devices produced by the Prentke Romich Company. Minspeak and Unity are based on a visual language method called semantic compaction that uses a bank of carefully selected icons that can be easily combined to mean different things. The icons were selected deliberately to have multiple meanings and to be easily remembered. For example, to say the name of an animal, a user presses the "zebra" icon first. To say colors, a user presses the "rainbow" key first. Figure 9.2 contains examples of icon sequences. Learning the meanings of these icons and remembering how they are sequenced to convey different messages is known as **encoding**. Encoding enables an augmentative user to construct messages with less effort and time by striking fewer keys.

The Unity series has a consistent set of icons for several levels, with consistent patterns for forming words and phrases. Each stage of Unity builds on the skills a student has already learned. The most advanced Unity system comprises a core vocabulary that represents the few hundred words that make up 85% of common conversation. High-end devices using Unity also include text-based features such as a QWERTY spelling keyboard and word prediction to facilitate the addition of custom vocabulary.

From this brief discussion it is clear that symbols vary in complexity from higher order symbol sets such as Unity and text to less complex symbols such as object cues that represent single activities. Determining which symbol set best matches a student's

FIGURE 9–1 Sample Boardmaker symbols

Boardmaker Symbol	Typical Meaning	Degree of Iconicity
	"ice cream"	Transparent
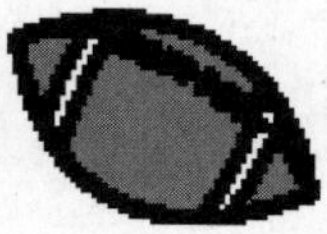	"football"	Transparent
	"run"	Transparent
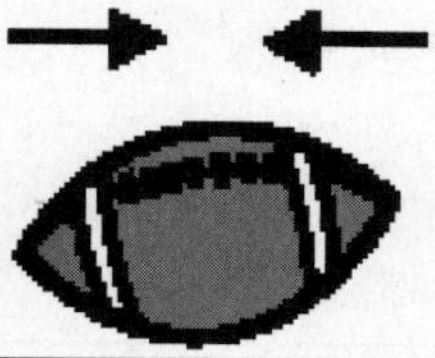	"football game"	Translucent
	"I don't like that show."	Translucent
	"I am so angry!"	Translucent

(continued)

FIGURE 9–1 (continued)

	"That's so funny!"	Translucent
	"How do you play?" or "I don't know how to play this game."	Translucent
	"Can I play?"	Translucent
	"I have no one to play with."	Translucent
	"Please repeat that."	Opaque
	"I would like some more."	Opaque
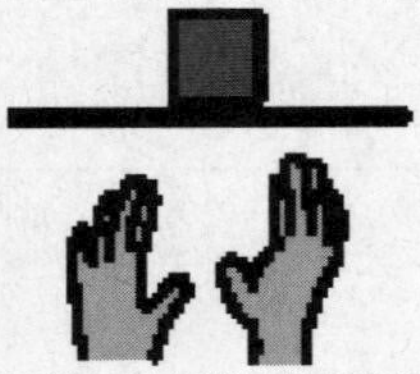	"I want . . ."	Opaque

	"Have you heard . . . ?"	Opaque
	"Let's go home."	Opaque
	"Let's talk later."	Opaque

Source: The Picture Communication Symbols © 1981–2006 by Mayer-Johnson LLC. All rights reserved worldwide. Used with permission.

needs is, therefore, an important part of the augmentative communication assessment process.

The symbol assessment process begins with evaluating whether the student has a basic ability to determine the function of objects. At this stage, the team observes the student for evidence that he or she understands the fundamental link between an item and its use. For example, a cup is used for drinking or keys are used to start a car and go on a trip. From this point, the team progresses to transferring object symbols to less iconic representations such as photographs or line drawings. If the student successfully masters the match between objects and pictures, then the team further assesses the student's ability to understand and utilize more iconic symbol representations. Augmentative communication candidates who demonstrate an ability to understand language and words are better positioned to learn more sophisticated symbol systems than candidates who have not yet developed these skills.

In addition to the team's assessment of the type of symbol system to use, they must consider other variables that will influence its effectiveness. These variables include:

- Will the initial symbol system change as the student demonstrates more complex symbolic abilities? For example, will the symbol system change from simple objects to pictures or from pictures to line drawings?
- Will the symbol system reflect the student's skills in encoding messages?
- What is the most appropriate size for the symbols?
- How many symbols can be displayed at one time?
- How many symbols will be introduced at first?
- Can the student access multiple categories of symbols?

FIGURE 9–2   Unity's natural language structure

Building Basic Phrases and Sentences

With Unity, a client can select an icon to express single words and easily progress to building short phrases and complete sentences by using the same icons. The examples demonstrate how the natural language structure of Unity is used to build vocabulary.

The **action man** icon (or **verb** as it is labeled) is associated with verbs or things you do, such as **"drink."**

The **juice** icon plus the **adjective** icon communicates **"thirsty."**

The **he** icon represents the subject. The universally popular **sun** with a pleasant smiley face icon represents **"like."**

How Is Vocabulary Selected?   Once the appropriate symbol system is identified and the devices are identified, an initial vocabulary must be selected. It is especially important that the student continue or heighten his or her active role in the decision-making process. Vocabulary selection is a large factor in the successful use of any augmentative communication system (Balandin & Iacono, 1998). Many teams make the mistake of identifying vocabulary that is important to caregivers or teachers rather than to the student who will be using the system. Instead, the team must work to select vocabulary that is empowering to the individual. This means communication must begin with messages that are highly motivating, such as requests for preferred objects or activities, questions that will enable the student to initiate conversation with another student, and comments that will get a reaction from other people. The selection of specific words and phrases should fit with the student's culture and age group. Teenagers, for example, do not want to sound like their (older) speech therapists or teachers; they want to use the same slang expressions that their peers are using.

For example, most teenagers do not say "How are you today?" or "I am fine, thank you." Instead, they have their own way of greeting each other and answering these kinds of questions, and the augmentative communication system's vocabulary should

The **apple** icon followed by **action man** products the verb **"eat."**

The **apple** icon followed by **action man** products the verb **"eat."**

$$\text{apple} + \text{action man} = eat$$

Apple plus **adjective** produces the adjective **"hungry."**

$$\text{apple} + \text{adjective} = hungry$$

Statements or questions can be easily created by simply reversing certain icon sequences.

$$\text{he} + \text{sun} + \text{drink} + \text{coffee} = He\ likes\ coffee.$$

$$\text{sun} + \text{he} + \text{drink} + \text{coffee} = Does\ he\ like\ coffee?$$

How It Works

In Unity, the core vocabulary icons are simply used to teach an association. For example, the apple is associated with the concept of eating and the rainbow is associated with colors. Eventually, the communicator doesn't think "apple"; rather, he or she automatically touches the apple icon as part of saying the word "eat."

Source: From the Prentke Romich Company, http://www.prentrom.com/language/unity/index.php?page=5. Reprinted with permission.

reflect this "kid-talk." Teachers need to become familiar with the slang their students use and incorporate these phrases in the device's vocabulary. Humor is often very motivating for students, so including jokes and sarcastic comments is often effective.

The following guidelines may be used to identify meaningful vocabulary:

- Provide messages that enable the student to greet other students and begin a conversation.

- Include vocabulary that enables the student to comment on events and activities, both as a way to express his or her opinion and as a way to continue a conversation.

- Provide vocabulary that includes specific people who are important in the student's life and enables the student to call them.

- Include favorite activities or objects and the vocabulary that enables the student to request them.

Student using an augmentative communication device to participate in a classroom activity.

Kevin J. Cohen. Used with permission.

- Make sure the student has a way of conveying his or her feelings, such as "That makes me really angry."
- Include a method for protest. Provide a way of refusing or saying no. For example, "I don't want to do that," "I need a break," or "I want to be alone."
- Use age-appropriate and culturally sensitive words and phrases, including slang.
- Incorporate humor and sarcasm if age appropriate.

Identifying preferred vocabulary and words that have significance for the student may not be a simple task. Many individuals do not have the ability to express the circumstances in which they would find communication the most powerful. Therefore, it is necessary for the team to look outward to other people in the student's life and from other assessment initiatives (Yorkston, Honsinger, Dowden, & Marriner, 1988). The team must employ multiple assessment strategies that may include the following:

- Interviews with family members, including siblings and grandparents
- Interviews with friends and same-age peers
- Preference inventories that detail an individual's likes and dislikes
- Direct observation across environments, activities, and people
- Analysis of challenging behavior

How Are Symbols Grouped or Arranged? In addition to selecting the symbol system, the vocabulary, and an access method, the collaborative team must decide how to arrange the symbols on the device. Because efficiency in communicating is the greatest

USER PROFILE: Life Skills Classroom

The day begins in this Life Skills classroom much like in other classrooms at the elementary school in this town. The students arrive, hang up their coats and bags, and greet the teacher and the assistant. However, here is where a difference arises. Of the 12 students in the class, ages 8–12, four of the students proceed to take their augmentative communication devices out of their backpacks and put on their speech wallets. The whole class puts on name tags imprinted with their name and favorite symbol. The name tags help develop sight words, and the symbols are cues for the students who use the augmentative devices to know which key to press to address that child.

Vocabulary Selection

Ms. G., the special education teacher, has learned that to motivate her students to communicate she must provide vocabulary which interests them. Before selecting vocabulary for a device, she works with the parents and the student to determine appropriate vocabulary. She makes a point of including favorite activities, expressions of emotions, humorous messages, and if appropriate, sarcastic comments. Ms. G. recommends listening to other students in the school to find out what expressions are current and popular. Some of her favorites include "Yea, no school!" "See you later, alligator," and "Stop being a crybaby." Other high interest messages which are stored on the students' devices are listed below:

Sample Age-Appropriate Messages Stored on Students' Augmentative Communication Devices

- Wow, that was so cool!
- I don't want to play.
- We did something fun at school.
- School was yucky today.
- Don't tell me what to do.
- Will you help me call someone?
- That's great news.
- Can I go with my friends?
- I'm going to tell on you.
- I can do it myself.
- What's your problem?
- No way, man!
- Oh no. I have homework.
- She really makes me mad.
- He's so funny.

A Collaborative Effort

Ms. G. notes that it takes time and commitment on the part of the teacher, the speech-language specialist, the parents, and the students to integrate augmentative communication devices into the classroom. She attends training workshops with the parents, and she spends a good deal of prep time each week programming the devices with appropriate vocabulary for classroom activities. She makes a corresponding speech wallet for each student which hooks to a belt loop to serve as a nonelectronic backup to their high-tech devices. These manual backups are essential for those times when devices break or batteries run down.

(continued)

Her efforts, however, have reaped many benefits in her classroom. She has seen communication initiation increase as her students now have a way to express emotions and ask for help. "I need to see the nurse," "I need help," and "Please leave me alone" are some of the initiations she has observed. The students also communicate with each other now. Christopher likes to stop students in the hallway to say, "Hi! How are you today?" When Seth killed a spider that the class had been watching, Christopher said, "Seth, I'm mad at you. That was not very nice. It is dead. Spider."

The class recently began a campaign to educate the regular education staff and students in their school about augmentative communication. Classes visit Ms. G.'s room to hear her students explain their devices and read the story *Brown Bear, Brown Bear, What Do You See?* Christopher describes his device as follows:

> This machine is called a Liberator. I use it to help me talk. Sometimes the battery gets low, and I have to plug it in. I can do it on my own. I wear a WalkerTalker [a simpler, low-tech device] around my waist. I wear it all the time.

Christopher, Eli and Bobby then take turns reading pages of *Brown Bear, Brown Bear.* This experience gives the other classes an opportunity to learn about augmentative communication, see the devices in action, ask questions about them, and make some new friends.

From "Functional Communication in a Life Skills Class," by Regina Quinn, 1996. *TECH-NJ*, pp. 6, 15. *7*(2). Reprinted with permission.

challenge to an augmentative communication user, the arrangement of symbols should maximize the student's rate of communication. Preferred layouts include those that allow the user easy access to words, phrases, and full sentences that are likely to be used often, and ease in constructing novel messages. A student who has control over only one hand, for example, needs frequently used words and phrases placed on the side of the device closest to a functioning hand. Decisions about symbol arrangement should consider the student's current developmental stage. For children whose language is still developing, a symbol array that provides practice in typical language skills may be helpful. For example, a child who is learning the rules of word order in sentences may benefit from a symbol array that groups parts of speech together—nouns on the left, verbs in the middle, adjectives on the right. As the child constructs a sentence he or she moves from left to right, an essential skill in literacy development. Children who are learning about classifying items by attributes may need an array that groups categories of items together, such as foods, toys, and family members (Beukelmen & Mirenda, 2005).

Visual scene display is a symbol arrangement that is effective with beginning communicators and those with more complex challenges. Instead of simply arranging symbols in rows and columns, a visual scene display begins with a large picture or photograph that provides a context for more detailed information (Blackstone, 2004). As the student clicks on part of the large picture, vocabulary related to that selection appears. For example, a picture of a classroom is shown on a computer screen. When the child places the mouse over a section of the room, detailed vocabulary is shown with additional choices. Using visual scene displays in augmentative communication devices creates a shared context for vocabulary. Research suggests it reduces the learning demands on young users and shifts the focus away from simple requests for desired objects to social interaction (Blackstone, 2004).

How Is the Access Method Determined? During the assessment process, the team is involved in discussions regarding the appropriate features of the system. In addition to the symbol system and vocabulary selection, the team must consider the manner in which the student will access the vocabulary (i.e., the selection method) and the manner in which the messages will be displayed (i.e., the system's output). Access to computers and selecting the most appropriate access methods were discussed in detail in Chapters 7 and 8. Many computer access methods discussed in these chapters are also available on augmentative communication systems. Therefore, this section focuses on access issues that are unique to augmentative communication.

Students who have a reliable point (the index finger extended at something) can use direct selection to construct messages on either low-tech language boards or high-tech computer-based systems. Direct selection may be accomplished in a variety of ways, including using direct finger pressure on specific keys; using a pointing device such as a head stick or chin stick; using an infrared beam that is mounted on the head; or pointing with the eyes (eye control, or eye gaze). However, many students do not have reliable motor abilities to use direct selection, and the team must collaborate to select and design a system that can be accessed through scanning.

Lori's user profile illustrates one alternative to direct selection for students to access their communication devices. Other methods include encoding systems such as Morse code that can be activated with two switches (one for dots and one for dashes) or the use of scanning with multiple switches or a joystick. It is critical that the team determines the most efficient and effective access method for the student with a focus on enhancing the rate of message development.

What Other Features Need to Be Considered? Other important features are for the team to consider the physical nature of the system and its compatibility with the natural environments in which the student will use it. The size, weight, mountability,

Student using direct selection to access her augmentative communication device.
Photo by Vicki Spence

USER PROFILE: Lori

Lori is a first-year high school student who uses a computerized voice output device that she accesses via single-switch scanning. She operates the device with a foot switch that when activated stops the scanning on her device at the desired selection. When she has completed composing a message, Lori scans to the Speak key and her device speaks the message using synthesized speech. Although this system is slower than direct selection, it is the most efficient system for Lori. This selection system enables Lori to construct any message she wants and gives her the freedom to communicate independently.

degree of water resistance, and other characteristics must be considered during the selection process. A student who uses a wheelchair does not need a lightweight system, but needs a system that can easily mount on his or her wheelchair. A student who is ambulatory (i.e., walks for mobility) needs a system that is portable. A student who walks and has behavior problems probably needs a system that is not only portable, but rugged as well. Last, selection of a dedicated versus a nondedicated system must be decided. A dedicated system is a stand-alone device designed specifically for augmentative communication. A nondedicated system is a computer, usually a laptop computer, that has been equipped with symbol system software and speech output so that it can be used for communication. This issue is decided primarily by personal preference. Most high-tech dedicated devices can be easily connected to a computer and students can use the device in place of the standard keyboard. This gives them access to the Internet and other applications in which they are interested. Dedicated devices tend to be more durable than laptop computers. The main advantage to laptop computers is that they are less expensive than dedicated devices.

As the team identifies the current skills of the student, the most appropriate symbol system, and the most efficient access method, consideration of specific devices—low, mid, and high tech—begins. It is at this point that the team begins to try out specific augmentative communication solutions that match the student's skills and needs. As the most appropriate and effective system becomes clear, the team then works to customize the system for the student's particular needs and interests.

EVALUATING THE EFFICIENCY AND EFFECTIVENESS OF A STUDENT'S AUGMENTATIVE COMMUNICATION SYSTEM

After an augmentative communication system is selected and designed for a student, the team's work is not over. Communication ability is a work in progress. Most beginner augmentative communication users need years to develop their communication skills and to progress through a hierarchy of skill levels until true independent communication is realized. Therefore, ongoing evaluation of the effectiveness and efficiency of a system must be conducted. As students' skills improve or become more challenging, devices become outdated, students' environments change, and students' needs change. For these reasons there needs to be an ongoing assessment effort that continues to engage the student and his or her family and teachers.

Anthony, who has cerebral palsy, uses the Pathfinder (Prentke Romich Company) to communicate. See his User Profile in Chapter 4.

Alberta Arnold. Reprinted with permission from Anthony Arnold.

CONCLUSION

Although the process of designing and selecting an augmentative communication system is always individualized, the underlying components are the same. The complicated nature of this task mandates the use of a team approach that takes direction from the student who is being considered for an augmentative communication system. The primary emphasis of this collaborative team is to create a system that will result in independent and functional communication by the student. The process is inclusive and centered on the needs, wants, and desires of the students themselves. In the next chapter we will discuss the emergent stages of early communication that lead students to more sophisticated systems of interaction. Chapter 11 focuses on strategies for supporting the communication of students who are augmentative communication users in the classroom.

SUMMARY

- There are no prerequisites to augmentative communication. All people with communication difficulties can achieve enhanced communication abilities through the use of augmentative communication.

- Teachers need to be aware of the myths and realities surrounding augmentative communication so that they can provide appropriate supports for students who are—or soon will be—augmentative communication users in their classes.

- The process for selecting and designing an augmentative communication system must involve a collaborative team that includes a professional, such as a speech-language therapist, who is trained and experienced in augmentative communication assessment and applications; the student; his or her parent(s) or family members; and his or her teacher(s). Additional team members may include a physical therapist, occupational therapist, tech support person, a peer, or anyone else who works closely with the student.

- Factors to consider during an augmentative communication assessment include the student's developmental status, current communication skills, attributes of the environment, and the student's current and future communication needs.

- The three major components of an augmentative communication system that must be determined are the symbol system, the vocabulary, and the student's access method. Other features to consider are portability, ruggedness, and the question of a dedicated device or a generic laptop computer.

- Ongoing evaluation of the effectiveness of the augmentative communication system is essential.

WEB RESOURCES

For additional information on the topics listed, go to the following websites:

More from Michael Williams, Writer and AAC User

AAC 101: A crash course for beginners
http://www.augcominc.com/articles/as_1_1.html

AT/AAC Enables: How Assistive Technology (AT) and Augmentative and Alternative Communication (AAC) Enable Individuals with Disabilities to Participate in All Aspects of Life

Dispelling myths
http://depts.washington.edu/enables/myths/myths_intro.htm

Profiles of Augmentative Communication Users
http://depts.washington.edu/enables/profiles/profiles_at_aac.htm

Augmentative Communication Users Join the Working World
http://depts.washington.edu/enables/myths/myths_aac_people_working.htm

Augmentative Communication Devices

Prentke Romich Company
http://www.prentrom.com

DynaVox Technologies
http://www.dynavoxtech.com/

Words+, Inc.
http://www.words-plus.com/index.htm

Assistive Technology, Inc.
http://www.assistivetech.com/prod-index.htm

Collaborative Teaming for Assessment

QIAT Consortium: Quality Indicator #2
http://www.qiat.org

Cerebral Palsy

National Institute of Neurological Disorders and Stroke
http://www.ninds.nih.gov/disorders/cerebral_palsy/cerebral_palsy.htm

Symbol Systems

BoardMaker
http://www.mayer-johnson.com/
Overboard
http://www.gusinc.com/Overboard/?gclid=COTaoLqxrooCFRRsSgod5kVbqw
Minspeak
http://www.minspeak.com
Unity
http://www.prentrom.com/language/unity/index.php?page5
Visual Scene Display
http://www.imakenews.com/aac-rerc/e_article000344804.cfm?x=b11,0,w
Create your own Visual Scene Display
http://www.spectronicsinoz.com/downloads/faqs/dynavox/Creating-VSD-in-DynaVox-Speaking.pdf

Research & Resources

AAC Institute
http://www.aacinstitute.org/index.html
AAC Rehabilitation Engineering Research Centers (RERC)
http://www.aac-rerc.com/

SUGGESTED ACTIVITIES

1. *Read Profiles of Augmentative Communication Users:* Visit the website of the Prentke Romich Company: www.prentrom.com/index.html and click on 40 Heroes of AAC. Read the archived profiles of five augmentative communication users and write a three- to five-page paper on the themes that run through these personal stories. For example, consider the users' lives *before* they had access to augmentative communication, and the power and control they gained after they became skilled augmentative communication users.

2. *Interview an Augmentative Communication User.* Find an adult augmentative communication user in your community and interview him or her regarding his or her life story.

   a. What have been the highlights of the individual's life? When did augmentative communication become a part of his or her life, and how has it contributed to the individual's accomplishments?

   b. Describe the augmentative system used by the person. For aided systems indicate the brand name of the equipment and the means of indication used. What symbol system is used? Describe the layout of the overlay(s). Describe how the student is positioned to use the system.

   c. Describe the person's vocabulary *on the augmentative communication device.* Include specific examples of vocabulary use that you observed and other vocabulary the person is reported to use.

   d. How effective were the user's attempts at communicating with the system? What problem areas can you identify? What factors, such as the vocabulary available or the behavior of the communication partner, influenced the success of the communicative exchanges?

3. *Participate in a Discussion Board on Augmentative Communication.* Participate in an online discussion board that focuses on augmentative communication. Each week a new question or topic should be posted by either the instructor or students. Topics should reflect issues or practices that relate to the selection and design of augmentative communication systems, such as the teacher's role in the decision-making process; data collection procedures for monitoring a student's use of an augmentative communication system; the use of an augmentative communication system at home; the role of related services staff (e.g., speech therapist, occupational therapist) in selecting an augmentative communication system; and issues in identifying an appropriate symbol system.

4. *Attend a Vendor Exhibit.* Attend a vendor exhibit that features augmentative communication devices from several manufacturers, and spend time exploring a variety of mid-tech to high-tech systems. Vendor displays are found at consumer shows such as the Abilities Expo, and at state, regional, and national conferences of professional organizations such as the American Speech-Language-Hearing Association (ASHA). They are also featured at the three national conferences on assistive technology: Closing the Gap in Minneapolis in October, the Assistive Technology Industry Association (ATIA) in Orlando in January, and California State University–Northridge (CSUN) in Los Angeles in March. Gather literature on current augmentative communication systems, and inquire about devices under development. Add this literature to your assistive technology portfolio.

5. *Simulate and Reflect.* Using a low-tech augmentative communication device such as an alphabet board, complete a routine activity within the community. You are to act as a nonspeaking person and utilize *only* the system that you have created for yourself. For example, you can order a meal at a restaurant using the device. Write a three- to five-page reaction paper that describes your experiences and outlines your further insights into the lives of augmentative communication users.

REFERENCES

Balandin, S., & Iacono, T. (1998) A few well-chosen words. *Augmentative and Alternative Communication, 14,* 147–161.

Beukelman, D. R., & Mirenda, P. (2005). *Augmentative and alternative communication* (3rd ed.). Baltimore: Brookes.

Beukelman, D. R., Yorkston, K., & Dowden, P. (1985). *Communication augmentation: A casebook of clinical management.* Austin, TX: Pro-Ed.

Blackstone, S. W. (2004, August). Visual scene displays. *Augmentative Communication News, 16*(2).

Bruder, M. B. (1994). Working with members of other disciplines: Collaboration for success. In M. Wolery & J. S. Wilbers (Eds.), *Including children with special needs in early childhood programs* (pp. 45–70). Washington, DC: National Association for the Education of Young Children.

Daniels, M. (1994). The effect of sign on hearing children's language. *Communication Education, 43,* 291–298.

Downey, D., & Hurtig, R. (2003, July). Augmentative and alternative communication. *Pediatric Annals, 32*(7), 467–474.

Erickson, K. A. (2000). All children are ready to learn: An emergent versus readiness perspective in early literacy assessment. *Seminars in Speech and Language, 213,* 193–203.

Finch, A., & Romski, M. (2004). *The myths of AAC.* Presentation at the American Speech-Language-Hearing Association 2004 Augmentative Communication Leadership Conference, Sea Island, GA.

Grady, A. P., Kovach, T., Lange, M., & Shannon, L. (1993, February). "Consumer knows best": Promoting choice in assistive technology. *PT: Magazine of Physical Therapy, 1*(2), 50–56.

Hetzroni, O. E. (2004). AAC and literacy. *Disability and Rehabilitation, 26*(21/22), 1305–1312.

Hourcade, J., Everhart-Pilotte, T., West, E., & Parette, P. (2004, Winter). A history of augmentative and alternative communication for individuals with severe and profound disabilities. *Focus on Autism and Other Developmental Disabilities, 19*(4), 235–244.

Kangas, K., & Lloyd, L. (1988). Early cognitive skills as prerequisites to augmentative and alternative communication use: What are we waiting for? *Augmentative and Alternative Communication, 4,* 211–221.

Kroth, R., & Bolson, M. D. (1996). Family involvement with assistive technology. *Contemporary Education, 68,* 17–20.

Musselwhite, C., & King-DeBaun, P. (1997). *Emerging literacy success: Merging whole language and technology for students with disabilities.* Park City, UT: Creative Communicating.

Quinn, R. (1996). Functional communication in a life skills class. *TECH-NJ, 7*(2), pp. 6, 15.

Schlosser, R. (2003). Effects of augmentative communication on natural speech development. In R. Schlosser, *The efficacy of augmentative and alternative communication: Toward evidence-based practice* (pp. 404–426). San Diego: Academic Press.

Snell, M. E., & Janney, R. (2000). *Teacher's guide to inclusive practices: Collaborative teaming.* Baltimore: Brookes.

Vanderheiden, G. C., & Yoder, D. E. (1986). Overview. In S. W. Blackstone (Ed.), *Augmentative communication: An introduction* (pp. 1–28). Rockville, MD: American Speech-Language-Hearing Association.

Van Tatenhove, G. M. (1987). Teaching power through augmentative communication: Guidelines for early intervention. *Journal of Childhood Communication Disorders, 10,* 185–199.

Williams, M. B. (2005, March 16). *Why I use more than one communication device.* Presentation at California State University–Northridge's 20th annual international conference, Technology and Persons with Disabilities, Los Angeles, CA.

Yorkston, K. M., Honsinger, M. J., Dowden, P. A., & Marriner, N. (1988). Vocabulary selection: A case report. *Augmentative and Alternative Communication, 5*(2), 101–108.

CHAPTER 10

Low-Tech Approaches to Teaching Early Communication and Emergent Literacy

FOCUS QUESTIONS

1. What is the difference between communication and language?
2. What are the factors that promote communication and language development?
3. What are low-tech solutions to enhancing early communication in children with disabilities?
4. What is emergent literacy?
5. How can assistive technology be used to facilitate emergent literacy?

INTRODUCTION

In the previous chapter we discussed how assistive technology can be used to provide a voice for students with disabilities who cannot speak. Some children who cannot speak have multiple and severe intellectual disabilities that interfere with the overall development of communication. These children have not yet learned the very early skills necessary to support the development of speech or language. Therefore, they do not, and may never, possess the necessary abilities to use the sophisticated augmentative communication systems discussed in Chapter 9. For these children, there are other appropriate and effective applications of simple technology that can contribute to further development of their communication skills.

The example of Clara demonstrates several ways in which a teacher can use assistive technology to influence the early communication development of children with severe disabilities. However, although the technology itself may be simple, the appropriate application involves careful consideration and understanding of communication and language development. There is an abundance of professional literature that substantiates the importance of early communication to the development of more complex forms of communication such as language (Beukelman & Mirenda, 1998; Calandrella & Wilcox 2000; Warren & Yoder, 1998). Although a review of this literature is beyond the scope of this text, it is important to understand some basic concepts and parameters in order to use assistive technology as an instructional strategy for early communication.

USER PROFILE: Clara

Clara is a 6-year-old girl with significant developmental disabilities. She is a social and pleasant youngster who uses smiles, gestures, and vocalizations to indicate when she is happy, sad, or displeased with something. Because Clara has not developed speech, cannot walk, and has cognitive impairments, the experiences she needs in order to develop more effective communication skills are provided through the use of assistive technology. For example, Clara is presented with a variety of favorite toys that are activated by large single switches. She is given opportunities to choose from among these toys, allowing Clara to demonstrate her understanding that her deliberate actions (hitting the switch) can cause specific results or effects (activating a toy). There are other ways in which simple technology is infused into Clara's educational program to support her growing abilities to interact with others. A one-step digitized voice output device is programmed with a little girl's voice saying "Excuse me, but can someone come here for a minute?" Clara activates this simple augmentative communication device to get attention. It is available to her at all times so that she can use it as an alternative to gaining attention in negative ways such as by screeching.

WHAT IS COMMUNICATION?

Communication may be broadly defined as the exchange of information between people (Siegel-Causey & Guess, 1989). More specifically, it is

- the process of transmitting and receiving messages between two people; and
- occurs within the context of a socially supportive environment.

Communication occurs when one individual sends a message to another individual, who then acknowledges receipt and understanding. When this communication interaction is continued or sustained, it is called a **conversation**.

Although this description of the communication process is simple and most children develop communication with ease, a more detailed examination reveals a complex interdependent set of variables. These variables include the following:

1. The presence and participation of one or more partners
2. A socially and physically supportive environment
3. The ability and desire to send an intentional message and receive a message (Stremel-Campbell & Matthews, 1988)

Messages are created for a reason, have specific content, are communicated through some set of rules, and take some structure that can be expressed. The structure or mode of communication can be either symbolic (e.g., speech) or nonsymbolic (e.g., a gesture). This distinction represents the difference between communication and language. Language is a form of communication that uses a set of symbols with rules for ordering that we all agree have a specific meaning. (See Chapter 9 for an explanation of symbols.)

It is important to understand that communication is not limited to language (Downing & Siegel-Causey, 1988). People communicate with each other in a variety of nonsymbolic ways—through eye contact, body movements, facial expressions, gestures, and nonverbal vocalizations. Consider two friends unexpectedly running into each other at the mall. As they recognize each other from a distance they wave enthusiastically and smile broadly, while their eyes widen and light up with excitement. Not a single word is exchanged, yet the meaning of their messages is clear without the use of language. This is **nonsymbolic communication**.

Nonsymbolic communication regularly occurs between babies and their parents. A baby's cry conveys hunger or tiredness or some kind of discomfort. Cooing communicates contentment. As the baby becomes a toddler, the point becomes a very effective gesture. The simplicity of the toddler's point does not compare to its power. With a single point, everyone in that toddler's environment understands that he or she wants *this*, not that, or wants to go *there*, not stay here.

HOW DO COMMUNICATION AND LANGUAGE DEVELOP?

Infants and early communicators (children with delayed speech and language) progress through a series of stages from unintentional to intentional forms of nonsymbolic communication. This comes about as a result of interactions and relationships with caregivers (Siegel-Causey, Ernst, & Guess, 1988). An **unintentional** form of communication is defined as a behavior that is merely *suggested* to have meaning or intent, such as a baby's first smile. These forms are then shaped into intentional

Child pointing to indicate his choice.
Photo by Tammy Cordwell

communicative behaviors by the adults in the child's environment. (Consider the adults' reactions to the baby's first smile.) These early communication forms, or prelinguistic communicative behaviors, are important precursors to later language development (Warren & Yoder, 1998).

Infants then develop deliberate behaviors to influence others in their environments through a developmental process involving reciprocity between babies and their caregivers. For example, a baby responds to a familiar vocal cue and facial expression of his or her mother by gazing back in her eyes and smiling, cooing, or mimicking her facial expression. This is called a **reciprocal interaction** because it involves the basic back-and-forth elements of a conversation. These elements include someone sending a message, another person receiving and responding to a message, and then continuing the exchange until someone stops the exchange or ends the conversation. This game is played over and over and, in effect, establishes the back-and-forth (reciprocal) nature of communication.

Children need practice to learn to communicate and interact. Infants enjoy and benefit from repeating routines involving familiar objects or toys and adults. For example, babies never seem to tire of playing a game of peek-a-boo while getting dressed in the morning or getting dried off after a bath. Peek-a-boo games are good illustrations of the fact that communication and language development are rooted in social behavior and are dependent on the social environment (Bates, 1976; Bloom, 1993; Moore & Corkum, 1994; Wetherby & Prizant, 1992). Children interact with people and objects within their environments to learn the rules and patterns of effective communication (see Figure 10.1). Eventually, language is generated, and in place of the prelinguistic forms of communication are words, sentences, and language-based conversations.

What Factors Promote Communication and Language Development?

The factors that promote communication and language are both within children and outside them. A child's capacity to interact with people and objects in the environment is influenced by his or her ability to see, hear, touch, smell, move, and problem solve. When these abilities are severely compromised, the development of communication and language is interrupted.

However, it is the factors *outside* the child that may have the greatest effect on communication development. Communication is developed by parents, siblings, and other more competent communicators being responsive and interactive with the child.

FIGURE 10–1
Communication model

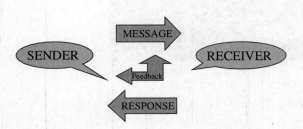

It is the child's environment and the behavior of those people within it that can be influenced or changed to promote the communication development of the child.

Communication is stimulated within the context of routines, people, and objects that are present in the child's environment. An environment that is rich in activities and interesting objects gives children and their partners more opportunities to communicate or interact. It also supports the development of critical cognitive concepts such as cause and effect. Cause and effect is the understanding that your behavior can deliberately cause something to occur. ("If I do X, then Y will happen.") For example, "If I shake this rattle, it will make a funny noise," or "If I point at the cookie jar, Grandma will give me a cookie." This is increasingly important for children who are nonspeaking and in the early stages of developing communication skills. Children need to be *provided with opportunities* for frequent communicative interactions *with competent partners for a variety of reasons* so they, in turn, will learn to communicate for a variety of purposes.

Choice making is a powerful skill that presents a context for early communication development. Children are motivated to communicate their wants and needs when presented with a choice. For example, a toddler is more ready to get dressed in the morning when given an opportunity to choose between a selection of two outfits. This reinforces individual control and power, as well as provides a meaningful opportunity to interact with another person.

Another example of communication as power is when a child initiates a communicative exchange. Typical children learn to initiate and express intentions; they do not wait to be asked by an adult. This is usually done in an environment that contains interesting and novel objects and activities, as well as people who are able to interact with the child. For students who have severe disabilities, simple technology can be harnessed to provide opportunities to initiate communication, as illustrated in the following user profile.

Attention to both initiated communication and the response from a caregiver are equally critical in creating optimal environments for the development of early communication (Noonan & Siegel-Causey, 1997). Caregivers such as parents and teachers must be deliberate and consistent in their initiating and sustaining conversations with young children. Typically developing children require thousands of exchanges to gain the skills of having a conversation, and children with disabilities will need as many or more.

USER PROFILE: Justin

Justin is a nonambulatory 3-year-old who does not speak and has limited use of his hands. At home, his parents appear to know when he needs comfort, is hungry, or wants attention. However, in preschool Justin's intentions are not as well understood. Therefore, he uses a colorful BIGmack (AbleNet, Inc.), a single-message communication device that will ask for someone to attend to him when he presses it with his fist. Justin presses the switch, a recorded voice says "I need someone to come over here," and a teacher approaches, inferring that he either wants attention or needs something. This is teaching Justin the beginning skills of initiating communication.

PROBLEMS STUDENTS WITH DISABILITIES HAVE WITH EARLY COMMUNICATION DEVELOPMENT

Children with severe social, cognitive, motor, and sensory disabilities are at risk for delays in developing effective communication and language skills (Stremel-Campbell & Matthews, 1988). As stated, early communication development requires that children participate actively in their environment. Children participate actively through play, interactions with other children, interactions with adults during daily routines (e.g., dressing, eating, bathing), and other activities that are repeated over and over. This becomes extremely challenging for children who have significant social, cognitive, motor, and sensory disabilities. They often (1) cannot independently interact with people and objects in the environment due to hearing, vision, or motor difficulties; (2) do not present the cognitive abilities to become fully symbolic communicators independently; and (3) are not provided with multiple opportunities to engage in communicative-rich environments with a variety of competent partners.

As a result of these delays in developing language, children with severe disabilities may remain dependent on nonsymbolic behaviors as their primary system of communication (Ogletree, 1996). For example, they use facial grimaces to express dislike, protest through the use of crying, or exhibit problematic behavior as a means to communicate their needs.

Table 10.1 offers a view of these limitations as they relate to the critical elements of communication and language development already discussed. The barriers represent attributes often recognized in children with severe or profound disabilities.

TABLE 10–1   Supports and barriers to early communication

Factors Supporting Communication Development	Barrier	Effect
Intentionality and causality	Motor, sensory, and cognitive disabilities limit the number of opportunities to engage in routines that support intentionality and causality	Child does not develop skills that promote early nonsymbolic communication
Choice making	Direct instruction in choice making and/or multiple opportunities for choice making are not provided to the child	Child either does not develop the skills for choice making or does not make choices
Frequent and rich interaction with objects and people	Motor, sensory, and cognitive disabilities limit the availability of objects and people	In cooperation with a communication partner, the child does not gain joint attention to objects or other people in the environment

Factors Supporting Communication Development	Barrier	Effect
Frequent and consistent practice of having conversations with others	Limited and inconsistent opportunities to practice the give and take of a conversation	Child does not initiate or sustain a communication exchange
The overall presence of early communication forms	No way to communicate basic needs effectively	Child exhibits inappropriate and problematic behavior

TECHNOLOGY TOOLS THAT SUPPORT EARLY COMMUNICATION DEVELOPMENT

Whereas most children learn communication skills through typical daily interactions, children with significant disabilities often require direct, systematic instruction (Noonan & Siegel-Causey, 1997). They must be taught the fundamental concept that their actions can influence the environment and that their deliberate interactions can achieve desired ends (i.e., cause and effect). The use of assistive technology can bridge this gap for many children with cognitive, motor, and sensory impairments. It offers solutions to the problem of providing these children with the same opportunities to communicate and make choices. Through the use of devices to request attention, develop understandings of consequences, and stimulate the sensory system, children with disabilities can be provided with opportunities to access environments rich in interesting objects and people.

Direct instruction in cause and effect can be provided through the use of simple technology. **Switches** enable students who have limited motor control to activate battery-operated toys and other electronic equipment with a single movement. They enable students with disabilities to achieve positive interactions with their immediate surroundings and exert control over relevant stimuli (Lancioni et al., 2002; Langley, 1990). For example, a simple switch can be used to turn on a model race car that moves, makes sounds, and displays lights; a vibrating pillow that tickles; or a CD player that plays a child's favorite songs. Each time the child presses the switch, the enjoyable consequence results. To be effective in teaching cause and effect, it is essential that switches are connected to toys, CDs, or objects that the child finds entertaining.

In addition to cause and effect, switches can be used to teach choice making to children with disabilities (Lancioni et. al., 2002). Typically developing children learn to make choices over time through multiple opportunities provided within natural settings, but many children with disabilities are limited in their ability to express a choice and do not have the equivalent opportunities. Choice making is an important developmental skill that must be exercised often, especially for the student who is still developing intentional communication. The use of switches can be an excellent

Two types of switches from AbleNet, Inc.—Microswitch & Big Red switch
Courtesy of AbleNet, Inc.

USER PROFILE: Daniel

Daniel is a 3-year-old toddler who has motor and cognitive disabilities. He is nonverbal and cannot ambulate independently, but he can reach and grasp with one hand. He attends a preschool program with typically developing children and is provided special education support services. His special education teacher has developed a variety of activities using assistive technology to provide Daniel with opportunities to understand that his deliberate actions can influence a desired effect. Daniel operates a remote control train set by activating a switch connected to the train and turns the pages of a computer storybook that reads to him and his peers by pressing a large Jelly Bean switch. Using switch technology, the special education teacher has provided multiple opportunities for Daniel to participate in his preschool routines and learn the power of his direct influence.

strategy to assist in the development of choice-making behavior and in providing opportunities to practice making choices. Choice making provides students with a sense of power. For example, during free play or break time, a student can make a choice of what he or she would like to listen to: a rap CD or a classical music CD, or perhaps a book-on-tape. Other students will use multiple switches to choose one battery-operated toy (a dancing pig, perhaps) over another (a noisy truck). In the following user profile, Jane uses two switches for choice making, learning that she can have deliberate influence on her environment.

In addition to promoting students' prelinguistic skills of cause and effect and choice making, switches can be used as simple augmentative communication devices. Building on the switch activation skills a student has been taught, a single-message communication device (e.g., BIGmack, LITTLEmack [both by AbleNet, Inc.]) can be used to deliver a recorded message. Single-message communication devices look very similar to switches but contain sound chips that can be recorded with spoken

Switch-operated toy with a Jelly Bean switch.

USER PROFILE: Jane

Jane is another child in Daniel's preschool class. She receives similar special education services within the context of the general preschool program. Jane has been identified with a developmental disability that manifests limited speech, global difficulties in problem solving, and fine motor delays. Each activity in Jane's preschool program includes the use of some assistive technology that reinforces the fundamental understanding of cause and effect and choice making. For example, Jane is offered two switches that advance or reverse a page in a computerized storybook. In addition, she is provided with a choice of two switches to answer simple yes and no questions. The teacher asks, "Do you want to play a game with Daniel?" and Jane can make a choice. At first, it was not clear if Jane's selection was random or deliberate, but as time went on and she had more exposure to choice-making opportunities using switches, it became clear that her choices were real.

messages. Students with disabilities can activate these prerecorded devices to initiate communication or respond to another person. For example, a child can use a single-step communication device to invite another person to play a game or read a story by pressing a single-message communication device that asks, "Does anyone want to play a game?" or "Will someone read me a story?" Single-message communicators are often used as calling or alerting devices that enable a student to request attention in an appropriate manner.

As students with severe disabilities are being educated within general education settings, single-switch communication devices can be extremely useful. Such devices can be programmed so that students with disabilities can actively participate in groups of typical peers. For example, a single-switch communication device can be programmed for participation in a morning exercise such as asking the other children what they did over the weekend. Single-switch communication devices can

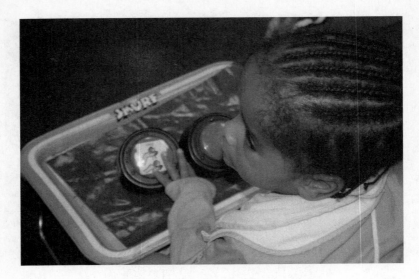

Student using a single-message communication device.

Photo by Vicki Spence

be programmed to provide anticipated answers to questions within an activity, such as "It's snowing today" during morning circle time. A student can use a single switch to answer questions during a social studies lesson; for example, "What is the capital of our state?" or "Who was the first president of our country?" These devices are very easy to program, enabling teachers to be creative in finding ways for students to participate within their classrooms.

Multiple-step communication devices are available for use by children who are early communicators and present complex disabilities. These devices look just like a single-step communicator or switch but can be programmed with a sequence of messages. For example, the first activation says, "I have a secret!" The second hit of the switch says, "Come closer and I will tell you." And the third activation says, "It is Mrs. Jones's birthday." The use of multiple-step communication devices enables nonverbal children to experience a conversation rather than a simple one-turn communication episode.

Types of Switches to Promote Early Communication

An array of options are available to meet the unique needs of every student. Some switches are large and can be pressed with a fist or foot. Others are tiny and require only a light touch; they can be activated with a single finger movement. Commercially available switches are usually categorized by their activation features (see Table 10.2). Students must have a reliable movement to activate the switch independently, such as flexing a fist, extending a hand, or turning their head to the side. Physical or occupational therapists should be consulted to determine a student's most functional movement. (See Chapter 8 for a detailed discussion of how to select appropriate technology.)

TABLE 10–2 Types of commercially available switches

Switch	Activation Features
Generic push	This switch comes in all sizes, shapes, and colors. The student pushes down on the switch and it activates the toy it is connected to. Some of these switches are designed for use as head switches, foot switches, or positioned in unique access points such as a student's knee or thigh.
Toggle/Flexible	This switch is activated by moving a stick or bending a flexible piece of rubber (sometimes referred to as a wand switch).
Leaf	A plastic flap that is activated by swiping lightly against the leaf in one direction.
Squeeze/Pinch	A soft rubber ball-like or thin plastic switch that is activated by squeezing or pinching.
Mercury	A switch that is activated by tilting; usually mounted on a headband or hat and activated by head movement.
Pneumatic	This switch operates by changing air pressure. The student puffs air into a tube, or in the case of the sip and puff switch, blows into a tube for one activation and sucks air out of tube for a second activation.
Muscle/Twitch	The muscle/twitch switch is activated by small muscle movement, such as wrinkling the forehead, and can be adjusted to increase or decrease the amount of muscle movement needed to easily activate it.
Light sensitive	The light switch activates by a change in lighting. Students can place a finger or hand over a sensor with no pressure and activate the switch.
Vibration	This switch activates by movement or vibration and can be calibrated for sensitivity.
Wireless	The wireless feature can be added to many of the switches or purchased solely as a wireless activation device.

Switches may be mounted or positioned in a variety of ways to facilitate activation. Many of the switches and multiple-step communication devices mentioned in this chapter can be mounted for activation by a hand, head, foot, elbow, or any other available body part.

Commercially available battery-operated toys can be easily adapted for use with switches. Companies that produce switches, such as AbleNet, Inc., market a "battery device adapter" that is inserted in the battery compartment between the battery and the leads; it connects to the switch by a simple jack. In addition, there are switch interfaces that allow for the use of multiple switches for choice making.

Determining the Use of Switches for Early Communication

The decision to use switch technology must be made by a team of professionals such as the collaborative team discussed in Chapter 9. The teacher needs to collaborate with colleagues such as a speech-language specialist, whose expertise includes early communication; an occupational therapist, whose expertise is in fine motor development; a physical therapist, whose expertise involves seating and other gross motor skills; and with the student's parents, whose expertise includes knowledge of their child's likes and dislikes. Because switches are not an end result in themselves—they are employed within the broader context of an activity—they must have a specific function within a child's educational program (see Figure 10.2).

Once it is determined that a switch will be used for a specific activity, the time and place the child will engage in the activity need to be decided. As York, Nietupski, and Hamre-Nietupski (1985) suggest, the decision-making process then needs to address the following:

1. The optimal position the child will be placed in for the activity
2. The specific motor behavior that the child will use for activation
3. The best type of switch to use
4. The instructional procedures that will be used to teach the student to use the switch set-up, such as a prompting hierarchy or modeling

Each of these decision-making steps must involve the team, and consideration should begin with the least complex solutions. In addition, a record-keeping system should be designed and implemented to determine if expected progress is being made. In the absence of this kind of systematic approach, students are often saturated by the endless presentation of the same switch and switch-activated device, and learning fails to take place.

FIGURE 10–2 Suggested inquiry for determining the use of switches for early communication development

- At what stage of communication development is the child?
  - Understanding cause and effect
  - Making choices
  - Interacting with his or her environment
  - Initiating communication
  - Beginning conversations
- How can this child's communication development be enhanced through the use of switches?
- In which activities within the child's educational program can you embed communication through the use of switches?
- How can the use of switch technology support the child's participation in the classroom, school, community, and home?

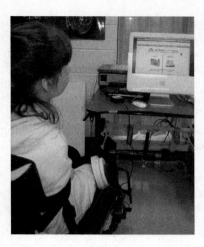

Student activating a switch with her knee.
Photo by Vicki Spence

Examples of Switch Technology for Early Communication in the Classroom

There are hundreds of ways in which switch technology can be used within the class-room to promote the early communication development of children with disabilities. Although most of the examples within this chapter have focused on early childhood, many older children and adults remain rooted in the use of simple communication systems. There is debate within the professional community on whether or not there should be prerequisites for using more sophisticated augmentative communication systems. However, the fact remains that for many older children the use of switches continues to be a viable assistive technology solution to participation in classroom

USER PROFILE: Joel

Joel is a 16-year-old, nonverbal student who attends a special education program within his local high school. He uses a power wheelchair with supervision and participates in school activities with his typical peers. Joel has been using switch technology for commu-nication since he was in elementary school. Within his secondary education program he continues to show effective use of communication through the use of switch technology.

- To greet his peers in the morning, Joel activates a one-step communication device with his foot. Using his foot leaves his left hand free so he can use it to independently navigate his power wheelchair.
- Joel opens his locker with a remote control switch that is positioned on his wheel-chair tray.
- During physical education Joel activates a spin dial device with a single switch that randomly chooses teams for the other students.
- Joel calls for his personal care attendant by hitting a big button switch that activates the attendant's vibrating beeper.

activities and expressive communication. The following user profile highlights the use of switch technology for a high school student's communication in the classroom.

Students with disabilities who are early communicators can be provided with an array of simple technology solutions to enhance their expressive communication. They need to be provided with multiple opportunities to use these solutions as they develop the skills to use additional options in augmentative communication. The next chapter presents strategies for integrating augmentative communication into the classroom and discusses the roles of the classroom teacher in supporting students who use technology to communicate.

USER PROFILE: Peter

Peter is a friendly, curious, and attentive 7-year-old who attends his local elementary school. For the majority of the day he is included in a first-grade classroom and has been assigned a one-to-one aide who provides instructional support and personal care services. Peter has significant challenges due to global developmental disabilities of prematurity, cerebral palsy, and birth trauma He is nonspeaking, uses a wheelchair with assistance, and has limited use of his hands. Peter has peers who interact with him; however, he rarely initiates an interaction. Because Peter does not have conventional symbolic communication strategies, his interactions are often not sustained. However, his peers indicate that Peter uses a reliable yes and no response by shaking his head. A combination of several switches has been incorporated into Peter's educational program to foster his communication and provide opportunities for him to initiate communication with his peers.

- Peter activates a single-message communication device, which is recorded by his brother, to greet his peers and ask questions. For example, in the morning when he presses the device it says, "Hey! Ask me what I did last night!" and he is prepared with an object or picture that represents what he did last night (e.g., an advertisement for the movie he saw). Thus, a simple conversation takes place between Peter and his classmates.
- When Peter needs help, he calls his aide with another single-step communication device that is programmed with the aide's name.
- Peter uses a talking photo album to share a weekend experience. He chooses among a sequence of four pictures, each of which has a message recorded on its sound chip. When he activates each message it retells his experience.

EMERGENT LITERACY

Closely related to the development of language and communication is the development of literacy. In the past, literacy was defined only as the ability to read and write. However, the definition has been expanded to include skills regarding the ability to locate, evaluate, use, and communicate using a wide range of resources including text, visual, audio, and video sources (Erickson & Koppenhaver, 1995). Current theory and practice demonstrate that the behaviors of reading and writing begin to develop at a very young age, much earlier than was previously realized. In the past, students with disabilities who experienced difficulties in the development of communication were not considered candidates for learning to read or write. Consequently, no effort was made to teach them early literacy skills (Koppenhaver & Yoder, 1993).

However, reading, writing, and oral language develop concurrently within children (Sulzby & Teale, 1991). Early reading and writing skills are identified as **emergent literacy.** The term *emergent literacy* refers to a range of behaviors related to reading and writing that occur prior to conventional literacy (Sulzby & Teale, 1991). For example, many infants enjoy turning the pages of a book and following along with an adult. In the popular book *Pat the Bunny* (Kunhardt, 1940) very young children follow directions such as, "Judy can pat the bunny. Can you pat the bunny?" Toddlers often page through books and bring familiar books to an adult to be read over and over again. Toddlers and preschoolers often use crayons and markers to imitate writing. Preschoolers are exposed repeatedly to print and the behaviors involved in reading and writing. With subsequent reading instruction, most children become literate adults with multiple abilities to express themselves.

However, for children with severe disabilities, the motor, cognitive, and sensory impairments that interfere with their communication development also interfere with their access to early reading and writing activities. Often nonverbal children are not viewed as literate and are not provided with opportunities to exercise communication through reading and writing. Therefore, it is essential that, along with learning to use simple technology to communicate, children with severe disabilities are actively engaged in activities that promote emergent literacy (Erickson & Koppenhaver, 1995; Koppenhaver, Coleman, Kalman, & Yoder, 1991; Koppenhaver, Pierce, Steelman, & Yoder, 1994; Light & McNaughton, 1993; Musselwhite & King-DeBaun, 1997). These

BookWorm, a voice output reading device, engages students in early literacy activities.

Courtesy of AbleNet, Inc.

children need direct and deliberate instruction and exposure to early literacy activities regardless of the severity of their disabilities (Musselwhite & King-DeBaun, 1997).

With the use of assistive technology, students who have significant disabilities can engage in literacy-focused activities. Switches and other low-tech strategies can be used to enhance early literacy activities such as participating in story reading and storytelling. For example, preschool stories often include repetitive refrains that children remember and enjoy reciting as the story is retold. This repeat or choral verse, such as "He huffed and he puffed and he blew the house in" from the *Three Little Pigs* can be stored in a one-step communication device and activated by a child at the appropriate time. Tufte and Maro (1999) present several suggestions for facilitating communication development through literature-based activities and the use of simple switches. These include using several one-step communication switches that have been programmed with generic story-reacting vocabulary such as "Turn the page," "I can't see," and "I know what happens next!"

USER PROFILE: Angela

Angela is a 7-year-old first grader who attends her neighborhood elementary school. As a result of a rare genetic syndrome, she has a variety of challenges that affect her development and learning. She began to walk at 3 years old but remains non-speaking due to a combination of factors related to cognition and oral motor functioning. Angela has developed an understanding of cause and effect and accurately uses a variety of switches and a four-panel voice output device. She participates in the following literacy-based activities:

- A story bag of objects are collected for the weekly storybook that the teacher reads to the class. These objects are representations for events that occur in the story. They reinforce the story line and can be used to indicate order of events or to reinforce a component of the story. By selecting or arranging the objects, Angela can comment or provide information to others. In addition, an overlay for her four-panel communication device is created for each story. Angela presses a button to answer the teacher's story comprehension questions such as "What do you think will happen next?"
- Angela's speech therapist comes in the classroom during the students' free time and reads familiar stories to a small group of children who require articulation therapy. These stories are engineered for the children to practice specific sounds; for Angela they provide instruction in early phonics. She uses her one-step communicator to answer questions about initial consonant sounds. For example, Angela presses the communicator when the therapist asks, "What sound does 'Silly Sam the Snake' make?"
- On all of her switches, one-step communicators, and four-panel communication device, the written word appears along with the picture symbols. This creates a text-rich environment and contributes to Angela's beginning understanding of the use of words as symbols.
- Angela engages in "imaginary writing" exercises in which meaning is inferred from her "kid writing." She uses an alternative keyboard with a custom overlay to create simple stories on a computer.

With the use of switch technology, augmentative communication, and computer access, many children who previously were not provided with opportunities to read and write are now accessing print and developing early literacy skills (Musselwhite & King-DeBaun, 1997). The following user profile provides a good example of this.

All of the activities discussed in Angela's user profile illustrate how the appropriate integration of assistive technology can help develop communication within the context of speaking, reading, and writing.

SUMMARY

- All children, regardless of the severity of their disabilities, can communicate. However, opportunities and supportive environments must be established and provided.
- Children can communicate in the absence of language. The goal of intervention and education is to encourage the further development of communication through symbolism or language.
- Children with motor, cognitive, and sensory disabilities require deliberate and systematic intervention to develop a functional system of communication.
- Assistive technology can be used to enhance the early communication efforts of children with significant disabilities.
- The use of switch technology for communication must be infused within the context of daily routines and classroom activities throughout the day.
- Communication is further developed by teaching the emergent literacy skills of early reading and writing.
- Children with significant disabilities should be exposed to print and writing to enhance their communication development and abilities.

For additional information on the topics listed, go to the following websites:

Low-Tech Communication Devices

Go Talk (Attainment Company)
http://www.attainmentcompany.com/xcart/home.php?cat=277
Other communication aids from Attainment Company
http://www.attainmentcompany.com/xcart/home.php?cat=278
Hawk, Blackhawk, Lighthawk, Superhawk
http://www.adamlab.com/
Step-by-Step Communicator (AbleNet, Inc.)
http://www/ablenetinc.com/communication.asp
Communication Builder
http://enablingdevices.com/subcat.aspx?id=6&session=child

Early Language Development

Child Development Institute
http://www.childdevelopmentinfo.com/development/language_development.shtml

Tangible and Tactile Symbols

Design to Learn
http://www.designtolearn.com/pages/ts.html
Tactile Systems from the Texas School for the Blind
http://www.tsbvi.edu/Education/vmi/tactile_symbols.htm

Strategies to Teach Early Communication

Learning to Communicate: Strategies for Developing Communication with Infants
Whose Multiple Disabilities Include Visual Impairment and Hearing Loss (PDF)
http://www.osepideasthatwork.org/parentkit/Learning_EngVer.asp

Emergent Literacy

Center for Literacy and Disability Studies at UNC
http://www.med.unc.edu/ahs/clds/
Literacy for All! By Gretchen Hanser
http://www.cs.unc.edu/Research/assist/et/2006/attach/HanserNotes/EnginTalkHO.pdf
Caroline Musselwhite's website: Activities & Materials
http://www.aacintervention.com/
Do To Learn
http://www.dotolearn.com
News-2-You: Subscription service to newspapers written at beginning literacy levels,
including with communication symbols
http://www.news-2-you.com/about.aspx

SUGGESTED ACTIVITIES

1. *Observe a Classroom.* In small groups of two or three students, conduct a 2–3 hour observation of a child who has significant disabilities and is nonspeaking. During this observation, collect data regarding the following: (1) the frequency and types of expressive communication of the child; (2) the frequency in which the child has an opportunity to communicate with others; (3) the content of the communication that is presented (for example, how often is the child given the opportunity to comment or protest?); and (4) the number and types of people who are available and who interact with the child. Based on this data, develop recommendations for the classroom teacher to enhance communication for this student.

2. *Develop an Early Communication Parental Workbook.* Develop a workbook that guides parents in understanding their child's early communication development.

The workbook should provide a framework to promote communication within the home and community. In addition, include a list of references and resources in the workbook.

3. *Explore a Toy Store.* Take a trip to a local toy store and inventory the various battery-operated toys and games that could be adapted with switches to be used to promote interactive play with typical peers. Develop an annotated list including the name of the toy or game; the company that produces the toy or game; the suggested manner in which it can be adapted; and your suggested uses as independent activities or activities with typical peers.

4. *Create an Object Story Bag.* Select two children's books appropriate for early elementary school students. Create a story bag of objects that can be used as the books are being read out loud.

REFERENCES

Bates, E. (1976). *Language and context: The acquisition of pragmatics.* New York: Academic Press.

Beukelman, D., & Mirenda, P. (1998). *Augmentative and alternative communication: Management of severe communication disorders in children and adults* (2nd ed.). Baltimore: Brookes.

Bloom, L. (1993). *The transition from infancy to language.* Cambridge, England: Cambridge University Press.

Calandrella, A. M., & Wilcox, M. J. (2000). Predicting language outcomes for young prelinguistic children with developmental delay. *Journal of Speech, Language, and Hearing Research, 43,* 1061–1071.

Downing, J. E., & Siegel-Causey, E. (1988). Enhancing the nonsymbolic communicative behavior of children with multiple impairments. *Language, Speech, and Hearing Services in Schools, 19,* 338–348.

Erickson, A., & Koppenhaver. (1995). Developing a literacy program for children with severe disabilities. *The Reading Teacher, 48*(8) 676–684.

Koppenhaver, D. A., Coleman, P. P., Kalman, S. L., & Yoder, D. E. (1991). The implications of emergent literacy research for children with developmental disabilities. *American Journal of Speech-Language Pathology, 1*(1), 38–44.

Koppenhaver, D., & Yoder, D. (1993). Classroom literacy instruction for children with severe speech and physical impairments (SSPI): What is and what might be? *Topics in Language Disorders, 13,* 1–15.

Koppenhaver, D. A., Pierce, P. L., Steelman, J. D., & Yoder, D. E. (1994). Contexts of early literacy intervention for children with developmental disabilities. In M. E. Fey, J. Windsor, & S. F. Warren (Eds.), *Language intervention in the early school years* (pp. 241–274). Baltimore: Brookes.

Kunhardt, D. (1940). *Pat the bunny.* New York: Golden Books.

Lancioni, G. E., O'Reilly, M. F., Singh, N. N., Oliva, D., Piazzolla, G., Pirani, P., et al. (2002). Evaluating the use of multiple microswitches and responses for children with multiple disabilities. *Journal of Intellectual Disability Research, 46*(4), 346–351.

Langley, M. B. (1990). A developmental approach to the use of toys for facilitation of environmental control. *Physical and Occupational Therapy in Pediatrics, 10,* 69–91.

Light, J., & McNaughton, D. (1993). Literacy and augmentative and alternative communication (AAC): The expectations and priorities of parents and teachers. *Topics in Language Disorders, 13*(2), 33–46.

Moore, C., & Corkum, V. L. (1994). Social understanding at the end of the first year of life. *Developmental Review, 14,* 349–372.

Musselwhite, C., & King-DeBaun, P. (1997). *Emergent literacy success: Merging technology and whole language for students with disabilities.* Park City, UT: Creative Communicating.

Noonan, M. J., & Siegel-Causey, E. (1997). Special needs of young children with severe handicaps. In L. McCormick, D. Loeb, & R. Schiefelbusch (Eds.), *Supporting children with communication difficulties in inclusive settings: School-based language intervention* (pp. 405–432). Boston: Allyn & Bacon.

Ogletree, B. T. (1996). Assessment targets and protocols for nonsymbolic communicators with profound disabilities. *Focus on Autism and Other Developmental Disabilities, 11*(1).

Owens, R. E. (2000). *Language development: An introduction.* Boston: Allyn & Bacon.

Pineau, K. A. (2001). *Including AT in literacy instruction: Inclusive emergent literacy programming for language disabled students.* California State University, Northridge conference proceedings.

Rowland, C., & Schweigert, P. (1993). *The early communication process using microswitch technology.* Tucson, AZ: Communication Skills Builders.

Siegel, E., & Wetherby, A. (2000). Nonsymbolic communication. In M. Snell & F. Brown (Eds.), *Instruction of students with severe disabilities* (pp. 409–451). Columbus, OH: Merrill/Prentice Hall.

Siegel-Causey, E. (1997). Responses to Reichle. *The Journal of Special Education, 31*(1), 135–136.

Siegel-Causey, E., Ernst, B., & Guess, D. (1988). Nonsymbolic communication in early interactional processes and implications for interventions. In M. Bullis (Ed.), *Communication in young children with deaf-blindness: Literature review III.* Monmouth, OR: Teaching Research.

Siegel-Causey, E., & Guess, D. (1989). *Enhancing nonsymbolic communication interactions among learners with severe disabilities.* Baltimore: Brookes.

Stremel-Campbell, K., & Matthews, J. (1988). Development of emergent language. In M. Bullis (Ed.), *Communication in young children with deaf-blindness: Literature review III.* Monmouth, OR: Teaching Research.

Sulzby, E., & Teale, W. (1991). Emergent literacy. In R. Barr, M. L. Kamil, P. B. Mosenthal, & P. D. Pearson (Eds.), *Handbook of reading research* (Vol. 2, pp. 727–757). New York: Longman.

Tufte, L. and Maro, J. (1999). Creating Literature Based Communication Boards. Retrieved April 26, 2007, from http://www.aacintervention.com/litboards.htm

Warren, S. F., & Yoder, P. J. (1998). Facilitating the transition from preintentional to intentional communication. In A. Wetherby, S. Warren, & J. Reichle (Eds.), *Transition in prelinguistic communication* (Vol. 7, pp. 365–385). Baltimore: Brookes.

Wetherby, A. M., & Prizant, B. M. (1992). Profiling young children's communicative competence. In S. F. Warren & J. Reichle (Eds.), *Communication and language intervention: Vol. 1. Causes and effects in communication and language intervention* (pp. 217–251). Baltimore: Brookes.

York, J., Nietupski, J., & Hamre-Nietupski, S. (1985). A decision-making process for using microswitches. *Journal of the Association for Persons with Severe Handicaps, 10*(4), 214–223.

Integrating Augmentative Communication in the Classroom, Home, and Community

FOCUS QUESTIONS

1. How can teachers effectively integrate a student's use of his or her augmentative communication system within the classroom and school?
2. How can peers provide support for students who use augmentative communication?
3. What are some strategies for teachers to use to overcome "learned helplessness"?
4. How can augmentative communication be infused in the IEP?
5. Why is it important to support the use of augmentative communication systems at home and in the community?
6. How can a student's augmentative communication system be designed to meet the communication demands of home and the community?

INTRODUCTION

Chapter 4 introduced the benefits of augmentative communication for students with disabilities who cannot speak. Chapter 9 described the primary components of augmentative communication systems and outlined the collaborative process for selecting and designing a system for a specific student. Chapter 10 discussed specialized issues related to low-tech approaches to augmentative communication for early communicators. This chapter focuses on the teacher's critical role in teaching effective communication skills by integrating augmentative communication into the curriculum and daily classroom routines.

Too often, students who have been equipped with augmentative communication systems attend school in environments that do not provide a range of communication opportunities. As a result, the systems are used only minimally or may be abandoned completely. As students with disabilities are being educated within general education settings, there are many opportunities to weave augmentative communication users within the fabric of their schools and communities. In these settings students are surrounded by a milieu of functional and social communication, and they have access to competent communication partners. This presents both opportunities and challenges to the ongoing development of their augmentative communication skills.

SUPPORTIVE ENVIRONMENTS FOR AUGMENTATIVE COMMUNICATION USERS: THE TEACHER'S ROLE

Neighborhood schools and general education classrooms represent the context in which all students achieve and progress in academic and social learning. Central to this context for any beginner or seasoned augmentative communication student user is the classroom teacher. The teacher may be the single most influential variable in ensuring that students who use augmentative communication are successful. Once a system is designed by the collaborative team, it is the teacher who guides the implementation. It is the teacher (and other teaching staff) who create classroom environments that facilitate social interaction and communication.

What specifically can teachers do to support augmentative communication users? Locke and Mirenda (1992) studied the responsibilities of special education teachers who serve on collaborative teams for augmentative communication. They found that teachers have many key roles to play. Table 11.1 lists these roles, each of which is discussed below.

Curriculum Issues

Many units of study taught in school use specialized terms and proper nouns. If students who are augmentative communication users are to be able to answer their teachers' questions and participate in classroom activities in these subjects, they need this specialized vocabulary added to their augmentative communication systems. For example, students studying the American Revolution in social studies class will need to be able communicate names like George Washington, Thomas Jefferson, Paul Revere, and the battles of Lexington and Concord. In English class students need access to the names of literary characters and literary terms. The teacher is the one person who knows what new vocabulary will be covered. Therefore, it is the teacher's role to add curriculum-related vocabulary to students' augmentative communication systems or provide this vocabulary ahead of time to a staff person who has been designated to do this task. Depending on the school staffing, this person could be a speech-language therapist or a teacher's aide (paraeducator).

TABLE 11–1   Teachers' roles in augmentative communication

- Adapting the curriculum
- Writing goals and objectives for augmentative communication users
- Acting as a liaison between the team and the student's parents
- Providing for ongoing skill development in communication
- Identifying appropriate vocabulary
- Determining students' communication needs
- Training others in using the augmentative communication system

Source: Adapted from "Roles and Responsibilities of Special Education Teachers Serving on Teams Delivering AAC Services," by P. A. Locke and P. Mirenda, 1992, *Augmentative and Alternative Communication, 8,* pp. 200–214.

Child using a Springboard augmentative communication device (Prentke Romich Company) in the classroom to play a board game.

Photo by Vicki Spence

Ongoing Skill Development in Communication

Teachers must seek every opportunity for students to practice their communication skills and conduct conversations throughout the school day. They need to provide deliberate interventions that support the use of augmentative communication systems. Using the context of daily routines and naturally occurring events in the classroom and other school environments is recognized as a powerful approach to communication skill development. A specific protocol for this practice, **environmental communication teaching (ECT),** was developed by Karlan (1991). This method focuses on identifying the communication demands of natural environments, providing partners to prompt communication messages, and systematically arranging to expand communication exchanges. The user profile provides a clear illustration of ECT in use.

There are a variety of strategies for the promotion of communication using augmentative and alternative communication that have their roots in effective instruction. The use of positive social reinforcement through a hierarchy of prompting or modeling is an approach to instruction in any skill. Therefore, often skill development training in the use of a communication device and system will require the teacher to provide direct instruction by fading from physical coactive prompting to complete independent use of the device. This systematic use of instruction shares its efficacy with a host of other behaviorally oriented approaches to instruction. Students with autism have responded positively to the use of such techniques as pivotal response training.

Pivotal response training (PRT) is a behavioral strategy based on the principles of applied behavior analysis (Koegel & Koegel, 2006; Koegel, O'Dell, & Dunlap, 1988; Koegel, O'Dell, & Koegel, 1987). The assumption is that motivation and

USER PROFILE: Teaching Communication in Natural Environments

"Bernie, stand up. Are you buying lunch? Did you bring a lunch?"

"*I am buying lunch.*"

"Ashley, stand up. Are you buying lunch? Did you bring a lunch?"

"*I brought my lunch.*"

Taking the lunch count is a daily ritual performed by most elementary teachers, so at first glance this communication exchange seems quite ordinary. However, lunch count in this Life Skills class is not just another teacher-directed routine that has to be completed before learning can occur. In this class, lunch count *is* learning.

Implementing Environmental Communication Teaching

The classroom teacher, assistant teacher, and speech-language consultant have been implementing environmental communication teaching (ECT). ECT is designed to assist classroom teams in delivering communication intervention within the context of existing natural environments. The teams learn to develop activity-based objectives; sequences of cues, prompts, and feedback; and techniques to integrate augmentative communication in their classrooms. Teachers and parents who attend ECT training learn to change communication interactions from being teacher directed to being student directed, and to target communication skills in every classroom activity. Team members also learn to reduce the number of verbal and nonverbal prompts they give to students, and to change prompts when needed from yes/no questions and directives to open-ended questions and indirect prompts.

One of the hardest lessons of ECT is learning to pause to allow students the opportunity to process and initiate or respond. "We thought we were pausing to give the kids a chance to answer," reported the classroom teacher. "But we were amazed to see [on a videotape recorded in the classroom] just how quickly we jumped in to help the kids. Before ECT, we never would have waited as long as we do now, but the wait is worth it when a student finally answers a question on his own."

Integrating Augmentative Communication into the Classroom

Of the 10 students in this Life Skills class, only 4 have speech that is somewhat intelligible. Therefore, several students are learning to use augmentative communication devices. The devices in the room are on the low-tech end of the spectrum—devices such as the Hawk (Adamlab, LLC) that offers about 32 messages. One of the opportunities created for the students to learn and practice communication skills is the daily lunch count.

On the blackboard are photos of each student and a poster with a symbol for "lunchbox" on the left, "cafeteria tray" on the right; Velcro strips run vertically beneath the symbols for "They're not here" and "I'm finished." Next to the augmentative communication devices are laminated strips with the children's names. Jamillah, the lunch count taker of the day, removes Ashley's photo from the board and presses Ashley's picture on her device. As the device says "Ashley, stand up," Jamillah deposits Ashley's photo in the "All Done" box, then presses the question marks to ask "Are you buying lunch? Did you bring lunch?" Ashley presses the symbol of the cafeteria tray to answer, "I am buying lunch." She then finds her name and places it on the poster under the tray symbol.

Jamillah continues this routine until all students have been called. If a child is absent, Jamillah puts his or her photo in the "All Done" box and presses "They're not here." When the job is done, she tells the teacher "I'm finished" and sits down. The entire student-directed routine has once again been initiated, maintained, and completed by a 6-year-old student who has Down syndrome, visual and hearing impairments, and unintelligible speech.

Increasing Independence and Competence

Julie, another 6-year-old student, has also achieved a new level of independence. Julie's job is to go to the office to get the mail from the teacher's mailbox. Analyzing the task and Julie's educational objectives, the team determined that Julie had to (1) identify the teacher's mailbox, (2) handle both the mail and her augmentative communication device, and (3) communicate socially and request help if needed. Solution #1: The teacher's mailbox is now labeled with her picture instead of her name. Solution #2: Julie's augmentative communication device sits in the top basket of a three-tiered rolling cart so her communication system is readily available and the mail can be carried in the second basket to be wheeled back to the classroom. Solution #3: Julie uses the device to communicate to the office staff: "Hello," "It's time to get the mail," "I need help," and "Thank you." Upon returning to the classroom, she reports, "The mail is here" or "There wasn't any mail today." Julie completes this job entirely on her own; she no longer requires adult assistance.

The augmentative communication devices and manual communication boards are now an important component of a classroom that was already filled with line-drawn symbols, photographs, and words attached to the objects they represent. The team believes in using pictures with students in the Life Skills program to augment verbal messages from both the teachers and the students. "Symbols or pictures provide another avenue for the children to communicate, and also for understanding what we say to them," explains the teacher. As a result, all storage bins and cabinets are labeled with symbols for the objects they contain. The daily schedule is displayed in symbols on Velcro; changing the schedule is part of the morning routine, and following the schedule throughout the day is a lesson in sequencing.

Creating and Organizing All the Overlays and Symbols

Using Boardmaker (Mayer-Johnson), the team creates a plethora of communication materials for every activity and lesson, including overlays for the students' communication devices, manual picture boards for students who are moderately intelligible but who have limited expressive vocabularies, and enlarged individual symbols for object-symbol matching activities as new vocabulary is introduced. Because they use these materials during snack, crafts, story time, music, morning circle, cooking, grooming, and free play, a clear system for organization is a must. All device overlays and manual boards, along with manila envelops of the related individual symbols, are kept in a three-ring binder, one for each month of the school year.

Positive Results

With ECT the team has learned new instructional and implementation strategies, as well as the value of the team approach. "We've proved the old saying, 'Three heads are better than one.' Each one of us has contributed insights and ideas that have benefited the kids." The acquisition of Boardmaker has opened up a world of creative possibilities for symbol use in the classroom, and the use of augmentative communication systems has given children who would have little chance of effective communication independence a means to both.

From "Teaching Communication in Natural Environments," by P. L. Mervine, 1995, *TECH-NJ, 6*(1), pp. 3, 16. Reprinted with permission.

responsiveness to a variety of cues affect behaviors that are central to a wide area of functioning. PRT promotes motivation by combining skill development (including skills in communication) with highly motivating variables such as child choice, taking turns, and other reinforcing events.

Another behavioral approach to promoting the use of augmentative communication systems for students with autism that are nonspeaking is the use of the picture exchange communication system and other similar visual communication strategies. The **picture exchange communication system (PECS)** is a method for teaching children with autism and related developmental disabilities a functional communication system. Its theoretical roots combine principles from applied behavior analysis and guidelines established within the field of augmentative communication. It uses direct instruction and modeling of an exchange of simple to more complex symbol/picture exchanges (Bondy, 2001; Bondy & Frost, 2001; Frost & Bondy, 2006).

Although direct behavioral intervention is an important vehicle in the development of language and effective communication, it must accompany an understanding that this occurs within a social context (see Chapter 10). Therefore, consistent and frequent social exchanges that represent an appropriate balance of pragmatic structure and turn taking are critical to the success of using any communication system. Teachers can employ various strategies to ensure that communication is being used by developing an ongoing need. One such strategy is the use of sabotage to stimulate a need for communication. For example, a teacher may pretend not to see the attendance sheet that is behind him or her. "Where did I put that attendance sheet?" "I wonder where it could be." This creates an opportunity for students to respond using their devices, "I see it!" and then pointing.

Importance of Selecting Appropriate Vocabulary

As illustrated in the user profile, routine daily activities that occur in schools present excellent opportunities for communication. Other infrequent but planned activities such as pep rallies present additional opportunities. To ensure full participation in these activities, appropriate vocabulary needs to be added to the augmentative communication system. For example, a teacher or aide can work with the student user to construct a stored daily announcement that can be transmitted via the school's public address system. Low-tech language boards can be constructed for field trips so that the student has access to specific vocabulary related to that specific destination. For example, on a field trip to the zoo, a student will probably want to communicate his or her reactions to the strange sights and smells (e.g., "Oh boy, that stinks!," "That is so ugly!" "Gross!"). The vocabulary for a visit to an art museum, however, will likely be different. The student will probably want to express opinions about the paintings and sculpture ("That's beautiful," "I really like/don't like that") and possibly ask questions about the artists.

The school environment offers hundreds of opportunities to communicate and interact with peers. In addition to their regular classroom setting, students need to

TABLE 11–2 Examples of vocabulary and communicative functions

Function of the Communication Message	Sample Vocabulary
Commenting	"That's cool!" "I am not a fan." "No fair!"
Questioning	"What did you watch last night?" "What is your favorite TV show?" "What do you mean?"
Protesting or rejecting	"No, I don't wanna." "Leave me alone." "I hate this!"
Requesting	"Ms. C., I need help." "Can I play?" "Can I have a snack?" "Could you explain that again?"
Commanding	"Cut it out!" "Stop bothering me!" "Get out of the way!" "Change the channel."

respond to the demands of the playground, hallways, and lunchrooms. Therefore, vocabulary made available to students in their augmentative communication systems needs to be ecologically sound; that is, it must reflect the needs of the environment. Because it is difficult to predict the needed vocabulary for every school-related event or activity, teachers and classroom staff need to observe other children talking. Peer-referenced vocabulary is easily obtained by documenting frequently used phrases (e.g., "awesome," "cool," "no way") and by directly involving peers in vocabulary selection. Table 11.2 includes examples of age-appropriate vocabulary. Table 11.3 provides a checklist regarding the effectiveness of an augmentative communication system for supporting students' participation in general education classrooms.

Use of Peers as Communication Facilitators

Deliberate training of peers is important to ensure that they feel competent in communicating with someone who uses an augmentative communication system. This can occur in natural ways through teacher or peer guidance. One strategy that may be used is to establish a **communication circle of peer support**. Building on the concept of peer support to facilitate inclusion (Falvey, Forest, Pearpoint, &

TABLE 11–3 Augmentative communication checklist for participation in general education classrooms

Yes	A Little	No	
❏	❏	❏	Does the student's system enable him or her to participate in classroom discussions?
❏	❏	❏	Does the student's system enable him or her to answer questions?
❏	❏	❏	Can the student use his or her system for quick responses or messages?
❏	❏	❏	Is there a way for the student to gain attention from a distance?
❏	❏	❏	Does the student's system enable him or her to initiate a conversation?
❏	❏	❏	Does the student have a way to use unique and personalized vocabulary?
❏	❏	❏	Does the student have ways to express feelings and opinions?
❏	❏	❏	Is the student communicating efficiently with his or her peers?
❏	❏	❏	Is the student successfully communicating in other areas of the school, such as the playground, at lunch, or in the gym?
❏	❏	❏	Is the student increasing his or her overall skills in functional communication?
❏	❏	❏	Are there communication demands of specific activities that are not being met?
❏	❏	❏	Does there seem to be a need to expand the system to include additional solutions?

Rosenberg, 1994), the communication circle involves identifying a small group of peers who meet regularly to discuss and problem solve issues related to providing communication opportunities for the augmentative communication user. A communication circle of peer support can be an effective tool for refreshing available vocabulary and identifying needed new vocabulary (see Figure 11.1). To set up the circle, a teacher requests peer volunteers. This small group of peers is taught how to use the augmentative communication device and how to engage other students in social interactions with the augmentative communication user. The group meets weekly with the teacher and the student to review communication progress and brainstorm solutions to problems.

Child using his tango! (Blink-Twice) augmentative communication device to order a snowcone.

Courtesy of Blink-Twice Inc.

Other Strategies

Students who use augmentative communication must be *active* participants—not passive nonparticipants—within the classroom (Beukelman & Mirenda, 2005). If the user is not actively involved in an activity, lesson, or social event, his or her presence alone is not participation. Beginning users are often unskilled in initiating active participation, so teachers need to model effective ways to invite them into the process. Also, some nonspeaking students may be unable to participate fully in an activity because of the nature and scope of their disabilities. In these cases, partial participation is better than no participation. The sidebar provides specific examples of using partial participation to develop communication skills.

In addition to understanding the value of partial participation, teachers need to recognize that some students may have developed a pattern of learned helplessness through years of disempowerment (Reichle, York, & Sigafoos, 1991; Scherer, 2000).

FIGURE 11–1 Communication circle of peer support summary protocol

Chris's Communication Support Circle

Today's Date: _____
Circle Members: _____
_____
_____
_____

Description and Feeling Words about This Week

Were there any communication challenges?

Challenges	What Did You Do about It?

How can Chris and his circle members make it a better week?

❏ No way! It was a perfect week.
❏ Keep trying what we have been doing.
❏ There are some ways to make things better.

Circle Members Can . . .	Chris Can . . .

It's a wrap. Any final thoughts?

SIDEBAR

Examples of Partial Participation

- During roll call the augmentative communication user announces the names of each student while another student records the attendance records.
- During read-aloud time the augmentative communication user repeats the refrain of a book or poem while other students read the entire book out loud. For example, when reading from *The Very Hungry Caterpillar* the refrain might be "But he was still hungry!" (Carle, 1969).
- During break time the augmentative communication user participates in a game of Simon Says by "being Simon," that is, by calling out the commands.

Example of partial participation: Although the child cannot physically "pick a card," he takes his turn by using a switch to spin the dial.
Photo by Vicki Spence

Providing students with a voice can be very powerful; however, many initial augmentative communication users do not know what to do with their new-found power. Therefore, teachers must be able to identify learned helplessness (Petersen, Maier, & Seligman, 1995) and provide support to overcome the passive responses of students who have yet to learn that they can exert control over their environments.

Need for Teacher Training

Another reason students experience missed opportunities or limited practice is that the teacher is often unfamiliar with the augmentative communication system or has little technical support for troubleshooting. If a system is a mystery to teachers and

SIDEBAR

Tips for Overcoming Learned Helplessness

- Build a daily expectation of communication through specific activities such as choosing the activity during recess, picking a book to read, or identifying where to eat lunch.
- Construct a brief daily report to parents that is communicated by the student.
- Allow natural consequences to occur and provide avenues for repair. This includes setups that alter the environment to provide less support or sabotage.
- Provide for choice making whenever possible that requires the student to use his or her augmentative communication system.
- Provide powerful phrases on the device for students to reject or protest something.

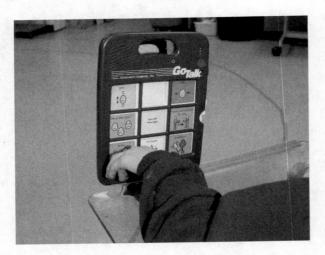

Child making a choice using the GoTalk augmentative communication device
Courtesy of Attainment Company.

other educational staff, the likelihood of the student being able to use it effectively is diminished. Therefore, it is important that the student's primary teacher and aide or paraeducator are involved in initial and ongoing training in the use of the augmentative communication system. In addition, a tech support staff member in the district should be designated as a technical assistance provider for the system to provide first-level troubleshooting and to address issues related to connecting to the school network.

Not Everything Is High Tech

Making simple communication more complex than necessary can be a mistake that teachers make in their attempts to be communication facilitators. Students need to be provided with an array of strategies to respond as efficiently as possible to simple communication demands. Students are often required to answer simple questions or make quick decisions regarding anything from lunch preferences to recess options. In these frequent and quick-moving situations, it is critical that the augmentative communication user have access to a simple no-tech or low-tech response such as using an unaided conventional gesture (e.g., shaking the head no) or a low-tech single-switch device that is easily accessible to the student at all times (Downey, Daugherty, Helt, & Daugherty, 2004).

INFUSING COMMUNICATION DEVELOPMENT WITHIN THE IEP

The teaching of communication skills is guided by the individualized education program (IEP) process. Augmentative communication evaluations should be a component of the program development process and must be carefully considered for all nonspeaking students. Once determined to be necessary for a student, the components of the system should be outlined within the IEP. In addition to specifying the system components, the IEP should also include the *use* of the augmentative communication system within the student's educational program. This will ensure that fundamental opportunities are provided for the student to practice communication skills within the context of his or her overall program. A student's academic goals and objectives should assume that his or her participation and evaluation will be achieved through the use of the augmentative communication system. However, every student user must have goals and objectives that reflect the use and continued

TABLE 11–4 Sample IEP goals related to augmentative communication

- The student will increase his or her spontaneous use of appropriate communication with familiar partners for at least three communicative purposes (e.g., initiating, rejecting, and commenting).
- The student will increase his or her use of appropriate communication with unfamiliar partners within the community.
- The student will independently navigate the augmentative communication device without assistance or prompts.
- The student will independently change his or her augmentative communication device overlay to increase available vocabulary and complexity of expression.
- The student will communicate more complex messages by selecting a three-icon sequence.

development of the system. Table 11.4 presents sample IEP goals related to augmentative communication.

TRANSITION FROM SCHOOL TO SCHOOL AND TEACHER TO TEACHER

When a student is transitioning from one school to another or from one teacher to another, it is critical to apply the protocols of comprehensive transition planning to ensure continued progress in the student's communication skills. Every effort should be made to ensure that the student does not experience regression or diminished opportunities for communication and participation. Training and technical assistance to the new teaching staff should be provided. Other effective practices include teacher observations in the current environment, written protocols for the support that new teachers can expect, training of new peers, and the designation of a central point person for troubleshooting.

HOME AND COMMUNITY USE

Although students receive direct instruction and guidance in developing augmentative communication skills in the school, they must practice and use their system at home and within their communities. Using their systems in these other places reinforces the communication skills learned in school and helps generalize them to other settings. This requires expanded consideration of family involvement, issues related to culture, and the identification of places or activities in which the student is active. Teachers must be actively involved in ensuring that there is appropriate carry-over and use within the home, among the family, and across community sites.

The importance of developing a working relationship between school and home is critical to the success of augmentative communication. Both environments reflect different and varied communication demands, and coordinated efforts can significantly increase the likelihood of effective communication. Training in the use of augmentative communication systems should be provided to families. This may include strategies for expanded use of the system and providing new vocabulary for the unique communication demands of home and community. For example, the family may like their nonspeaking child to participate in family birthday celebrations, religious activities, or a community group like scouting.

It is strongly recommended that patterns of family functioning and cultural diversity be actively considered at the initial stages of development and throughout the implementation process (VanBiervliet & Parette, 2002). Family members, including siblings, grandparents, and extended family, must be included in the evaluation and implementation process. Parents are familiar with the need to have conversations with their children and to facilitate their appropriate interaction with others. They do this with ease and consistency when at home or in other settings. However, this parenting skill is more challenging when a system of augmentative communication is introduced into the process. School personnel must provide direct instruction to the parents, who in turn can teach other family and

SIDEBAR

Tips for Guiding Parents to Promote the Use of Augmentative Communication

- **Provide Direct Instruction on the Use of the System:** A select group of family members should be assigned as primary at-home support for the student. This enables the school to provide intense and comprehensive training to a few people who will provide support at home. The more that family members can appropriately troubleshoot technical and pragmatic problems, the less likely they will need to depend on school staff.

- **Identify Vocabulary That Is Relevant to the Home:** Phrases such as "What's for dinner?" or "Change the channel" should be available for home use. A guided interview with the family can identify the specific communication demands of the home and most frequented community environments.

- **Teach Family Members to Provide Opportunities for Communication and to Wait:** Parents tend to anticipate the needs of their children and thereby create no real need to communicate. This tendency to speak for their child or assume that they know what the child wants must be replaced with strategies that encourage communication.

- **Provide Simple Data and Evaluation Sheets for Home and Community Use:** School staff should request families to report on their child's augmentative communication system use. Providing simple report protocols will enable the team to monitor the system's use outside the school and determine if and where assistance is needed.

- **Give Parents Permission to Expand the Child's Communication:** Parents should be reinforced for reported occurrences of communication practice and moving their child to expand his or her communication partners and experiences. The more novel people and places the student can communicate about and among, the better.

- **Keep It Simple:** If parents are expected to promote the use of augmentative communication to others, then the explanation of the system's use must be simple. Provide parents with clear, simple descriptions of their child's device—what it does and how the student uses it.

community members to interact with their child. Because some augmentative communication systems can be quite complicated to operate, consideration should be given to the current level of the family members' familiarity with computers and technology and their willingness to learn, prior to deciding on the most appropriate system. This will enable the school staff to plan the most appropriate home supports and expectations. It is important for the family to feel comfortable with the system and to understand the impact that communication practice will have on future success.

Using Augmentative Communication in the Community

Using augmentative communication systems in school and at home has the advantage of involving people who are interested in making sure it is successful. In contrast, the community at-large is less familiar with the augmentative communication user and may be less willing to accept the unfamiliar approach to communication. Communicating with unfamiliar partners is extremely challenging for most users. Unfamiliar partners are people who have no shared knowledge with the user, no understanding of the system, and no understanding of the rules of communicating with an augmentative communication user (Wagner, Musselwhite, & Odom, 2005). Teachers can facilitate positive experiences with novel communication partners through schoolwide special activities or assemblies and through planned field trips in the community. In this case, the devices can be programmed to ask specific questions and guests can be directed toward the augmentative communication user to answer a question. This will enable the student to practice interacting with unfamiliar partners.

SIDEBAR

Augmentative Communication Resources for Teachers

Providing new opportunities for communication for students who use low-tech communication devices does not need to entail time-consuming construction of communication boards. A wealth of resources have been developed to infuse the practice of augmentative communication within activities in school, home, and the community. *I Can Cook, Too!* (Mervine, Mark, & Burton, 1995) and *Art for Me, Too!* (Mervine, Burton, & Wood, 1996) are two collections of classroom activities that are designed to encourage communication. In addition to providing detailed instructions for implementing the cooking and art activities, these volumes provide communication boards that were designed using Boardmaker (Mayer Johnson) for augmentative communication users. The vocabulary on each of these communication boards matches the communication demands of each activity. Teachers are encouraged to copy the boards, laminate them, and use them in the context of the cooking and art activities to provide multiple opportunities for students to practice their communication skills. Figures 11.2, 11.3, and 11.4 illustrate the communications materials that are provided for one cooking activity in *I Can Cook, Too!*

FIGURE 11–2 Sample picture recipe for "Dirt Cups"

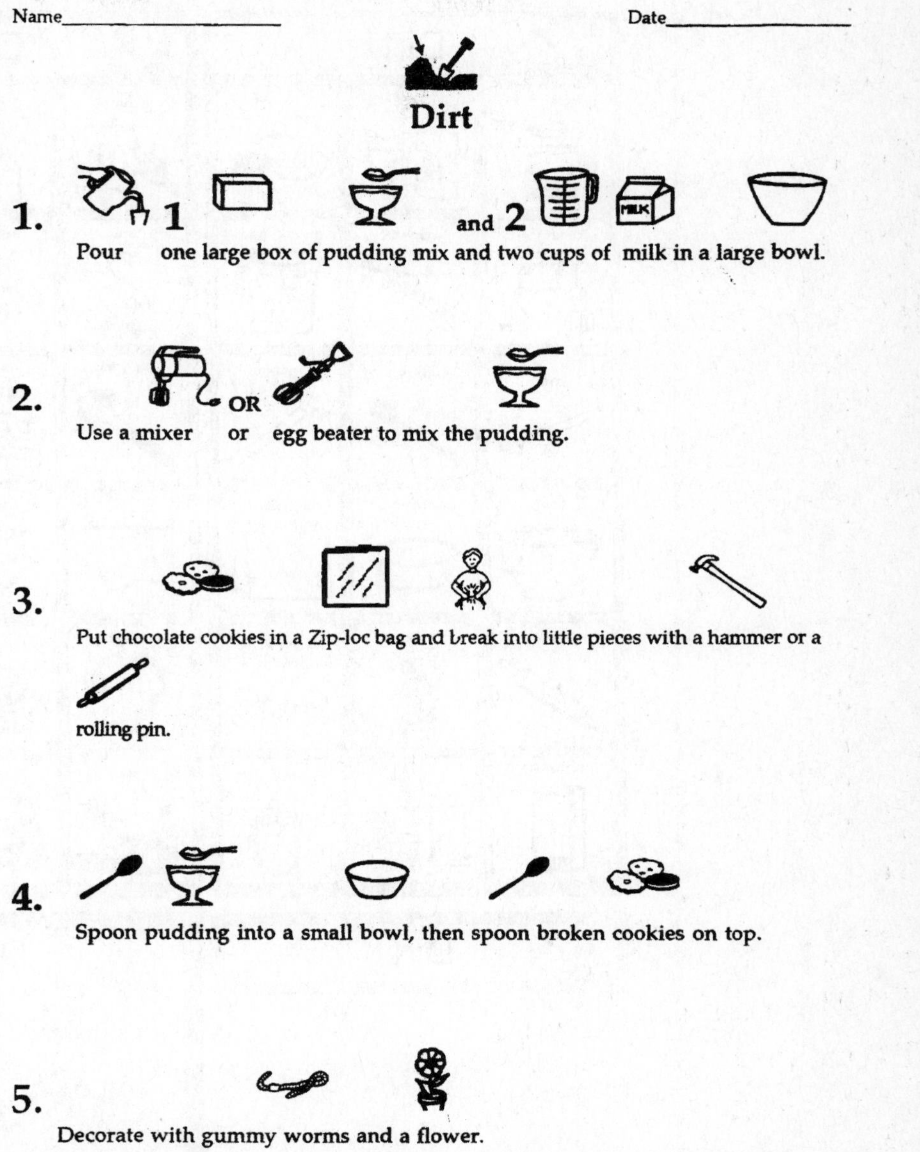

Name_____ Date_____

Dirt

1. **1** and **2**
    Pour   one large box of pudding mix and two cups of milk in a large bowl.

2. **OR**
    Use a mixer   or   egg beater to mix the pudding.

3. Put chocolate cookies in a Zip-loc bag and break into little pieces with a hammer or a
    rolling pin.

4. Spoon pudding into a small bowl, then spoon broken cookies on top.

5. Decorate with gummy worms and a flower.

Source: From *I Can Cook, Too!* by P. L. Mervine, M. Mark, and M. Burton, 1995, Solana Beach, CA: Mayer-Johnson. Reprinted with permission.

FIGURE 11–3 Communication board that accompanies Dirt Cups recipe

Source: From *I Can Cook, Too!* by P. L. Mervine, M. Mark, and M. Burton, 1995, Solana Beach, CA: Mayer-Johnson. Reprinted with permission.

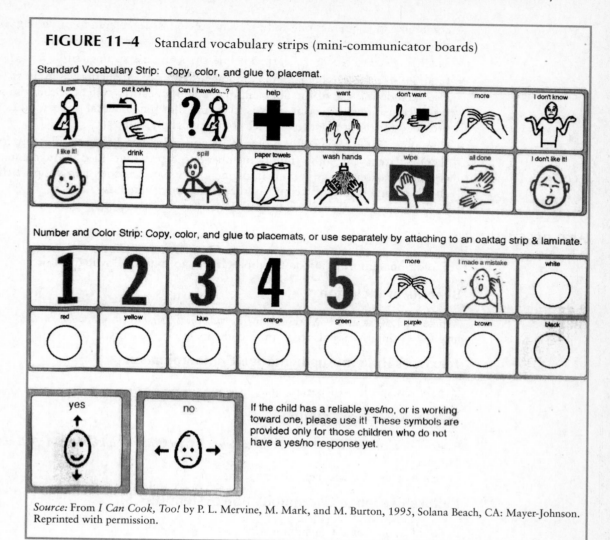

FIGURE 11–4   Standard vocabulary strips (mini-communicator boards)

Source: From *I Can Cook, Too!* by P. L. Mervine, M. Mark, and M. Burton, 1995, Solana Beach, CA: Mayer-Johnson. Reprinted with permission.

SUMMARY

- The teacher has a critical role to play in teaching effective communication skills by integrating augmentative communication into the curriculum and daily classroom routines.
- Of the many roles teachers fill, providing opportunities for communication and teaching communication skills are among the most important.
- Peers also have an important role to play in teaching communication skills. Organizing a communication circle of peer support is one way to involve peers in

communicative interactions and problem-solving issues related to providing communication opportunities for the augmentative communication user.

- Teachers need to recognize learned helplessness and use strategies to overcome it.
- In addition to specifying system components, IEPs of augmentative users should also include the use of the augmentative communication system within the student's educational program. This is to ensure that fundamental opportunities are provided for the student to practice communication skills.
- Communication demands of home and community can differ considerably from school. Parents and other family members need to be included in augmentative communication planning and implementation so that they can support their child's communication attempts in these other environments.

WEB RESOURCES

For additional information on the topics listed, go to the following websites:

Benefits of Inclusion

Article by J. Katz and P. Mirenda in *International Journal of Special Education*
http://www.internationalsped.com/documents/Educ._Benefits(2).doc

Teacher's Role in Augmentative Communication

http://www.speakingofspeech.com

Pivotal Response Training

R. Koegel, et al., *How to Teach Pivotal Behaviors to Children with Autism: A Training Manual*
http://www.users.qwest.net/~tbharris/prt.htm

Picture Exchange Communication System (PECS)

Pyramid Educational Consultants, Inc
http://www.pecs.com/

Joke Telling to Encourage Social Interaction

Linda Burkhart's recommendations: websites for jokes and riddles
http://www.lburkhart.com/jokes.htm

Augmentative Communication Listservs

SpeakShare: Hosted by the Prentke Romich company
http://www.speakshare.com
ACOLUG (Augmentative Communication OnLine Users Group): Hosted by Temple University's Institute on Disabilities
http://listserv.temple.edu/archives/ACOLUG.html

General Information Regarding Advancements in Augmentative Communication

Rehabilitation Engineering Research Center (RERC)
http://www.aac-rerc.com

Parent Advocacy and Home-School Collaboration

PACER Center (Parent Advocacy Coalition for Educational Rights) and Simon Technology Center at PACER
http://www.pacer.org/stc/index.htm

SUGGESTED ACTIVITIES

1. *Conduct an Ecological Inventory.* Conduct an ecological inventory or assessment of a classroom, identifying the communication demands and opportunities presented to the students. Using the questions *Who, What, Where, Why,* and *How,* analyze the opportunities for communication available. Discuss additional strategies that the teacher can use to promote communication.

2. *Develop a Peer Support Training Manual.* Develop a peer support training manual that focuses on creating understanding of and skills in supporting the communication efforts of augmentative communication users. What do peers need to know about communicating with a fellow student who uses augmentative communication? Write the manual for a specific age group and be sure it reflects age-appropriate and practical advice. The manual should be written without jargon and in easy-to-understand language.

3. *Infuse Augmentative Communication in the IEP.* Review three sample IEPs that are available on the Family Village website: http://www.familyvillage.wisc.edu/education/iepsamples.html. Modify the goals and objectives to infuse and operationalize the use of an augmentative communication system.

4. *Brainstorm for Vocabulary Selection.* The class will be divided into three groups, with each group assigned a grade level and an activity:
   a. Group A: Kindergarten, story time
   b. Group B: Fourth and fifth grade, nature hike
   c. Group C: High school, at the mall

Brainstorm with the members of your group and develop a list of vocabulary that would be needed for an augmentative communication user to participate actively in the activity. Remember to include vocabulary that is age appropriate and that provides a variety of communicative functions.

REFERENCES

Beukelman, D. R., & Mirenda, P. (2005). *Augmentative and alternative communication* (3rd ed.). Baltimore: Brookes.

Bondy, A. (2001). PECS: Potential benefits and risks. *The Behavior Analyst Today, 2,* 127–132.

Bondy, A., & Frost, L. (2001). The picture exchange communication system. *Behavior Modification, 25,* 725–744.

Carle, E. (1969). *The very hungry caterpillar.* New York: Philomel.

Downey, D., Daugherty, P., Helt, S., & Daugherty, D. (2004, September 21). Integrating AAC into the classroom: Low-tech strategies. *The ASHA Leader,* 6–7, 36.

Falvey, M. A., Forest, M., Pearpoint, J., & Rosenberg, R. (1994). *All my life's a circle. Using the tools: Circles, MAP's and PATH.* Toronto, Ontario, Canada: Inclusion Press.

Frost, L., & Bondy, A. (2006). A common language: Using B.F. Skinner's verbal behavior for assessment and treatment of communication disabilities in SLP-ABA. *The Journal of Speech-Language Pathology and Applied Behavior Analysis, 1,* 103–110.

Karlan, G. (1991). *Environmental communication teaching training.* Field-Initiated Research Grant Award No. H023C9005, Office of Special Education Programs, U.S. Department of Education. Lafayette, IN: Purdue University.

Koegel, R. L., & Koegel, L. K. (2006). *Pivotal response treatments for autism.* Baltimore: Brookes.

Koegel, R. L., O'Dell, M. C., & Dunlap, G. (1988). Motivating speech use in nonverbal autistic children by reinforcing attempts. *Journal of Autism and Other Developmental Disorders, 18,* NA 525–537.

Koegel, R. L., O'Dell, M. C., & Koegel, L. K. (1987). A natural language teaching paradigm for nonverbal autistic children. *Journal of Autism and Developmental Disorders, 17,* 187–200.

Locke, P. A., & Mirenda, P. (1992). Roles and responsibilities of special education teachers serving on teams delivering AAC services. *Augmentative and Alternative Communication, 8,* 200–214.

Mervine, P. L. (1995). Teaching communication in natural environments. *TECH-NJ, 6*(1), 3, 16.

Mervine, P. L., Burton, M., & Wood, L. (1996). *Art for me, too!* Solana Beach, CA: Mayer-Johnson.

Mervine, P. L., Mark, M., & Burton, M. (1995). *I can cook, too!* Solana Beach, CA: Mayer-Johnson.

Petersen, C., Maier, S. F., & Seligman, M. E. P. (1995). *Learned helplessness: A theory for the age of personal control.* New York: Oxford University Press.

Reichle, J., York, J., & Sigafoos, J. (1991). *Implementing augmentative and alternative communication: Strategies for learners with severe disabilities.* Baltimore: Brookes.

Scherer, M. J. (2000). *Living in the state of stuck: How assistive technology impacts the lives of people with disabilities.* Newton, MA: Brookline Books.

VanBiervliet, A., & Parette, H. P. (2002). Development and evaluation of the families, cultures and augmentative and alternative communication (AAC) multimedia program. *Disability and Rehabilitation, 24*(1/2/3), 131–143.

Wagner, D., Musselwhite, C., & Odom, J. (2005). *Out and about: AAC in the community.* Litchfield Park, AZ: C. Musselwhite.

PART IV

Making It Happen

CHAPTER 12
Implementation of Assistive Technology in Schools

CHAPTER 13
Implementation of Assistive Technology in Transition Planning

CHAPTER 12

Implementation of Assistive Technology in Schools

FOCUS QUESTIONS

1. What laws influence assistive technology provision in P–12 education?
2. How can assistive technology be integrated into the IEP?
3. What are some of the barriers to assistive technology implementation?
4. How does each barrier affect assistive technology implementation?
5. What are the major funding sources of assistive technology for students?
6. What do professional standards of educational personnel require with regard to assistive technology?

INTRODUCTION

Assistive technology offers numerous benefits for students with disabilities, as discussed in the preceding chapters. However, many students with disabilities are not being provided with the assistive technology tools and training that they need. Many students with learning disabilities continue to struggle with reading and writing, falling further and further behind in their work because their schools have not made talking word processing, word prediction, or scan/read software available to them. Many students with physical disabilities or autism continue to be frustrated by their inability to communicate and are unable to demonstrate their intelligence because their schools have not provided them with appropriate augmentative communication systems. The gap between the *possibilities* of assistive technology and the actual implementation of it in our schools is substantial. This chapter focuses on the key issues that need to be addressed to get assistive technology into the hands of the students who will benefit from it. The place to start is in examining the legal basis for assistive technology.

LEGAL BASIS FOR ASSISTIVE TECHNOLOGY

The United States Congress has underscored the importance of assistive technology to the education of students with disabilities by stating:

> Almost 30 years of research and experience has demonstrated that the education of children with disabilities can be made more effective by . . .
>
> (H) supporting the development and use of technology, including assistive technology devices and assistive technology services, to maximize accessibility for children with disabilities. (IDEA 2004)

We can say, therefore, that provision of assistive technology is not only a good idea, it is the law. Students with disabilities are entitled to assistive technology if it is essential for accessing education and education-related resources. The Individuals with Disabilities Education Improvement Act of 2004 (IDEA 2004), Section 504 of the Rehabilitation Act of 1973 (Section 504), and the Americans with Disabilities Act (ADA) ensure that students with disabilities have access to education and that they are protected from discrimination based on having a disability. Each of these laws is relevant to our discussion of assistive technology (see Chapter 1 for detailed information). However, IDEA 2004 is the law that has the greatest impact on Preschool through Grade 12 students with disabilities because it requires consideration of students' needs for assistive technology during the development of their individualized education programs (IEPs).

INTEGRATING ASSISTIVE TECHNOLOGY INTO THE IEP

Because the IEP drives the provision of special education services to students with disabilities, any discussion of assistive technology implementation must address the need to integrate assistive technology into the IEP. Assistive technology is one of the special factors that must be considered when developing each student's IEP. (See Chapter 8 for a discussion of assistive technology consideration.) The IEP must document that assistive technology has been considered. If the IEP team determines that assistive technology is not needed, this must be noted, along with the reason for this determination. If the IEP team determines that assistive technology is needed, this needs to be documented as well.

The documentation of the need for assistive technology may be incorporated throughout the IEP; however, there are three places in the IEP where specific assistive technology needs usually appear:

1. In the description of specially designed instruction
2. In the description of supplementary aids and services
3. In the description of related services (Bauder, Lewis, Bearden, & Gobert, 1997, p. 19)

It is also common to integrate assistive technology into the IEP in the section addressing present levels of academic achievement and functional performance. In IDEA 1997, this section was called the present level of educational performance (PLEP). The name change makes more explicit the intended purpose of this section which is (and has been) to provide information about "the present level at which the student is functioning

FIGURE 12–1 Sample statements for the Present Level of Academic Achievement and Functional Performance (PLEP)

- Uses adapted pencil grip for all written work.
- Uses slant board for all written work.
- Can complete written work using a computer adapted with a mini-keyboard.
- Completes written work using a word processing program with speech feedback and headphones.
- Completes % of written work compared to peers when using assistive technology and % if not using assistive technology.
- Uses adapted chair for toileting.
- Self-propels adapted wheelchair for mobility in school.
- Plays with other students in competitive games using assistive technology.
- Uses a voice output device to communicate within the classroom.
- Uses a communication board to interact with peers.
- Uses a personal FM amplification system to comprehend classroom instruction.
- Uses an FM sound field system to improve his or her attention to spoken messages.
- Completes written assignments using a computer with a voice recognition program.
- Uses a closed-circuit television (CCTV) to read printed material.
- Completes functional tasks using environmental controls.
- Participates in leisure activities using an environmental control unit.
- Accesses emergency evacuation information using visual, auditory, and tactile cues.

Source: From *Assistive Technology in the IEP*, by the Pennsylvania Training and Technical Assistance Network, no date, Harrisburg, PA: Pennsylvania Department of Education. Reprinted with permission.

in physical, social, academic, emotional, and transitional areas" (Wallace, 1999, p. 10). *Assistive Technology in the IEP* (Pennsylvania Training and Technical Assistance Network [PaTTAN], n.d.) provides many examples of acceptable statements (see Figure 12.1), along with the following guidance: "If the student is currently using assistive technology in his/her educational program, summarize how it is being used and how it relates to the student's performance" (p. 10).

Specially Designed Instruction

Assistive technology is often included in the goals or objectives of students' IEPs. Goals are relatively broad statements related to achievement expectations for students. "Goals should relate to the general education curriculum with assistive technology used as a tool to reach the curriculum goals" (PaTTAN, n.d., p. 14). That is, "assistive technology may be a means to help the child reach a goal. It should not be the goal itself" (Connecticut State Department of Education and Connecticut Birth to Three System, 1999, p. 32).

Objectives or benchmarks are the intermediary steps that must be reached in order to achieve the goals. Assistive technology is often included in objectives. This is good practice if using assistive technology is the means by which students will be able to demonstrate they have successfully accomplished their objectives. Another reason for including assistive technology is that "with objectives that include the specific technology, everyone involved in implementing the IEP knows and understands what is expected and what will be used" (Connecticut, 1999, p. 33).

Assistive technology may also be included in the IEP section dealing with accommodations and modifications. Any modifications to instructional methods or materials that will be required to make the general education curriculum accessible to students with disabilities should be noted. It is often beneficial to list assistive technology in this section even if it was mentioned in other sections of the IEP.

Supplementing Aids and Services, and Related Services

The sections of the IEP concerned with supplementary aids and services and related services are appropriate places to integrate assistive technology. IDEA 2004 defines supplementary aids and services as "aids, services, and other supports that are provided in regular education classes or other education-related settings to enable children with disabilities to be educated with nondisabled children to the maximum extent appropriate" (IDEA, 2004).

Related services are defined as

transportation, and such developmental, corrective, and other supportive services . . . as may be required to assist a child with a disability to benefit from special education. . . . The term does not include a medical device that is surgically implanted, or the replacement of such device. (IDEA, 2004)

Clearly, assistive technology can provide students with access to the curriculum, enable them to be educated in the regular education classroom, and help them benefit from special education. For these reasons assistive technology can be considered supplementary aids and services or a related service and included as such in the IEP.

OBSTACLES TO ASSISTIVE TECHNOLOGY IMPLEMENTATION

The Digital Divide

Educational and civil rights laws apply to all students with disabilities in P–12 settings. However, professionals and parents recognize the existence of a basic inequity with regard to application of these laws. In many respects this equity gap mirrors the "digital divide," a phrase that is often used to identify the gap between people who have access to information technology and people who do not. There is also a digital divide in terms of access to assistive technology.

A clear understanding of the digital divide is essential for understanding its impact on assistive technology. Webopedia (n.d.), an online dictionary focusing on computer technology, provides the following definition of *digital divide*:

A term used to describe the discrepancy between people who have access to and the resources to use new information and communication tools, such as the Internet, and people who do not have the resources and access to the technology. The term also describes the discrepancy between those who have the skills, knowledge and abilities to use the technologies and those who do not.

As you might surmise, many school districts serving upper- and middle-class students are among the "haves," and many districts serving predominantly low-income and minority students are among the "have-nots." Brown, Higgins, and Hartley (2001) identify the have-nots as

> students from diverse ethnic backgrounds, students living in inner cities, female students, students with disabilities, rural children, English language learning (ELL) children and their families, and students unlikely to graduate or who leave school without an adequate level of basic skills. (p. 33)

Not surprisingly, many of those who are have-nots with respect to information technology are also have-nots with respect to assistive technology. The financial resources of school districts account in large part for both forms of digital divides; Districts that have extremely limited funds simply have less money to invest in information technology and assistive technology. However, other factors also contribute to the inequity. Culture, access to information, and advocacy skills are among the factors that strongly influence assistive technology implementation.

Culture

Your culture can have a tremendous impact on your view of disabilities as well as acceptance of interventions, including assistive technology. **Culture** can be broadly defined as a system of learned and shared standards for perceiving, interpreting, and behaving in interactions with others and the environment (Jezewski & Sotnik, 2001, p. 3). Jezewski and Sotnik identify dietary practices, religion and religious practices, language, child-rearing practices, and family and social relations among the elements of a culture system; some of these elements have a stronger influence on how disabilities are viewed and treated than others. In some cultures disabilities are considered shameful because they are viewed as punishment for sins or actions of the parents or sins committed in past lives. Individuals subscribing to this cultural view may simply accept the disability as predetermined and not seek medical or rehabilitation services to address the disability. When disabilities are considered shameful, families may prefer to have their children with disabilities keep a low profile; they may not embrace the use of assistive technology because it would call attention to their child.

Some cultures are more collectivist than individualistically oriented. The American culture values independence and self-reliance, whereas other cultures put the needs of the family above the individual. People from these cultures may live with extended family, and there are many family members to help an individual with a disability. They do not value independence and do not see a need to use assistive technology to increase independent functioning. For monographs related to 11 specific cultures, go to the Center for International Rehabilitation Research Information and Exchange (CIRRIE website, http:// cirrie. buffalo. edu/mseries. html.)

Parents of students with disabilities from diverse cultures and lower economic status may have less access to information about assistive technology and their children's rights under IDEA, including an entitlement to assistive technology consideration. It may be difficult or impossible to access available print and online resources because they may not be available in the parents' native languages. Online information is less accessible to those who do not have Internet access in the home or those who have slower Internet connectivity, which is the case for many low-income families. The National Center for Education Statistics (DeBell & Chapman, 2003) reports the following:

> There are racial/ethnic gaps in home use: 41 percent of Blacks and Hispanics use computers at home and 54 percent of American Indians do so, compared to 76–77 percent of Whites and Asians. There is also a difference in home use between children and adolescents from the lowest and highest family incomes. Only 31 percent of those from families with incomes less than $20,000 use computers at home, compared to 89 percent of those living in families with annual incomes over $75,000.
>
> Larger still is the gap between children and adolescents whose parents have the least and the most education: while 26 percent of those whose parents did not complete high school use computers at home, 90 percent of those living with at least one parent who has attended graduate school use a computer at home. (p. 11)

Well-informed parents are better able to advocate for their children's rights and to bring important assistive technology information to the attention of IEP teams. As mentioned in Chapter 8 and discussed in the following text, IEP team members may have received little, if any, preservice or in-service training in assistive technology. This problem is compounded by rapidly changing technological advances, making it difficult to keep abreast of the latest products and developments. Parents can be instrumental in bringing categories of assistive technology or specific products to the attention of IEP teams, thereby increasing the probability that their children will benefit from appropriately selected and implemented technology. Whites (non-Hispanics), higher income earners, and those with higher educational attainment have greater access to computers (Horrigan & Rainie, 2002) and to high-speed, broadband connections (Horrigan, 2006). Therefore, they will have increased access to information and be better able to contribute to the assistive technology consideration process and advocate for their children's technology needs during IEP meetings.

Consideration Misunderstood

Despite the clear mandate to consider the assistive technology needs of all students receiving special education services, many obstacles prevent this ideal situation from becoming a reality. One problem stems directly from the language used in IDEA. Although assistive technology consideration is required, *consideration* is not clearly defined. State and local education agencies may have disparate interpretations and actualizations of *consideration*. Some educational agencies include a checklist of assistive technology solutions along the full assistive technology continuum as part of the IEP document and have policies and procedures in place to obtain an evaluation if team members feel they cannot adequately consider a student's needs. In other districts consideration is reduced to a statement on the IEP that assistive technology has been considered and is accompanied by checkboxes to indicate that technology is or is not necessary. "Is not" may be checked routinely simply because those doing the considering lack the necessary knowledge and skills in assistive technology.

SIDEBAR

Resources for Teachers, IEP Teams, Administrators, and Parents

Good resources on considering assistive technology during the IEP process and implementing assistive technology in the classroom are available from the Technology and Media Division (TAM) of the Council for Exceptional Children (CEC). The monograph *Considering the Need for Assistive Technology Within the Individualized Education Program* (Center for Technology in Education at Johns Hopkins University and Technology and Media Division of CEC, 2005) provides essential information on the process for IEP teams. A second monograph, *A School Administrator's Desktop Guide to Assistive Technology* (Bowser & Reed, 2004), is specifically geared to principals and other educational leaders so they will be prepared to support assistive technology use in their schools.

A kit called the *Assistive Technology Planner: From IEP Consideration to Classroom Implementation* (Bausch, Ault, & Hasselbring, 2006) consists of a form for assistive technology implementation planning and three informative manuals: one for teachers, one for administrators, and one for families. Each booklet is tailored to its audience with information on their particular roles in the process and specific strategies that are relevant to those roles. For example, the guide for teachers lists the following roles: (1) familiarizing oneself with assistive technology tools; (2) organizing the classroom environment and routines to support the use of assistive technology; (3) arranging for assistive technology to be used consistently; (4) monitoring student progress on assistive technology use; (5) maintaining communication with colleagues and parents about students' use of assistive technology; and (6) committing to further professional development on assistive technology. These resources are all available from http://www.tamcec.org/products.htm.

Professionals' Lack of Knowledge and Skills

A major obstacle to assistive technology implementation arises due to a lack of knowledge and skills in assistive technology among educational professionals. Although IDEA 2004 mandates assistive technology consideration, many of the educational personnel who are responsible for considering students' technology needs are unprepared to do so (Bausch & Hasselbring, 2005; Derer, Polsgrove, & Rieth, 1996). Additionally, simply identifying the assistive technology needed by a student does not equate to successful implementation. Levin (2005) cautions that "teachers may not have the training and support they need to help their students to make the most effective use of the technology tools and resources at their disposal" (p. 32). This barrier occurs because of a lack of assistive technology training. At both the preservice and in-service levels, training for special education teachers is either missing entirely or is inadequate. Often assistive technology training focuses on learning to use *devices*, not on using the devices *to learn*. "Training does not typically include using assistive technology to access the general-education curriculum, which is a key component to the successful use of assistive technology" (Bausch & Hasselbring, 2005, p. 9). Consequently, a lack of training for professionals continues to hinder the successful implementation of assistive technology in our schools (Gruner et al., 2000). Special education teachers entering the field today may be no more informed about, able to use, or skilled at identifying appropriate assistive technology than were teachers ten years ago.

Opportunities for *quality* in-service assistive technology training are often not made available to increase the competency of teachers and other educational personnel. This may be the case despite the fact that technology training may be provided during school district professional development days. Newton and Shiller (2005) report that special education teachers and staff are often required to attend the same technology trainings as general education teachers, regardless of whether the training is appropriate for them or not.

Failure to Implement Assistive Technology Recommendations

A common complaint is that recommendations for the use of assistive technology fail to get implemented despite the technology having been acquired and delivered to the student's classroom (Bell & Blackhurst, 1999). Even ensuring that professionals have the requisite technological knowledge and skills does not equate to successful implementation. A number of other issues must be addressed, or assistive technology implementation within students' educational programs is unlikely to happen.

Consider, for example, that a scan/read system has been recommended for a high school student with a learning disability to compensate for an inability to decode printed text. The system is purchased and everyone maintains high expectations for the student's academic success because of this acquisition. However, as the school year starts, the student's textbooks and other required reading materials are not available in electronic format. No one had been assigned to investigate whether there is a source for obtaining the needed materials in electronic format, and if so, to acquire them. Indeed, aside from the textbooks, no one even knows what other materials will be needed (e.g., the novels that will be read in English classes or the genre of books required for book reports). The textbooks have not been scanned because no one was assigned responsibility for this task, and it becomes apparent that scanning will be a lengthy and time-consuming process because the school does not have a high-speed scanner. No provisions have been made for scanning day-to-day printed materials such as handouts, worksheets, and study guides.

The need for addressing the wide variety of issues necessary to ensure successful assistive technology implementation has been recognized by the QIAT Consortium. As stated in Chapter 8, the QIAT (Quality Indicators for Assistive Technology) Consortium is comprised of assistive technology professionals and other stakeholders throughout the country. The *Quality Indicators for Assistive Technology Implementation: Research-Based Revisions, 2004* established by the QIAT Consortium sets standards for effective technology implementation (see Figure 12.2). Perusal of this document clearly reveals that planning for assistive technology implementation is considered vital to success, but that implementation planning is commonly not done effectively or not done at all.

FIGURE 12–2 Quality Indicators for Assistive Technology Implementation

Assistive technology implementation pertains to the ways that assistive technology devices and services, as included in the IEP (including goals/objectives, related services, supplementary aids and services, and accommodations or modifications), are delivered and integrated into the student's educational program. Assistive technology implementation involves people working together to support the student using assistive technology to accomplish expected tasks necessary for active participation and progress in customary educational environments.

1. **Assistive technology implementation proceeds according to a collaboratively developed plan.**
   Intent: Following IEP development, all those involved in implementation work together to develop a written action plan that provides detailed information about how the technology will be used in specific educational settings, what will be done, and who will do it.

2. **Assistive technology is integrated into the curriculum and daily activities of the student across environments.**
   Intent: Assistive technology is used when and where it is needed to facilitate the student's access to, and mastery of, the curriculum. Assistive technology may facilitate active participation in educational activities, assessments, extracurricular activities, and typical routines.

3. **Persons supporting the student across all environments in which the assistive technology is expected to be used share responsibility for implementation of the plan.**
   Intent: All persons who work with the student know their roles and responsibilities, are able to support the student using assistive technology, and are expected to do so.

4. **Persons supporting the student provide opportunities for the student to use a variety of strategies—including assistive technology—and to learn which strategies are most effective for particular circumstances and tasks.**
   Intent: When and where appropriate, students are encouraged to consider and use alternative strategies to remove barriers to participation or performance. Strategies may include the student's natural abilities, use of assistive technology, other supports, or modifications to the curriculum, task, or environment.

5. **Training for the student, family, and staff are an integral part of implementation.**
   Intent: Determination of the training needs of the student, staff, and family is based on how the assistive technology will be used in each unique environment. Training and technical assistance are planned and implemented as ongoing processes based on current and changing needs.

6. **Assistive technology implementation is initially based on assessment data and is adjusted based on performance data.**
   Intent: Formal and informal assessment data guide initial decision making and planning for implementation. As the plan is carried out, student performance is monitored and implementation is adjusted in a timely manner to support student progress.

7. **Assistive technology implementation includes management and maintenance of equipment and materials.**
   Intent: For technology to be useful it is important that equipment management responsibilities are clearly defined and assigned. Though specifics may differ based on the technology, some general areas may include organization of equipment and materials; responsibility for acquisition, setup, repair, and replacement in a timely fashion; and assurance that equipment is operational.

(continued)

FIGURE 12–2 (continued)

Common Errors
1. Implementation is expected to be smooth and effective without addressing specific components in a plan. Team members assume that everyone understands what needs to happen and knows what to do.
2. Plans for implementation are created and carried out by one IEP team member.
3. The team focuses on device acquisition and does not discuss implementation.
4. An implementation plan is developed that is incompatible with the instructional environments.
5. No one takes responsibility for the care and maintenance of devices so they are not available or in working order when needed.
6. Contingency plans for dealing with broken or lost devices are not made in advance.

Source: QIAT Consortium (2005). Quality Indicators for assistive technology services: Research-based update. Retrieved April 16, 2007 from http://www.qiat.org

Information Technology Policies

Assistive technology practitioners and teachers lament the fact that policies established to protect information technology (IT) systems can become barriers to assistive technology implementation (Newton, 2002). Access to operating system resources (e.g., control panels) may be a privilege reserved for IT personnel. As a result, assistive technology practitioners and teachers are unable to implement simple modifications such as activating StickyKeys or MouseKeys (see Chapter 6), and they cannot install software programs or assistive devices that are mandated by students' IEPs. At times these problems are transitory and easily resolved when IT personnel respond to requests to provide required services. However, at other times the IT policies result in denying students the assistive technology to which they are legally entitled. Teachers and assistive technology practitioners report that requests for software or hardware installation are sometimes denied because IT policies dictate that every computer in a school or district be configured the same way; therefore, if a program is not on *every* computer it cannot be on *any* computer (Newton, 2002).

Funding

Lack of funding is one of the major barriers to the successful implementation of assistive technology (National Task Force on Technology and Disability [NTFTD], 2004). Although IDEA mandates assistive technology consideration, it does not provide adequate funding for the technology that may be considered appropriate. Whereas the cost of low-tech assistive technology is usually minimal, further along the assistive technology continuum the cost increases. In school districts already facing financial challenges, funding may be viewed as an insurmountable barrier to assistive technology implementation.

Funding issues negatively affect assistive technology implementation in ways other than simply the expense involved with acquiring the assistive technology. Purchase price does not represent the total cost of most assistive technology devices; there are costs associated with insuring, maintaining, repairing, transporting, and updating the purchased items. Of particular concern is providing training for the students and adults who support the students' use of the technology, and training costs money. Unfortunately, when funds are short, adequate training is not provided; in this case students end up with the assistive technology that they need, but do not benefit from it because no one knows how to use it correctly.

ASSISTIVE TECHNOLOGY STANDARDS FOR EDUCATIONAL PROFESSIONALS

Educational professionals who are familiar with and meet the standards of their professional organizations will be well equipped to support assistive technology use by students with disabilities. This in turn increases the probability that students with disabilities will realize the benefits of the technology. Teachers, occupational therapists, physical therapists, and speech-language pathologists have professional organizations that advocate adherence to established standards of practice or knowledge and skill expectations for practitioners. The standards of each of the professions already mentioned include references to assistive technology.

SIDEBAR

Assistive Technology for Occupational Therapists, Physical Therapists, and Speech-Language Pathologists

To view standards and skills related to assistive technology for occupational therapists, physical therapists, and speech-language pathologists, go to the following websites:

American Occupational Therapy Association
http://www.aota.org/featured/area6/index.asp#otfact
AOTA's *Fact Sheets*

American Physical Therapy Association
http://www.apta.org/AM/Template.cfm?Section=Search&section=Governance
&template=/CM/ContentDisplay.cfm&ContentFileID=4916
Minimum Required Skills of Physical Therapist Graduates At Entry-Level.

American Speech-Language-Hearing Association
http://www.asha.org/about/membership-certification/new_standards.htm
2005 Certification Standards for Speech-Language Pathology.

What Every Special Educator Must Know: International Standards for the Preparation and Certification of Special Education Teachers, 5th ed.
http://www.cec.sped.org/Content/NavigationMenu/ProfessionalDevelopment/
ProfessionalStandards/

The following discussion concentrates on assistive technology–related standards of the Council for Exceptional Children (CEC) and the National Educational Technology Standards for Teachers (NETS for Teachers), established by the International Society for Technology in Education (ISTE). Other educational professionals are advised to go to the website of their professional organization to review the current standards.

Council for Exceptional Children Standards

CEC, the international professional organization for special education teachers, strives to improve educational outcomes for students with disabilities, as well as for students who are gifted and talented. Among the ways CEC seeks to accomplish its mission is by setting professional standards. Two types of standards are identified in CEC's Standards of Professional Practice: (a) content standards and (b) knowledge and skills standards. Content standards apply to all special educators, whereas the knowledge and skills standards vary according to teachers' areas of specialization. CEC explains that the knowledge and skills standards are "distinct sets of validated knowledge and skills [that] inform and differentiate the respective specialty areas and provide minimum knowledge and skills that special educators must master for safe and effective practice" (Council for Exceptional Children [CEC], 2003, p. 7). Assistive technology standards are referenced in both content and knowledge and skills standards, but not in every one of the 10 domain areas for which standards have been established.

Reference to assistive technology is found in the content standards under the language domain, identified as Standard #6: Language. This standard states:

> Special educators understand typical and atypical language development and the ways in which exceptional conditions can interact with an individual's experience with and use of language. Special educators use individualized strategies to enhance language development and teach communication skills to individuals with exceptional learning needs. Special educators are familiar with augmentative, alternative, and assistive technologies to support and enhance communication of individuals with exceptional needs. (CEC, 2003, p. 9)
>
> Standard #7: Instructional Planning includes a reference to technology, which includes assistive technology, stating, "Special educators are comfortable using appropriate technologies to support instructional planning and individualized instruction." (CEC, 2003, p. 9)

Because these are content standards, the implication is that *every* special educator should be familiar with assistive technologies to meet students' communication and instructional needs.

Assistive technology is also included in the knowledge and skills standards for every category of entry-level special education teacher. Every teacher of students with disabilities is expected to have proficiencies with assistive technology as specified in the standards for his or her specialty. Figure 12.3 lists the specific assistive technology expectations for entry-level special education teachers in the various specialty areas. Special education teachers are required to demonstrate competency with using, maintaining, incorporating, or integrating assistive technology into students' educational

FIGURE 12–3 CEC knowledge and skills standards for entry-level special education teachers

All Entry-Level Special Education Teachers of Students with Exceptionalities in Individualized General Curriculums (most closely aligns with a Mild/Moderate licensure framework)	
Standard #5: Learning Environments and Social Interactions	
GC5S2	Use and maintain assistive technologies.
Standard #7: Instructional Planning	
CC7S9	Incorporate and implement instructional and assistive technology into the educational program.
All Entry-Level Special Education Teachers of Students with Exceptionalities in Individualized Independence Curriculums (most closely aligns with a Severe/Profound licensure framework)	
Standard #4: Instructional Strategies	
IC4S2	Use appropriate adaptations and assistive technology for all individuals with disabilities.
Standard #5: Learning Environments and Social Interactions	
IC5S2	Use and maintain assistive technologies.
Standard #7: Instructional Planning	
CC7S9	Incorporate and implement instructional and assistive technology into the educational program.
All Entry-Level Special Education Teachers of Students Who Are Deaf and Hard of Hearing	
Standard #5: Learning Environments and Social Interactions	
DH5S3	Manage assistive/augmentative technology for individuals who are deaf or hard of hearing.
Standard #7: Instructional Planning	
CC7S9	Incorporate and implement instructional and assistive technology into the educational program.
All Entry-Level Special Education Teachers of Students in Early Childhood	
Standard #5: Learning Environments and Social Interactions	
EC5S4	Provide a stimuli-rich indoor and outdoor environment that employs materials, media, and technology, including adaptive and assistive technology.
Standard #7: Instructional Planning	
CC7S9	Incorporate and implement instructional and assistive technology into the educational program.
Teachers of Students with Emotional and Behavioral Disorders	
Standard #7: Instructional Planning	
CC7S9	Incorporate and implement instructional and assistive technology into the educational program.
All Entry-Level Special Education Teachers of Students with Learning Disabilities	
Standard #7: Instructional Planning	
CC7S9	Incorporate and implement instructional and assistive technology into the educational program.
All Entry-Level Special Education Teachers of Students with Mental Retardation/Developmental Disabilities	
Standard #5: Learning Environments and Social Interactions	
MR5S3	Use and maintain assistive technologies.

(*continued*)

FIGURE 12–3   (continued)

Standard #7: Instructional Planning	
CC7S9	Incorporate and implement instructional and assistive technology into the educational program.
All Entry-Level Special Education Teachers of Students with Physical and Health Disabilities	
Standard #4: Instructional Strategies	
PH4K2	Sources of specialized materials, equipment, and assistive technology for individuals with physical and health disabilities.
PH4S1	Use adaptations and assistive technology to provide individuals with physical and health disabilities full participation and access to the general curriculum.
Standard #6: Language	
CC6K4	Augmentative and assistive communication strategies.
Standard #7: Instructional Planning	
CC7S9	Incorporate and implement instructional and assistive technology into the educational program.
PH7S1	Develop and use technology plan based on assistive technology assessment.
All Entry-Level Special Education Teachers of Students with Visual Impairment	
Standard #7: Instructional Planning	
CC7S9	Incorporate and implement instructional and assistive technology into the educational program.

Source: From *What Every Special Educator Must Know: Ethics, Standards, and Guidelines for Special Educators* (5th ed.), by the Council for Exceptional Children, 2003, Arlington, VA: Author.

programs. This implies that their entry-level skills go beyond simply knowing about assistive technology hardware and software; they must be able to competently apply that knowledge to enhance the educational outcomes for students with disabilities.

International Society for Technology in Education Standards

ISTE states its mission as "providing leadership and service to improve teaching and learning by advancing the effective use of technology in education" (International Society for Technology in Education [ISTE], n.d.). This nonprofit professional organization engages in many initiatives, either independently or in collaboration with other organizations, to promote its mission. Among the collaborative initiatives is the National Education Technology Standards (NETS) Project, which has the goal of enabling "stakeholders in PreK–12 education to develop national standards for educational uses of technology that facilitate school improvement in the United States" (ISTE, 2002).

Between 1998 and 2001 ISTE released three sets of National Educational Technology Standards—NETS for Students (1998), NETS for Teachers (2000), and NETS for Administrators (2001). The NETS specify the technology-related standards and performance indicators that students, teachers, and administrators should be prepared to meet.

FIGURE 12–4 Performance profile assistive technology standards

---

Professional Preparation Performance Profile: Prior to the culminating student teaching or internship experience, prospective teachers:

24. identify and use assistive technologies to meet the special physical needs of students.

Student Teaching/Internship Performance Profile: Upon completion of the culminating student teaching or internship experience, and at the point of initial licensure, teachers:

5. design and facilitate learning experiences that use assistive technologies to meet the special physical needs of students.

First-Year Teaching Performance Profile: Upon completion of the first year of teaching, teachers:

19. enforce classroom procedures that guide students' safe and healthy use of technology and that comply with legal and professional responsibilities for students needing assistive technologies.

Source: From *National Educational Technology Standards for Teachers: Preparing Teachers to Use Technology*, by the International Society for Technology in Education, 2002, Eugene, OR: Author.

The NETS for Teachers are guidelines for all classroom teachers. Terms such as *assistive technology*, *special education*, or *students with disabilities* do not appear in the NETS for Teachers. However, the wording of the standards clearly conveys the expectation that classroom teachers will develop the skills to meet the needs of *all* students, including students with special needs. The inclusive nature of the standards is most evident in the standards related to social, ethical, legal, and human issues, which state: "Teachers . . . apply technology resources to enable and empower learners with diverse backgrounds, characteristics, and abilities . . . [and] facilitate equitable access to technology resources for *all* students" (NETS Project, 2001, p. 306, italics added). For more information on the NETS for Teachers, go to the ISTE website, http://cnets.iste.org.)

The inclusiveness of the NETS for Teachers is made explicit in the ISTE document *Technology Performance Profiles for Teacher Preparation*. This document provides guidelines for teacher preparation programs to support the development of technology-literate teachers who are capable of meeting NETS for Teachers. Specific performance profiles are provided for progressive stages of teacher development—General Preparation, Professional Preparation, Student Teaching/Internship, and First-Year Teaching; assistive technology standards are included in the profiles for the last three stages. Figure 12.4 displays the assistive technology competencies that teachers are expected to exhibit as they advance from preservice to in-service teaching. The NETS for Teachers carry the message that classroom teachers bear the responsibility for meeting the technology needs of all students, including students with disabilities.

FUNDING FOR ASSISTIVE TECHNOLOGY

The issue of finding the funds to support assistive technology was discussed as one of the major barriers to assistive technology implementation. This section addresses possible funding sources for assistive technology. School district budgets, public and private insurance, and other sources may be accessed to pay for assistive technology for P–12 students.

IDEA requires that **school districts** provide assistive technology devices and services at no charge to students' families if the assistive technology is necessary for students to benefit from a free appropriate public education (FAPE). School districts must provide any assistive technology that is identified in students' IEPs regardless of cost. School districts also are obligated to provide the technology services that students need to benefit from the devices provided. However, simply providing devices does not meet the legal obligations mandated by IDEA. Assistive technology *services*, such as technology evaluations; training for students, school personnel, and others who will support students' use of assistive technology for academic purposes; and repair and maintenance of technology must be provided at no charge to students' families.

Often special education budgets are the source of funds for purchasing assistive technology; however, this need not, and in fact should not, be the sole source of funding for devices and services. The Connecticut State Assistive Technology Guidelines add emphasis to this by stating:

> Assistive technology should be a part of every district's technology plans and purchases so that schools begin to deal with assistive technology needs pro-actively instead of reactively. In setting up technology plans, districts should incorporate basic assistive technology software, for example, when setting up computer labs. They should take into account student access to computers and carefully examine the environment so that at least some of the equipment is accessible to all students in terms of scheduling, workstation access, keyboard use, etc. Districts ought to include awareness level training in assistive technology use as part of their in-service technology training sessions, requiring that all teachers and support personnel become aware of the full range of assistive technology devices and services. (Connecticut, 1999, p. 41)

IDEA provides an option for acquiring medically necessary assistive technology through funding sources other than school districts. Use of Medicaid and parents' private health insurance to purchase assistive technology was authorized by IDEA 1997, and IDEA 2004 does not change this. However, because assistive technology must be provided at no cost, parental agreement to the use of these alternate funding sources is voluntary.

Medicaid is a joint federal–state program that provides funding for medical care, rehabilitation, and other services to individuals who meet eligibility requirements that include financial need. The Medicaid program varies from state to state: Each state's program must provide a certain set of mandatory services, and then the state can elect to provide a number of optional services for adult beneficiaries. Children with disabilities receive Medicaid benefits under Early Periodic Screening, Diagnosis, and Treatment (EPSDT) provisions and are eligible for the full range of Medicaid services, even those that may not be available to adult beneficiaries in their state (Sheldon & Hager, 1997). Regardless of a beneficiary's age, Medicaid provides assistive technology only if it is judged to be "medically necessary." At times, assistive technology deemed medically necessary, such as an augmentative communication device, also enables students to benefit from FAPE. In such cases, Medicaid funds, with parental approval, can be used to purchase the assistive technology.

For students who do not qualify for Medicaid, assistive technology that is medically necessary may be covered under the **family's private health insurance.** Parents may elect to use their private insurance to pay for assistive technology rather than school funds. If parents elect to do this, they own the assistive technology device, but that does not negate the school's obligation to provide associated assistive technology services. When private insurance is used, schools are still obligated to meet IDEA's mandate that assistive technology be provided at no cost to families; therefore, they may need to reimburse parents for copayments or deductibles (Hager & Smith, 2003).

Despite reimbursement for out-of-pocket expenses, there is often an unseen cost to parents when they agree to use private insurance to pay for assistive technology—a reduction in the annual or lifetime cap for medical benefits. Hager and Smith (2003) state, "For some students with significant needs, even a very substantial lifetime cap could be quickly used up, requiring the family to be very careful about when the insurance policy is used" (p. 38). School districts are required to inform parents that the use of private insurance is voluntary, and schools must provide the assistive technology if parents decline to use their private insurance.

Vocational rehabilitation (VR) agencies and the services they provide vary from state to state. In some states VR may be a funding source for assistive technology for students with disabilities. An **individual transition plan (ITP)** must be established as part of the IEP process when students are 16 years old. As part of the ITP, agencies that will be needed to support students after high school graduation should be involved in the transition planning process. State VR agencies are often involved in the transition plans of students with disabilities, especially those with the most severe disabilities. VR agencies may provide assistive technology while students are still in high school if the assistive technology will increase the students' chances for successful employment or pursuit of postsecondary education. Because VR funds must be targeted to improved employment outcomes, Kemp, Hourcade, and Parette (2000) suggest that "requests made for assistive technology through a state's Department of Vocational Rehabilitation might especially highlight the contributions that the technology will make towards the student's potential for vocational independence and/or productivity" (p. 7).

School district budgets, Medicaid, private insurance, and VR agencies are the major funding options available to school districts for purchasing assistive technology, but some districts pursue additional resources in their local communities. **Local civic organizations** such as the chamber of commerce, Lions club, Kiwanis club, and Rotary clubs are often tapped for support of assistive technology purchases. School and community fund-raisers may be other sources of funding (Bauder et al., 1997; Connecticut, 1999; Montana Office of Public Instruction, 2004). Renting or borrowing assistive technology, rather than outright purchase, can be considered as well. Regardless of the source of funding, "it is important to note . . . that the implementation of the devices and services required in the IEP cannot be delayed while the school system tries to find alternative funding sources" (Connecticut, 1999, p. 55).

SUMMARY

- The Individuals with Disabilities Education Improvement Act of 2004 (IDEA 2004), Section 504 of the Rehabilitation Act of 1973 (Section 504), and the American with Disabilities Act (ADA) are the laws that entitle students in P–12 education to assistive technology in order to access education and education-related resources.

- Assistive technology must be considered for each student receiving special education services.

- Because the IEP drives the provision of special education services to students with disabilities, any discussion of assistive technology implementation must address the need to integrate technology into the IEP.
- Despite the legal mandates, there are many obstacles impeding successful consideration and implementation of assistive technology. Major obstacles include the digital divide, cultural issues, misunderstandings about what constitutes assistive technology consideration, a dearth of assistive technology skills among educational professionals, failure to implement technology recommendations, information technology policies, and lack of funding to purchase technology and provide necessary training.
- It is important to recognize these obstacles because that is a necessary first step to overcoming them.
- The QIAT Consortium sets standards for effective assistive technology implementation.
- School district budgets, Medicaid, private insurance, and vocational rehabilitation agencies are the major funding options available to school districts for purchasing assistive technology, but some districts pursue additional resources in their local communities.

WEB RESOURCES

For additional information on the topics listed, go to the following websites:

Making It Work: Implementation Issues

National Center for Technology Innovation
http://www.nationaltechcenter.org/index.php/category/i-can-soar/

Assistive Technology and the Law

U.S. Department of Education: Building the Legacy: IDEA 2004
http://idea.ed.gov/
Texas Assistive Technology Network: *Providing Assistive Technology: A Legal Perspective* (PDF)
http://www.texasat.net/docs/Legal.Persp.Guides.pdf

Digital Divide

ISTE Educator Resources
http://www.iste.org → Educator Resources → Equity → Digital Divide
Digital Equity Service Center
http://www.digitalequity.org/index.php

Digital Equity Toolkit
http://www.nici-mc2.org/de_toolkit/pages/print.htm
Digital Divide Network
http://www.digitaldividenetwork.org/

Cultural Influences

Family Information Guide to Assistive Technology
http://www.fctd.info/resources/fig_summary.php

Building Assistive Technology Skills

The Early Childhood Technology Integrated Instructional System
http://www.wiu.edu/users/ectiis/
Videos of assistive technology from Valdosta State University
http://coefaculty.valdosta.edu/spe/ATRB/Video_Tips.htm

Resources for Assistive Technology Implementation

Georgia Project for Assistive Technology: Implementation and Intervention
http://www.gpat.org/Resources%20Main.htm
Oregon Technology Access Program: Assistive Technology Model Operating Guidelines
http://www.otap-oregon.org/media/pdf/AMOG.PDF

Collaboration between Assistive Technology and Information Technology Staff

Consortium for School Networking (CoSN)
http://www.accessibletech4all.org/index.cfm

Technology Standards for Teachers

Council for Exceptional Children: *What Every Special Educator Must Know: International Standards for the Preparation and Certification of Special Education Teachers—5th ed.*
http://www.cec.sped.org/Content/NavigationMenu/ProfessionalDevelopment/ProfessionalStandards/
International Society for Technology in Education: NETS for Teachers
http://cnets.iste.org/getdocs.html#teachers

SUGGESTED ACTIVITIES

1. *Check out the QIAT Listserv.* Monitor the messages posted to the QIAT listserv by reviewing the archived postings available at http://lsv.uky.edu/archives/QIAT .html. Be prepared to discuss or write about the postings during class sessions.

2. *Add to your Portfolio.* Add a copy of the standards of practice for your professional organization to your portfolio. Identify and highlight the standards related to assistive technology.

3. *Complete a Self-Evaluation.* Print a copy of the section titled "Knowledge and Skill Base for Special Education Technology Specialists" from the CEC publication *What Every Special Educator Must Know: Ethics, Standards, and Guidelines for Special Educators.* Access the publication by clicking on the "Professional Standards" link at the CEC website (http://www.cec.sped.org). Complete a self-assessment by reading each indicator, considering your skill level, and indicating whether you are at a novice or proficient level for each indicator. When you have completed the self-evaluation, create a professional development plan to address your area of greatest need.

4. *Integrate a Low-Tech Device in the IEP.* You have a student who requires the use of a slant board to complete handwriting tasks. In what sections of the IEP might you include reference to using a slant board? Write statements that would be appropriate for each section.

5. *Research Assistive Technology in the IEP.* Interview a member of a local IEP team. Ask the following questions as well as others that you feel are relevant. Submit a written summary of the interview and be prepared to discuss the interview in class.

   • Does the district have a prescribed process for assistive technology consideration while developing an IEP? If yes: What is the process?

   • How does the district document that assistive technology has been considered?

   • If assistive technology is included in the IEP, is an implementation plan developed? If yes: What is included in an implementation plan? If no: How do you make sure the assistive technology gets purchased and implemented?

   • Has any assistive technology training been provided for IEP team members?

6. *Conduct a School Profile Survey.* The School Profile of Assistive Technology Services is a survey designed to help improve assistive technology service delivery. Have at least two special education teachers at a school of your choice complete the survey. The school profile can be purchased from WATI (http://www .wati.org/products/products.html) or you can download a copy of the completed Wisconsin profile and edit it for your use (http://www.wati.org/AT_Services/pdf/ profile.pdf, permission granted by WATI). Summarize the data from the completed surveys, identifying areas of strengths and areas in greatest need of improvement.

REFERENCES

Bauder, D. K., Lewis, P., Bearden, C., & Gobert, C. (1997). *Assistive technology guidelines for Kentucky schools.* Frankfort: Kentucky Department of Education.

Bausch, M. E., Ault, M. J., & Hasselbring, T. S. (2006). *Assistive technology planner: From IEP consideration to classroom implementation.* Lexington, KY: National Assistive Technology Research Institute.

Bausch, M. E., & Hasselbring, T. S. (2005). Using assistive technology: Is it working? *Threshold, 2*(1), 7–9.

Bell, J. K. & Blackhurst, A. E. (1999). *How assistive technology services can go awry.* Report of the University of Kentucky Assistive Technology Project. Retrieved April 3, 2007 from http://natri.uky.edu/resources/reports/awry.html

Bowser, G., & Reed, P. (2004). *A school administrator's desktop guide to assistive technology.* Arlington, VA: Technology and Media Division of the Council for Exceptional Children.

Brown, M. R., Higgins, K., & Hartley, K. (2001). Teachers and technology equity. *Teaching Exceptional Children, 33*(4), 32–39.

Center for Technology in Education at Johns Hopkins University and Technology and Media Division of CEC. (2005). *Considering the need for assistive technology within the individualized education program.* Arlington, VA: Technology and Media Division of CEC.

Connecticut State Department of Education and Connecticut Birth to Three System. (1999). *Guidelines for assistive technology.* Hartford, CT: Author.

Council for Exceptional Children. (n.d.). Retrieved from http://www.cec.sped.org/ab/purpose.html

Council for Exceptional Children. (2003). *What every special educator must know: Ethics, standards, and guidelines for special educators* (5th ed.). Arlington: VA: Author.

DeBell, M. & Chapman, C. (2003). Computer and Internet use by children and adolescents in 2001, NCES 2004-014, Washington, DC: U.S. Department of Education, National Center for Education Statistics. Retrieved April 30, 2007 from http://nces.ed.gov/pubsearch/pubsinfo.asp?pubid=2004014

Derer, K., Polsgrove, L., & Rieth, H. (1996). A survey of assistive technology applications in schools and recommendations for practice. *Journal of Special Education Technology, 13*(2), 62–80.

Gruner, A., Fleming, E., Carl, B., Diamond, C. M., Ruedel, K. L. A., Saunders, J., et al. (2000). *Synthesis on the selection and use of assistive technology* (Final report). Washington, DC: U.S. Department of Education.

Hager, R. M., & Smith, D., (2003). *The public school's special education system as an assistive technology funding source: The cutting edge.* Buffalo, NY: Neighborhood Legal Services.

Horrigan, J. B. (2006). *Home broadband adoption 2006: Home broadband adoption is going mainstream and that means user-generated content is coming from all kinds of Internet users.* Washington, DC: Pew Internet & American Life Project.

Horrigan, J. B., & Rainie, L., (2002). *The broadband difference: How online Americans' behavior changes with high-speed Internet connections at home.* Washington, DC: Pew Internet & American Life Project.

Individuals with Disabilities Education Act of 2004, 20 U.S.C. § 1401D.

International Society for Technology in Education. (n.d.). Retrieved from http://www.iste.org/

International Society for Technology in Education. (2002). *National educational technology standards for teachers: Preparing teachers to use technology.* Eugene, OR: Author. Retrieved April 26, 2007, from http://www.iste.org/template.ctm?section=NETS

Jezewski, M. A., & Sotnik, P. (2001). *The rehabilitation service provider as culture broker: Providing culturally competent services to foreign born persons.* Buffalo, NY: Center for International Rehabilitation Research Information and Exchange.

Kemp, C. E., Hourcade, J. J., & Parette, H. P. (2000). Building an initial information base: Assistive technology funding resources for school-aged students with disabilities. *Journal of Special Education Technology, 15*(4), 15–24.

Levin, D. A. (2005). From promise to practice: Honoring leadership in using technology for improved learning. *Threshold, 2*(1), 32.

Montana Office of Public Instruction. (2004). *A special education guide to assistive technology.* Helena, MT: Division of Special Education.

National Task Force on Technology and Disability. (2004). *Within our reach: Findings and recommendations of the National Task Force on Technology and Disability.* Flint, MI: The Disability Network.

NETS Project, (2001). *National Educational Technology Standards for Teachers: Preparing Teachers to Use Technology.* Eugene, OR: International Society for Technology in Education.

Newton, D. (2002). *The impact of a local assistive technology team on the implementation of assistive technology in the school setting.* Unpublished doctoral dissertation, University of Cincinnati.

Newton, D., & Shiller, B. (2005, October 21). *When assistive technology meets IT: The good, the bad, and the ugly.* Paper presented at the 23rd annual Closing the Gap Conference, Minneapolis, MN.

Pennsylvania Training and Technical Assistance Network. (n.d.). *Assistive technology in the IEP.* Harrisburg, PA: Pennsylvania Department of Education, p. 10.

QIAT Consortium (2005). *Quality Indicators for assistive technology services: Research-based update.* Retrieved April 16, 2007 from http://www.qiat.org

Sheldon, J. R., Jr., & Hager, R. M. (1997, May–June). Funding of assistive technology for persons with disabilities: The availability of assistive technology through Medicaid, public school special education programs and state vocational rehabilitation agencies. *Clearinghouse Review.* Retrieved February 25, 2006, from http://www.nls.org/atart.htm

Wallace, J. (1999). *Assistive technology in the student's Individualized Education Program: A handbook for parents and school personnel.* Richmond: Virginia Assistive Technology System. Retrieved from the Virginia Assistive Technology System website: http://www.vats.org/athandbook.htm

Webopedia. (n.d.). Digital divide [Definition]. Retrieved from http://www.webopedia.com/TERM/D/digital_divide.html

CHAPTER 13

Implementation of Assistive Technology in Transition Planning

FOCUS QUESTIONS

1. How can assistive technology serve as a reasonable accommodation for students with disabilities in college?

2. What are the differences between the rights and requirements of the Individuals with Disabilities Education Act (IDEA) in the P–12 world and the rights and responsibilities under the Americans with Disabilities Act (ADA) in higher education?

3. What are the implications of assistive technology needs in college for transition planning and implementation in high school?

4. How can assistive technology help students who have autism, cognitive disabilities, or multiple disabilities achieve independence in home, work, and community settings?

PREPARATION FOR TRANSITION FROM HIGH SCHOOL TO COLLEGE

The 1990s saw the first group of children with disabilities who had received a free appropriate public education (FAPE) under the Individuals with Disabilities Education Act (IDEA) graduate from high school. For many of these adolescents, going on to college was a logical next step, and, in fact, research reveals that the employment rate is substantially higher for people with disabilities who complete 4 years of college (50.3%) compared to those who complete only high school (30.2%) (Yelin & Katz, 1994). The number of students with disabilities attending college has increased significantly in the last decade. In one study, 9.3% of all undergraduates self-identified as having a disability (U.S. Department of Education Office for Civil Rights, 2002). Fifty-nine percent of these students were attending 2-year programs. In another study, a breakdown by disability category revealed the following: 16% of first-year students with disabilities identified themselves as being blind or partially sighted, 15.4% self-reported health-related impairments, 8.6% reported deafness or hearing impairment, and 7% reported having orthopedic disabilities. The largest percentage reported among first-year students was learning disabilities—40.4% in 2000, in contrast to 16% in 1988 (Henderson, 2001).

Problems Students with Disabilities Face in College

Consider the typical tasks college students must complete in order to be successful in their academic endeavors. College students do a lot of reading—textbooks, journal articles, literary works, websites, and exams, to name a few. Many course assignments involve writing papers that require students to organize their thoughts, express themselves clearly, and demonstrate their knowledge. Students need to be able to attend lectures and discussions and simultaneously take notes. And finally, college students need to keep themselves organized and manage their time responsibly (e.g., turn in their assignments on time). (See Brinckerhoff, McGuire, & Shaw, 2002, p. 285 for a comprehensive list of the common demands placed on college students.)

Now consider the typical characteristics of students with learning disabilities. The National Joint Committee on Learning Disabilities (NJCLD; 1994), which developed the definition of learning disabilities that is accepted in higher education, defines **learning disabilities** as

> a heterogeneous group of disorders manifested by significant difficulties in . . . listening, speaking, reading, writing, reasoning, or mathematical abilities. . . . Problems in self-regulatory behaviors, social perception, and social interaction may exist with learning disabilities but do not by themselves constitute a learning disability. (pp. 65–66)

In other words, these are students who tend to read slowly at best and struggle with reading comprehension; they have significant difficulties organizing their thoughts and expressing themselves in writing; they dread writing because they are poor spellers and the writing process is so frustrating; many cannot listen and take notes at the same time; some find math to be incomprehensible; some cannot master the intricacies of social interactions; and many students with learning disabilities are especially weak in executive functions such as task organization and time management.

Students with other disabilities also face obstacles in completing college-level work. For students with visual impairments the tasks of reading, taking notes, researching information, and using a computer may be barriers to success. For students who are deaf or hard of hearing, listening to lectures and taking notes in class may present problems; communicating with faculty and peers, and participating in group discussions pose additional obstacles for students who are deaf or hard of hearing. Students with physical disabilities may be extremely slow typists or may not be able to type on a computer at all.

Assistive technology offers solutions to these obstacles. With the right hardware, software, and assistive device, computers can help college students complete academic tasks in a timely fashion; decrease the anxiety and frustration associated with reading, writing, and communicating; gain access to and participate in the full range of learning opportunities; and maximize their independence (Burgstahler, 2003).

Typical Accommodations at College That Meet These Needs

Assistive technology can be used to assist college students during classes, testing situations, and in completing assignments. Chapters 2 and 3 of this text described specific ways computer technology can assist with writing, organizing, and reading;

Chapter 4 addressed assistive technology tools that can enhance communication; and Chapters 6, 7, and 8 described multiple ways of accessing computers for students who cannot type on a regular QWERTY keyboard. All of these assistive technology tools may be helpful to college students *if* the tools meet the following criteria:

1. The assistive technology tool must be **easy to use** and **easy to customize.** The technology must make accomplishing the task *easier*, not more difficult, for the student with a disability. Software that takes hours to set up or days to learn how to use is not appropriate. The device or software must also be easily customized to the student's specific needs or styles. If choosing a word prediction program, for example, the user will want to make sure he or she can add specialized vocabulary to the dictionary quickly and efficiently.

2. The technology tool must be **age appropriate.** Although there are many assistive technology devices and software programs that are effective at the elementary school level, college students will refuse to use them if they appear childish. The assistive technology tool chosen should blend in with the college environment. For example, college students who need word prediction (see Chapter 2) prefer using a word prediction program that works along with Microsoft Word (a standard word processor) rather than a stand-alone program that has a simplified, juvenile-looking interface.

3. Closely related to the previous point, the assistive technology selected must be the **student's own choice.** It is extremely important that personal preference be a major criterion in technology selection in higher education (Burgstahler, 2003). The student has an understanding of his or her strengths and needs and goals and priorities, which can be very helpful in determining appropriate technology solutions. It is also likely that the student has particular likes and dislikes. If these personal preferences are not honored, the student is unlikely to use the technology.

4. The technology tool must carefully **match the specific task** that needs to be accomplished and the **environment** in which it will take place. Notetaking, for example, is a specialized form of writing. It needs to be done quickly, while the instructor is speaking or showing a video. Notetaking takes place in a lecture hall or classroom, where there are other students present. Often there is no power source available. How does this affect the selection of assistive technology? Voice recognition is not likely to be a good choice because dictation will bother other students. Typing notes on a laptop that requires charging every 3 hours may not be effective because the course is in the afternoon, the laptop's power will be used up, and there may be no power outlet accessible to the student. In this case the technology solution may be a portable notetaker like Neo that runs for 700 hours on three AAA alkaline batteries.

5. The assistive technology tool must be installed in a place that the student can **access easily,** whenever he or she needs it for completing college work. College students without disabilities usually have access to their institution's computers

at least 16 hours a day; many colleges offer computer access 24/7. Assistive technology solutions must be available during the same time period as other technology resources. Computers and devices such as video magnifiers may be set up in a centrally located place like the college library or a computer lab, or in a student's dormitory room. Software may be installed in computer labs or on students' own computers—this will vary by college. What must be avoided is installing the assistive technology in an office that is open only limited hours or a room that is inaccessible to the student who needs it.

6. **Training** and ongoing **technical support** must be provided to students and staff. Even if students already are skilled in using a particular piece of software, it is not unusual for technical problems to arise, especially on college computers that are set up for many different uses. Software and network conflicts are commonplace; therefore provisions for providing technical support must be in place.

USER PROFILE: Serena

Assistive Technology as a Reasonable Accommodation in College

A desktop computer, screen-reading software, a scanner with an automatic document feed, scan/read software, a talking Braille notetaker, a Braille embosser (printer), digital books, books-on-tape, and a tape player: These are the technology tools that Serena uses to complete her academic requirements in college. Serena, who is blind, is a first-year student who plans to major in either psychology or sociology, and to pursue her interest in Spanish. She takes notes in class using her lightweight Braille notetaker, which has both speech output and a refreshable Braille display. It is also equipped with a Spanish module so she can write and print out in Spanish as well as English. She writes papers using the Braille notetaker or the desktop computer (she learned to touch-type in second grade); she can print Braille copies on the Braille embosser for her own reading and standard text copies on an inkjet printer for her professors.

Reading textbooks and other assigned readings requires a more elaborate arrangement. Some textbooks are available as digital books or books-on-tape from Recording from the Blind and Dyslexic (RFB&D); others are borrowed as Braille books or books-on-tape from the state Library for the Blind and Handicapped. Books and other reading material that are in the public domain are downloaded as electronic text from a variety of websites and then read aloud by Serena's screen-reading program. A few textbook publishers have provided electronic files of their texts so they can be read by the screen-reading software. Reading assignments that are not available in any of these formats are scanned into her computer and read aloud via the scan/read software. The scan/read program can also send documents to the Braille notetaker, which gives Serena the option of reading the books herself using the notetaker's refreshable Braille display. This array of technology tools provides Serena with complete access to her college coursework.

Adapted from "Utilizing Blindness Skills in College," by S. Cucco, *TECH-NJ, 16*(1), p. 6.

There Are No IEPs in College

Although many of the technology tools used at the college level are the same as those used in the P–12 environment, the laws affecting students with disabilities and the process of obtaining assistive technology are completely different. IDEA is not in effect in higher education. Colleges have no legal responsibility to identify students with disabilities or involve parents in decision making. There are no IEPs in college (Varrassi, 2004). In fact, there is no *right* to college; no one in this country—with or without disabilities—is *entitled* to a higher education.

Rather, in higher education the relevant law is a civil rights law that protects people with disabilities from discrimination in admission to college and participation in college activities. The two federal laws that provide this protection are:

- Section 504 of the Rehabilitation Act (originally passed in 1973, with subsequent reauthorizations)
- The Americans with Disabilities Act (ADA, passed in 1990)

The ADA upholds and extends the compliance standards of Section 504, which had been passed years earlier (AHEAD, 2001). Section 504 pertains only to those colleges and universities that receive federal funds, whereas the ADA applies to all entities—public, under Title II, and private under Title III. The ADA states:

> No otherwise qualified individual with a disability shall, by reason of such disability, be excluded from participation in or be denied the benefits of the services, programs, or activities of a public entity, or be subjected to discrimination by any such entity (www.wrightslaw.com/info/sec504.summ.rights.htm).

In other words, a disability cannot be grounds for excluding a person from a college, an academic program, a class, a residence hall, or a college activity, if the person is qualified. The ADA guarantees access to equal opportunity; you could say that it entitles students with disabilities to "an opportunity to compete with their non-disabled peers" (Rothstein, 2002, p. 77).

Reasonable Accommodations

Under Section 504 and the ADA, colleges must provide—at no cost to the student—reasonable accommodations to make their programs accessible to students with disabilities. Examples are scheduling a class in a first-floor classroom to accommodate a student who uses a wheelchair, providing sign language interpreters for a student who is deaf, and arranging for extended time on tests for a student who has learning disabilities. The second column in Table 13.1 lists typical accommodations that colleges provide matched to the corresponding task needing to be completed.

In many cases, providing an effective assistive technology tool is considered a reasonable accommodation. As in Section 504, Title II of the ADA uses the phrase

TABLE 13–1 Accommodations for college students with disabilities linked to tasks required in college coursework

Task	Typical Nontechnology Accommodations	Technology-Based Accommodations
Notetaking	Student notetakers using carbonless paper	Use of a portable notetaker (e.g., Neo or Dana) Tape-recording lectures Whiteboard capturing devices
Understanding lectures	Sign language interpreters	C-print captioning Assistive listening system
Taking tests	Extended time on tests Distraction-free environment for testing	Talking word processing software for essay exams (with earphones) Use of spell-check feature or handheld speller Use of a calculator Text-to-speech software for reading support
Accessing course materials	Sign-language-interpreted videos Arranging for materials to be Brailled	Captioning videos Providing handouts in electronic format Making course websites accessible
Reading	Providing readers	Scan/read systems with highlighting and text-to-speech Books-on-tape Digital books and e-text Video magnifiers
Completing papers and other assignments		Screen magnification software Screen-reading software Talking word processing and word prediction software Voice recognition software Graphic organizer software
Accessing the Internet		Providing screen magnification, screen reading, or text-to-speech software Making college Web pages accessible
Registering for classes	Priority registration	Making college Web-based systems accessible
Telecommunicating		Providing a telecommunications device for the deaf (TTY) E-Mail Text messaging Instant messaging

"auxiliary aids and services" to refer to devices and services that make programs and materials available to people with disabilities:

> A public entity shall furnish appropriate aids and services where necessary to afford an individual with a disability an equal opportunity to participate in . . . a service, program, or activity. (U.S. Department of Education, 1998)

Section 504 regulations state that auxiliary aids and services "are not required to produce the identical result or level of achievement" for people with and without disabilities, but must afford people with disabilities "*equal opportunity* to obtain the same result, to gain the same benefit, or to reach the same level of achievement" (U.S. Department of Education, 1998, italics added). Similarly, the *effectiveness* of an auxiliary aid or service is determined by whether or not it succeeds in equalizing the opportunity for the student with a disability to participate in the educational program.

For example, auxiliary aids and services for a student who is hard of hearing may include the use of an assistive listening system (see Chapter 4) because this device offers the student an equal opportunity to learn from a lecture. Auxiliary aids for a student who is blind and a Braille reader may include a Braille printer and Braille translation software so that the student has an equal opportunity to produce written assignments (see Chapter 2). For a student who has visual impairments, providing screen magnification software provides access to the college's library's services and to computers for reading, writing, and research (see Chapters 2, 3 and 7). For students who struggle with reading and writing, providing text-to-speech programs (e.g., talking word processing software or scan/read systems) for class assignments and testing may be an effective auxiliary aid (see Chapters 2 and 3). The third column in Table 13.1 lists common technology-based accommodations in college.

Of particular relevance to the topic of assistive technology is that although colleges are required to provide auxiliary aids and services, they are not required to provide the most sophisticated technology available. A college "has flexibility in choosing the specific aid or service it provides to the student, as long as the aid or service selected is effective" (U.S. Department of Education, 1998). This means that a student may be provided with a different technology product from that which he or she requested. For example, the college may provide a different brand of screen-reading software than requested or an FM system instead of a digital assistive listening device.

The term *reasonable* in the phrase "reasonable accommodation" is not defined in the law and is still being debated in the courts. It is generally understood to mean that providing the accommodation will not cause "undue burden" to the institution. Colleges would be hard-pressed to claim that purchasing a piece of software or a $100 flatbed scanner represents undue burden, considering the millions of dollars most spend annually on technology. Therefore, under Section 504 and the ADA many college students with disabilities are finding access to assistive technology tools to be an important accommodation (Bryant, Bryant, & Rieth, 2002).

Procedures for Obtaining Assistive Technology in College

How is assistive technology provided to students with disabilities in college? To answer this question we must examine the procedural requirements of the ADA. In higher education the responsibility for documenting a disability and requesting

TABLE 13–2 College and student obligations under the Americans with Disabilities Act (ADA)

College's Obligations Under the ADA	Student's Obligations Under the ADA
Ensure that qualified applicants and students have access to the college's programs.	Self-identify that he or she has a disability (following the specific college's stated policies and procedures). Provide appropriate documentation of the disability.
Provide reasonable accommodations for the student's documented disabilities.	Request specific accommodation(s).
Demonstrate a good-faith effort to provide the student with meaningful access.	Follow the agreed-upon procedures for using the accommodations.

accommodations falls on the *student*, not on the educational institution. The college is not required to find or assess students who have disabilities. If a student chooses to keep his or her disability a secret, that is the student's prerogative and the college is not required to provide any kind of auxiliary aid. If a student does not follow through on his or her obligations under the law, the institution is also not required to provide accommodations. Table 13.2 summarizes the obligations of colleges and students with disabilities under the ADA.

What is particularly important to note is that the student must specifically *request* a piece of assistive technology as an accommodation if he or she believes it will provide access to the curriculum and an equal opportunity to demonstrate his or her knowledge. The accommodation must be clearly linked to the student's particular needs. Table 13.1 illustrates the link between specific tasks students must complete and technology-based accommodations that may assist students in successfully completing those tasks.

Legal and Procedural Differences Between ADA and IDEA

Learning that the IDEA does not apply to higher education and that college students have a much greater responsibility if they are to receive accommodations (and parents have a greatly reduced role) is often a shock for students and their parents. Unlike the IDEA, which, under its zero reject policy, guarantees an education to all school-aged children regardless of ability, the ADA protects only those individuals who meet the stated qualifications of a college or program. The phrase "otherwise qualified" in the ADA means that only those people who are able to meet the technical and academic qualifications for entry into a school, program, or activity are protected by the ADA. This means that although colleges are required to make what are called minor academic adjustments, they are *not* required to make substantial modifications to their curricula or course requirements. A good example of how this differs from the P–12 world is that although a reasonable accommodation may be extended time on tests or a distraction-free environment for testing, the law does *not* require colleges to modify the *contents* of an exam. Another example is that colleges are not obligated to provide students with disabilities more intensive tutoring services than they provide to students without disabilities. Table 13.3 summarizes the major differences between the requirements and procedures of the IDEA and the ADA.

TABLE 13–3   Comparison of the requirements and procedures of the Individuals with Disabilities Education Act (IDEA) and the Americans with Disabilities Act (ADA)

	IDEA (K–12)	ADA (College)
Rights guaranteed by the law	Free appropriate public education (FAPE)	Prohibits discrimination on the basis of disability.
Who is covered	Every child; concept of zero reject	Students who are "otherwise qualified."
Identification and evaluation of students with disabilities	District responsible for identifying students with disabilities, evaluating them, and covering the costs	College has no such responsibility. Students must self-identify and provide appropriate documentation. If an evaluation is needed, the expense is the student's responsibility.
Determining services	Individualized education plan (IEP) developed by team Curriculum modifications and special programs are common	Reasonable accommodations, including auxiliary aids and services, must be requested by student. Academic adjustments that equalize opportunity for participation are required; substantial modifications to curriculum and lowering standards are not required.
Personal devices and services such as wheelchairs, hearing aids, and personal care attendants	Provided by district if determined to be necessary (and included in IEP)	Colleges are not required to provide these.
Role of parents	Parents must be included in decision making	College students are over 18 and are considered adults. No parent consultation is required.
Appeals process	Right to due process as spelled out in the law	College grievance procedure and then a complaint with U.S. Department of Education's Office of Civil Rights must be filed.

IMPORTANCE OF TRANSITION PLANNING IN HIGH SCHOOL

Because many of you are primarily concerned with the P–12 world, you may be wondering why this chapter focuses on students with disabilities who have exited high school. The reason is that in order to access and use technology tools effectively in college, students with disabilities must be adequately prepared in high school. Technology access that leads to greater success in high school and postsecondary environments "has the potential to improve career outcomes for people with disabilities" (Burgstahler, 2003, p. 8). However, the differences between the protections and procedures of the IDEA and the ADA described previously have been identified as a serious barrier to technology access for people with disabilities (National Council on Disability, 2000). These differences make transition planning in high school especially important for students in special education who want to go on to college.

IDEA mandates that transition planning begin at age 16; starting at age 16 means that most students will have 2 to 3 years in which to learn the skills they will need to succeed in college. What skills do they need to learn? Transition plans for students with disabilities who want to attend college must include the development of two kinds of skills:

1. Assistive technology skills
2. Self-advocacy skills

Assistive Technology Skills

High schools must make it a high priority to identify assistive technology tools that will help students with disabilities work more independently and efficiently. High school is the perfect time and place to *teach* students how to use the assistive technology tools that will help them. Brinckerhoff, McGuire, and Shaw (2002) provide a detailed timetable for transition planning in high school that recommends that students "try out auxiliary accommodations and auxiliary aids" (pp. 38–39) and learn about technology tools in Grades 9 and 10. Once appropriate technology tools have been identified (see the chapters in Parts I and II of this text), students need to be given multiple opportunities to *practice* their new technology skills so that they become comfortable with the technology, they learn to customize it to their specific needs and preferences, and they are able to use it quickly and effortlessly. If this kind of training begins in high school, by the time students enter college, they will be prepared to use assistive technology to meet the academic demands they will face in college.

SIDEBAR

Implementation Details

Reread the paragraph in Serena's user profile that describes the ways she obtains accessible textbooks. No fewer than five methods are utilized, including scanning one page at a time. This is a much more involved and time-consuming process than the traditional method sighted students use to obtain their textbooks—a trip to the college bookstore or a few mouse clicks at a website. It takes Serena up to 3 months to locate and obtain accessible versions of all of her textbooks. This means she must get reading lists from her professors well in advance, and she must contact the various organizations and check out several websites to see if the books are already available as recordings or electronic text. These tasks require Serena to manage her time carefully, keep track of all the information, and advocate for herself. Without her attending to these implementation details, the technology tools themselves would be ineffective.

Self-Advocacy Skills

Being skilled in using specific assistive technology tools, however, is not enough. In order to receive accommodations in higher education, college students need to be able to articulate which technology tools are effective for them. Students need to be able to advocate for themselves so that they will be prepared for their increased responsibilities in accessing accommodations in college. This means that self-advocacy skills need to be taught in high school. Barr, Harttnan, and Spillane (1995) provide a good explanation of self-advocates:

> People who can speak up in logical, clear and positive language to communicate about their needs. Self-advocates take responsibility for themselves. To be a self-advocate, each student must learn to understand his or her particular type of . . . disability, and the resultant academic strengths and weaknesses . . . Most importantly, high school students with . . . disabilities need to become comfortable with describing to others both their disability and the academic related needs. (p. 3)

In order to advocate for themselves in college, students with disabilities need to be able to explain the nature of their disabilities and to articulate the strategies and adaptations that will support their learning. Empowering adaptations often include assistive technology tools, so students need to learn—in high school—the advocacy skills they will need to request specific assistive technology solutions as reasonable accommodations in college. Brinckerhoff and colleagues (2002, pp. 38–39) recommend that students learn about the nature of their disability, their preferred learning styles, and their rights and responsibilities under Section 504 and the ADA in Grades 9 and 10. Combining the teaching of strong self-advocacy skills with appropriate assistive technology skills will enable students with disabilities to transition to the college environment smoothly and successfully.

TRANSITION FROM HIGH SCHOOL TO HOME, WORKPLACE, AND COMMUNITY

Students with disabilities who are not headed for college also need careful planning for their transition from high school to adult life, and they, too, can benefit from the use of assistive technology. Many of these students have cognitive disabilities, autism, or multiple disabilities, and their transition plans often focus on the enhancement of their communication, social, self-care, leisure, and work skills. Chapters 9, 10, and 11 addressed the use of augmentative communication technology to support students whose speech is not adequate to meet their communication needs. This section summarizes other kinds of assistive technology that can help students who have severe disabilities develop skills for living and working in the community.

Personal Digital Assistants

Personal digital assistants (PDAs or handhelds) like Palm Pilots, BlackBerrys, and Treos have become ubiquitous in the workplace. For students who have cognitive disabilities, autism, or multiple disabilities, a new line of specialized PDAs offers

FIGURE 13–1   Specialized PDAs that assist students in the workplace and at home

The Pocket Coach provides customized audio prompts to help students complete tasks independently. The Visual Assistant provides customized digital photos in addition to audio prompts to help students complete tasks independently

Courtesy of AbleLink Technologies.

support for completing vocational and self-care activities (see Figure 13.1). For students who rely on verbal prompts to complete multistep tasks, the Pocket Coach (AbleLink Technologies, Inc.) may be an age-appropriate option. The Pocket Coach is a PDA that uses speech output to provide verbal prompts for specific tasks in the natural environment. Teachers or job coaches record a series of step-by-step instructions for whatever task a student is learning. Students then play back the instructions in the environments in which they need to complete the tasks. The Pocket Coach is appropriate for community situations because it is easily carried and it increases students' independence by fading the direct assistance of a job coach.

Another PDA, called Visual Assistant (AbleLink Technologies, Inc.), also provides task-prompting support with recorded audio messages, but this product adds digital pictures to the step-by-step support. Instead of just displaying pictures of objects, it is recommended that the digital photos be of the students themselves performing the steps in the actual environment in which they will be completing the task. This provides multimodal cues for task completion and is especially helpful for students who respond to visual prompts such as those with autism.

A third specialized PDA, Schedule Assistant (AbleLink Technologies, Inc.), is a scheduling application for students who have significant literacy problems that prevent them from using conventional text-based PDAs. Appointments or events are entered into the device by recording audio messages and designating the day(s) and time(s) for the messages to activate. A digital picture can be displayed when the message is spoken. This combination of time-based audio prompts and picture cues help students who cannot read meet bus schedules, take appropriate work breaks, maintain school schedules, or complete morning and nighttime routines in a timely fashion.

Computer-Generated Visual Supports

Technology can also be used to create visual supports in a simple paper format. Picture schedules (see Figure 13.2) and activity schedules are sequential, pictorial representations of events or tasks that cue a student to complete them (McClannahan & Krantz, 1999). Similar to a "to-do" list, they provide a visual reminder of what happens next and what will occur later. (For students who are strong readers, text can be used instead of pictures.) Picture schedules help students see the day's structure at a glance and can reduce the anxiety that some students experience when it is time to transition from one activity to another. By helping students understand what is to come and what is expected of them, picture schedules can reduce confusion and acting-out behaviors (McClannahan & Krantz, 1999). This kind of visual information is also helpful to students whose skills in sequential memory or receptive language are weak.

For students who need concrete symbols, picture schedules can be created by taking digital photos of each activity or environment, printing the photos, and placing them—in sequence—in an inexpensive mini-photo album. Or, the photos can be laminated on a plain file folder. In preparing a student for the next activity, the teacher or aide provides a verbal prompt such as "What happens next?" and the student "checks his schedule" by turning the page in the photo album or looking at the next image in the photo list.

For students who understand less transparent symbols (see Chapter 9), picture schedules can be created using Boardmaker (Mayer-Johnson) or Overboard (Gus Communications, Inc.). These can be printed and laminated and made easily available for students to refer to. Some teachers tape a student's daily schedule to a corner of his or her desktop. For students who are in the community, the picture schedules can be folded up and put in a pocket.

Activity sequences (see Figure 13.3) are step-by-step pictorial representations of a particular task like brushing teeth, cooking popcorn in the microwave, or taking out the trash. They are an effective strategy for shifting students from a reliance on verbal prompts (adult assistance) to more independent completion of self-care and vocational tasks (McClannahan & Krantz, 1999). Activity sequences are easily constructed in software programs like Boardmaker and Overboard, both of which include templates for picture schedules and activity sequences, but they can also be easily created in Microsoft Word or PowerPoint using clip art.

FIGURE 13–2
Sample picture schedule of a school day, made with Boardmaker

Source: The Picture Communication Symbols © 1981–2006 by Mayer-Johnson, LLC. All rights reserved worldwide. Used with permission.

FIGURE 13–3
Sample on-the-job activity sequence, made with Boardmaker

Source: The Picture Communication Symbols © 1981–2006 by Mayer-Johnson, LLC. All rights reserved worldwide. Used with permission.

Computer-Generated Social Stories

Digital photos, PowerPoint, Boardmaker and other graphics programs can also be used to create social stories (see Figure 13.4). Social stories are teacher- (or parent) authored short stories that are written to help a student who has autism learn "the social information he may be lacking" (Gray, 2000, p. 13-1). They are often used as part of a social skills training curriculum to teach students how to interact with other people, and they address skills such as reading body language, looking at situations from another person's perspective, and responding in socially acceptable ways. Many teachers use them to help students cope with changes in classroom routines, such as the presence of a substitute teacher, an upcoming school assembly, or a planned fire drill (Gray, 2000).

FIGURE 13–4   Sample pages from a social story

How Should I Act During Rug Time?

Rug time is a time where we do calendar, sing songs, and read stories. I will sit and listen. When I listen to the teacher I learn.

When it is rug time, I may choose which shape on the rug to sit on. Usually two people can sit on a big shape, like a rectangle, but only one person can sit on a small shape, like a triangle, square, and circle.

Gray (2000) presents clear guidelines for the content and format of social stories, including the specific kinds of sentences that need to be included. Technology makes the creation and production of social stories easier, and it presents the added advantage of being able to personalize the story for each particular student. For example, if a student has problems waiting in line and acts out whenever the class is told to "line up," the teacher could write a simple social story and illustrate it with digital photos of the teacher standing at the door giving instructions, the other children lining up appropriately, this particular student getting in line appropriately, and the entire class, including this student, walking appropriately down the hall. Another option afforded by social stories created in PowerPoint is that the story can be recorded and read aloud in the student's own voice.

Simple Technology for Self-Care and Leisure Activities

For many students who have severe physical disabilities that interfere with normal movement patterns, functional curriculum goals often involve increasing their participation in everyday activities such as self-care, food preparation, leisure, and vocational tasks. Although these students may not be able to complete tasks completely independently, they can benefit from—and should be given opportunities to engage in—**partial participation**—completing a portion of the activity (Baumgart et al., 1982). Simple technology using adapted switches, which were discussed in Chapters 7 and 10, can be used to facilitate partial participation. Adapted switches can be connected to battery-operated devices such as audio players, funny toy animals that sing and dance, remote control cars, or other entertaining electronic gadgets. Through a special interface, they can also be connected to table-top appliances such as hair dryers, fans, and kitchen mixers.

For example, a student who has spastic cerebral palsy that causes her hands to be fisted most of the time can participate in self-grooming by turning a hair dryer and a lighted makeup mirror on and off with an adapted switch that she activates with her fist (Levin & Scherfenberg, 1990). Although someone else needs to do the actual styling of her hair and putting on of makeup, the use of simple technology enables this student to be an active participant in these grooming tasks. This same student can help her mother bake cookies by turning the electric mixer on and off with the same adapted switch. Using simple technology for partial participation in vocational activities, this student could activate an electric stapler, electric three-whole punch, or a paper shredder if she works with a partner in an office environment (Levin & Scherfenberg, 1990).

For students who cannot use their hands at all, the switches can be mounted so that they are accessible to whatever body part the student can control. Some students have better head control than hand control, so a switch can be mounted next to their cheek

Example of using a switch for partial participation

or the side of their head for activation by a turn of their head. Switches can also be positioned to be activated by a foot, elbow, or knee. Smaller, more sensitive switches are also available for students who have only very limited, weak movements.

PLANNING FOR TRANSITION TO HOME, WORKPLACE, AND COMMUNITY

Just as students with learning disabilities need to be prepared for college by learning assistive technology tools in high schools, students with severe disabilities must learn to use the assistive technology tools that will help them function more independently in their homes and communities. In addition to the technology applications discussed in this chapter, students with severe disabilities can benefit from many of the tools discussed in Part I of this text (writing tools, reading tools, and instructional tools). They also need and benefit from many of the augmentative communication systems discussed in Chapters 4, 5, 9, 10, and 11). These students' transition plans need to include the identification of appropriate technology supports, and the students need to be given multiple opportunities to *practice* their new technology skills while they are in high school. Then, when they exit high school at age 21, they will be better prepared for their lives in their communities.

SUMMARY

- The number of students with disabilities attending college has increased significantly in the last decade, and assistive technology offers solutions to the obstacles they face in meeting the academic demands of college.

- The assistive technology tools discussed in this text can help college students with disabilities if they are easy to use, easy to customize, age appropriate, reflect the students' preferences, match the specific task that needs to be completed, are accessible to the students, and are supported with training and ongoing technical support.

- There are no IEPs in college. The laws and procedures governing services to college students with disabilities are very different from those in the P–12 world.

- Students need to learn about these differences and need to be taught self-advocacy skills so that they will be prepared to articulate their assistive technology needs and request tools as reasonable accommodations when they get to college.

- Assistive technology can also support students with disabilities who are not headed for college. Specialized personal digital assistants offer age-appropriate support for completing vocational and self-care activities. Graphics programs can be used to easily create visual supports such as picture schedules, activity schedules, and social stories. Simple technology using adapted switches can be used to facilitate partial participation in self-care, grooming, domestic, leisure, and vocational activities.

- Careful transition planning is essential so that students learn these assistive technology skills in high school before they make the transition to adult life.

WEB RESOURCES

For additional information on the topics listed, go to the following websites:

Students with Learning Disabilities in College

TECH-NJ at The College of New Jersey
http://www.tcnj.edu/~technj/2004/horne.htm
http://www.tcnj.edu/~technj/2004/farr.htm

Legal Issues in Higher Education

U.S. Department of Education Office for Civil Rights Students with Disabilities Preparing for Postsecondary Education: Know Your Rights and Responsibilities
http://www.ed.gov/about/offices/list/ocr/transition.html
Heath Resource Center: Online Clearinghouse on Postsecondary Education for Individuals with Disabilities
http://www.heath.gwu.edu

Transition Planning in High School

TECH-NJ at The College of New Jersey
www.tcnj.edu/~technj/2007/plancollegesuccess.htm
www.tcnj.edu/~technj/2007/makingtransition.htm
Schwab Learning: Preparing for Life After High School
http://www.schwablearning.org/resources.aspx?g=4&s=7

Self-Advocacy

Advice for high school students
http://www.tcnj.edu/~technj/2007/advice.htm
Wrightslaw: Self-Advocacy: Know Yourself, Know What You Need, Know How to Get It
http://www.wrightslaw.com/info/sec504.selfadvo.ld.johnson.htm

Personal Digital Assistants (PDA's) for Students With Disabilities

Ablelink Technologies
http://www.ablelinktech.com
Dana from Alphasmart, Inc.
http://www.alphasmart.com/k12/K12_Products/dana-w_K12.html

Visual Supports

Use Visual Strategies website
http://www.usevisualstrategies.com/index.html

Child Autism Parent Cafe
http://www.child-autism-parent-cafe.com/visual-pictureschedule-example.html

Social Stories

Carol Gray's website
www.thegraycenter.org/socialstorywhat.cfm
Simple technology at home Linda Burkhart's Simplified Technology website
http://www.lburkhart.com/index.html

Self-Determination

ERIC Digest: Promoting the Self-Determination of Students with Severe Disabilities, by M. Wehmeyer
http://www.ericdigests.org/2003-4/severe-disabilities.html

SUGGESTED ACTIVITIES

1. *Research Accommodations at Your College.* Research the policies and procedures at your college regarding making its programs and services accessible to students who have disabilities. At which office does a student self-identify and provide documentation of a disability? How does your college publicize the procedure for requesting accommodations? What kinds of assistive technology does your college provide to make its programs and services accessible to students with disabilities?

2. *Investigate Assistive Technology and Self-Advocacy Training in a High School.* Arrange to visit a high school in your area and interview a transition coordinator or a teacher who teaches transition skills. What kinds of assistive technology are students being taught to use? What is the curriculum for teaching self-advocacy skills? Based on what you have learned in this course, will these students have the assistive technology skills they will need to succeed academically in college?

3. *Create a Picture Schedule.* Locate a high school student who has autism, cognitive disabilities, or multiple disabilities. Work with his or her teacher to find out which tasks related to transition are presenting challenges to this student that might be addressed with the aid of a visual support such as a picture schedule. Using Boardmaker or a digital camera, create a picture schedule that will support this student. Write a brief narrative explaining your decision making in designing and creating the picture schedule.

4. *Create a Social Story.* Go to Carol Gray's website at http://www.thegraycenter .org/socialstorywhat.cfm. After reading about social stories, go to the section titled "How Do I Write a Social Story?" Follow the instructions to create a social story in PowerPoint that specifically addresses a problem faced by one of your own students.

REFERENCES

Association on Higher Education and Disability (AHEAD) (2001). *The Americans with Disabilities Act: The law and its impact on postsecondary education* (brochure). Boston: Author.

Barr, V. M., Harttnan, R., & Spillane, S. (1995). *Getting ready for college: Advising high school students with learning disabilities.* Retrieved from the George Washington University HEATH Resource Center. Website: http://www.heath.gwu.edu

Baumgart, D., Brown, L., Pumpian, I., Nisbet, J., Ford, A., Sweet, M., et al. (1982). Principle of partial participation and individualized adaptations in educational programs for severely handicapped students. *Journal of the Association for the Severely Handicapped, 7,* 17–27.

Brinckerhoff, L. C., McGuire, J. M., & Shaw, S. F. (2002). *Postsecondary education and transition for students with learning disabilities* (2nd ed.). Austin, TX: Pro-Ed.

Bryant, B. R., Bryant, D. P., & Rieth, H. J. (2002). The use of assistive technology in postsecondary education. In L. C. Brinckerhoff, J. M. McGuire, & S. F. Shaw (Eds.), *Postsecondary education and transition for students with learning disabilities* (2nd ed., pp. 389–429). Austin, TX: Pro-Ed.

Burgstahler, S. (2003). The role of technology in preparing youth with disabilities for postsecondary education and employment. *Special Education Technology, 18*(4), 7–19.

Cucco, S. (2005). Utilizing blindness skills in college. *TECH-NJ, 16*(1), 6.

Gray, C. (2000). *The new social story book, illustrated.* Arlington, TX: Future Horizons.

Henderson, C. (2001). *College freshmen with disabilities: A Biennial statistical profile.* Washington, DC: American Council on Education.

Levin, J., & Scherfenberg, L. (1990). *Selection and use of simple technology in home, school, work, and community settings.* Minneapolis, MN: AbleNet.

McClannahan, L. E., & Krantz, P. J. (1999). *Activity schedules for children with autism: Teaching independent behavior.* Bethesda, MD: Woodbine House.

National Council on Disability. (2000). *Federal policy barriers to assistive technology.* Washington, DC: Author.

National Joint Committee on Learning Disabilities. (1994). *Collective perspectives on issues affecting learning disabilities: Position papers and statements.* Austin, TX: Pro-Ed.

Rothstein, L. (2002). Judicial intent and legal precedents. In L. C. Brinckerhoff, C. Loring, J. M. McGuire, & S. F. Shaw (Eds.), *Postsecondary education and transition for students with learning disabilities* (2nd ed., pp. 71–106). Austin, TX: Pro-Ed.

U.S. Department of Education Office for Civil Rights. (1998). *Auxiliary aids and services for postsecondary students with disabilities: Higher education's obligations under Section 504 and Title II of the ADA.* Retrieved January 29, 2004, from http://www.ed.gov/about/offices/list/ocr/docs/auxaids.html

U.S. Department of Education Office for Civil Rights. (2002). *Students with disabilities preparing for postsecondary education: Know your rights and responsibilities.* Retrieved from http://www.ed.gov/about/offices/list/ocr/transition.html

Varrassi, V. (2004). *Personal communication.* Trenton, New Jersey.

Yelin, E., & Katz, P. (1994). Labor force trends of persons with and without disabilities. *Monthly Labor Review, 117*(10), 36–42.

Index

Note: Figures and illustrations are indicated by italics; *t* indicates a table.